LANGUAGE, CULTURE, AND PERSONALITY

EDWARD SAPIR 1884–1939

LANGUAGE, CULTURE, AND PERSONALITY

Essays in Memory of Edward Sapir

EDITED BY

LESLIE SPIER
A. IRVING HALLOWELL
STANLEY S. NEWMAN

PUBLISHED BY
SAPIR MEMORIAL PUBLICATION FUND
MENASHA, WISCONSIN

1941

In a casual conversation in the fall of 1956 the then director of the University of Utah Press, Dr. Phillip Sturges, expressed an interest in the reprinting by offset of standard anthropological books now out of print. I immediately proposed that the *Sapir Memorial Volume* would be an excellent choice for the beginning of such a project. Following Dr. Sturges' tentative agreement to publish, I got in touch with the original editors, Drs. Leslie Spier, Dave Mandelbaum and Vern F. Ray. They enthusiastically endorsed the proposal and gave their full permission, when a tentative arrangement with another publisher failed to materialize. The Publications Committee of the University of Utah of which Dr. Leland Creer head of the department of history is chairman authorized the reprinting.

However, funds were not immediately available. In June of 1959 upon the resignation of Dr. Sturges, Dean Bentley of the Extension Division (to which the Press it attached administratively) interested himself in the project. Finally, in 1959, money for the reprinting became available and later the long-laid plans for publication were put in motion.

I proffer my thanks and that of the anthropological profession to Messrs. Spier, Mandelbaum, Ray, Sturges, Bentley and Creer for uniting to make this classic volume again available and at a modest price. Further I express the hope that other rare volumes may appear in this reprint series. Suggestions from colleagues for the next volume to be reprinted can be made directly to the University of Utah Press.

Jesse D. Jennings

Reprinted by Photolithography
University of Utah Press
1960

FOREWORD

EDWARD SAPIR, to whose memory this volume is dedicated, had exceptional gifts: an artistic intuition, a scholar's acuteness and erudition, a shrewd synthesizing capacity, an extraordinary clarity of expression and a fertility of suggestiveness and enthusiasm that communicated itself to his students and colleagues. His originality and boldness of mind led him beyond the conventional limits of a single department of study. Although he is often thought of primarily as a student of language, he was equally concerned with the analysis of cultural behavior and the interplay of both on the development of personality. To be sure, he was peculiarly adept at descriptive linguisitics, but his quickness of insight led to a coordination of languages seemingly far apart and, even more important, to novel formulations of the essence of language. He saw language as verbal symbol of human relations. Hence his records of other types of cultural behavior, derived largely from an approach through language, have emphasis as frequently on thought and expression as on form. He held that the understanding of cultural behavior was difficult or impossible unless its course of development was minutely traced. What interested him even more than establishing a solid factual basis—on which he was insistent—were the nuances of interrelation between personality, verbal expression, and socially determined behavior. And especially was he aware of the subtle balance between social dictates and the aims and satisfactions of the individual. In short, language, culture, and personality were for him coordinate.

The delight of the teaching scholar is to know that his ideas have taken root among his students, have fertilized their thought, and that from these beginnings have arisen healthy, vigorous, and independent growths. It was for the purpose of revealing to Edward Sapir that his students had pride in acknowledging the impetus he gave them and demonstrating their ability to produce in turn, that this volume was conceived.

The enterprise was launched at a gathering of his former and current students in attendance at a meeting of the American Anthropological Association in New York, December 28, 1938, under the leadership of David G. Mandelbaum, Murray B. Emeneau, Verne F. Ray, Morris Swadesh, and Willard Z. Park. Thanks to the energy of a host of Dr Sapir's students, who saw here an opportunity for indicating their devotion, a publication fund was soon in hand. For the many contributors, this was a welcome opportunity to express their friendship and admiration of Dr Sapir. It was part of the plan to devote any excess of the publication fund, together with royalties, to publishing some of Dr Sapir's manuscripts.

Knowing he was gravely ill, we decided to tell him of our plan. With characteristic modesty, he disclaimed the significance which we knew attached to his work but nonetheless expressed his deep pleasure, appreciation, and thanks. We wished to greet Dr Sapir with a completed volume in his honor, but to our profound sorrow he died on February 4, 1939 before it was fairly under way.

It is our intention in this volume to show something of Dr Sapir's influence, as well as to pay tribute to his memory. Had it been possible, we would have liked to have called on everyone of his scores of students for articles, but with our limited resources this was out of the question. We have, therefore, drafted a panel of contributors to represent them all, with the implication that each author would speak for others beside himself. Our choice has been not only among those who had been formal students to Dr Sapir, but also among others profoundly influenced by him and hence his "students" in the wider, more vital sense. It was hoped that in this way some representative problems in linguistics, ethnology, and psychology in which he inspired research could best be exhibited. To cover the complete range of the subtle and varied problems which occupied Dr Sapir's widely inquiring mind was, of course, impossible, nor could full justice be done to the coherence he saw in them.

We asked each contributor to write on a topic of his own choice, using his own data, but bearing in mind that we expected to see Dr Sapir's influence on himself and his fellows reflected in his article. It was distinctly understood that the authors were not of necessity to agree with him either in views or conclusions. Dr Sapir himself would have insisted on their independence, their right to move on to new viewpoints. These are discrete contributions, yet threading through them in some measure are those interconnections which Dr Sapir saw between language, culture, and psychology.

Edward Sapir's career was abruptly terminated in mid-course. This volume in his memory is an earnest that his influence will endure.

LESLIE SPIER
A. IRVING HALLOWELL
STANLEY S. NEWMAN

CONTRIBUTORS TO THE PUBLISHING FUND

A. S. ALSCHULER
CHARLES AMSDEN
ELIZABETH E. BACON
LEO H. BARTEMEIER
RALPH BEALS
GEORGE BECHTEL
MARTHA W. BECKWITH
K. T. BEHANEN
RUTH BENEDICT
DOROTHY BENNETT
WENDELL BENNETT
Mr and Mrs ARTHUR BERGHOLZ
BEATRICE BLACKWOOD
ROBERT W. BLISS
Mr and Mrs N. LIONEL BLITZSTEN
LEONARD BLOOMFIELD
HERBERT BLUMER
FRANZ BOAS
A. A. BRILL
BRYN MAWR COLLEGE LIBRARY
ERNEST W. BURGESS
CHARLES W. BURR
EDWIN G. BURROWS
Mr and Mrs MORTON CAHN
CAMBRIDGE UNIVERSITY ANTHRO-
   POLOGY CLUB
ROSS McCLURE CHAPMAN
IRVIN CHILD
WALTER CLINE
HELEN F. CODERE
FAY-COOPER COLE
ANNE M. COOKE
JOHN M. COOPER
GEORGE E. DANIELS
WAYNE DENNIS
FREDERICA DE LAGUNA
THORNE DEUEL
MYLES DILLON
FREDERIC DOUGLAS
J. H. DRIBERG
CORA DU BOIS
FRANKLIN EDGERTON
FRED EGGAN

GORDON F. EKHOLM
EDWIN R. EMBREE
M. B. EMENEAU
HENRY EPSTEIN
ETNOGRAFISKA MUSEET, GÖTEBORG
   (Gothenburg Ethnographical Mu-
   seum)
E. E. EVANS-PRITCHARD
WILLIAM N. FENTON
MARJORIE C. FLINN
GUY STANTON FORD
JEROME FRANK
L. K. FRANK
ERICH FROMM
FRIEDA FROMM-REIHMANN
VIOLA GARFIELD
A. H. GAYTON
NAOMI GIFFEN
ALBRECHT GOETZE
GRENVILLE GOODWIN
HARRY GOTTLIEB
GROSVENER LIBRARY
Mr and Mrs ERNEST GRUNSFELD
ERNA GUNTHER
MARY R. HAAS
ERNEST E. HADLEY
BERARD HAILE
A. IRVING HALLOWELL
CHAUNCEY J. HAMLIN
MILES L. HANLEY
ZELLIG S. HARRIS
HAWAIIAN ANTHROPOLOGICAL SO-
   CIETY
CLARENCE L. HAY
CHARLES W. HENDEL
MELVILLE HERSKOVITS
Mr and Mrs GEORGE HERZOG
HARRY HOIJER
ALLAN R. HOLMBERG
EARNEST ALBERT HOOTON
W. W. HOWELLS
ALFRED E. HUDSON
MELVILLE JACOBS

DIAMOND JENNESS
EUGEN KAHN
A. G. KELLER
WILLIAM H. KELLEY
SARAH R. KELMAN
HAYWARD KENISTON
RAYMOND KENNEDY
ROLAND G. KENT
JOHN KEPKE
EDWARD KERR
FENTON KEYES
DALE KING
OTTO KLINEBERG
CLYDE KLUCKHOHN
FRANK H. KNIGHT
NATHANIEL KNOWLES
Mrs ALEXANDER KOHUT
A. L. KROEBER
WESTON LABARRE
DOROTHY D. LEE
F. W. LEON
DAVID M. LEVY
A. B. LEWIS
J. G. LEYBURN
AN-CHE LI
FANG-KUEI LI
ELI LILLY
E. J. LINDGREN
RALPH LINTON
ABRAM LIPSKY
EDWIN M. LOEB
ROBERT LOWIE
J. GILBERT McALLISTER
URSULA McCONNELL
CLINTON P. McCORD
THEODORE McCOWN
T. F. McILWRAITH
KENNETH MacLEISH
DAVID G. MANDELBAUM
PAUL S. MARTIN
J. ALDEN MASON
MARK A. MAY
H. SCUDDER MEKEEL

ix

SOURCE OF THE QUOTATIONS

The quotations on the title pages of the four sections of this book have been drawn from the writings of Edward Sapir, as follows:

Language: An Introduction to the Study of Speech (New York, 1921), pp. 183–84.
The Status of Linguistics as a Science (Language, Vol. 5, pp. 207–14, 1929), pp. 209–10.
Cultural Anthropology and Psychiatry (Journal of Abnormal and Social Psychology, Vol. 27, pp. 229–42, 1932), p. 241.
The Contribution of Psychiatry to an Understanding of Behavior in Society (American Journal of Sociology, Vol. 42, pp. 862–70, 1937), p. 868.

A full bibliography of Dr Sapir's scientific works will be found in American Anthropologist, Vol. 41, pp. 469–77, 1939.

CONTENTS

PROBLEMS OF LINGUISTIC CLASSIFICATION

"*Nothing is perfectly static. Every word, every grammatical element, every locution, every sound and accent is a slowly changing configuration, molded by the invisible and impersonal drift that is the life of language. The evidence is overwhelming that this drift has a certain consistent direction. . . . The general drift of a language has its depths. At the surface the current is relatively fast. In certain features dialects drift apart rapidly. By that very fact these features betray themselves as less fundamental to the genius of the language than the more slowly modifiable features in which the dialects keep together long after they have grown to be mutually alien forms of speech.*"

Language

METHODS IN THE CLASSIFICATION OF AMERICAN INDIAN LANGUAGES

By HARRY HOIJER

THE FIRST comprehensive classification of the American Indian languages north of Mexico was made by J. W. Powell in 1891.[1] Concerning the method employed in establishing this classification, Powell states:

Languages are said to be cognate when such relations between them are found that they are supposed to have descended from a common ancestral speech. The evidence of cognation is derived exclusively from the vocabulary. Grammatic similarities are not supposed to furnish evidence of cognation, but to be phenomena, in part relating to stage of culture and in part adventitious. It must be remembered that extreme peculiarities of grammar, like the vocal mutations of the Hebrew or the monosyllabic separation of the Chinese, have not been discovered among the Indian tongues. It therefore becomes necessary in the classification of Indian languages into families to neglect grammatic structure, and to consider lexical elements only.[2]

It is clear from this statement that the Powell classification could only be a first step in the problem of defining the linguistic families of America. Neither Powell nor his associates claimed that their classification was final. On the contrary, Powell definitely stated, in speaking of the lingusitic map which accompanied his report:

. . . It is hardly necessary to add that the accompanying map does not purport to represent final results. On the contrary, it is to be regarded as tentative, setting forth in visible form the results of investigation up to the present time, as a guide and aid to future effort.

. . . Unquestionably, future and more critical study will result in the fusion of some of these families. As the means for analysis and comparison accumulate, resemblances now hidden will be brought to light, and relationships hitherto unsuspected will be shown to exist.[3]

The publication of the Powell classification marked the end of what Goddard has called the first period of linguistic research in America.[4] During this period, most of the work was done by missionaries and others who were not primarily linguists. Apart from the practical necessity of learning Indian languages that confronted these students, their main interest was in securing enough data on a language to reveal its immediate cognates.

A. S. Gatschet and J. O. Dorsey, Powell's collaborators, may be said to have initiated the second period of linguistic research in America. The dominant interest of this period was in the collection of detailed grammatical and lexical data on individual languages. Franz Boas soon became a leader in this work; he and his students published many volumes of textual material as well as numerous grammatical treatises.[5] It was not until the later por-

---

[1] Powell, *Indian Linguistic Families of America.*   [2] *Ibid.*, p. 11.
[3] *Ibid.*, p. 26.   [4] Goddard, *Present Condition*, p. 559.   [5] *Ibid.*, pp. 560–61.

3

tion of this period that interest in comparative studies was revived, primarily through the influence of Edward Sapir.[6]

Unlike the majority of the American Indian linguists of this period, Sapir was thoroughly trained in Indo-European linguistics. He was, furthermore, convinced that the historical problems presented by the American languages could only be solved by applying to them the methods developed by Indo-European scholars.

The methods developed by the Indo-Europeanists have been applied with marked success to other groups of languages. It is abundantly clear that they apply just as rigorously to the unwritten primitive languages of Africa and America as to the better known forms of speech of the more sophisticated peoples. It is probably in the languages of these more cultured peoples that the fundamental regularity of linguistic processes has been most often crossed by the operation of such conflicting tendencies as borrowing from other languages, dialectic blending, and social differentiations of speech. The more we devote ourselves to the comparative study of the languages of a primitive linguistic stock, the more clearly we realize that phonetic law and analogical leveling are the only satisfactory key to the unravelling of the development of dialects and languages from a common base. Professor Leonard Bloomfield's experiences with Central Algonkian and my own with Athabaskan leave nothing to be desired in this respect and are a complete answer to those who find it difficult to accept the large scale regularity of the operation of all those unconscious linguistic forces which in their totality give us regular phonetic change and morphological readjustment on the basis of such change. It is not merely theoretically possible to predict the correctness of specific forms among unlettered peoples on the basis of such phonetic laws as have been worked out for them—such predictions are already on record in considerable number. There can be no doubt that the methods first developed in the field of Indo-European linguistics are destined to play a consistently important role in the study of all other groups of languages, and that it is through them and through their gradual extension that we can hope to arrive at significant historical inferences as to the remoter relations between groups of languages that show few superficial signs of a common origin.[7]

By the rigorous application of these methods, Sapir was able to establish, tentatively at least, a number of relationships between stocks hitherto considered independent. His main contributions[8] to this field of research may be summarized as follows:

1. The Na-dene stock, which combined the Haida, Tlingit, and Athapaskan stocks set up by Powell.[9]

2. The Hokan (or, more accurately, the Hokan-Coahuiltecan) stock, which united the Hokan (of California) first proposed by Dixon and Kroeber[10] with the Coahuiltecan languages of Texas and the Subtiaba-Tlappanec group of Nicaragua.[11]

[6] Boas, *Classification of American Languages*, p. 367.

[7] Sapir, *Status of Linguistics as a Science*, p. 208.

[8] I am omitting from consideration in this paper Sapir's far-reaching classification of American languages published in the 14th edition of the *Encyclopædia Britannica* under the title "Central and North American Indian Languages" because Sapir never found the time to publish data substantiating these relationships.

[9] Sapir, *Na-dene Languages*.

[10] Dixon and Kroeber, *New Linguistic Families of California*. See also Dixon and Kroeber, *Linguistic Families in California*.   [11] Sapir, *Position of Yana; Hokan and Coahuiltecan Languages; Hokan Affinity of Subtiaba*.

ERRATA

On page v, lines 5 and 6 which read: " . . . I got in touch with the original editors, Drs. Leslie Spier, Dave Mandelbaum and Vern[e] F. Ray. . . . " should be changed to read " . . . I got in touch with the chief editor, Dr. Leslie Spier and Drs. Dave Mandelbaum and Verne F. Ray. . . . "

3. The Uto-Aztekan stock, combining Nahuatl, Piman, and Shoshonean into a single genetic group.[12]

4. The Algonkin-Ritwan stock, which grouped Algonkin with the Wiyot and Yurok languages of California.[13]

The criteria whereby genetic relationship between two or more linguistic stocks may be established are of two types, phonetic and morphological. Identities and regular correspondences of sound feature are clearly of the most importance. Where such phonetic correspondences[14] can be established between a greater portion of the phonemes of the languages under consideration, those languages can only be regarded as descendants from a single common ancestor. It must be remembered, however, that phonetic correspondences of this sort, particularly in the case of languages only remotely related, are difficult of formulation. The correspondences are rarely obvious; indeed, obvious resemblances in sound feature must be viewed with suspicion, since they may be either purely fortuitous (as, for example, in the case of English *day* and Latin *dies*) or the result of borrowing (e.g., English *dental*, Latin *dentalis*).

Sapir's method in establishing phonetic correspondences may be illustrated from his paper on the Na-dene languages.[15] Available for comparison were over 300 Athapaskan reconstructions attested by forms from the northern, Pacific coast, and southern Athapaskan languages, and the Haida and Tlingit materials collected by Swanton.[16] In his comparative vocabulary, Sapir included only a selected list of cognates, about one hundred in number. From this list of cognates he was able to demonstrate thirty phonetic correspondences most of which could be illustrated by three or more examples.[17] It is evident, then, that the lexical resemblances pointed out by Sapir, though few in number, are not haphazard or chance similarities but can be systematized.

The possibility that these phonetic and lexical correspondences are due to borrowing is remote. It should be re-emphasized that the correlations were drawn between Haida, Tlingit, and Athapaskan reconstructions, not between Haida, Tlingit, and the neighboring Athapaskan languages. Since the Athapaskan forms compared exist in the Pacific coast and southern Athapaskan languages as well as in the northern languages, any borrowing of lexical traits between Tlingit and Athapaskan must have taken place at a time before the dispersal of the primitive Athapaskan speech community.

---

[12] Sapir, *Southern Paiute and Nahuatl, a Study in Uto-Aztekan; Southern Paiute and Nahuatl, a Study in Uto-Aztekan, Part II; Southern Paiute and Nahuatl, a Study in Uto-Aztekan, Part II* [contd.].

[13] Sapir, *Wiyot and Yurok; Algonkin Affinity of Yurok and Wiyot.* The first of these papers was severely criticised: see Michelson, *Two Alleged Algonquian Languages of California.* Sapir's reply to this criticism, Michelson's "Rejoinder," and Sapir's final rebuttal will be found in the American Anthropologist, Vol. 17, pp. 188–98, 1915.

[14] I use the term "phonetic correspondences" in place of the older and less accurate "phonetic laws." See Bloomfield, *Language*, p. 347.   [15] Sapir, *Na-dene Languages.*

[16] Swanton, *Social Condition of the Tlingit Indians; Tlingit Myths and Tales; Tlingit; Haida.*

[17] Sapir, *Na-dene Languages*, p. 551 et seq.

It is therefore evident that the phonetic correspondences established by Sapir can only be the result of a genetic relationship between Haida, Tlingit, and Athapaskan. Verification of this relationship must await more detailed knowledge of the three groups but the evidence at hand is sufficient—especially when it is remembered that Haida, Tlingit, and Athapaskan are strikingly similar in morphology—to justify an hypothesis of genetic relationship.

Languages belonging to the same stock may also possess structural or morphological features in common. It is well to remember, however, particularly in regard to languages remotely related, that the divergences of grammatical form are always more obvious than the resemblances. To quote Sapir on this point:

When one passes from a language to another that is only remotely related to it, say from English to Irish or from Haida to Hupa or from Yana to Salinan, one is overwhelmed at first by the great and obvious differences of grammatical structure. As one probes more deeply, however, significant resemblances are discovered which weigh far more in a genetic sense than the discrepancies that lie on the surface and that so often prove to be merely secondary dialectic developments which yield no very remote historical perspective. In the upshot it may appear, and frequently does appear, that the most important grammatical features of a given language and perhaps the bulk of what is conventionally called its grammar are of little value for the remoter comparison, which may rest largely on submerged features that are of only minor interest to a descriptive analysis. Those who find this a paradox think descriptively rather than historically. It would be an instructive experience in method to compare English grammar with that of the Indo-European language reconstructed by philologists. Whole departments of Indo-European grammar find no analogue in English, while a very large part of what English grammar there is is of such secondary growth as to have no relevance for Indo-European problems. To anticipate from another field, a curiously large proportion of those features that make up "Haida grammar" turn out on closer study to be dialectic developments, on a common Na-dene basis, that are peculiar to it as distinct from Tlingit-Athapaskan; it appears, moreover, that some of the most significant evidence serving to link Haida with Tlingit-Athapaskan is not so much as mentioned in the formal remarks on Haida grammar that have been published. It would not seem necessary to make these self-evident remarks if so much of our work in American linguistics were not heavily biased in favor of a purely descriptive method and against all attempts at reconstructing the historical perspective.[18]

It should also be pointed out that resemblances in what Graff calls "general structure"[19] are not necessarily indicative of genetic relationship. To have value for comparative purposes, morphological resemblances must be found in "concrete morphological systems or in coherent parts of them"[20] and not in such general grammatical procedures as inflection, reduplication, and the like.

To illustrate these points, let us turn to Sapir's paper on the Hokan affinity of Subtiaba in Nicaragua.[21] The purpose of this paper was to follow up W. Lehmann's suggestion that Subtiaba is related to certain languages in California. Sapir finds, after examining Lehmann's

[18] Sapir, *Hokan Affinity of Subtiaba*, pp. 491–92.   [19] Graff, *Language and Languages*, p. 345.
[20] *Ibid.*, p. 351.   [21] Sapir, *Hokan Affinity of Subtiaba*.

material, "that he is essentially correct but that Subtiaba and Tlappanec are to be regarded as a southern outlier of the Hokan-Coahuiltecan stock as a whole, not of a sub-division of this group to which Washo belongs in particular."[22]

Sapir begins by preparing a comparative lexicon, listing those forms from the Hokan and Coahuiltecan languages which seem to bear a resemblance to Subtiaba words. This lexicon contains over one hundred comparisons, including body-part nouns, numerals, kinship terms, and other such words of basic importance for comparison. In addition, he points out lexical resemblances between pronominal stems, particles, and a number of grammatical elements. In the next section on phonology, Sapir draws a number of interesting and highly convincing parallels between the sound features of the languages considered. Though he is unable to establish any great number of phonetic correspondences, the few that are formulated can be well illustrated from the material at hand.

The third section of this paper deals with the comparative morphology of the Hokan-Coahuiltecan languages with particular reference to Subtiaba. Sapir begins this section by pointing out that:

We need not be surprised to find that some of the more superficial facts about Subtiaba morphology, enumerated in Lehmann's study, find no direct parallels in the northern Hokan languages. Subtiaba, for instance, has a "preterit tense" formed by prefixed *ni-* or *ci-*, a "present tense" in *na-*, a "future" in *ga-*; while Pomo has a past in suffixed *-hi* or *-hi-ba*, a present in *-a*, and a future in *-eya*; and Yana a preterit in suffixed *-ha* or *-'ni-*, a present in *-si*, and a future in *-si-*. As soon as we realize, however, that the Subtiaba "tense prefixes" are merely proclitic elements, probably of demonstrative or adverbial origin . . . , they cease to be of major morphological interest for the comparative point of view. As a matter of fact, some of the most important grammatical elements and features of Subtiaba have not been isolated by Lehmann and it is precisely these that prove it to possess a fundamentally Hokan grammar.[23]

The "important grammatical elements and features of Subtiaba" that "prove it to have a fundamentally Hokan grammar" may briefly be summarized as follows:

1. *Stem form.* There are many stems in the Hokan-Coahuiltecan languages which begin with a vowel and in which the vowel has a tendency to drop out, either in other forms of the same word or in cognate words of other languages. Thus, for example, Pomo *uyu* "eye" becomes *yu-* in such compounds as *yu-xa* "tear" (literally: "eye-water"). Similar stem forms and alternations exist in large numbers in Subtiaba.

2. *Noun prefixes.* A number of noun prefixes occur in many Hokan-Coahuiltecan languages as well as in Subtiaba. By comparing occurrences of these in the Hokan-Coahuiltecan languages and Subtiaba, Sapir is able to reconstruct no less than eight such prefixes for primitive Hokan-Coahuiltecan, and to give some idea of their distribution in the modern Hokan-Coahuiltecan languages.

3. *Adjective and verb class-prefixes.* "One of the most far-reaching, as well as interesting, features of Hokan morphology is the use of a set of consonantal class-prefixes in the verb

[22] *Ibid.*, p. 404.   [23] *Ibid.*, pp. 492–93.

and adjective. Probably none of the dialects keeps the old system intact, but it is not difficult to get an inkling of what it must have been like from the survivals we still possess.''[24] After bringing together the data on this morphological feature for all the Hokan-Coahuiltecan languages, Sapir concludes:

> The material that we have passed in review, scanty as it is, seems to leave little room for doubt that Hokan originally possessed a set of consonantal verb prefixes of a generic type. The elements that have the best claim to be recognized as archaic rather than as of secondary dialectic origin are:
>
>   *m-*, adjectival, (static intransitive)
>   *t-*, adjectival
>   *k-*, intransitive, (adjectival)
>   *p-*, transitive
>
> Other elements, like transitive or causative *s-*, may well be equally archaic, but the evidence is too scattering to justify a definite statement. Salinan and Subtiaba seem to preserve the old system of prefixes as a live mechanism where the other languages can apparently show only survivals, but it is quite possible that if we had reasonably full data for Washo and Seri, we should have to number these among the archaic languages as well.[25]

Morphological correlations such as these, indicating a systematic parallelism in grammatical procedures, are clearly strong evidence of genetic relationship. When it is remembered that great distances separate the Hokan languages of California from the Coahuiltecan of Texas and the Subtiaba of Nicaragua, these correspondences take on vastly more significance.

It is evident from this brief survey of Sapir's work that he achieved his revisions of the Powell classification by the strict application of the comparative method to American Indian materials. Because these materials, in many cases, were fragmentary or otherwise unsatisfactory, his formulations lack completeness and, at least to some of his critics, validity.[26] It is clear, however, that the ultimate verification (or disproof) of Sapir's hypotheses will come, not by a refinement or major change in the methods he employed, but when additional data on the languages concerned are made available.

In the case of three of the problems here discussed, additional data is now available though, in greater portion, yet unpublished. Whorf's work on the Uto-Aztekan languages has not only supplied additional data but has further verified Sapir's hypothesis of relationship.[27] My own work on Tonkawa[28] and that of A. M. Halpern on Yuma[29] has made available the data for testing Sapir's Hokan-Coahuiltecan connection. And, finally, Sapir's unpublished data on the Athapaskan languages plus what has been collected in recent years by Fang-Kwei Li and myself have further confirmed, in many particulars, Sapir's Na-dene stock.

[24] *Ibid.*, p. 504.   [25] *Ibid.*, pp. 522–24.

[26] See, for example, Goddard, *Has Tlingit a Genetic Relation to Athapascan?*

[27] Whorf, *Comparative Linguistics of Uto-Aztecan.*   [28] Hoijer, *Tonkawa.*

[29] Mr Halpern is now completing a manuscript on Yuma grammar to be presented as a doctoral thesis at the University of Chicago.

The efforts of Sapir and others to demonstrate genetic relations between stocks hitherto considered independent has led Boas, on various occasions,[30] "to state briefly the theoretical points of view on which . . . [his] attitude [on the problem of classifying American Indian languages] has been and still is based."[31] This point of view is briefly summarized in the following statements.

1. A survey of American Indian languages, particularly those of California and the North Pacific coast,"has demonstrated the occurrence of a number of striking morphological similarities between neighboring stocks which, however, are not accompanied by appreciable similarities in vocabulary."[32] Boas is not inclined to interpret these similarities as due to a common genetic origin.

2. It appears from what is known of the history of human languages "that the present wide distribution of a few linguistic stocks is a later phenomenon, and that in earlier times the area occupied by each linguistic family was small."[33] Because of the recent extensions of some linguistic families, Boas holds that "it seems reasonable to suppose that the number of languages that have disappeared is very large."[33] Therefore, "if there was a common source of several modern languages, they have become so much differentiated, that without historical knowledge of their growth, the attempts to prove their interrelation cannot succeed."[34]

3. Boas points out that "the problem of the study of languages is not one of classification but that our task is to trace the history of the development of human speech. Therefore, classification is only a means to an end."[34] Later, he says: "From this point of view the linguistic phenomena cannot be treated as a unit, but the manifestations of linguistic activity must be studied first each by itself, then in their relations to other linguistic phenomena."[34]

4. If we examine the distribution of phonetic features, grammatical features, and lexical features, we find, in America at least, that certain of these features have a limited and well-defined distribution which is, on the whole, continuous. From a survey of such distributions, Boas concludes:

While I am not inclined to state categorically that the areas of distribution of phonetic phenomena, of morphological characteristics, and of groups based on similarities in vocabularies are absolutely distinct, I believe this question must be answered empirically before we can undertake to solve the general problem of the history of modern American languages. If it should prove true, as I believe it will, that all these different areas do not coincide, then the conclusion seems inevitable that the different languages must have exerted a far-reaching influence upon one another. If this point of view is correct, then we have to ask ourselves in how far the phenomena of acculturation extend also over the domain of languages.[35]

5. After considering some of the means by which phonetic, morphological, and lexical features might be diffused from language to language, Boas points out:

---

[30] Boas, *Introductory; Classification of American Languages; Classification of American Indian Languages.*
[31] Boas, *Classification of American Languages*, p. 367.
[32] *Ibid.*, pp. 367–68.   [33] *Ibid.*, p. 368.   [34] *Ibid.*, p. 369.   [35] *Ibid.*, p. 371.

The distribution of these phenomena the world over is so irregular, that it would be entirely unwarranted to claim, that all similarities of phonetics, classification of concepts, or of morphology, must be due to borrowing. On the contrary, their distribution shows that they must be considered as due to psychological causes such as the unavoidable necessity of classification of experience in speech, which can lead to a limited number of categories only, or the physiological possibilities of articulation, that also limit the range of possible sounds which are sufficiently distinct to the ear for clear understanding.[36]

6. But, in contiguous areas at any rate, diffusion would seem to occur.

If these observations regarding the influence of acculturation upon language should be correct, then the whole history of American languages must not be treated on the assumption that all languages which show similarities must be considered as branches of the same linguistic family. We should rather find a phenomenon which is parallel to the features characteristic of other ethno-logical phenomena—namely, a development from diverse sources which are gradually worked into a single cultural unit. We should have to reckon with the tendency of languages to absorb so many foreign traits, that we can no longer speak of a single origin, and that it would be arbitrary whether we associate a language with one or the other of the contributing stocks. In other words, the whole theory of an "Ursprache" for every group of modern languages, must be held in abeyance until we can prove that these languages go back to a single stock and that they have not originated, to a large extent, by the process of acculturation.[37]

7. Boas concludes, then, that a critical attitude toward the general historical problem

. . . makes it necessary to approach our task from three points of view. Firstly, we must study the differentiation of dialects like those of the Sioux, Muskoki, Algonquin, Shoshoni, Salish, and Athapascan. Secondly, we must make a detailed study of the distribution of phonetic, grammatical, and lexicographical phenomena, the latter including also particularly the principles on which the grouping of concepts is based. Finally, our study ought to be directed not only to an investigation of the similarities of languages, but equally intensively towards their dissimilarities. Only on this basis can we hope to solve the general historical problem.[38]

Perhaps Boas' point of view is better summarized in the following quotation from a more recent article on the same subject. After reviewing data on the distribution of gram-matical features in native American languages, he concludes:

Considering these data as a whole, we may say that in a considerable number of native languages of the North Pacific Coast we find, notwithstanding fundamental differences in structure and vo-cabulary, similarities in particular grammatical features distributed in such a way that neighboring languages show striking similarities. The areas in which similar features are found do not coincide in regard to the various traits compared.

It seems to me almost impossible to explain this phenomenon without assuming the diffusion of grammatical processes over contiguous areas. Stress must be laid here upon the contiguity of dis-tribution, because comparative grammar shows clearly that similar features may develop independ-ently in different parts of the world. . . . On the other hand the distribution of the same particular

---

[36] *Ibid.*, p. 373.   [37] *Ibid.*, pp. 374–75.   [38] *Ibid.*, pp. 375–76.

grouping of concepts, or of the same methods of expression over contiguous areas can hardly be explained on the basis of independent origin.

So far as I can see an attempt to bring together the different languages of contiguous areas which have similar processes, is not feasible on account of the fundamental differences in conceptualization, in grammatical processes, and in vocabulary. . . .

If the view expressed here is correct, then it is not possible to group American languages rigidly in a genealogical scheme in which each linguistic family is shown to have developed to modern forms, but we have to recognize that many of the languages have multiple roots.[39]

Boas bases his conclusion that grammatical elements may diffuse over contiguous areas upon certain facts of distribution in native America. Thus, for example, he finds that, in Chinook and the neighboring but unrelated Sahaptin languages, diminutives are expressed by consonantal changes; that pronominal gender is found in Chinook and the coastal Salish languages adjoining the Chinook; that, in Quileute, Kwakiutl, and Tsimshian, "the pronominal representation of the noun (or article) is treated differently for proper nouns and for common nouns."[40] It would admittedly be difficult to dispute the conclusion drawn from such facts as these, viz., that grammatical elements may and do diffuse over contiguous areas. It is, however, equally difficult to believe that one or two traits taken over by one language from another can exert any profound influence on its basic structure.

It is also claimed, moreover, that, in some cases at least, there is evidence that diffusion has so affected two or more contiguous stocks as to make them strikingly similar in morphology. Boas states quite definitely, for example, that, though the morphology of Tlingit and Athapaskan "shows the most far-reaching similarities" and though "it is inevitable that these similarities must be due to historical causes," he "should not be inclined to claim . . . that Tlingit and Athapaskan are members of the same linguistic family."[41] The implication of this statement is clear: Boas considers that the similarities between Tlingit and Athapaskan are due to mutual borrowings.

Let us assume for the moment that Boas' interpretation of the facts in the case of Tlingit and Athapaskan is a valid one. Michelson has pointed out "that if the morphological resemblances between two supposedly distinct but contiguous stocks were entirely due to borrowings, by the doctrine of chances we should expect to find similar borrowings in another supposedly distinct but contiguous stock."[42] But, in this case certainly, such borrowings have not taken place. "Thus, Athapascan, so far as is known, has been in just as intimate contact for a very long period with Salishan and Esquimauan as with Tlingit, but there is but slight resemblance structurally between Athapascan, Salishan and Esquimauan."[42] Michelson goes on to point out that

. . . Algonquian, so far as we know, has been in just as intimate contact with Iroquoian, Siouan,

[39] Boas, *Classification of American Indian Languages*, pp. 6–7. Compare this statement with that quoted from Sapir on p. 4 of this paper.   [40] *Ibid.*, pp. 3–4.

[41] Boas, *Classification of American Languages*, p. 375.

[42] Michelson, *Classification of American Languages*.

and Muskhogean for at least several hundred years as it has with Esquimauan. Yet structurally Esquimauan and Algonquian resemble each other, and similarly Siouan and Muskhogean: but observe that the first pair does not resemble the second pair nor does either member of the first group resemble either one of the second. . . . Now if the above were entirely due to borrowing we should expect to find resemblances equally distributed where supposedly distinct stocks are contiguous. If the resemblances are confined to one or two features, they may be safely ascribed to acculturation; but when there are far-reaching structural resemblances between two or more supposedly distinct (and especially contiguous) stocks we may legitimately infer an ancient genetic connection which perhaps can no longer be proved owing to very early differentiation.[42]

It may also be pointed out that, though the languages of our modern civilizations are probably much more subject to borrowing and dialectic blending than are any of the so-called primitive languages, there is no direct evidence in what we know of the history of the Indo-European tongues of extensive morphological diffusion. Indeed, quite the contrary is indicated, at least by the history of English. Though English has borrowed tremendous numbers of words from other languages, there is no evidence that it has directly taken over any basic grammatical elements. The morphological innovations that did arise in English as a result of French contact were a direct result of extensive lexical borrowings. "Thus, the Latin-French suffix -ible, -able as in *agreeable, excusable, variable,* has been extended to forms like *bearable, eatable, drinkable,* where the underlying verb is native."[43] It is not likely, then, that we shall find evidences of extensive morphological borrowings in primitive languages unaccompanied by lexical borrowings of far greater extent.

These factors, taken with the evidences presented by Sapir for the genetic relationship of Haida, Tlingit, and Athapaskan, make it evident that structural similarities of a really far-reaching nature are probably more indicative of genetic relationship than of diffusion. We may, then, conclude with Sapir that

So long as such direct historical testimony as we have gives us no really convincing examples of profound morphological influence by diffusion, we shall do well not to put too much reliance in diffusion theories. On the whole, therefore, we shall ascribe the major concordances and divergences in linguistic form—phonetic pattern and morphology—to the autonomous drift of language, not to the complicating effect of single, diffused features that cluster now this way, now that. Language is probably the most self-contained, the most massively resistant of all social phenomena. It is easier to kill it off than to disintegrate its individual form.[44]

BIBLIOGRAPHY

BLOOMFIELD, LEONARD *Language* (New York, 1933).
BOAS, FRANZ *The Classification of American Languages* (American Anthropologist, Vol. 22, pp. 367–76, 1920).
    Classification of American Indian Languages (Language, Vol. 5, pp. 1–7, 1929).
    Introductory (International Journal of American Linguistics, Vol. 1, pp. 1–8, 1917).

[43] Bloomfield, *Language,* p. 454.   [44] Sapir, *Language,* p. 220.

DIXON, R. B., and A. L. KROEBER *Linguistic Families in California* (University of California Publications in American Archaeology and Ethnology, Vol. 16, No. 3, 1919).

New Linguistic Families in California (American Anthropologist, Vol. 15, pp. 647–55, 1913).

GODDARD, PLINY EARLE *Has Tlingit a Genetic Relation to Athapascan?* (International Journal of American Linguistics, Vol. 1, pp. 266–79, 1917–20).

The Present Condition of our Knowledge of North American Languages (American Anthropologist, Vol. 16, pp. 555–601, 1914).

GRAFF, WILLEM L. *Language and Languages* (New York, 1932).

HOIJER, HARRY *Tonkawa, an Indian Language of Texas* (In *Handbook of American Indian Languages*, Part 3, pp. 1–148, New York, 1933).

MICHELSON, TRUMAN *The Classification of American Languages* (International Journal of American Linguistics, Vol. 2, p. 73, 1921–23).

Two Alleged Algonquian Languages of California (American Anthropologist, Vol. 16, pp. 361–67, 1914).

POWELL, J. W. *Indian Linguistic Families of America North of Mexico* (Seventh Annual Report, Bureau of American Ethnology, pp. 7–148, 1891).

SAPIR, EDWARD *The Algonkin Affinity of Yurok and Wiyot Kinship Terms* (Journal, Société des Américanistes de Paris, n. s., Vol. 15, pp. 36–74, 1923).

The Hokan Affinity of Subtiaba in Nicaragua (American Anthropologist, Vol. 27, pp. 402–35, 491–527, 1925).

The Hokan and Coahuiltecan Languages (International Journal of American Linguistics, Vol. 1, pp. 280–90, 1917).

Language, an Introduction to the Study of Speech (New York, 1921).

The Na-dene Languages, a Preliminary Report (American Anthropologist, Vol. 17, pp. 534–58, 1915).

The Position of Yana in the Hokan Stock (University of California Publications in American Archaeology and Ethnology, Vol. 13, No. 1, 1917).

Southern Paiute and Nahuatl, a Study in Uto-Aztekan (Journal, Société des Américanistes de Paris, n. s., Vol. 10, pp. 379–425, 1913; Vol. 11, pp. 443–88, 1914).

Southern Paiute and Nahuatl, a Study in Uto-Aztekan, Part II [contd.] (American Anthropologist, Vol. 17, pp. 98–120, 306–28, 1915).

The Status of Linguistics as a Science (Language, Vol. 5, pp. 207–14, 1929).

Wiyot and Yurok, Algonkin Languages of California (American Anthropologist, Vol. 15, pp. 617–46, 1913).

SWANTON, JOHN R. *Haida* (In *Handbook of American Indian Languages*, Part 1, Bulletin, Bureau of American Ethnology, No. 40, pp. 205–82, 1911).

Social Condition, Beliefs, and Linguistic Relationship of the Tlingit Indians (Twenty-sixth Annual Report, Bureau of American Ethnology, pp. 391–486, 1908).

Tlingit (In *Handbook of American Indian Languages*, Part 1, Bulletin, Bureau of American Ethnology, No. 40, pp. 159–204, 1911).

Tlingit Myths and Tales (Bulletin, Bureau of American Ethnology, No. 39, 1909).

WHORF, B. L. *The Comparative Linguistics of Uto-Aztecan* (American Anthropologist, Vol. 37, pp. 600–608, 1935).

UNIVERSITY OF CALIFORNIA
AT LOS ANGELES

NORTH AMERICAN INDIAN LANGUAGES STILL SPOKEN AND THEIR GENETIC RELATIONSHIPS

By C. F. VOEGELIN

THE GROUPING of the separate languages which follows is according to demonstrated genetic relationships (linguistic families), and where this is uncertain, according to postulated linguistic families. If comparative work means the comparison of a few or several languages each of which has been studied synchronically, then such work can be said to have begun definitely for the Algonquian and Athabascan families, less definitely for the Uto-Aztecan family, possibly for the Siouan and Salish families.[1]

For the other languages north of Mexico, there have been numerous comparisons between word lists, and relationships have been suggested based on this kind of evidence, but not on the kind of evidence which the comparative method in linguistics can yield. Certain languages of the large remaining group have been described morphologically, including in isolated instances an adequate statement of phonology which is a *sine qua non* for comparative work, strictly speaking; dictionaries are generally lacking. The result of all this is that together with languages compared on the basis of word lists without structure, there are also comparisons on the basis of structure without word lists.

The number of language families north of Mexico was found to be half a hundred by Powell, half a dozen by Sapir.[2] The great reduction in one generation was possible, by and large, through relying on structural rather than lexical evidence for the comparison of languages. The six unnamed groups (I to VI, below) represent the reduced scheme; the named sub-headings (ALGONQUIAN, SALISH, etc.) are used where lexical material at least shows unquestionable and generally very close relationship; important dialects are given in a hyphenated name for a language (e.g., Fox-Sauk-Kikapoo).

A list of closely related languages is merely a statement of pretty obvious relationships between sister languages; further grouping of language families into a few divisions is, in

---

[1] For example, for ALGONQUIAN: Bloomfield, *Sound-System of Central Algonquian* and *Algonquian Sketch;* Michelson, *Preliminary Report* and *Phonetic Shifts;* for ATHABASCAN: Sapir, *Type of Athabaskan Relative* and *Comparative Athabaskan Grammar;* Li, *Mattole* and *Chipewyan Consonants;* Hoijer, *Southern Athapaskan Languages;* for UTO-AZTECAN: Kroeber, *Shoshonean Dialects of California;* Sapir, *Southern Paiute and Nahuatl;* Whorf, *Comparative Linguistics;* for SIOUAN: Dorsey, *Comparative Phonology;* Boas and Swanton, *Siouan.* In *Problems in Comparative Siouan Linguistics,* I have listed the surprisingly rich store of lexical materials available; much of this is published but the greater part remains in manuscript in the archives of the Bureau of American Ethnology. Beyond Boas and Haeberlin, *Sound Shifts,* there is little direct comparative work in SALISH; but there are an increasing number of grammatical and lexical studies being published which will permit a fuller application of the comparative method to Salish.

[2] Powell, *Indian Linguistic Families;* Sapir, *Central and North American Languages.* For the status of the relationship problem in the interim between Powell and Sapir, see Goddard, *Present Condition.*

contrast, a statement of less direct relationships between parent languages rather than between the sister languages as such. The more obvious relationships do not enjoy a greater scientific respectability than the subtle and less direct relationships; the Powell list and the Sapir list are not contradictory statements. The comparative method can be just as well applied to two reconstructed parent languages as to two sister languages, and for North America we have an architect's blue-print for such a procedure. This is the great reduction of language families which was initiated in part by Sapir, who contributed more to its plan than any other worker. Since we lack extensive texts such as those available in Semetic, further work can be carried on in the New World only when languages are still spoken; and the basic unit for comparative work is always the individual language.

Accordingly, the first interest of the present paper is to assemble a documented list of languages still spoken north of Mexico. Extinct languages are not counted. Our linguistic census takes separate languages (not dialects) as its primary unit. This cannot be determined with absolute certainty, but a review of the relevant literature and generous response to requests for supplementary data from both linguists and ethnographers shows that field workers have been on the whole much interested in eliciting information on the separability of languages, checking the generalizations of informants by observing attempts at communication between members of different tribes, and in favorable cases having a personal command of one or more dialects.[3] In doubtful cases, dialects which are said to be possibly intelligible are grouped together as one language. If we had full information, we should count dialects as belonging to one language when speakers of neighboring dialects understand one another, even though visitors from geographically separated dialects of the same language might have considerable difficulty in making themselves understood. This viewpoint has been consistently kept in mind in reading the literature. What error there is in counting will probably turn out to be on the understatement side. No comparisons can be made with other estimates of the number of languages north of Mexico, for this is the first serious attempt to count separate languages; Powell and others merely list tribal names (political divisions) under family headings.

NUMBER OF LANGUAGES

I

Eskimo (2 languages). That most Eskimo dialects are mutually intelligible is attested by Rasmussen who travelled across arctic America from Greenland to Alaska expecting to but failing to find numerous different Eskimo languages. "Yet the remarkable thing I found

[3] Grateful acknowledgement is made to anthropologists for supplying names of languages spoken and extinct, and for distinguishing with greater or less emphasis the degree of intelligibility between dialects. Sources for this information are specifically acknowledged as "personal communications" (abbreviated to p. c.). In trying to maintain a consistent viewpoint in estimating the number of separate languages, I have combined some few names given to me as representing pretty distinct dialects in one hyphenated language. I am alone responsible for possible errors in such arrangements. Grateful acknowledgement is also made to Erminie W. Voegelin who joined me in reviewing much of the ethnographic literature.

was that my Greenlandic dialect served to get me into complete understanding with all the tribes."[4] Our authority cites characteristic experiences on his journey. When he arrived at the Lyon Inlet Eskimo, west of Baffinland, he says, "I was delighted to find that the differ-ence in language was so slight that we had not the least difficulty in understanding one another. Indeed, they took us at first for tribesmen of kindred race from somewhere up in Baffin Island."[5] Rasmussen found that the majority of place names on the Melville Peninsula coast "were identical with some of the familiar place names from that part of Greenland where I was born."[6] The Eskimo of Cape Krusenstern, across Coronation Gulf, found Ras-mussen's Greenlandic dialect completely intelligible.[7] The Mackenzie Eskimo "spoke a language which was almost exactly like that of the Eskimos in Greenland."[8] At Point Barrow Rasmussen says, "My Greenland accent and idiom occasioned no difficulty among the na-tives here; a fact which promised well for future work."[9] All in all, we may conclude that essentially one Eskimo language is spoken all the way from Greenland to Alaska.

The first real break in languages is found in Alaska where Rasmussen says, "The Eskimo from the south and west of the Yukon spoke a dialect differing so considerably from the others that I found it, contrary to all previous experience, impossible . . . without the aid of an interpreter."[10]

No one is very definite about the precise nature of the dialectic differences between the numerous local groups which are treated as units in the ethnographic literature. Thal-bitzer emphasizes the difference between the dialect of an East Greenlander and West Greenlander, and of both to the Baffinland Eskimo, and indeed says that one must learn some "peculiarities of the dialect" of the other, but does not define the nature of the peculiarities.[11] There are Greenland dialects, Central dialects (Cumberland Sound, Iglulik, Netsilik, Coronation Gulf, Barren Grounds group), and Labrador dialects; Birket-Smith vouches for Rasmussen's ability to use Greenlandic among the Central dialects, and adds, "neither had the rest of us any difficulty in our daily intercourse with the Canadian Eskimos."[12] As to diversity, "The difference between the individual groups may, perhaps, be compared with the difference between standard English and Scotch, and between stand-ard Danish and Jutlandic. . . . Neither Jacob Olsen, a native of West Greenland, nor our Polar Eskimos had spent many days among the Canadian Eskimos, before they were able to talk freely with them upon all everyday subjects."[13]

Returning to Alaska, we find Dall reporting significant change of dialect at the Yukon delta group of Ekogmut.[14] This was about where Rasmussen's Greenlandic Eskimo failed him. Until further work is done, particularly in Alaska, we may conclude that there are two Eskimo languages, Central-Greenlandic and Alaskan.

ALEUT (2 languages). Dall lists a few grammatical differences between the two Aleutian

[4] Rasmussen, *Across Arctic America*, p. x.   [5] *Ibid.*, p. 6.   [6] *Ibid.*, p. 11.   [7] *Ibid.*, p. 282.
[8] *Ibid.*, p. 292.   [9] *Ibid.*, p. 305.   [10] *Ibid.*, p. 349.   [11] Thalbitzer, *Eskimo*, p. 971.
[12] Birket-Smith, *Five Hundred Eskimo Words*, p. 5.   [13] *Ibid.*, p. 43.
[14] Dall, *Tribes of the Extreme Northwest*, p. 17; cf. Barnum, *Grammatical Fundamentals*.

languages spoken on the Aleutian Islands.[15] Jochelson points out that these two languages are unintelligible, and that Russian is used as a *lingua franca*.[16]

II

ALGONQUIAN (13 languages). There is a vast literature on Algonquian languages. Michelson and more recently Bloomfield have summarized the known facts and given bibliographies.[17] The following six languages are sometimes referred to as Central Algonquian: (1) Cree-Montagnais-Naskapi, (2) Menomini, (3) Fox-Sauk-Kickapoo, (4) Shawnee, (5) Potawatomi, and (6) Ojibwa-Ottawa-Algonquin-Salteaux. The next four languages are sometimes distinguished as Eastern Algonquian, but this distinction rests on very little linguistic evidence: (7) Delaware, (8) Penobscot-Abnaki, (9) Malecite-Passamaquoddy, (10) Micmac. All the preceding languages are spoken in the Eastern Woodlands. The remaining three languages belong to the Great Plains and, while divergent lexically, are surprisingly like Woodlands Algonquian in inflectional and compositional features: (11) Piegan-Blood-Blackfoot, (12) Northern-Southern Cheyenne, (13) Arapaho-Atsina-Nawathinehena.

WIYOT and YUROK. The variations or family habits which Reichard notes for Wiyot may be reflexes of former dialects. Despite the fact that the territories of the Wiyot and Yurok are contiguous in northwestern California, the two languages are most distantly related. And knowledge of Yurok remains most fragmentary.[18]

KUTENAI. This language, spoken in two dialects, is found on the eastern slopes of the Rocky Mountains at the international line.[19]

QUILEUTE. This is perhaps the only remaining language of the Chemakuan family of Washington.[20]

WAKASHAN (6 languages). All members of this family are on Vancouver Island and the adjacent mainland:[21] Nootka proper,[22] Nitinat, and Makah; Kwakiutl proper,[23] Bella Bella, and Kitamat.

SALISH (15 languages). The relationship of the numerous Salish dialects in Oregon, Washington, Idaho, and British Columbia is uncertain. A lexical comparison shows that most of the coast dialects belong to a "tc" group but the "tc" in the words compared corresponds to "k" in Bella Coola, also a coast dialect; there are many inland dialects of the "tc" group as well as of the "k" group.[24] Linguistic classifications of this kind do not necessarily correlate with degrees of intelligibility.

Teit spoke the Thompson dialect fluently, and is a reliable authority for all the interior

---

[15] Dall, *op. cit.*, p. 116.   [16] Jochelson, *History of the Aleut*, p. 43.

[17] Michelson gave scattered bibliographic references in his numerous publications; Bloomfield (*Algonquian Sketch*) gives a systematic bibliography of all Algonquian papers published since Pilling.

[18] Reichard, *Wiyot Grammar*, p. 6; Waterman, *Yurok Affixes*.

[19] Canestrelli, *Grammar of Kutenai Language;* Boas, *Kutenai Grammar*.   [20] Andrade, *Quileute*, p. 151.

[21] Sapir and Swadesh, *Nootka Texts*, p. 10.   [22] Swadesh, *Nootka Internal Syntax*.

[23] Boas, *Kwakiutl*.   [24] Boas and Haeberlin, *Sound Shifts*, p. 120.

Salish. He regards Lillooet, Shuswap, and Thompson as separate languages.[25] In addition, some dialects have been recently yielding to others so that an earlier picture might well have shown greater diversity.[26] Shuswap, like Thompson and Lillooet, is a name covering several bands, each of which may have some slight dialectic peculiarity.[27]

Teit lists as a fourth Salish language or group of closely related dialects Okanagon-Sanpoil (Nespelim)-Colville-Lake, or more briefly Okanagon dialects, for which the natives had one term meaning "Salish speaking;"[28] sometimes this term is used to include all the interior languages.[29]

Whereas Teit's first four languages, as given, belong to the interior "k" group, his fifth language, Flathead-Pend d'Oreille-Kalispel-Spokan, belongs to the interior "tc" group.[30] Dialect differences are especially notable among the Flathead and Spokan bands; however, Teit is perfectly clear in insisting that all the tribes "had little or no difficulty in understanding one another."[31]

Coeur d'Alène is somewhat removed, although in the interior "tc" group, and must be counted as a sixth Salish language.[32]

Middle Columbia-Wenatchi, of the "k" group, is similar to Okanagon dialects but not intelligible; it counts as a seventh Salish language, and the last of our interior tribes.[33]

Tillamook, of the coastal "tc" group, is absolutely unintelligible to any of the others.[34] Likewise, on the authority of Franz Boas, Chehalis-Cowlitz-Lower Chehalis-Quinault are mutually intelligible but Twana appears to be less readily intelligible to neighboring tribes; the group of dialects from Olympia to the Lummi are mutually intelligible; so also are Lummi-Songish-Clallam; so also are Lower Fraser River-Nanaimo; Squamish is a group by itself; Comox-Sishiatl is another; Bella Coola another.[35]

Of the 15 Salish languages, 7 are spoken in the interior, 8 on the coast. The family as a whole, like Wakashan and Eskimo but unlike Algonquian and most of the remaining larger families, extends over a more or less continuous area.

III

ATHABASCAN (19 languages). Athabascan languages are spoken in three widely separated areas: the Mackenzie River drainage, the Pacific Coast, and the Southwest.[36]

The Mackenzie area has been recently surveyed ethnographically by Osgood, who sug-

[25] Teit, Lillooet Indians, p. 195; Dawson, Notes on the Shuswap, p. 5; Franz Boas corroborates this (p. c.).

[26] Teit, op. cit., p. 200. [27] Teit, The Shuswap, p. 456.

[28] Teit, Salishan Tribes, p. 199. [29] Ibid., p. 203; Ray, Sanpoil and Nespelem, p. 9.

[30] Teit, Salishan Tribes, p. 295. [31] Ibid., p. 303.

[32] Teit, loc. cit.; Franz Boas (p. c.); Reichard, Coeur d'Alene, pp. 630–34, 682–86.

[33] Teit, Middle Columbia Salish, p. 93. [34] Franz Boas (p. c.); Edel, Tillamook Language.

[35] Franz Boas, Distribution of Salish Dialects and of Languages spoken in the Adjoining Territory before 1800, based on information collected by James A. Teit, Franz Boas, and Leo J. Frachtenberg (In: Haeberlin, Teit, and Roberts, Coiled Basketry, map); Haeberlin and Gunther, Indians of Puget Sound, pp. 7, 11.

[36] Sapir, Internal Linguistic Evidence.

gests a few groupings of tribal dialects in terms of mutual intelligibility. (1) Dogrib-Hare-Bear Lake is almost certainly one language; (2) Chipewyan-Yellowknife-Slave.[37] Birket-Smith's report suggests that the intertribal relationships did not make for much linguistic practise between dialects; between the Chipewyan and "the closely related Yellow Knife intercourse was in the best of cases cool."[38] (3) Kutchin is a language spoken by eight tribes in various dialects.[39] (4) Tanana-Koyukon-Han-Tutchone; perhaps the first pair and the second pair of dialects form two languages.[40] Dall sees little difference between Koyukon and the Ingalik languages.[41] Allen gives additional local or band names for members of this language.[42] (5) Sekani-Sarsi-Beaver-Stonies. That the dialect of the last tribe belongs in this group is known from Teit.[43] Goddard, with reservations, gives Sarsi-Beaver as akin.[44] Jenness gives Sekani-Beaver as almost the same dialect.[45] (6) Carrier-Chilcotin is given by Farrand, Osgood, and Teit.[46] (7) Tahltan-Kaska is given by Emmons, Osgood, and Teit.[47] (8) Osgood places Tanaina-Ingalik as one language; [48] Ingalik has also been associated with language 4, above.

Perhaps five Athabascan languages are still spoken in northwest California and southwest Oregon: Hupa, Kato-Wailaki, Chasta-Costa, and Mattole may be regarded as separate languages on the authority of Li,[49] but Kato and Wailaki no doubt have important dialectic differences;[50] Tolowa seems to have some speakers remaining.[51]

Hoijer finds that the southwestern Athabascans speak six separate languages: Jicarilla, Lipan, and Kiowa Apache, with Navaho dialects, San Carlos dialects, and Chiricahua-Mescalero dialects to the west of the first three languages.[52] Goddard appears to say that with the possible exception of Navaho and Lipan, southern Athabascan is one language.[53] This is no doubt an overstatement occasioned by a wider comparison of Southern Athabascan with Pacific Athabascan and Mackenzie Athabascan languages.

[37] Cornelius Osgood (p. c.); Li, *List of Chipewyan Stems.*

[38] Birket-Smith, *Chipewyan Ethnology,* p. 34.

[39] Osgood, *Ethnography of the Kutchin,* p. 13; Sapir, *Kutchin Lexical Materials.*

[40] Cornelius Osgood (p. c.).   [41] Dall, *Tribes of the Extreme Northwest,* pp. 24 ff.

[42] Allen, *Report of an Expedition,* pp. 137–40.

[43] Teit, *The Shuswap,* p. 451. These Stonies are not to be confused with the Siouan Stoney (Assiniboine). Cf. Sapir, *Pitch Accent in Sarcee,* p. 185; Li, *Sarcee Verb-stems.*

[44] Goddard, *Beaver Indians,* p. 209; *Sarsi Texts,* p. 190.

[45] Jenness, *Sekani Indians* (Transactions, Royal Society), pp. 21, 23; *Sekani Indians* (Bulletin, National Museum), p. 6.

[46] Farrand, *Traditions of the Chilcotin,* p. 3; Osgood, *Distribution of Northern Athapaskan,* p. 22; Teit, *The Shuswap,* p. 763; Morice, *Carrier Language.*

[47] Emmons, *Tahltan Indians,* p. 5; Osgood, *Distribution of Northern Athapaskan,* p. 22; Teit, *Notes on the Tahltan,* p. 340.   [48] Osgood, *Distribution of Northern Athapaskan,* p. 22; *Tanaina Culture,* p. 716.

[49] Fang-kuei Li (p. c.); Goddard, *Athapascan (Hupa),* p. 92; Sapir, *Notes on Chasta Costa.*

[50] Goddard, *Elements of the Kato Language,* pp. 3, 67, 68.   [51] Drucker, *The Tolowa,* p. 222.

[52] Hoijer, *Southern Athapaskan Languages,* p. 86; Franciscan Fathers, *Ethnologic Dictionary; Vocabulary of Navaho Language;* Sapir, *Navaho Grammar;* Hoijer, *Chiricahua and Mescalero Apache Texts,* pp. 71–140.

[53] Goddard, *Jicarilla Apache Texts,* p. 8; cf. Goddard, *Similarities and Diversities.*

EYAK. This language, discovered as recently as 1930, was spoken by less than 200 individuals in two main villages at the Copper River Delta, Alaska.[54]

TLINGIT. This language is spoken over a considerable area in southeastern Alaska.[55] Swanton minimizes local dialectic peculiarities. Some neighboring Eskimo groups, and possibly other linguistically unrelated groups, have allowed their native languages to become supplanted by Tlingit. Possible reflexes of a relatively recent substratum in these new Tlingit languages present a problem not without theoretical interest.

HAIDA. Two important dialects remain, Skidegate and Masset, both on the Queen Charlotte Islands off the coast of British Columbia; the latter is also spoken on the adjacent mainland of Alaska.[56]

IV

UTO-AZTECAN (10 languages in the United States). A few years ago a summary statement of our knowledge of Uto-Aztecan relationships would have been simple. North of Mexico. one had merely to account for the Shoshonean languages, and add Pima-Papago.[57]

The only part of this scheme which remains usable today is Pima-Papago, a very divergent member of its family and a single dialect spoken by a "River People" (Pima) and by a "Desert people" (Papago).[58] For the rest, Whorf has shown that Shoshonean languages do not form a homogeneous group in contrast to the Nahuatl of Mexico: any one Shoshonean language may be more closely related to Nahuatl than to another neighboring Shoshonean language.[59] The essential problem of Uto-Aztecan relationships remains to be worked out.

Uto-Aztecan languages north of Mexico are spoken in California, Nevada, Utah, and contiguous states. In Southern California, Luiseño, Cahuilla, Serrano, and Cupeño are presumably to be counted as four separate languages; the last two are on the verge of extinction.[60] A fifth language is Tübatulabal, spoken in a southern enclave of the Sierra Nevada.[61] Spilling over into Arizona from Mexico is the divergent Pima-Papago, already mentioned.[62] This, with Hopi, spoken in an Arizona pueblo, makes seven Uto-Aztecan languages.[63]

Turning back to an area generally east of the Sierras in California, in Nevada and Utah and extending north, we are less certain as to where differences of a dialectic order end and where unintelligibility begins. Sapir says, "It is doubtful if even the geographically extreme Ute-Chemehuevi dialects . . . are not mutually intelligible. . . . "[64] This would make Ute-Southern Paiute-Chemehuevi-Kawaiisu an eighth Uto-Aztecan language,[65] but Whorf regards these dialects as falling together into three languages, Ute-Southern Paiute, Kawaiisu,

[54] De Laguna, Preliminary Sketch of Eyak, pp. 63–64.

[55] Swanton, Tlingit, p. 163; Boas, Grammatical Notes on Language of Tlingit.

[56] Swanton, Haida, p. 209.   [57] Sapir, Southern Paiute Language, p. 6.

[58] Underhill, Autobiography of Papago, p. 1.

[59] Whorf, Comparative Linguistics, pp. 606–608; Origin of Aztec TL.

[60] E. W. Gifford (p. c.); A. L. Kroeber (p. c.).   [61] Voegelin, Tübatulabal Grammar.

[62] Dolores, Papago Verb Stems; Papago Nominal Stems.

[63] Whorf, Punctual and Segmentative Aspects; Some Verbal Categories.

[64] Sapir, Southern Paiute Language, p. 5.   [65] Ibid., pp. 1–730.

Chemehuevi.[66] Likewise, (9) Shoshoni-Comanche-Gosiute-Wind River-Panamint (Koso) can be taken as another language only with reservations; and (10) Mono-Bannock-Snake-Northern Paiute (Paviotso) may possibly be another language.[67] Bands speaking these last dialects extend into the Rocky Mountains and even into the Great Plains.

TANOAN (4 languages). Tanoan languages are spoken only in the Pueblos, as follows: Tiwa (Isleta-Sandia; Taos-Picuris), Tewa (San Juan-Santa Clara-San Ildefonso-Tesuque-Nambe-Hano), Towa (Jemez). It is not certain whether Tiwa should be counted as one or two languages. Trager says, "Taos and Picurís are much alike, and mutually intelligible. Sandía and Isleta are almost identical. A speaker of the southern languages can manage to understand the northern two, but the reverse is not true. The northern languages are more archaic (Taos apparently most so)."[68] Parsons, says "So great are the dialectical differences in the Tanoan speech of the two towns [Isleta and Taos] that when the Isletan cousin of this Taos man . . . visited Taos he had to speak either Spanish or English with his hosts."[69] This is not an isolated instance of what may be a more general problem of non-reciprocal intelligibility (see Achumawi-Atsugewi, under VI, below); perhaps in such instances of partial intelligibility a *lingua franca* is used if available.

KIOWA. In historic times, the Kiowa were found in the Plains east of the Pueblo country.[70]

ZUNI. This language is spoken in a single pueblo in western New Mexico.[71]

V[72]

YOKUTS (3 languages). Stanley Newman regards the southernmost foothill dialects, the Buena Vista group, as a separate Yokuts language on the basis of Kroeber's statement of divergence. On the basis of his own experience, Newman is able to say that Chukchansi and Dumna (Northern Foothill dialects) are intelligible to Gashowu and Choinimni (Kings River Foothill dialects), and that these are intelligible to Wükchumni and Yaudanchi (Tule-Kaweah Foothill dialects), and less certainly to Paleuyami (of the Poso Creek Foothill). In other words, there are two Yokuts Foothill languages: Buena Vista in the south, with all the dialects north of Buena Vista constituting a second language. The Valley dialects, Chauchila-Yauelmani, constitute a third Yokuts language.[73]

MAIDU (4 languages). The Nisenan or Southern Maidu language has some dialectic peculiarities.[74] Of the Valley, Foothill, and Mountain Maidu, the remaining languages are probably Northwest Maidu and Mountain Maidu; one or two Valley Maidu remain.[75]

MIWOK (2 languages). Of the formerly numerous Miwok dialects, there are now no speak-

---

[66] B. L. Whorf (p. c.).   [67] Sapir, *Southern Paiute Language*, p. 5.
[68] Trager, *Kinship and Status Terms*.   [69] Parsons, *Isleta*, p. 205.
[70] Harrington, *Vocabulary of Kiowa*.   [71] Bunzel, *Zuni*, p. 393.
[72] The language families in this group are listed in general geographic order from the Yokuts in central California through Oregon and Washington to the Tsimshian in British Columbia.
[73] Stanley S. Newman (p. c.); Kroeber, *Yokuts Language*; Newman, *Yawelmani Dialect*.
[74] Ralph Beals (p. c.).   [75] A. L. Kroeber (p. c.); Dixon, *Maidu*; Erminie W. Voegelin (p. c.).

ers along the southern Marin County coast, only two or three speakers at Bodega Bay, and a few speakers representing the Lower Lake dialect which was formerly in constant contact with the Coast Miwok. There were formerly a few interior dialects on the Sierra slope from Fresno River to Cosumnes, extending into the San Joaquin valley; these did not know of the existence of the geographically separated Miwok on both sides of the Coast range. Freeland regards the Miwok of the Coast range and the Miwok of the Sierra as two distinct languages.[76] Gifford also distinguishes the Sierra from the Lake and Coast language.[77]

WINTUN (2 languages). Wintun-Wintu is on the borderline of being two languages or two dialects of one language. There is no doubt that Patwin is a separate Wintun language.[78]

KLAMATH-MODOC (Lutuami). Spier has discovered five local groups for the Klamath alone, but only one of his informants thought of dialectic differentiation in connection with these five groups: it is pointed out that Gatschet recorded no linguistic differences for the various groups.[79] Barrett also had a single informant tell him of dialectic variation within Klamath, and while this is regarded as not impossible it is none the less argued that differences between Klamath groups must be inconsiderable because lexical differences between Klamath and Modoc are slight.[80] The Gúmbatwas group of Modoc differed from other Modoc groups.[81] Klamath and Modoc have remarkably different grammatical resources and yet are intelligible to each other.[82]

MOLALE. Molale is still spoken. Another language of the family, Cayuse, is considered to be in effect extinct.[83]

SAHAPTIN (2 languages). There are numerous dialects of Northern Sahaptin: Warmspring (Tenino)-Wallawalla-Umatilla-Palus-Skin-Yakima-Pswanwapam-Wanapam-Klikitat-Upper Cowlitz-Upper Nisqually. These all constitute one language. Nez Percé is the second Sahaptin language.[84]

TAKELMA. When Sapir studied Takelma in 1906 there were only a few speakers of the language remaining.[85] Two speakers remain today.[86]

LOWER UMPQUA-SIUSLAW. These dialects may be more or less distinct or practically identical; one language is involved and this language is spoken by not more than three or four people.[87]

ALSEA. Jacobs has checked over Frachtenberg's manuscript grammar with the last remaining speaker of Alsea.[88]

---

[76] Freeland, *Miwok Grammar*; Kroeber, *Languages of Coast of California North of San Francisco*, pp. 278–319.   [77] E. W. Gifford (p. c.).

[78] E. W. Gifford and A. L. Kroeber (p. c.); Du Bois, *Wintu Ethnography*, p. 5.

[79] Spier, *Klamath Ethnography*, p. 22.   [80] Barrett, *Material Culture of Klamath*, p. 241.

[81] Spier, *op. cit.*, p. 2, with footnote reference to Gatschet, *Klamath Indians*, Vol. 1, p. xxxiv.

[82] Voegelin, *Study of Paradigmatic Differences*.   [83] Melville Jacobs (p. c.).

[84] Jacobs, *Northern Sahaptin Grammar*, p. 96; Spinden, *Nez Percé Indians*, p. 172.

[85] Sapir, *Takelma Language*.   [86] Melville Jacobs (p. c.).

[87] Frachtenberg, *Siuslawan (Lower Umpqua)*; Melville Jacobs (p. c.).

[88] Melville Jacobs (p. c.); Frachtenberg, *Alsea Texts and Myths*.

Coos. This family is now represented by two dialects, Hanis and Miluk.[89]

KALAPUYA (2 languages). The Santiam-Mackenzie dialects are still spoken by a few individuals; the Yonkalla dialect of another language is spoken by one woman; a third Kalapuya language became extinct two years ago.[90]

CHINOOK (2 languages). Lower Chinook is spoken by one or two old men.[90] It is an entirely separate language from Upper Chinook. The latter is known by speakers as Kikct and includes such dialects as Cascades, Multnomah, Wasco, Wishram, as well as others now extinct, as Clackamas.[91]

TSIMSHIAN. The three dialects of Tsimshian are said to be mutually intelligible.[92]

VI

WASHO. Detached political units formerly embraced only six or seven families, and these ranged about Lake Tahoe, chiefly on the eastern slopes of the Sierra Nevada. There were some local differences in culture; it seems probable that local dialectic differences might be found.[93]

POMO (4 languages). The most recent field report divides the numerous Pomo settlements according to three contiguous natural areas: Clear Lake, Russian River, and Coast to the west of the first two areas.[94] The Coast Pomo speak a Southwestern dialect (language). It is not certain whether the intermediate Russian River settlements had a language unintelligible to other Pomo. Kniffen questions Barrett's division of a dialect area into Coast and River divisions.[95] Three distinct Pomo languages are found about Clear Lake, and this together with Southwestern (Coast) makes four Pomo languages. Kroeber shows additional dialects, presumably intelligible to one or another of the four separate languages.[96] It is possible that one of the Clear Lake languages, Northeast Pomo, has become extinct.[97]

YUKI (2 languages). Yuki proper and Wappo are still spoken.[98]

SHASTA-ACHUMAWI (3 languages). Of the nine Achumawi dialects spoken in northeastern California, at least Atwandjini-Ilmawi-Adjumawi-Hammaawi still retain their dialectic peculiarities.[99] These, and indeed all nine dialects, are or were mutually intelligible. No Achumawi speaker could understand speakers of Atsugewi immediately to the south. Conversely, Atsugewi speakers either learned Achumawi or some special relationship existed between these two languages comparable to the non-reciprocal intelligibility between cer-

---

[89] Frachtenberg, *Coos;* Jacobs, *Coos Narrative and Ethnologic Texts.*   [90] Melville Jacobs (p. c.).

[91] Spier and Sapir, *Wishram Ethnography,* p. 159; Jacobs, *Structure of Chinook Jargon;* Boas, *Chinook.*

[92] Garfield, *Tsimshian Clan and Society,* p. 173; Boas, *Tsimshian.*

[93] Lowie, *Ethnographic Notes on Washo;* Kroeber, *Washo Language.*   [94] Kniffen, *Pomo Geography.*

[95] *Ibid.,* p. 385. However, A. M. Halpern says his own recently collected lexical material corroborates Barrett's seven-fold classification of the Pomo languages (p. c.).

[96] Kroeber, *Handbook of Indians of California,* p. 227.

[97] E. W. Gifford and A. L. Kroeber (p. c.).

[98] A. L. Kroeber (p. c.); Radin, *Grammar of Wappo.*

[99] C. F. Voegelin, Unpublished field notes, 1936.

tain Tanoan languages.[100] A divergent member of this family is Shasta, of the upper Klamath River to the west.[101]

KAROK. Between the Shasta and the Yurok, on the Klamath River, there were a number of Karok settlements. These had a substantially uniform speech, according to Kroeber who would isolate the dialect of the uppermost Karok as somewhat differentiated from the speech of the settlements on the lower reaches of the Klamath.[102]

YUMAN (4 languages). The following dialects are still spoken; the boundaries between "dialect" and "language" are tentative: Havasupai-Walapai-Yavapai; Mohave-Yuma-Maricopa-Kaveltchadom-Halchidhoma; Kohuana-Halyikwamai-Cocopa; Diegueño-Kamia-Akwaala.[103] Extending from the Grand Canyon in Arizona to the Pacific at the international boundary, Yuman languages are believed to show nearer relationship to the California languages listed above (except Yuki) than to the remaining languages of Group VI which are all east of the Rocky Mountains.

IROQUOIAN (6 languages). Ashur Wright, in a work dated 1842, speaks of Onondaga and Cayuga as idioms of Seneca;[104] present day Senecas can understand Cayuga and Onondaga after a few hours.[105] The three may possibly be taken as very distinctive dialects of one language, Seneca-Cayuga-Onondaga;[106] three other languages were spoken in contiguous territory centering in New York state: Mohawk, Oneida, and Wyandot, the last also known as Huron.[107] Tuscarora was spoken in Virginia, and Cherokee dialects in the Carolinas.[108] Most of the Iroquois tribes, as other tribes east of the Mississippi still speaking native languages, are now removed from their early homes to reservations and allotments.

SIOUAN (8 languages). Siouan tribes of the Gulf and Atlantic slope areas are extinct except for Catawba which still remains on a reservation in South Carolina; Catawba, as a dying language, is now being freshly studied.[109] Of Siouan languages belonging to the fringe of the Woodlands and Plains, Iowa-Oto is practically one dialect; Iowa-Oto speakers say they cannot understand the Woodlands Winnebago to the north.[110] Omaha-Ponca-Osage-Kansa (extinct?)-Quapaw are more or less distinct dialects of a fourth Siouan language. It

---

[100] De Angulo and Freeland, *Achumawi Language*, p. 78; Kniffen, *Achomawi Geography*, p. 303; Uldall, *Sketch of Achumawi Phonetics.*   [101] Dixon, *Shasta-Achomawi.*

[102] Kroeber, *Handbook of Indians of California*, p. 100; cf. the striking dialectic differences between Harrington, *Karuk Texts*, and De Angulo and Freeland, *Karok Texts.*

[103] Leslie Spier and E. W. Gifford (p. c.); Gatschet, *Der Yuma-Sprachstamm;* Spier, *Havasupai Texts;* Kroeber, *Phonetic Elements of Mohave;* Kroeber and Harrington, *Phonetic Elements of Diegueño.*

[104] Anonymous, *Spelling-Book in Seneca Language.* William N. Fenton, of the Bureau of American Ethnology, has been able to identify the author of this work as Ashur Wright.   [105] William N. Fenton (p. c.).

[106] Rather, each of these names would then represent groups of still closer dialects. Thus, Fenton finds four sub-dialects for Seneca: Allegany-Tonawanda-Grand River-Cattaraugus; slight differences, such as relative speed in speaking, distinguish the sub-dialects.

[107] Mohawk, Oneida, and Wyandot certainly appear to be separate languages in the comparisons of Barbeau, *Classification of Iroquoian Radicals.*   [108] Olbrechts, *Two Cherokee Texts.*

[109] Speck, *Catawba Texts*, pp. x–xv; Morris Swadesh (p. c.); Raven McDavid (p. c.).

[110] C. F. Voegelin, Unpublished field notes, 1938; Whitman, *The Oto*, p. xi.

may be questioned whether the dialects of the last language (Dorsey's Dhegiha) are mutually intelligible. Fortune says, "The cognate tribes [to the Omaha] are the Ponca, who speak the same language and have approximately the same institutions, and the Osage, the Kansa, and the Quapaw who speak the same language with dialectical differences."[111] Dorsey's list of words common to these Dhegiha languages would certainly make mutual intelligibility expectable. For the Dakota-Assiniboine language Lowie says, "At the same time the question raised by Powell whether the speech of the Assiniboine represents a distinct language of the Siouan stock, must be answered negatively as the dialectic variations do not transcend the limits of mutual intelligibility."[112] In addition to these five languages, there are three Siouan languages in the northern Plains: Mandan,[113] Hidatsa,[114] and Crow.[115]

CADDOAN (4 languages). The divergent Caddo, together with the Wichita and the now almost extinct Kitsai, belong in the southern Plains. Arikara of the northern Plains and Pawnee of the central Plains are highly divergent dialects of one language.[116]

KERESAN. This is one language spoken in several Pueblos. White says, "The western dialect of the Keres language, represented by Acoma and Laguna, may be understood only with some difficulty by the eastern section, comprising Santo Domingo, San Felipe, Sant' Ana, Cochiti, and Zia."[117]

MUSKOGEAN (4 languages). All the languages were spoken in contiguous areas in the southeast: Choctaw-Chickasaw; Alabama-Koasati; Mikasuki-Hitchiti; Muskogee (Creek)-Seminole.[118]

The following isolated languages also belong to the Southeast and Gulf region; all are on the verge of extinction, except Yuchi.

TUNICA[119]

NATCHEZ[120]

CHITIMACHA[121]

YUCHI[122]

TONKAWA[123]

[111] Fortune, *Omaha Secret Societies*, p. 9; Dorsey, *Comparative Phonology*.
[112] Lowie, *The Assiniboine*, p. 10.
[113] Kennard, *Mandan Grammar*.
[114] Lowie, *Hidatsa Texts*.
[115] Lowie, *Crow Grammatical Sketch*.
[116] Lesser and Weltfish, *Caddoan Linguistic Stock*.
[117] White, *Summary Report*, p. 559; Boas, *Keresan Texts*; Parsons, *Pueblo Indian Religion*, Vol. 1, map 1.
[118] Mary R. Haas (p. c.); Byington, *Dictionary of Choctaw*.
[119] Swanton, *Tunica Language*; Haas, *Tunica Grammar*.
[120] Two speakers remaining: Haas, *Nachez and Chitimacha*, p. 598.
[121] Swadesh, *Phonetics of Chitimacha*.
[122] Wagner, *Yuchi*.
[123] Hoijer, *Tonkawa*.

DISTANT RELATIONSHIPS

In the following sections, I to VI, which parallel the listing of language families as given above, a distinction is made between impressionistic classifications and classifications based on published evidence. Earlier classifications on a smaller scale were combined in the great reduction which, in consequence, silently summarizes much linguistic opinion.

I

Rask recorded samples of Aleut, probably from natives visiting in Petrograd in 1818 and 1819; he either recorded or studied Greenlandic Eskimo in Copenhagen in his early youth.[124] Thalbitzer says, "By means of these examples from Rasmus Rask's records, and from later material, I think I have given a renewed and strengthened basis for the assertion of the affinity between the Aleutian and Eskimo languages."[125]

Rask was also the first to point out similarities between Eskimo and languages of the Ural-Altaic family, including Finnish, Hungarian, Lappish, Turkish, and Manchu.[126]

II

The inclusion of Kutenai, Quileute, Wakashan, and Salish in this group is impressionistic.

Of all of Sapir's linguistic work, nothing quite so dazzled Americanists as the evidence presented to show that Californian Yurok and Wiyot, distantly related to one another, are also distantly related to the Algonquian family.[127] Ethnographers appear to regard the relationship as more or less established. The California languages can be found listed by them as Algonquian without qualifying comment; more cautiously, some of the literature gives Yurok or Wiyot as "possibly Algonquian."

In the linguistic literature, two Algonquianists have argued against recognizing the proposed genetic relationship even after Reichard's fuller material appeared for Wiyot.[128] If a relationship has not been demonstrated, despite numerous points of similarities which have been marshalled, there remains only one thing to do: to return to the individual languages and provide adequate synchronic materials so that fresh comparisons may be made. The units of comparison, when areas are widely separated as in the case of Yurok-Wiyot and Algonquian, should certainly be reconstructed parent languages and not random languages selected from the families involved.

III

Evidence has been presented to show that Tlingit, Haida, and Athabascan are related.[129] Those who do not agree that a genetic relationship has been established admit nevertheless

---

[124] Thalbitzer, *Aleutian Language*, p. 41.   [125] *Ibid.*, p. 55.

[126] *Ibid.*, p. 40; cf. Sauvageot, *Esquimalt et Ouralien*.

[127] Sapir, *Wiyot and Yurok; Algonkin Affinity of Yurok and Wiyot*.

[128] Uhlenbeck, *Algonkisch-Klinkende Woorden*, p. 25, also reviews Michelson's position.

[129] Sapir, *Na-dene Languages*.

that similarities do exist, at least between Athabascan and Tlingit.[130] The recent discovery of Eyak promises well for the Na-Dene hypothesis: Sapir pointed out to de Laguna that Eyak might prove to be "coördinate with Athabaskan on the one hand and Tlingit on the other."[131]

IV

Comparisons have been made between Kiowa and Tanoan languages.[132] For Tanoan and Uto-Aztecan, Whorf and Trager have attempted a method of comparison which is without doubt superior to the usual comparisons of isolated languages of one family with isolated languages of another family: "by reconstructing the ancestral forms of each family . . . we discover the common ancestor of both."[133] The reconstructed forms for Uto-Aztecan were established by the comparative method, those for Tanoan not, for at the time the comparisons were made only fragmentary notes and word lists for Tanoan languages were available; Taos was taken as a type for Tanoan phonetics and morphology.[134]

The inclusion of Zuni in this group is impressionistic.

V

Comparative evidence for this group has been geographically restricted. Thus, Dixon's and Kroeber's comparisons of Yokuts, Maidu, Miwok (and Costanoan, now extinct), and Wintun are the basis for California Penutian.[135] Frachtenberg's comparisons of Chinook, Kalapuya, and Takelma are the basis for Oregon (and Washington) Penutian.[136] Sapir extended this to include Lower Umpqua-Siuslaw and Coos, and indeed showed that Oregon and California Penutian have some morphological features in common.[137]

The inclusion of Klamath-Modoc, Molale, Sahaptin, Alsea (Yakonan), and Tsimshian in this group is impressionistic. However, unpublished comparisons have been made.[138]

Comparative work in the usual sense, restricted to languages within one family rather than extended to distant relationships between families, appears to have been neglected in this group except for a special paper or two in Chinook and for some dialect comparisons in Yokuts.[139]

VI

This group combines more languages and more language families than any other. Comparative evidence for its support has been marshalled chiefly in California and in the South-east.

[130] Boas, *Classification of American Languages*, p. 375; Goddard, *Has Tlingit a Genetic Relation to Athapascan?*   [131] De Laguna, *Preliminary Sketch of Eyak*, p. 64.   [132] Harrington, *Vocabulary of Kiowa.*
[133] Whorf and Trager, *Relationship of Uto-Aztecan and Tanoan*, p. 610.   [134] *Ibid.*, p. 612.
[135] Dixon and Kroeber, *New Linguistic Families; Linguistic Families.*
[136] Frachtenberg, *Comparative Studies in Takelman, Kalapuyan and Chinookan.*
[137] Sapir, *A Characteristic Penutian Form;* cf. Freeland, *Relationship of Mixe.*
[138] Frachtenberg, *op. cit.*, p. 176; Melville Jacobs (p. c.).
[139] Sapir, *Chinookan Phonetic Law;* Stanley S. Newman (p. c.).

Dixon and Kroeber cited similar words from Washo, Pomo, Shasta-Achumawi, Karok, Yuman, and other families as the basis for Hokan.[140] Sapir compared 192 elements from Yana, now extinct, with languages from the families already compared by Kroeber and Dixon, and presented for the first time details of comparative phonology and morphology; he also extended Hokan to include Tonkawa and other languages.[141]

California Hokan affinities reach out to the Gulf of Mexico. The Gulf region was a point of juncture between the western (almost entirely Hokan) and eastern (chiefly Southeastern) members of this most extended group.

Gallatin in 1836 compared Muskogee-Choctaw words with Catawba words, without realizing that Catawba was a Siouan language; Swanton has summarized not only Siouan work of the last century but also all other work bearing on Southeastern languages.[142] In addition, Swanton has provided evidence to extend the Muskogean family to include Natchez,[143] and evidence to show a special relationship between Chitimacha and Tunica.[144] Allen has compared words from Siouan languages with words from Iroquoian languages.[145]

The inclusion of Yuki, Caddoan, Keresan, and Yuchi in this group is impressionistic. Special sub-relationships, such as Caddoan to Iroquoian, are also impressionistic.

An exceptional difficulty was encountered in placing the Yuki family with other families. Paul Radin announced that Yuki belonged with Penutian (our Group V), but credited this insight to Kroeber.[146] Kroeber refused the honor.[147] Sapir finally classified Yuki with Hokan-Siouan (our Group VI), possibly because Yuki would not fit in any other group. That is to say, this final group is loosely enough characterized to admit languages otherwise unclassifiable.[148]

INTERPRETATION

It will come as a surprise to most anthropologists to realize there are fewer than 150 separate languages still spoken in America north of Mexico. This does not mean that most of the aboriginal languages have become extinct. Certain areas have suffered heavy losses: the Atlantic coast in general, particularly Florida; the Gulf coast region; the California coast south of San Francisco; and sporadic losses are known throughout the continent. But it seems safe to estimate that well over half the aboriginal languages are still spoken, a sample sufficient to yield a realistic picture of aboriginal linguistic complexity, especially since some of the languages now extinct have been described.

The kind of complexity meant can be measured on different levels, chiefly (1) contempo-

[140] Dixon and Kroeber, op. cit.; Kroeber, Serian, Tequistlatecan, and Hokan.

[141] Sapir, Position of Yana; Hokan and Coahuiltecan Languages; Supplementary Note on Salinan and Washo; Hokan Affinity of Subtiaba.

[142] Swanton, Early History, p. 371; Weer, Preliminary Notes on Muskhogean.

[143] Swanton, Muskhogean Connection of Natchez.

[144] Swanton, Structural and Lexical Comparison.   [145] Allen, Siouan and Iroquoian.

[146] Radin, Genetic Relationship of North American Indian Languages, p. 490.

[147] Kroeber, Handbook of Indians of California, p. 159, fn. 1.

[148] Sapir, Central and North American Languages.

rary languages in a given area; (2) language families in a given area, in which each language family is descriptively summarized by a single reconstructed language which was spoken at some earlier period. Much of what actually lies on the first level is tantalizingly elusive unless approached through the second level.

This means, in effect, that areal studies, which are on the first level, can not be as directly approached when words are involved as when ethnographic items are involved. Nothing remotely comparable to culture areas or Nordenskiöld spot maps has been done in linguistic distributions for North America. Velarized and glottalized consonants are pretty consistently found in western languages, irrespective of family affiliations, but these sounds are only less consistently found and perhaps less intensively produced throughout the continent: the Munsee dialect of Delaware, on the Atlantic coast, exhibits both sound types. And these two sound types are among the most clear cut of the various types suggested from time to time for delimiting phonetic areas. Muskogean languages in the southeast and Iroquoian and Siouan languages to the north and west have nasalized vowels, but since there is some reason for believing that these three families are distantly related, it is questionable whether the nasalized vowels can be counted as examples of phonetic diffusion. In practically all cases where instances of morphological borrowing have been postulated, as between Tlingit and Athabascan, the alternative explanation of historical descent from a single prototype is also possible.

Boas and Goddard have favored the explanation of borrowing on the analogy of the diffusion of culture in cases where similarities between languages do not suggest close relationships. Sapir and others would take as *prima facie* evidence for borrowing only isolated features which stand out aberrantly against the native groundwork of a language; in contrast, similarities between languages, however few, which configurate systematically would be taken as *prima facie* evidence for genetic relationship. Sapir operated with an ancillary postulate ("drift") to account for parallel independent developments in the daughter languages where a generalized prototype appeared to give rise to specialized reflexes.

The factor of personal preference in the alternative explanations is perhaps weaker than the professional prejudices of two disciplines: linguistic similarities can be treated as ethnographic data, as instances of borrowing; or linguistic similarities can be treated as linguistic data, subject to the comparative method, and described in terms of parent languages and daughter languages.

When the parent languages of an area are known, the direction of borrowing and the chronology of borrowing can be established. Words which are reconstructed in Proto-Algonquian and are also known to exist in one or two Siouan languages can be safely said to have been borrowed by the Siouan languages. If some of these words have archaic forms while others show recent sound changes, the relative time of borrowing can be established. Such chronology is often demonstrable in borrowing between the daughter languages of one family. Interpretations of this kind are obviously useful to ethnographers.

Linguistic interpretation can, in favorable cases, throw light on the movement of peoples. In support of the northern origin of the Athabascan family, Sapir cited such words as the one meaning "snow lying on the ground" which was the prototype for the Navaho term meaning "the seed lies." A reconstructed language necessarily implies that the speakers of a single language dispersed from one area. On a smaller scale, it is impossible for one dialect to influence another dialect without direct contact between speakers.

In general, comparative work between sister languages has a direct bearing on the history of a restricted area. Comparative work between parent languages, which is the essential task in the combined or consolidated classifications, has a wider bearing on the continent as a whole and ultimately on aboriginal migrations to the New World. Sapir has suggested principles for such interpretations which state that linguistic diversity is a chronological index, and that the geographic point of greatest diversity localizes the pre-dispersal area. These principles require the corroboration of biological and cultural evidence in actual application.

Accounts of early European history do not hesitate to relate linguistic with biological and cultural data. In contrast, reconstructions of American history either relate one field of data to another hesitantly, to say the least, or more commonly, treat each field in complete isolation. One of the famous negative generalizations of American anthropology is to the effect that there are no expectable correlations between race, language, and culture.

A typical Americanist example would be the Plains area which has been demonstrated to be fairly homogeneous in its cultural manifestations; this same area is represented by language families from five of the six groups in the great reduction: Algonquian from II, the Athabascan Sarsi from III, the Uto-Aztecan Comanche from IV, the Penutian Nez Percé from V, Siouan and Caddoan from VI. When the unit of comparison is the language family on the one hand and the culture area on the other, it can be said that each area is characterized by one general culture but not always restricted to one language family. As the historical sweep widens in reconstructing parent languages, the areas appear less and less restricted in their linguistic representation.

However, the language family is not the only linguistic unit. Equally important is the individual language or group of mutually intelligible dialects of which each one may be the speech of a politically separate tribe. With such a unit, a converse generalization can be made in respect to culture areas. Each separate language is spoken in only one culture area. Thus, the distinct dialects of the Keresan language (Acoma-Laguna and Santo Domingo-San Felipe-Santa Ana-Cochiti-Zia) are spoken only in the Southwest area and even are restricted to the specialized Pueblo culture of that area. Likewise, the various dialects spoken by widely separated tribes of the Dhegiha language are really restricted to a region of homogeneous culture. This suggests that a partial correlation does after all exist between language and culture.

The oft stated lack of correlation between language and race is obviously true when a few primary races are taken as units in comparison; work on smaller racial units has just begun in the New World. But physical anthropologists have already spoken of a Delaware race (the Delaware people were probably divided into three politically separate tribes, speaking at least two distinct dialects).

When still smaller units are taken, such as a single dialect with linguistic peculiarities of different individuals as variables, even closer correlations with race and culture will result. By definition, an individual's idiosyncrasies in speech, his own adaptation of culture, his physical make-up (resulting from amalgamation, selection, and environmental response) represent a complete correlation between language, culture, and race. We can therefore relate the three fields from the ideal correlations as expressed in a single individual to the less perfect correlation when a given dialect is taken as a unit, to the partial correlation when a given language of several dialects is taken as a unit. Proceeding from the better to the less known, it is even possible that some correlations may be shown in a wider historical sweep when language families are taken as primary units; or at any rate, disturbing factors may be discovered where expectable correlations fail.

BIBLIOGRAPHY

ALLEN, HENRY T. *Report of an Expedition to the Copper, Tananá, and Koyukuk Rivers in the Territory of Alaska, in the Year 1885* (Washington, 1887).

ALLEN, LOUIS *Siouan and Iroquoian* (International Journal of American Linguistics, Vol. 6, pp. 185–93, 1931).

ANDRADE, MANUEL J. *Quileute* (In *Handbook of American Indian Languages*, Part 3, pp. 151–292, New York, 1933).

ANGULO, JAIME DE, and L. S. FREELAND *The Achumawi Language* (International Journal of American Linguistics, Vol. 6, pp. 77–120, 1930).

    Karok Texts (International Journal of American Linguistics, Vol. 6, pp. 194–226, 1930–31).

ANONYMOUS [ASHUR WRIGHT] *A Spelling-Book in the Seneca Language: with English Definitions* (Buffalo Creek Reservation, N. Y., 1842).

BARBEAU, C. M. *Classification of Iroquoian Radicals with Subjective Pronominal Prefixes* (Memoir, Canada Department of Mines, Geological Survey, No. 56; Anthropological Series, No. 7, 1915).

BARNUM, F. *Grammatical Fundamentals of the Innuit-Language, as Spoken by the Eskimo of the Western Coast of Alaska* (Boston and London, 1901).

BARRETT, S. A. *The Material Culture of the Klamath Lake and Modoc Indians of Northeastern California and Southern Oregon* (University of California Publications in American Archaeology and Ethnology, Vol. 5, No. 4, 1910).

BIRKET-SMITH, KAJ *Contributions to Chipewyan Ethnology* (Report, Fifth Thule Expedition, 1921–24, Vol. 6, No. 3, Copenhagen, 1930).

    Five Hundred Eskimo Words (Report, Fifth Thule Expedition, 1921–24, Vol. 3, No. 3, Copenhagen, 1928).

BLOOMFIELD, LEONARD *Algonquian Sketch* (Ms., 1939).

On the Sound-System of Central Algonquian (Language, Vol. 1, pp. 130–56, 1925).

BOAS, FRANZ *Chinook* (In *Handbook of American Indian Languages*, Part 1, Bulletin, Bureau of American Ethnology, No. 40, pp. 559–677, 1911).

The Classification of American Languages (American Anthropologist, Vol. 22, pp. 367–76, 1920).

Grammatical Notes on the Language of the Tlingit Indians (Anthropological Publications, University of Pennsylvania Museum, Vol. 8, No. 1, 1917).

Keresan Texts (Publications, American Ethnological Society, Vol. 8, 2 parts, 1925–28).

Kutenai Grammar (Ms.).

Kwakiutl (In *Handbook of American Indian Languages*, Part 1, Bulletin, Bureau of American Ethnology, No. 40, pp. 423–557, 1911).

Tsimshian (In *Handbook of American Indian Languages*, Part 1, Bulletin, Bureau of American Ethnology, No. 40, pp. 283–422, 1911).

BOAS, FRANZ, and HERMAN HAEBERLIN *Sound Shifts in Salishan Dialects* (International Journal of American Linguistics, Vol. 4, pp. 117–36, 1927).

BOAS, FRANZ, and JOHN R. SWANTON *Siouan (Dakota)* (In *Handbook of American Indian Languages*, Part 1, Bulletin, Bureau of American Ethnology, No. 40, pp. 875–965, 1911).

BUNZEL, RUTH *Zuni* (In *Handbook of American Indian Languages*, Part 4, pp. 393–515, New York, 1935).

BYINGTON, CYRUS (JOHN R. SWANTON and HENRY S. HALBERT, eds.) *A Dictionary of the Choctaw Language* (Bulletin, Bureau of American Ethnology, No. 46, 1915).

CANESTRELLI, PHILIPPO (ANNOTATED BY FRANZ BOAS) *Grammar of the Kutenai Language* (International Journal of American Linguistics, Vol. 4, pp. 1–84, 1926).

DALL, W. H. *Tribes of the Extreme Northwest* (Contributions to North American Ethnology, Vol. 1, 1877).

DAWSON, GEORGE M. *Notes on the Shuswap Peoples of British Columbia* (Transactions, Royal Society of Canada, Vol. 9, Section 2, 1891).

DE LAGUNA, FREDERICA *A Preliminary Sketch of the Eyak Indians, Copper River Delta, Alaska* (Publications, Philadelphia Anthropological Society, Vol. 1, pp. 63–75, 1937).

DIXON, ROLAND B. *Maidu* (In *Handbook of American Indian Languages*, Part 1, Bulletin, Bureau of American Ethnology, No. 40, pp. 679–734, 1911).

Shasta-Achomawi: a New Linguistic Stock, with Four New Dialects (American Anthropologist, Vol. 7, pp. 213–17, 1905).

DIXON, ROLAND B., and A. L. KROEBER *Linguistic Families of California* (University of California Publications in American Archaeology and Ethnology, Vol. 16, No. 3, 1919).

New Linguistic Families in California (American Anthropologist, Vol. 15, pp. 647–55, 1913).

DOLORES, JUAN *Papago Nominal Stems* (University of California Publications in American Archaeology and Ethnology, Vol. 20, pp. 19–31, 1923).

Papago Verbal Stems (University of California Publications in American Archaeology and Ethnology, Vol. 10, No. 5, 1913).

DORSEY, J. OWEN *The Comparative Phonology of Four Siouan Languages* (Annual Report, Smithsonian Institution for 1883, pp. 919–29, 1885).

DRUCKER, PHILIP *The Tolowa and their Southwest Oregon Kin* (University of California Publications in American Archaeology and Ethnology, Vol. 36, No. 4, 1937).

DU BOIS, CORA *Wintu Ethnography* (University of California Publications in American Archaeology and Ethnology, Vol. 36, No. 1, 1935).

EDEL, MAY M. *The Tillamook Language* (International Journal of American Linguistics, Vol. 10, pp. 1–57, 1939).

EMMONS, GEORGE T. *The Tahltan Indians* (Anthropological Publications, University of Pennsylvania Museum, Vol. 4, No. 1, 1911).

FARRAND, LIVINGSTON *Traditions of the Chilcotin Indians* (Memoirs, American Museum of Natural History, Vol. 4, Part 1, 1909).

FORTUNE, R. F. *Omaha Secret Societies* (Columbia University Contributions to Anthropology, Vol. 14, 1932).

FRANCISCAN FATHERS *An Ethnologic Dictionary of the Navaho Language* (St. Michaels, Arizona, 1910).

A Vocabulary of the Navaho Language (2 vols., St. Michaels, Arizona, 1912).

FRACHTENBERG, LEO J. *Alsea Texts and Myths* (Bulletin, Bureau of American Ethnology, No. 67, 1920).

Comparative Studies in Takelman, Kalapuyan and Chinookan Lexicography, a Preliminary Paper (International Journal of American Linguistics, Vol. 1, pp. 175–82, 1918).

Coos (In *Handbook of American Indian Languages*, Part 2, Bulletin, Bureau of American Ethnology, No. 40, pp. 297–429, 1922).

Siuslawan (Lower Umpqua) (In *Handbook of American Indian Languages*, Part 2, Bulletin, Bureau of American Ethnology, No. 40, pp. 431–629, 1922).

FREELAND, L. S. *Miwok Grammar, Introduction* (Ms.).

The Relationship of Mixe to the Penutian Family (International Journal of American Linguistics, Vol. 6, pp. 28–33, 1930).

GARFIELD, VIOLA E. *Tsimshian Clan and Society* (University of Washington Publications in Anthropology, Vol. 7, No. 3, 1939).

GATSCHET, ALBERT SAMUEL *The Klamath Indians of Southwestern Oregon* (Contributions to North American Ethnology, Vol. 2, 2 parts, 1890).

Der Yuma-Sprachstamm nach den neuesten handschriftlichen Quellen dargestallt (Zeitschrift für Ethnologie, Vol. 9, pp. 365–418, 1877).

GODDARD, PLINY EARLE *Athapascan (Hupa)* (In *Handbook of American Indian Languages*, Part 1, Bulletin, Bureau of American Ethnology, No. 40, pp. 85–158, 1911).

The Beaver Indians (Anthropological Papers, American Museum of Natural History, Vol. 10, Part 4, 1916).

Elements of the Kato Language (University of California Publications in American Archaeology and Ethnology, Vol. 11, No. 1, 1912).

Has Tlingit a Genetic Relation to Athapascan? (International Journal of American Linguistics, Vol. 1, pp. 266–79, 1920).

Jicarilla Apache Texts (Anthropological Papers, American Museum of Natural History, Vol. 8, 1911).

The Present Condition of Our Knowledge of North American Languages (American Anthropologist, Vol. 16, pp. 555–601, 1914).

Sarsi Texts (University of California Publications in American Archaeology and Ethnology, Vol. 11, No. 3, 1915).

Similarities and Diversities within Athapascan Linguistic Stocks (Twenty-second International Congress of Americanists, Vol. 2, pp. 488–94, Rome, 1928).

HAAS, MARY R. *Natchez and Chitimacha Clans and Kinship Terminology* (American Anthropologist, Vol. 41, pp. 597–610, 1939).

Tunica Grammar (Ms.).

HAEBERLIN, HERMAN, and ERNA GUNTHER *The Indians of Puget Sound* (University of Washington Publications in Anthropology, Vol. 4, No. 1, 1930).

HAEBERLIN, H. K., JAMES A. TEIT, and HELEN H. ROBERTS (UNDER THE DIRECTION OF FRANZ BOAS) *Coiled Basketry in British Columbia and Surrounding Region* (Forty-first Annual Report, Bureau of American Ethnology, pp. 119–484, 1924).

HARRINGTON, J. P. *Karuk Texts* (International Journal of American Linguistics, Vol. 6, pp. 121–61, 1930–31).

Vocabulary of the Kiowa Language (Bulletin, Bureau of American Ethnology, No. 84, 1928).

HOIJER, HARRY *Chiricahua and Mescalero Apache Texts, with Ethnological Notes by Morris Edward Opler* (University of Chicago Publications in Anthropology, Linguistic Series, 1938).

The Southern Athapaskan Languages (American Anthropologist, Vol. 40, pp. 75–87, 1938).

Tonkawa, an Indian Language of Texas (In Handbook of American Indian Languages, Part 3, pp. 1–148, New York, 1933).

JACOBS, MELVILLE *Coos Narrative and Ethnologic Texts* (University of Washington Publications in Anthropology, Vol. 8, No. 1, 1939).

Notes on the Structure of Chinook Jargon (Language, Vol. 8, pp. 27–50, 1932).

A Sketch of Northern Sahaptin Grammar (University of Washington Publications in Anthropology, Vol. 4, No. 2, 1931).

JENNESS, DIAMOND *The Sekani Indians of British Columbia* (Transactions, Royal Society of Canada, Vol. 25, Section 2, pp. 21–35, 1931).

The Sekani Indians of British Columbia (Bulletin, National Museum of Canada, No. 84; Anthropological Series, No. 20, 1937).

JOCHELSON, W. *History, Ethnology and Anthropology of the Aleut* (Publication, Carnegie Institution of Washington, No. 432, 1933).

KENNARD, EDWARD *Mandan Grammar* (International Journal of American Linguistics, Vol. 9, pp. 1–43, 1936).

KNIFFEN, FRED B. *Achomawi Geography* (University of California Publications in American Archaeology and Ethnology, Vol. 23, No. 5, 1928).

Pomo Geography (University of California Publications in American Archaeology and Ethnology, Vol. 36, No. 6, 1939).

KROEBER, A. L. *Handbook of the Indians of California* (Bulletin, Bureau of American Ethnology, No. 78, 1925).

The Languages of the Coast of California North of San Francisco (University of California Publications in American Archaeology and Ethnology, Vol. 9, No. 3, 1911).

Phonetic Elements of the Mohave Language (University of California Publications in American Archaeology and Ethnology, Vol. 10, No. 3, 1911).

Serian, Tequistlatecan, and Hokan (University of California Publications in American Archaeology and Ethnology, Vol. 11, No. 4, 1915).

Shoshonean Dialects of California (University of California Publications in American Archaeology and Ethnology, Vol. 4, No. 3, 1906–07).

The Washo Language of East Central California and Nevada (University of California Publications in American Archaeology and Ethnology, Vol. 4, No. 5, 1906–07).

The Yokuts Language of South Central California (University of California Publications in American Archaeology and Ethnology, Vol. 2, No. 5, 1907).

KROEBER, A. L., and J. P. HARRINGTON *Phonetic Elements of the Diegueño Language* (University of California Publications in American Archaeology and Ethnology, Vol. 11, No. 2, 1914).

LESSER, ALEXANDER, and GENE WELTFISH *Composition of the Caddoan Linguistic Stock* (Smithsonian Miscellaneous Collections, Vol. 87, No. 6, 1932).

LI, FANG-KUEI *Chipewyan Consonants* (Ts'ai Yüan P'ei Anniversary Volume; Bulletin, Institute of History and Philology of the Academia Sinica, Suppl. Vol. 1, pp. 429–67, Peiping, 1933).

A List of Chipewyan Stems (International Journal of American Linguistics, Vol. 7, pp. 122–51, 1933).

Mattole, an Athabaskan Language (University of Chicago Publications in Anthropology, Linguistic Series, 1930).

A Study of Sarcee Verb-Stems (International Journal of American Linguistics, Vol. 6, pp. 3–27, 1930).

LOWIE, ROBERT H. The Assiniboine (Anthropological Papers, American Museum of Natural History, Vol. 4, Part 1, 1909).

Crow Grammatical Sketch (Ms.).

Ethnographic Notes on the Washo (University of California Publications in American Archaeology and Ethnology, Vol. 36, No. 5, 1939).

Hidatsa Texts, with Grammatical Notes and Phonograph Transcriptions by Zellig Harris and C. F. Voegelin (Prehistory Research Series, Indiana Historical Society, Vol. 1, No. 6, 1939).

MICHELSON, TRUMAN *Phonetic Shifts in Algonquian Languages* (International Journal of American Linguistics, Vol. 8, pp. 131–71, 1935).

Preliminary Report on the Linguistic Classification of Algonquian Tribes (Twenty-eighth Annual Report, Bureau of American Ethnology, pp. 221–90, 1906–07).

MORICE, A. G. *The Carrier Language* (2 vols., Mödling bei Wien, 1932).

NEWMAN, STANLEY S. *The Yawelmani Dialect of Yokuts* (International Journal of American Linguistics, Vol. 7, pp. 85–93, 1932).

OLBRECHTS, FRANS M. *Two Cherokee Texts* (International Journal of American Linguistics, Vol. 6, pp. 179–84, 1931).

OSGOOD, CORNELIUS *Contributions to the Ethnography of the Kutchin* (Yale University Publications in Anthropology, No. 14, 1936).

The Distribution of the Northern Athapaskan Indians (Yale University Publications in Anthropology, No. 7, 1936).

Tanaina Culture (American Anthropologist, Vol. 35, pp. 695–717, 1933).

PARSONS, ELSIE CLEWS *Isleta, New Mexico* (Forty-seventh Annual Report, Bureau of American Ethnology, pp. 193–466, 1932).

Pueblo Indian Religion (University of Chicago Publications in Anthropology, Ethnological Series, 1939).

POWELL, J. W. *Indian Linguistic Families of America North of Mexico* (Seventh Annual Report, Bureau of American Ethnology, pp. 1–142, 1891).

RADIN, PAUL *The Genetic Relationship of the North American Indian Languages* (University of California Publications in American Archaeology and Ethnology, Vol. 14; No. 5, 1919).

A Grammar of the Wappo Language (University of California Publications in American Archaeology and Ethnology, Vol. 27, 1929).

RASMUSSEN, KNUD *Across Arctic America* (New York and London, 1927).

RAY, VERNE F. *The Sanpoil and Nespelem: Salishan Peoples of Northeastern Washington* (University of Washington Publications in Anthropology, Vol. 5, 1932).

REICHARD, GLADYS A. *Coeur d'Alene* (In *Handbook of American Indian Languages, Part 3*, pp. 521–707, New York, 1938).

Wiyot Grammar and Texts (University of California Publications in American Archaeology and Ethnology, Vol. 22, No. 1, 1925).

SAPIR, EDWARD *The Algonkin Affinity of Yurok and Wiyot Kinship Terms* (Journal, Société des Américanistes de Paris, n. s., Vol. 25, pp. 1–44, 1923).

Central and North American Languages (In *Encyclopædia Britannica*, 14th ed., Vol. 5, pp. 138–41, 1929).

A Characteristic Penutian Form of Stem (International Journal of American Linguistics, Vol. 2, pp. 58–67, 1921).

A Chinookan Phonetic Law (International Journal of American Linguistics, Vol. 4, pp. 105–10, 1926).

Comparative Athabaskan Grammar (Ms., presented at Yale University, 1934).

Hokan Affinity of Subtiaba in Nicaragua (American Anthropologist, Vol. 27, pp. 402–35, 491–527, 1925).

The Hokan and Coahuiltecan Languages (International Journal of American Linguistics, Vol. 1, pp. 280–90, 1920).

Internal Linguistic Evidence Suggestive of the Northern Origin of the Navaho (American Anthropologist, Vol. 38, pp. 224–35, 1936).

Kutchin Lexical and Grammatical Materials (Ms.).

The Na-dene Languages, a Preliminary Report (American Anthropologist, Vol. 17, pp. 534–58, 1915).

Navaho Grammar (Ms., presented in seminar at Yale University, 1935).

Notes on Chasta Costa Phonology and Morphology (Anthropological Publications, University of Pennsylvania Museum, Vol. 2, No. 2, 1914).

Pitch Accent in Sarcee, an Athabaskan Language (Journal, Société des Américanistes de Paris, n. s., Vol. 17, pp. 185–205, 1925).

The Position of Yana in the Hokan Stock (University of California Publications in American Archaeology and Ethnology, Vol. 13, No. 1, 1917).

Southern Paiute, a Shoshonean Language (Proceedings, American Academy of Arts and Sciences, Vol. 65, No. 1, 1930).

Southern Paiute and Nahuatl, a Study in Uto-Aztekan (Journal, Société des Américanistes de Paris, n. s., Vol. 10, pp. 379–425, 1913; Vol. 11, pp. 443–88, 1914).

Southern Paiute and Nahuatl, a Study in Uto-Aztekan, Part II [contd.] (American Anthropologist, Vol. 17, pp. 98–120, 306–28, 1915).

A Supplementary Note on Salinan and Washo (International Journal of American Linguistics, Vol. 2, pp. 68–72, 1922).

The Takelma Language of Southwestern Oregon (In *Handbook of American Indian Languages*, Part 2, Bulletin, Bureau of American Ethnology, No. 40, pp. 1–296, 1922).

A Type of Athabaskan Relative (International Journal of American Linguistics, Vol. 2, pp. 136–42, 1923).

Wiyot and Yurok, Algonkin Languages of California (American Anthropologist, Vol. 15, pp. 617–46, 1913).

SAPIR, EDWARD, and MORRIS SWADESH *Nootka Texts, Tales and Ethnological Narratives, with Grammatical Notes and Lexical Materials* (William Dwight Whitney Linguistic Series, Yale University, 1939).

SAUVAGEOT, A. *Esquimalt et Ouralien* (Journal, Société des Américanistes de Paris, n. s., Vol. 16, pp. 279–316, 1924).

SPECK, FRANK G. *Catawba Texts* (Columbia University Contributions to Anthropology, Vol. 24, 1934).

SPIER, LESLIE *Havasupai (Yuman) Texts* (International Journal of American Linguistics, Vol. 3, pp. 109–16, 1924).

   Klamath Ethnography (University of California Publications in American Archaeology and Ethnology, Vol. 30, 1930).

SPIER, LESLIE, and EDWARD SAPIR *Wishram Ethnography* (University of Washington Publications in Anthropology, Vol. 3, No. 3, 1930).

SPINDEN, HERBERT JOSEPH *The Nez Percé Indians* (Memoirs, American Anthropological Association, Vol. 2, Part 3, 1908).

SWADESH, MORRIS *Nootka Internal Syntax* (International Journal of American Linguistics, Vol. 9, pp. 77–102, 1939).

   The Phonetics of Chitimacha (Language, Vol. 10, pp. 345–62, 1934).

SWANTON, JOHN R. *Early History of the Eastern Siouan Tribes* (In *Essays in Anthropology in Honor of Alfred Louis Kroeber*, Robert H. Lowie, ed., pp. 371–81, Berkeley, 1936).

   Haida (In *Handbook of American Indian Languages*, Part 1, Bulletin, Bureau of American Ethnology, No. 40, pp. 205–82, 1911).

   The Muskhogean Connection of the Natchez Language (International Journal of American Linguistics, Vol. 3, pp. 46–75, 1924).

   A Structural and Lexical Comparison of the Tunica, Chitimacha, and Atakapa Languages (Bulletin, Bureau of American Ethnology, No. 68, 1919).

   Tlingit (In *Handbook of American Indian Languages*, Part 1, Bulletin, Bureau of American Ethnology, No. 40, pp. 159–204, 1911).

   The Tunica Language (International Journal of American Linguistics, Vol. 2, pp. 1–39, 1922).

TEIT, JAMES A. *The Lillooet Indians* (Memoirs, American Museum of Natural History, Vol. 4, Part 5, 1907).

   The Middle Columbia Salish (University of Washington Publications in Anthropology, Vol. 2, No. 4, 1928).

   Notes on the Tahltan Indians of British Columbia (In *Anthropological Papers Written in Honor of Franz Boas*, pp. 337–49, New York, 1906).

   The Salishan Tribes of the Western Plateaus (Forty-fifth Annual Report, Bureau of American Ethnology, pp. 23–396, 1930).

   The Shuswap (Memoirs, American Museum of Natural History, Vol. 4, Part 7, 1909).

THALBITZER, WILLIAM *The Aleutian Language Compared with Greenlandic, a Manuscript by Rasmus Rask Dating from 1820, now in the Royal Library at Copenhagen* (International Journal of American Linguistics, Vol. 2, pp. 40–57, 1922).

Eskimo (In *Handbook of American Indian Languages*, Part 1, Bulletin, Bureau of American Ethnology, No. 40, pp. 967–1069, 1911).

TRAGER, GEORGE L. *The Kinship and Status Terms of the Tiwa Languages* (Ms.).

UHLENBECK, C. C. *Algonkisch-Klinkende Woorden in het Wiyot* (Mededeelingen, Koninklijke Akademie van Wetenschappen, Afdeeling Letterkunde, Deel 63, Serie A, No. 9, Amsterdam, 1927).

UNDERHILL, RUTH *The Autobiography of a Papago Woman* (Memoirs, American Anthropological Association, No. 46, 1936).

VOEGELIN, CHARLES F. *Comparative Siouan Linguistics* (Ms.)

    A Study of Paradigmatic Differences in Klamath-Modoc and Achumawi Dialects (Ms.).

    Tübatulabal Grammar (University of California Publications in American Archaeology and Ethnology, Vol. 34, No. 2, 1935).

WAGNER, GÜNTER *Yuchi* (In *Handbook of American Indian Languages*, Part 3, pp. 295–384, New York, 1934).

WATERMAN, T. T. *Yurok Affixes* (University of California Publications in American Archaeology and Ethnology, Vol. 20, pp. 369–86, 1923).

WEER, PAUL *Preliminary Notes on the Muskhogean Family* (Prehistory Research Series, Indiana Historical Society, Vol. 1, No. 7, 1939).

WHITE, LESLIE A. *Summary Report of Field Work at Acoma* (American Anthropologist, Vol. 30, pp. 559–68, 1928).

WHITMAN, WILLIAM *The Oto* (Columbia University Contributions to Anthropology, Vol. 28, 1937).

WHORF, B. L. *The Comparative Linguistics of Uto-Aztecan* (American Anthropologist, Vol. 37, 600–608, 1935).

    The Origin of Aztec TL (American Anthropologist, Vol. 39, pp. 265–74, 1937).

    The Punctual and Segmentative Aspects of Verbs in Hopi (Language, Vol. 12, pp. 127–31, 1936).

    Some Verbal Categories in Hopi (Language, Vol. 14, pp. 275–86, 1938).

WHORF, B. L., and G. L. TRAGER *The Relationship of Uto-Aztecan and Tanoan* (American Anthropologist, Vol. 39, pp. 609–24, 1937).

DEPAUW UNIVERSITY
GREENCASTLE, INDIANA

THE CLASSIFICATION OF THE MUSKOGEAN LANGUAGES

By MARY R. HAAS

OF SAPIR'S many and varied linguistic interests, not the least was his concern with his-torical problems. He laid particular stress upon the differences between the descriptive and the historical approaches to the study of languages, pointing out that "the most impor-tant grammatical features of a given language and perhaps the bulk of what is called its grammar are of little value for the remoter comparison, which may rest largely on submerged features that are of only minor interest to a descriptive analysis."[1] Moreover, he was among the first to adapt the rigid comparative methodology (developed by Indo-European scholars) to the problem of interrelationships of American Indian languages. Although his pub-lished works reflect largely his interest in the discovery of previously unrecognized rela-tionships between already established stocks,[2] he was not less interested in problems per-taining to the similarities and divergences exhibited between the various languages within these already established stocks. This is well attested by his voluminous unpublished notes on the Athapascan languages. The present paper has been stimulated particularly by this latter type of interest and also by the fact that of his proposed six major linguistic stocks in North America, he includes the Muskogean family as one of several families and languages within the Hokan-Siouan stock.[3]

I

The extant Muskogean languages are Choctaw, Chickasaw, Alabama, Koasati, Hitch-iti, Mikasuki, Creek (or Muskogee), and Seminole.[4,5] Of these Choctaw, Chickasaw, Creek,

[1] Sapir, *Hokan Affinity of Subtiaba in Nicaragua*, p. 492.

[2] Sapir, *Central and North American Languages.* [3] *Ibid.*

[4] Most of the material which forms the basis of this discussion is taken from my own field notes. Field work on Creek was made possible through two grants (in 1936 and 1937) from the Department of Anthropology, Yale University. During the second of these field trips certain materials on Hitchiti and Choctaw were also collected. The collection of materials on Koasati and on Creek and Seminole dialects comprised a part of the work done on the history of the towns of the Creek Confederacy under a grant from the Penrose Fund of the American Philo-sophical Society in 1938–39.

Much benefit has been derived from the study of an unpublished manuscript entitled *A Sketch of the Hitchiti Language*, by John R. Swanton, but the forms quoted herein are taken from my own notes on the language. Many Choctaw forms are quoted from Byington, *Dictionary of the Choctaw Language*. The Chickasaw forms and a part of the Mikasuki forms quoted herein are taken from Gatschet, *Migration Legend of the Creek Indians*, Vol. 1. The remaining Mikasuki forms are taken from a selected vocabulary which Mr Alexander Spoehr kindly filled out for me in Florida in the spring of 1939.

[5] This discussion is concerned with the Muskogean languages proper and does not include an evaluation of the relation of Natchez to these languages; see Swanton, *Muskhogean Connection of the Natchez Language*. A larger stock containing Natchez would consist of Natchez on the one hand as opposed to all of the Muskogean languages on the other.

and Seminole are now spoken in eastern Oklahoma in the Nations bearing their respective names. Choctaw is also spoken by a group living in eastern Mississippi and by scattered remnant groups in Louisiana, while Seminole is also spoken by a large part of the Seminole Indians living in Florida. Alabama and Koasati are spoken in eastern Texas and western Louisiana, respectively, but are no longer employed by the members of the tribal towns of the Creek Nation, Oklahoma, which bear their names. Hitchiti is practically extinct, being remembered by less than a half dozen individuals living in the Seminole Nation. Mikasuki is also spoken by a few individuals living in the Seminole Nation but the majority of speakers comprise a part of the Seminoles of Florida.

Of the languages mentioned above not all merit the rank of a separate "language." Choctaw and Chickasaw are actually subvarieties of the same language, and the same is true of Hitchiti and Mikasuki and of Creek and Seminole. This is not to imply that the subvarieties are identical at all points,[6] but in no case are the differences between them any greater than those existing between American English and British English. Hence the distinction between Choctaw and Chickasaw, Hitchiti and Mikasuki, Creek and Seminole is of a political rather than of a linguistic order.

Whether one observes them from the phonemic, the structural, or the lexicographical level, one finds that the various Muskogean languages are usually very close. On the phonemic level we find that all of the languages possess the voiceless stops p, t, č, and ḳ, which are fortis in Choctaw, Chickasaw, Alabama, and Koasati but lenis in Hitchiti, Mikasuki, Creek, and Seminole. (Note that except in Choctaw and Chickasaw, where it configurates with the spirant š, the writing of č is simplified to c.) In addition to the voiceless stops, Choctaw, Chickasaw, Alabama, and Koasati have an asymmetrical voiced stop b. All of the languages have the spirants f,[7] l, and h. Choctaw and Chickasaw have two sibilant spirants s and š, but the remaining languages have only one such spirant ranging from s, usual in Koasati, Hitchiti, Creek, and Seminole, to š, usual in Mikasuki and Alabama. (Note that to parallel the simplified writing of č as c, Mikasuki and Alabama š are written s.) All of the languages possess the semivowels y and w, the lateral l, and the nasals m and n. In addition Creek and Seminole employ the defective phoneme ŋ, occurring only before ḳ. All of the languages employ the three vowels i, a, and o, each of which may occur either with or without the length phoneme. When occurring without the length phoneme a is [a], o is [v], while i is [ɪ] everywhere except in final position in Alabama and Koasati where it is [e]. When accompanied by the length phoneme a· is [a·], o· is [o·], while i· is [i·] in Hitchiti, Mikasuki, Creek, and Seminole but [e·] in Choctaw, Chickasaw, Alabama, and Koasati. In addition Creek and Seminole have a defective vocalic phoneme e, which occurs only

---

[6] For a chart showing the virtual identity of the subvarieties of these three groups, see Gatschet, *op. cit.*, p. 56.

[7] The spirant f is generally bilabial, though some of the younger speakers of Creek have substituted the labio-dental f as the result of English influence.

before y in syllabic final position and which may not be accompanied by the length pho-neme.[8]

On the structural level it is observed that all of the languages employ the processes of word order, composition, affixation (prefixation, infixation, and suffixation), reduplication, and quantitative vocalic ablaut. In addition Creek and Seminole employ the process of tonal ablaut.[9] Composition, infixation, and suffixation are used in the formation of secondary stems; prefixation, infixation, and suffixation in inflection for person; reduplication, pre-fixation, and suffixation in inflection for number; and infixation, suffixation, and ablaut in the formation of tenses, aspects, and modes. However, it should be noted that the various languages do not necessarily employ all of the processes listed as serving in a given function nor do they all necessarily employ them to the same degree. For example, in Koasati pre-fixation and suffixation are much more important than reduplication in inflection for number while in Creek and Seminole reduplication and suffixation are the only processes used for this purpose. The above comments, then, are to be construed in the nature of a resumé for all of the languages taken together.

II

The primary subdivision of the Muskogean languages is into two groups, the Western and the Eastern. The Western division contains only Choctaw and Chickasaw while the Eastern division is composed of all of the remaining languages. The most important con-sonantic distinctions between the two groups are as follows:[10]

---

[8] In addition to the phonemes discussed above, all of the languages seem to possess certain tonal accents. However, except in the case of the Creek and Seminole languages, these are not at present fully understood. For this reason accents are marked in the case of words quoted from Creek and Seminole but omitted otherwise.

The tonal accents of Creek and Seminole may be briefly described as follows (see my article entitled *Ablaut and its Function in Muskogee*): "There are three phonemes of tonal accent which determine not only the tonal configurations of accented syllables but also those of the surrounding unaccented syllables. The three tonal ac-cents are the high, symbolized by an acute sign (') over the vowel of the accented syllable; the rising, symbolized by an inverted circumflex (ˇ); and the falling, symbolized by a circumflex (ˆ). The tonal configurations of the ac-cented syllables are described by the terms 'high,' 'rising,' and 'falling.' All unaccented syllables which follow an accented syllable are low in pitch. . . . All unaccented syllables which precede an accented syllable are high in pitch with the sole exception of a word-initial open syllable containing a short vowel; the latter type of syllable is low. . . . All polysyllabic (non-monosyllabic) words must have at least one tonal accent. A great many words have several accented syllables. . . . In this event the tonal level of each succeeding accented syl-lable will be slightly lower than that of the preceding accented syllable. . . . Moreover, unaccented syllables com-ing between two accented syllables accommodate their pitch to that of the second accented syllable . . ." (p. 150).

[9] See my article *Ablaut and its Function in Muskogee*. As is pointed out there (pp. 141–42), Creek employs all of the six main types of grammatical processes listed by Sapir for languages in general (*Language*, pp. 63–64).

[10] The Primitive Muskogean reconstructions are of course purely arbitrary; they will suffice until sufficient evidence is discovered for better reconstructions.

The following abbreviations are used: PM, Primitive Muskogean; Choc., Choctaw; Chick., Chickasaw; Ala., Alabama; Koas., Koasati; Hitch., Hitchiti; Mik., Mikasuki; Cr., Creek; Sem., Seminole. In addition capital G

TABLE 1

(1) PM *θ > Western n, Eastern ł; e.g.,

Choc., Chick. (G) nani "fish;" Ala., Koas. łało; Hitch., Mik. (G) ła·ł·i;[11] Cr., Sem. łáło.

Choc. (B) tana "to weave;" Ala. is·tał·ka; Koas. tała; Cr., Sem. tał·íta.

Choc. naki "arrow;" Ala., Koas. łaki; Hitch. in·łak·i, and possibly the Cr., Sem. word łi· is also related.

Choc. ninak "night;" Ala. niła·hasi "moon" (<"night·luminary"); Koas. niłak·hokki·ta "midnight" (<"night·middle"); Hitch., Mik. (S) ni·łak·i "night;" Cr., Sem. nił·í.

Choc. (B) inni "to bask;" Koas. hiłłi "to get warm."

(2) PM *c > Western s, Eastern c; e.g.,

Choc., Chick. (G) losa "black;" Ala., Koas. loca; Hitch., Mik. (S) lo·c·i. The Cr., Sem. word last·í· is probably unrelated.

Choc. nosi "to sleep;" Ala., Koas. noci; Hitch. no·c·i·ki; Cr., Sem. noc·íta.

Choc. naksi "side (over ribs);" Ala., Koas. nakci "rib;" Cr., Sem. ·náci "side (over ribs)."

Choc. sakli "trout;" Ala., Koas. ca·lo; Cr., Sem. cá·lo.

(3) PM *s > Western š, Eastern s; e.g.,

Choc. (B) šokča "sack;" Ala., Koas. sokca; Hitch. sokc·i; Cr., Sem. sókca.

Choc., Chick. (G) haši "sun, moon, month;" Ala., Koas. hasi "sun, month;" Hitch. ha·s·i; Cr., Sem. hasi.

Choc. šakči "crawfish;" Ala., Koas. sakco; Cr., Sem. sákco.

Choc. šokha "hog;" Ala., Koas. sokha; Hitch., Mik. (S) sok·i; Cr., Sem. sókha.

(4) PM *š > Western š, Eastern c; e.g.,

Choc. (B) šalontaki "cricket;" Ala. collo·ta; Koas. colo·tka; Hitch. colo·tk·i; Cr., Sem. coló·tka, calo·tka.

Choc. šokši "watermelon;" Ala., Koas. coksi "pumpkin;" Hitch. cos·talakc·i "water-melon." The Cr., Sem. word cási "pumpkin" is probably also related.

In all other cases so far investigated single consonantic sounds (including č < PM *č) are identical in the two groups, as is shown in the following examples.

TABLE 2

PM *y. Choc., Ala., Koas. yokpa "happy, pleased."

PM *w. Choc. (B) watonlak "crane;" Koas. watola; Hitch., watol·i; Cr., Sem. watóla.

PM *p. Choc. opa "hoot owl;" Ala., Koas. opa; Hitch. o·pa·k·i; Mik. (S) ho·pa·k·i; Cr. ópa.

---

in parentheses after the name of a language indicates that the form is quoted from Gatschet, *Migration Legend*. Similarly B indicates that it is quoted from Byington, *Dictionary*, while S refers to the aforementioned vocabulary recorded by Alexander Spoehr. Data on languages whose names are listed without a following initial are taken from my own notes, as in the case of the Choc., Ala., Koas., Hitch., Cr., and Sem. words quoted in the first ex-ample in Table 1. Certain transliterations have been introduced in the case of words quoted from other sources in order that their spelling may be consistent with that employed in the rest of the languages.

[11] All Hitchiti nouns end in a suffix ·i.

PM *b. Choc. ·bi·šakni "nose;" Ala., Koas. ·bisa·ni.

PM *f. Choc. fočoš "duck;" Hitch. fo·c·i; Cr., Sem. fóco.

PM *m. Choc., Chick. (G) minko "chief;" Ala., Koas. mi·kko; Hitch., Mik. (G) mik·i; Cr., Sem. mí·kko.

PM *t. Choc., Chick. (G) tali "stone;" Ala., Koas. tali; Hitch. tal·i.

PM *n. Choc. nakni "male;" Ala., Koas. na·ni; Hitch., Mik. (S) nakn·i; Cr., Sem. ho·nán·wa.

PM *ł. Choc. (B) pał·al·li "to split one;" Ala., Koas. pał·at·li; Hitch. pał·i·ki "to break;" Cr., Sem. pał·íta "to split."

PM *l. Choc. lakna "yellow;" Ala., Koas. la·na; Hitch. lakn·i; Cr., Sem. lá·n·i·.

PM *č. Choc. čokfi "rabbit;" Ala., Koas. cokfi; Hitch. cokf·i; Cr., Sem. cófi.[12]

PM *k. Choc. koni "skunk;" Ala., Koas. kono; Hitch., Mik. ko·n·i; Cr., Sem. kóno.

PM *h. Choc. (B) haklo "to hear;" Ala., Koas. ha·lo; Hitch. hakl·i·ki.

Turning now to the treatment of vowels, we find that there is one widespread phenomenon that sets off the Western group from the Eastern. This is the replacement in certain noun stems of Western final i by Eastern final o. Examples:

TABLE 3

Choc., Chick. (G) nani "fish;" Ala., Koas. łało; Cr., Sem., łáło.[13]

Choc. nipi "meat;" Ala., Koas., nipo.

Choc. (B) pakti "mushroom;" Ala., Koas., pakto; Cr., Sem. páto.

Choc. itti "tree;" Ala., Koas. itto; Cr., Sem. íto.

Choc. sakli "trout;" Ala., Koas. ca·lo; Cr., Sem. cá·lo.

In other cases, however, the final i is retained in both groups; e.g.,

Choc., Chick. (G) tali "stone;" Ala., Koas. tali.

Choc. nakni "male;" Ala., Koas., na·ni.

Aside from the i/o distinction just illustrated and aside from cases of qualitative ablaut to be illustrated later, we find that vowels in general are identical in the two groups. In illustration note the vowels of the initial syllables in the examples given immediately above.

There is still another trait which distinguishes the Western division from the Eastern. This is the phonomechanical rule whereby Western V plus a nasal corresponds to Eastern V·; e.g., (1) Choc. (B) pakanli "to bloom;" Ala., Koas. paka·li; (2) Choc., Chick. (G) minko "chief;" Ala., Koas. mi·kko; Cr., Sem. mí·kko; (3) Choc. ponfa "to blow;" Koas. po·f·ka; Hitch. po·f·k·i·ki; Cr., Sem. po·f·k·itá.

III

Whereas the Western division has no subgroups (Choctaw and Chickasaw being, as has already been shown, but subvarieties of the same language), the Eastern division con-

---

[12] As explained above the sound č is simplified in writing to c in Ala., Koas., Hitch., Cr., Sem.

[13] Hitchiti examples are not given because the vocalic finals of all Hitchiti nouns are lost before the suffix i.

tains three subgroups, as follows: (1) Alabama-Koasati; (2) Hitchiti, including as its sub-variety Mikasuki; (3) Creek, including as its subvarieties several Creek dialects and Seminole.

IV

Alabama and Koasati are to some extent mutually intelligible. On the phonemic level they are identical but on the lexical level they maintain quite a few differences. In many cases of lexical dissimilarities we find that Alabama agrees with Choctaw whereas Koasati agrees with Creek and sometimes with Hitchiti. Note the following instances:

TABLE 4

Ala. hacon-coba "alligator," agreeing with Choc. hačon-čoba, as against Koas. albata agreeing with Hitch. halpat-i, and Cr., Sem. alpatá, halpatá.

Ala. aka·ka "chicken" agreeing with Choc. akanka, as against Koas. kolo·si agreeing with Cr., Sem. tottolô·si.

Ala. hastola "winter," agreeing with Choc. haštola, as against Koas. łafi, agreeing with Hitch. ła·f-i and Cr., Sem. łáfo.

Ala. and Choc. tałła·pi "five," as against Koas. cahopp-a·ka, agreeing with Hitch. cahki·p-an and Cr., Sem. cahki·p-in.

Ala. and Choc. tałłi·pa "hundred," as against Koas., Hitch., Cr., Sem. cokpi·.

The lexical cleavage between Alabama and Choctaw on the one side and Koasati, Creek, and sometimes Hitchiti on the other is probably to be explained as the result of contact. In other words, the Alabama were probably at one time in closer association with the Choctaw or the Chickasaw while the Koasati and the Hitchiti were probably in closer association with the Creek.

In contrast to such lexical differences between Alabama and Koasati as were illustrated above, we find that there are also a considerable number of cases where the two languages share the same vocabulary components as against all the other languages, whose forms in turn may or may not be related to one another. Examples:

TABLE 5

Ala., Koas. co·skani "duck," as against Choc. fočoš, Hitch. fo·c-i and Cr., Sem. fóco.

Ala., Koas. satta "turtle," as against Choc. loksi, Hitch. yokc-i, and Cr., Sem. lóca.

Ala., Koas. i·sa "house," as against Choc. čokka, Hitch. cik-i, and Cr., Sem. cóko.

Ala., Koas. tikba "fire," differing in turn from Choc., Chick. (G) lowak, from Hitch. i·ti, and from Cr., Sem. tó·tka.

Ala., Koas. okwala "toad," differing in turn from Choc. šilokwa and from Cr., Sem. sopá·kta.

Ala., Koas. biłko "persimmon," differing in turn from Choc. onko·f and from Cr., Sem. sáta.

Ala, Koas. bayba "heavy," differing in turn from Choc. wi·ki and from Hitch. hokn·i, Cr., Sem. hónn·i·.

Ala., Koas. bitli "to dance," differing in turn from Choc. hiła and from Cr., Sem. opan·itá.

Having pointed out the lexical similarities and differences of Alabama and Koasati, it will now be pertinent to call attention to the fact that taken as a whole there are a great many more lexical similarities between these languages and Choctaw than there are between them and Hitchiti or Creek or both. These instances are, of course, over and above the instances in which all the languages are lexically similar. Note the following examples:

TABLE 6

Ala., Koas., nita "bear," Choc. nita, as against Hitch. nokos·i and Cr., Sem. nokósi.

Ala., Koas. cowahla "cedar," Choc. čowahla, as against Hitch. acin·i and Cr., Sem. acína.[14]

Ala., Koas. ayokpa "happy," Choc. (B) ayokpa "pleased," as against Hitch. a·fack·i·ki "to be happy," and Cr., Sem. a·fack·itá.

Ala., Koas. ibi "to kill it," Choc. abi, as against Hitch. ili·c·i·ki and Cr., Sem. ili·c·itá.

Ala., Koas. hapi "salt," Choc. hapi, as against Hitch. okcahn·i and Cr., Sem. okcán·wa.

Ala., Koas. hanna·li "six," Choc., Chick. (G) hanna·li, as against Hitch., Mik. (G) i·pa·k·in and Cr., Sem. i·pâ·k·in.

Ala., Koas. on·toklo "seven," Choc., Chick. (G) on·toklo, as against Hitch., Mik. (G) kol·apa·k·in and Cr., Sem. kol·apâ·k·in.[15]

Ala., Koas. cakka·li "nine," Choc., Chick. (G) čakka·li, as against Hitch., Mik. (G) osta·pa·k·in and Cr., Sem. osta·pâ·k·in.

Ala., Koas. okcakko "green, blue," Choc. okčakho, differing in turn from Hitch. honotp·i and from Cr., Sem. holá·tt·i· "blue."

Ala., Koas. homma "red," Choc. homma, differing in turn from Hitch. kitisc·i and from Cr., Sem. cá·t·i·.

Ala., Koas. on·oyya "one to climb," Choc. oyya, differing in turn from Hitch. ahon·i·ki and from Cr., Sem. acimk·itá.

Ala., Koas. cih·kafo "sassafras," Choc. kafi, as against Cr., Sem. wí·so.

Ala., Koas. lomhi "to hide," Choc. lohmi, as against Cr., Sem. i·h·k·itá.

Ala., Koas. sinapo "white ash tree," Choc. šinap, as against Cr., Sem. itohátka.

Ala., Koas. okca·ya "alive," Choc. okčanya, as against Cr., Sem. winá·k·i·.

Ala., Koas. okhica "door," Choc. okhisa, as against Cr., Sem. aháwki.

On the other hand, there are a few rare instances in which Alabama and Koasati are

[14] The Creek word is probably a borrowing from Cherokee ačina "cedar," in which case the Hitchiti word is probably in turn a borrowing from Creek.

[15] However, the element ·toklo in the Ala., Koas., Choc. and Chick. words is cognate with the element kol· in the Hitch., Mik., Cr. and Sem. words, as is shown later.

lexically similar to Creek or Hitchiti or both while being dissimilar to Choctaw. Examples:

TABLE 7

Ala., Koas., pokko "ball," Hitch., Mik. (S) po·k·i, Cr., Sem. pókko, as against Choc. to·wa.

Ala., Koas. cissi "mouse," Hitch., Mik. (S) cis·i "rat," Cr., Sem. císsi "rat," as against Choc. pinti.

Ala., Koas. coyyi "pine," Hitch., Mik. (S) co·y·i, Cr., Sem. cóli, as against Choc. tiyak.

Ala. wilo·wanha "shoes," Koas. wilo, Hitch., Mik. (S) wil·i, as against Choc. šološ.

Ala., Koas. limitka "to swallow," Hitch. limatk·i·ki, as against Choc. (B) nanabli.

There is an interesting type of contraction that Alabama and Koasati share with Creek in contrast to Choctaw and to Hitchiti. We find that Choctaw and Hitchiti ·Vk· followed by a liquid or nasal is represented by ·V·· in the Alabama-Koasati group and in Creek. Examples:

TABLE 8

Choc. lakna "yellow," Hitch. lakn·i, as against Ala., Koas. la·na, Cr., Sem. lá·n·i·.

Choc. sakli "trout," as against Ala., Koas. ca·lo, Cr., Sem. cá·lo.

Choc. nakni "male," Hitch. nakn·i, as against Ala., Koas. na·ni, Cr., Sem. ho·nán·wa.[16]

Choc. (B) haklo "to hear," Hitch. hakl·i·ki, as against Ala., Koas. ha·lo.

Choc. ·bi·takla "forehead," as against Koas. ·bita·la "face."

Choc. ·bi·šakni "nose," as against Ala., Koas. ·bisa·ni.

Choc. okla "people," Chick. (G) okla "town," Hitch. okl·i "town," as against Ala., Koas. o·la "town."

V

The Hitchiti subgroup has a few very definite traits which distinguish it from all of the other languages of the Muskogean family.

In two cases so far discovered Hitchiti replaces *l* with *y;* viz., (1) Hitch. ayikc·om·i "doctor," as against Choc. alikči, Ala., Koas. alikci, Cr., Sem. alikc·itá "to doctor," alí·kc·a "doctor;" (2) Hitch. yokc·i "turtle," as against Choc. loksi, Cr., Sem. lóca. The Mik. (S) form loc·i is a borrowing from Sem. The reason for this replacement is at present not clear, for in other cases Hitchiti retains *l;* e.g., Hitch. lakn·i "yellow;" Choc. lakna; Ala., Koas. la·na; Cr., Sem. lá·n·i·.

Hitchiti stems corresponding to Western division and other Eastern division stems lengthen the vowel of an initial open syllable. Examples:

TABLE 9

Hitch. lo·c·i "black," as against Choc., Chick. (G) losa; Ala., Koas. loca.

Hitch. ko·n·i "skunk," as against Choc. koni; Ala., Koas. kono; Cr., Sem. kóno.

[16] The short vowel in the Cr:, Sem. form is secondary.

Hitch. ha·s-i "sun, month," as against Choc., Chick. (G) haši; Ala., Koas. hasi; Cr., Sem. hási.

Hitch., Mik. (S) a·h-i "potatoes," as against Choc. ahi; Ala., Koas. aha; Cr., Sem. áha.

Hitch. ła·ł-i "fish," as against Choc. nani; Ala., Koas. łało; Cr., Sem. łáło.

Hitch. ni·łak-i "night," as against Choc. ninak; Ala., niła-hasi "moon" (<"night-luminary"); Koas. niłak-hokki·ta "midnight" (<"night-middle"); Cr., Sem. nił-í·.

Hitch. o·p-a·k-i "hoot owl"; Mik. (S) ho·p-a·k-i, as against Choc., Ala., Koas. opa; Cr., Sem. ópa.

Hitchiti ungeminates the geminate clusters of the other Eastern division languages. Examples:

TABLE 10

Hitch., Mik. (S) pił-i "boat," as against Ala., Koas. piłła; Cr., Sem. píłło. Cf. Choc. pi·ni.

Hitch., Mik. (G) mik-i "chief," as against Ala., Koas. mi·kko; Cr., Sem. mí·kko. Cf. Choc., Chick. (G) minko.

Hitch., Mik. (G) toci·n-in "three," as against Ala., Koas. tucci·na; Cr., Sem. toccî·n-in. Cf. Choc., Chick. (G) točči·na.

Hitch., Mik. (S) cis-i "rat," as against Ala., Koas. cissi "mouse;" Cr., Sem. císsi "rat."

Hitch. akcom-i "tobacco," as against Ala., Koas. hakcomma. Cf. Choc. hakčoma.

Hitch. poko·l-in "ten," as against Ala., Koas. pokko·li. Cf. Choc., Chick. (G) pokko·li.

Hitch. il-i·ki "to die," as against Ala., Koas. illi. Cf. Choc. illi. Here Cr., Sem. il-íta agrees with Hitch. in being ungeminated.

In certain cases Hitchiti preserves a stem final consonant that is lost in all of the other languages except Choctaw. Examples:

TABLE 11

Hitch. nihtak-i "day," Choc. nittak, as against Ala., Koas. nihta; Cr., Sem. nittá·.

Hitch. -hakcop-i "ear," Choc. -haksob-iš, as against Ala., Koas. -hakco; Cr., Sem. -hacko.

Hitchiti likewise shares with Choctaw the retention of -Vk- before a liquid or nasal whereas in Alabama, Koasati, and Creek it becomes -V·- (see the examples given in Table 8).

In its vocabulary Hitchiti agrees more often with Creek than it does with any of the other languages. In addition to the Hitchiti examples given in Table 6, note the following which lack cognates in the other groups:

TABLE 12

Hitch. oyok-i "lean," Cr., Sem. oyók-i·.

Hitch. inok-i·ki "to be sick," Cr., Sem. inókk-i· "sick."

Hitch. fa·y-i·ki "to hunt," Cr., Sem. fa·y-itá.

Hitch. apił-ac-i·ki "to laugh at," Cr., Sem. apił-eyc-itá.

Hitch. -ła·ł-i "(one's) back," Cr., Sem. -ła·.

In view of the long contact between the Hitchiti and the Creek, the likelihood is great that a number of these instances are borrowings, the more so since all present day speakers of Hitchiti also speak Creek, the same being true of a great many Mikasuki.

Cases wherein Hitchiti is lexically similar to Alabama and Koasati are given in Table 7. In addition note the following similarities to Alabama or Koasati or both:

TABLE 13

Hitch. ont-i·ki "one to come," Ala., Koas. onti.
Hitch. coko·l·i·ki "one to sit, dwell," Ala., Koas. coko·li.
Hitch. cayahl-i·ki "one to walk," Ala., ciyahli, Koas. cayahli.
Hitch. hayohk-i "deep," Ala. hayo·ki, Koas. hayohki.
Hitch. -halk-i "wife," Ala., Koas. -halki.
Hitch. -fo·s-i "grandfather," Ala. -fosi, as against Koas. -awo.
Hitch. fapli-hc-i "wind," Koas. fapli, as against Choc., Ala. mahli.

There are also notable instances wherein Hitchiti agrees in vocabulary with all of the languages except Creek. Examples:

TABLE 14

Hitch. sa·w-i "raccoon;" Choc. šawi; Ala., Koas. sawa; as against Cr., Sem. wó·tko.
Hitch. akcom-i "tobacco;" Choc. hakčoma; Ala., Koas. hakcomma; as against Cr., Sem. híci.
Hitch. hakl-i·ki "to hear;" Choc. haklo; Ala., Koas. ha·lo; as against Cr., Sem. poh-íta.
Hitch. solo·p-i "ghost;" Choc. šilo·p; Ala. silopi; as against Cr., Sem. poyafíkca.
Hitch. poko·l-in "ten;" Choc., Chick. (G), Ala., Koas. pokko·li; as against Cr., Sem. pâ·l-in.

In some additional cases Hitchiti is in lexical disagreement with all of the other languages. To mention only a few of such cases note the words for "green," "red," and "to climb" in Table 6.

VI

Having discussed the relation of the Alabama-Koasati and the Hitchiti subgroups to Creek in the two preceding sections, little remains to be said about the latter subgroup except that it is lexically more dissimilar to the Western division than any of the other subgroups. It should also be noted that it is sometimes similar to Choctaw and Hitchiti as against Alabama-Koasati (Table 5), sometimes similar to Hitchiti as against Choctaw and Alabama-Koasati (Tables 6 and 12), but at other times dissimilar to all of the other groups (Table 14). There are, however, two distinguishing features of Creek that deserve mention here.

There are at present a few unexplainable cases in which Creek drops ķ before another consonant. Examples:

TABLE 15

Cr., Sem. cófi "rabbit;" as against Choc. čokfi; Ala., Koas. cokfi; Hitch. cokf·i.

Cr., Sem. páto "mushroom;" as against Choc. (B) pakti; Ala., Koas. pakto.

Cr., Sem. ·náci "side (over ribs);" as against Ala., Koas. ·nakci "rib;" Choc. ·naksi "side (over ribs)."

Cr., Sem. cási "pumpkin;" as against Ala., Koas. coksi; Choc. šokši "watermelon."

But in other apparently similar cases, Creek retains ƙ before another consonant; e.g.,

Cr., Sem. sokca "sack;" Hitch. sokc·i; Ala., Koas. sokca; Choc. šokča.

Cr., Sem. sokha "hog;" Ala., Koas. sokha; Choc. šokha.

Cr., Sem. hokc·itá "to break wind;" Koas. hokco; Choc. (B) hokso.

As a second distinguishing feature we find that Creek is often characterized by meta-thesis as against the other languages. Examples:

TABLE 16

Cr., Sem. ·hacko "ear;" as against Hitch. ·hakcop·i; Ala., Koas. ·hakco; Choc. ·haksob·iš.

Cr., Sem. istikíni "horned owl;" as against Koas. kitini; Choc. (B) iškitini.

Cr., Sem. táph·i· "wide;" as against Ala., Koas., Choc. patha.

Cr., Sem. acokłán·wa "spider;" as against Choc. čołkan.

It should also be mentioned that metathesis often operates among the Creek subdialects, including Seminole, e.g., kapotoka vs. katopoká "hat." Creek, however, is not alone in having metathesis, as is shown in the next section.

VII

It will now be of interest to turn to some of the types of differences that are found between these languages without regard to subgroups. Since these differences may crop out in any of the subgroups and sometimes in the subdialects of the various languages (particularly Choctaw and Creek), it is to be assumed that they were characteristic of the primitive language. The differences are of a phonomechanical nature and consist of (1) gemination, (2) ungemination, (3) metathesis, (4) the interchange of initial h and zero, (5) alternative vocalic syncope, and (6) qualitative vocalic ablaut.

(1) Gemination frequently distinguishes the subdialects of Choctaw and Creek. In Choctaw the majority of subdialectical geminates arise from ƙ or h assimilating to a following consonant; e.g., oksak vs. ossak "hickory;" šolokpa vs. šiloppa[17] "liver;" yokpa (B) vs. yoppa[18] "happy, pleased;" ikfoka (B) vs. iffoka (B) "belly;" halakli (B) halalli (B) "to keep;" hohpi (B) vs. hoppi (B) "to bury;" hotihna (B) vs. hotinna (B) "to count;" fahpo (B) vs. fappo (B) "magic;" hohčifo (B) vs. hoččifo[18] "to name." But other types of gemination also occur, as in foyli (B) vs. folli (B) "to pick, take out."

---

[17] In this example and the preceding one the form containing the heterophonous cluster was recorded from a Louisiana Choctaw speaker, that containing the geminate cluster from an Oklahoma Choctaw speaker.

[18] Recorded from an Oklahoma Choctaw speaker.

In Creek a number of subdialectical geminates arise from the assimilation of ḳ to a following consonant, of h to a preceding consonant, or of a following consonant to s; e.g.,
·kpocí vs. ·ppocí "son (of a man);" sopá·kta vs. sopá·tta "toad;" ich·itá vs. icc·itá "to shoot;"
ichá·swa vs. iccá·swa "beaver;" tastasána vs. tassasána "kingfisher;" tafó·swa vs. tafó·sso
"red elm."

In addition gemination occurs at random in the various languages without regard to
their subgroups; hence the gemination in such cases is secondary. Examples:

TABLE 17

Ala., Koas. nihta "day;" Hitch. nihtak·i; as against Choc. nittak (<earlier *nihtak);
Cr., Sem. nittá· (< earlier *nihtá·).

Ala. Koas. yokpa "happy" as against Choc. dialect yoppa, older form preserved in Choc.
dialect (B) yokpa.

Choc. okčakho "green;" as against Ala., Koas. okcakko (<*okcakho).

Choc. (B) anči "to put on a cloak;" Koas. anci "to wrap around;" as against Cr., Sem.
acc·itá "to dress" (<*anc·itá).

Choc. sinti "snake;" Ala., Koas. cinto; Hitch. cint·i; as against Cr., Sem. cítto (<*cinto)

Ala. hasokmayli "to lighten;" as against Choc. (B) hašokmalli (<*hašokmayli); cf.
Choc. foyli vs. folli, quoted above.

Koas. halokpa "sharp;" as against Choc. (B) haloppa (<*halokpa).

Koas. olfa "to grow;" as against Choc. (B) offa (<*olfa).

Ala. bikno "ahead;" as against Koas. bikko (<*bikno).

Koas. kolo·si "chicken;" as against Cr., Sem. tottolô·si (<*totkolô·si).

Hitch. hokn·i "heavy;" as against Cr., Sem. hónn·i· (<*hókn·i·).

In one interesting instance we have assimilation in one direction in Choctaw and in the
opposite direction in Creek: Koas. histo "ashes," as against Choc. (B) hittok "potash" on
the one hand, and Cr., Sem. í·sso "ashes," on the other.

(2) Ungemination as a regular process in Hitchiti has been illustrated in Table 10. The
process also occurs sporadically in some of the other languages. Examples:

TABLE 18

Choc. oksak, ossak "hickory;" as against Ala., Koas. oca; Cr., Sem. ocí·.

Choc. (B) hossi "to pound;" as against Koas. hoci; Cr., Sem. hoc·íta.

Choc. issi "deer;" as against Ala., Koas. ico; Cr., Sem. íco.

Choc. itti "tree," Ala., Koas. itto; as against Cr., Sem. íto.

Choc., Ala., Koas. illi "to die;" as against Cr., Sem. il·íta.

Choc. (B) hohpi, hoppi "to bury;" as against. Cr., Sem. hopi·l·itá.

Ala., Koas. coyyi "pine" (prob. geminated <*coyli); as against Cr., Sem. cóli (prob.
ungeminated <*colli).

Koas. kotti "frog;" as against Cr., Sem. kóti.

(3) Metathesis is found in the subdialects of Choctaw, e.g., tohno vs. tonho (B) "to hire, engage;" toloski (B) vs. lotoski (B) "thick;" fannakla (B) vs. fallakna (B) "fox squirrel." Likewise in those of Creek; e.g., haloníski vs. hanolíski "devil's shoestring (herb);" kapotoká vs. katopoká "hat." Cases wherein Creek exhibits metathesis in contrast to the other languages have been illustrated in Table 16. Other instances of metathesis in the various languages are sporadic; e.g., Ala., Koas. lomhi "to hide," as against Choc. (B) lohmi; cf. Choc. tohno vs. tonho, quoted above.

(4) The interchange of initial h and zero occurs occasionally among the subdialects of Choctaw; e.g., haknip (B) vs. aknip (B) "body;" hofka (B) vs. ofka (B) "to sun, air," and even more frequently among the subdialects of Creek; e.g., hifólo vs. ifólo "screech owl;" hi·fkánco vs. i·fkánco "wood-tick;" haloníski vs. aloníski "devil's shoestring (herb);" ha·cofáka vs. a·cofáka "sinew;" hakłi·sk-itá vs. akłi·sk-itá "to sneeze." Similarly we find cases like Hitch. o·pa·k-i "hoot owl" vs. Mik. (S) ho·pa·k-i. The same type of interchange is occasionally found between the various languages; e.g., (1) Choc. (B), Ala., Koas. hopo·ni "to cook," vs. Cr. onip-itá; (2) Hitch. halpat-i "alligator," Cr. dialect halpatá, vs. Cr. dialect alpatá, Koas. albata; (3) Koas. hiłłi "to get warm," vs. Choc. (B) inni "to bask."

(5) We now come to the very interesting though rare process of alternative vocalic syncope. In the operation of this process the vowel of one syllable is elided in one language while the vowel of the following syllable is elided in another. In one case the first and third vowels are elided in one language while the second and fourth vowels are elided in another (see the first example below). In the examples given below the elided vowel is placed in parentheses.

*hotoko·lo "two." (1) *h(o)tok(o·)lo > Choc., Chick. (G), Ala., Koas. tokló; Hitch., Mik. (G) tokł-an. (2) *hot(o)ko·l(o) > Cr., Sem. *hotko·l- which by gemination > hokkô·l-in. A reduced form of this stem is also found in Hitch., Mik. (G) kol-apa·k-in and Cr., Sem. kol-apâ·k-in "seven" (< "two added").

*osi·ta "four." (1) *(o)si·ta > Hitch. si·t-a·kin. (2) *os(i·)ta > Choc. Chick. (G) ošta; Ala., Koas. ošt-a·ka; Cr., Sem. ô·st-in. The Cr., Sem. word represents a special lengthened form; for the unlengthened form note ost-apâ·kin "nine" (< "four added").

*čahoki·p- "five." (1) *čah(o)ki·p- > Hitch., Mik. (G) cahki·p-an; Cr., Sem. cahki·p-in. (2) *čahok(i·)p- > Koas. *cahokp- which by gemination > cahopp-, as in cahopp-a·ka.

*ifaθi/o "squirrel." (1) *(i)faθi > Choc. fani. (2) *if(a)θo > Ala., Koas. *ifło, which by change of spirant to stop > ipło. By elision of the p we get Cr., Sem. iło. (For other instances of the i/o alternation see Table 3.)

A similar example, which may be mentioned here, illustrates simple vocalic syncope rather than alternative vocalic syncope, viz., *točči·na "three," as in Choc., Chick. (G) točči·na; Ala., Koas. tocci·na; Cr., Sem. toccî·n-in; and by ungemination Hitch., Mik. (G) toci·n-an: *točč(i·)na > *tocna which by fricativization of c > Hitch., Mik. (G) tosn-, as in tosn-apa·k-in "eight" (< "three added"). A reduced form of this stem is also found in Cr., Sem. cin-apâ·k-in "eight."

(6) Several interesting instances of qualitative vocalic ablaut are preserved in Choctaw, e.g., taktaki (B) vs. tiktiki (B) "spotted;" yonyoki (B) vs. yinyiki (B) "crooked;" tanakbi (B) vs. tonokbi (B) "bent (as an oxbow)." The process is also occasionally found in Creek, e.g., kofo·y·itá "to scramble" vs. kafa·y·itá "to shake up, churn." Other instances occur between the various languages. Examples:

TABLE 19

Choc. (B) moǒo·li "to close the eyes;" Koas. misi·li; Cr., Sem. moso·l·itá.

Choc. (B) kisi·li "to bite one;" Koas. kaca·li "to bite several times;" Cr., Sem. kici·t·k·itá "to bite off a piece."

Choc. (B) toktoha "to cluck;" Koas. taktahka; Cr., Sem. to·kto·k·itá.

Choc. (B) pokpoki "to foam;" Koas. pakpaki; Cr., Sem. pakpak·íta.

Choc. (B) čikčiki "speckled;" Koas. cokcoki.

Choc. (B) taktaki, tiktiki "spotted;" Ala. toktoki. And perhaps Koas. tantaki also belongs here.

We now come to still another difference that occasionally distinguishes one or more of the languages from the rest, namely the presence of obscure prefixes. The instances are not numerous and are usually found when a given word begins in h in one or more of the languages but in some other consonant otherwise. Examples:

TABLE 20

Ala., Koas. hica "to see;" Hitch. hic·i·ki; Cr., Sem. hic·íta; as against Choc., Chick. (G) p·isa.

Choc., Ala., Koas. ha·hi "walnut;" Cr., Sem. aha·h·wa; as against Hitch. y·a·h·i.

Choc. (B) hiči "a boil;" Koas. hici; as against Cr., Sem. l·íci.

Koas. hoɫi "to cook done;" as against Choc. n·ona "to cook, ripen;" Cr., Sem. n·oɫ·íta "to cook done."

Choc. hina "road;" Ala., Koas. hini; Hitch., Mik. (S) hin·i; as against Cr., Sem. níni. But in this case the n of the first syllable of the Cr., Sem. word may have been induced by the presence of n in the second syllable.

In one case we seem to have an obscure prefix in both of two contrasting languages, viz. Choc. (B) l·apčo "earthworm," as against Koas. k·apco.

VIII

In summation of the previous sections we arrive at the following classification of the Muskogean languages:

> A. Western division
> > Old Choctaw
> > > New Choctaw subdialects, including Chickasaw
> B. Eastern division
> > 1. Old Alabama—a. New Alabama; b. Koasati

2. Old Hitchiti—New Hitchiti, including its subdialect Mikasuki

3. Old Creek—New Creek subdialects, including Seminole

In contrast to the genetic divisions listed above, it has been shown in sections IV, V, and VI that the various subgroups have influenced each other, particularly lexically. The following chart shows some of the more important of these cross-influences. (The numerals give references to the character of the relationships.)

$$\text{Choctaw} \quad 2 \quad \text{Hitchiti} \quad 4 \quad \text{Creek}$$

$$1 \qquad\qquad 3 \qquad\qquad 5$$

$$\text{Alabama} \quad + \quad \text{Koasati}$$

1. See Table 4
2. See Tables 8, 11
3. See Table 14
4. See Table 12
5. See Tables 4, 8

IX

It is still too soon to postulate definitely the inclusion of the Muskogean family in the Hokan-Siouan stock as envisioned by Sapir as early as 1921.[19] One of the reasons given by him for assuming a connection here is the possibility of explaining certain obscure Muskogean prefixes (of the type discussed at the end of section VII) as atavistic elements related to a set of nominal, adjectival, and verbal (transitive vs. intransitive) prefixes characteristic of Hokan.[20] In particular I might suggest that the prefixed p- in Choc. p-isa "to see" (as against Ala., Koas. hica; Hitch. hic-i·ki; Cr., Sem. hic-íta) may be related to the Hokan transitive prefix p-.[21] However, final proof of a connection must await the discovery of a great many cognates backed by demonstrable phonetic laws.[22] Spurred on by Sapir's hypothesis, I have found some thirty very plausible-appearing cognates between Muskogean, Natchez, Tunica, Chitimacha, Atakapa, Tonkawa, Coahuiltecan, and Siouan (or various combinations of these) with an occasional cognate between one or more of these and Hokan. However, materials of this sort will need to be augmented many times before we can completely rule out the possibility of coincidence. A serious drawback to the solution of the problem lies in the scarcity of published (or, in many cases, of even collected) materials on a number of these languages. When such materials become available, the most important desideratum, as Sapir so often insisted, will be a detailed study of each of the individual substocks involved; for the ideal approach to the problem can be made only when it is possible

[19] Sapir, Bird's-eye View of American Languages North of Mexico.

[20] Sapir, Hokan Affinity of Subtiaba, pp. 526–27. [21] Ibid., p. 524.

[22] Sapir, of course, had assembled a number of cognates, but since the time he did his work fuller materials on many of these languages have become available, e.g., Morris Swadesh's work on Chitimacha, Harry Hoijer's work on Tonkawa (see Tonkawa), and my own work on Tunica, Natchez, and the Muskogean languages. The work on all of these languages, except the Muskogean, has been carried out under the auspices of the Committee on Research in American Native Languages.

to compare Primitive Hokan with Primitive Coahuiltecan,[23] Primitive Muskogean, Primitive Siouan, Primitive Iroquoian, and Primitive Caddoan, and these in turn with the various isolated languages, such as Yuki, Keres, Tunica, Chitimacha, Atakapa,[24] Natchez, and Yuchi.

BIBLIOGRAPHY

BYINGTON, CYRUS A Dictionary of the Choctaw Language (Bulletin, Bureau of American Ethnology, No. 46, 1915).

GATSCHET, ALBERT S. A Migration Legend of the Creek Indians (2 vols., Philadelphia, 1884; St. Louis, 1888).

HAAS, MARY R. Ablaut and its Function in Muskogee (Language, Vol. 16, pp. 141–50, 1940).

    Geminate Consonant Clusters in Muskogee (Language, Vol. 14, pp. 61–65, 1938).

HOIJER, HARRY Tonkawa, an Indian Language of Texas (In Handbook of American Indian Languages, Part 3, pp. 1–148, New York, 1933).

SAPIR, EDWARD A Bird's-eye View of American Languages North of Mexico (Science, n.s., Vol. 54, p. 408, 1921).

    Central and North American Languages (In Encyclopædia Britannica, 14th edition, Vol. 5, pp. 138–41, 1929).

    The Hokan Affinity of Subtiaba in Nicaragua (American Anthropologist, Vol. 27, pp. 402–35, 491–527, 1925).

    Language, an Introduction to the Study of Speech (New York, 1921).

SWANTON, JOHN R. The Muskhogean Connection of the Natchez Language (International Journal of American Linguistics, Vol. 3, pp. 46–75, 1924).

    A Sketch of the Hitchiti Language (Ms.).

    A Structural and Lexical Comparison of the Tunica, Chitimacha, and Atakapa Languages (Bulletin, Bureau of American Ethnology, No. 68, 1919).

    Linguistic Material from the Tribes of Southern Texas and Northeastern Mexico (Bulletin, Bureau of American Ethnology, No. 127, 1940).

EUFAULA, OKLAHOMA

[23] The Coahuiltecan languages are extinct and hence it may never be possible to reconstruct Primitive Coahuiltecan. This is unfortunate, for, inasmuch as the proposed Hokan-Siouan stock stretches from the Pacific to the Atlantic, the more or less central position of the Coahuiltecan languages along the Texas coast suggests the possibility that they may have constituted a very important link between the languages of the West and those of the East. Since this article was written, Swanton has published a valuable monograph containing all the available manuscript materials on the Coahuiltecan and other extinct languages of the same general area (see Linguistic Material).

[24] Swanton has suggested the possibility that Tunica, Chitimacha, and Atakapa may have constituted a single stock which he calls Tunican (see Swanton, Structural and Lexical Comparison). However, the proposed stock does not constitute a tightly woven unit comparable to the Muskogean or Siouan languages, and hence it may turn out to be more profitable to compare each of these languages separately with the other constituents of the proposed Hokan-Siouan stock.

LINGUISTIC BEHAVIOR AND THOUGHT

"*Human beings do not live in the objective world alone, nor alone in the world of social activity as ordinarily understood, but are very much at the mercy of the particular language which has become the medium of expression for their society. It is quite an illusion to imagine that one adjusts to reality essentially without the use of language and that language is merely an incidental means of solving specific problems of communication or reflection. The fact of the matter is that the 'real world' is to a large extent unconsciously built up on the language habits of the group. . . . We see and hear and otherwise experience very largely as we do because the language habits of our community predispose certain choices of interpretation.*"

The Status of Linguistics as a Science

LINGUISTIC CHANGE AND THOUGHT

OBSERVATIONS OF PATTERN IMPACT ON THE PHONETICS OF BILINGUALS

By MORRIS SWADESH

THIS PAPER proposes to discuss the phonemics of bilinguals from the standpoint of their conceptions as well as their speech, an aspect which will be considered unscientific by such confirmed behaviorists as Twaddell, who criticized Sapir as a mentalist dealing with an "unknown and unknowable mind."[1] However, we offer as evidence only objectively observable behavior, what people say and what people do. Like all scientific evidence, introspective report requires critical handling. We do not offer as established fact every golden remark of the native informant, but check it against the phonetics of his utterance, his handling of an experimental alphabet, his facial and verbal reactions to our attempts to speak words of his language, his pronunciation of other languages we know, and any other item that may suggest something. This is Sapir's method, the critical use of every bit of evidence. It refuses to be restricted to using only half the observable facts, and is not frightened at such stigmas as "mentalist."

There are many problems of phonemics, such as the analysis of the system itself, that can be studied without involving a consideration of phonemic conceptions; in such cases, this class of evidence may still prove helpful in suggesting working hypotheses, and there is no reason to restrict oneself to more difficult techniques. There are other problems, that in their nature involve a consideration of phonemic conceptions. These latter problems include the basic thesis that phonemic conception is a factor in the history of the phonemic system, helping to determine the relative stability or extent of change in the system. Though this proposition has never been systematically investigated and quantitatively evaluated, it is generally accepted as true on the basis of much observed fact. To reassure the antimentalists, it may be pointed out that it is only a special case of the proposition that behavior tendencies affect behavior patterns.

Sapir, reaffirming Boas, stressed the role of the bilingual in linguistic change. It is the thesis of this paper that bilinguals have their own conception of the phonemics of both of the languages they speak; concrete cases are presented as proof and illustration. If bilinguals have a special conception of a phonemic system and if individual conceptions affect the development of phonemic systems, it is clear how the bilingual may be a factor in the history of language. The present paper does not attempt to prove the entire complex of propositions involved and to trace out the functioning of the different factors. It merely attempts some orientation of the problems.

[1] W. F. Twaddell, *On Defining the Phoneme* (Language Monographs, Vol. 16, 1935), p. 16.

DEFINITION

Basic to any discussion of any of these problems is an understanding of what a bilingual is. People who can be said to know two languages include those who handle both languages with equal ease and equal facility and those who handle one easily and the other with difficulty. The third possibility of a person who speaks both languages with difficulty is sometimes reputed to exist but is hardly possible in normal individuals.[2] We might define the bilingual idealistically as one who speaks both languages with such facility and accuracy that native speakers of either language sense nothing peculiar on hearing him speak. Or, we might include in a flexible definition all who have any knowledge whatever of two languages. If we use the latter definition we must recognize the varying connotation of our term, and always distinguish carefully what kind of bilingual we are discussing.

Bloomfield stresses the factor of time of learning, pointing out that a person ordinarily knows best the language he learned first in childhood. But there are cases of children who learn a language thoroughly and then largely or entirely lose the memory of it by constant use of another language.[3] To differentiate in terms of the actual control of the languages, we had therefore best operate with the concepts of primary languages and secondary languages, to distinguish the language that the individual controls fully and with ease and the one he controls partially and with difficulty. We recognize the possibility of essentially equal control. As already stated, the normal person will have at least one fully controlled language. We consider as an empiric fact the observation that the more fully adult a person is at the time he comes in contact with a new language, the less likely he is to attain full control of it.

Observed cases lead us to distinguish between the dominance of different aspects of a language. There are many people who have relatively complete mastery of the inflection or syntax or vocabulary of a language with little or no phonetic mastery, people, for example, who use German phonetics in talking a syntactically perfect English. Others,[4] much fewer in numbers, attain an adequate imitation of the phonetics of the new language before they have much vocabulary or any expertness in using the inflectional forms.

People who know two languages belong to the general class which also includes people who know three, four, or more languages. For this reason plurilingual might be a more correct term, but no important issue is involved and we continue to use the more common term bilingual.

The majority of language communities are essentially monolingual. But there are a great many border and enclave communities that are bilingual. In the United States, along the

---

[2] The incongruity of the bilingual who uses both languages awkwardly has made him a favorite subject of jokes in many languages. As a Mexican version, the story is told that the son of a prominent Mexican wrote home from New York, "I can't learn English and am rapidly forgetting Spanish." The father telegraphed back, "Come home at once before you can't speak at all."

[3] Leonard Bloomfield, *Language* (Chicago, 1933), pp. 55-56.

[4] Including well trained phoneticians as well as gifted imitators

Mexican border there are so many people who talk both English and Spanish that entire communities may be characterized as bilingual. In the large cities can be found immigrant groups the entirety of which talk English in addition to their original languages. On many Indian reservations, English shares with the native tongue the role of instrument of communication.

In some communities everyone from infancy learns two languages and the tradition may be maintained generation after generation. Examples are to be found in the Basque region of Spain, the Breton region of France, parts of Alsace-Lorraine and Switzerland. A country like Germany offers examples of communities where the local dialect and the standard language are spoken by everyone. The role of the two languages side by side is pretty definitely defined, the one being used in the home situation, the other for business and official relations.

In certain cases, the bilingual community is one in relatively rapid transition from the universal use of one language to the universal use of a second. The nature of the process is well illustrated by the Oneidas of Wisconsin. Oneida is the sole language of a few old people; English is the sole language of many children and a certain number of young and middle-aged adults. Perfect bilingualism (knowing both English and Oneida well) and graded bilingualism (knowing English well and Oneida partly or Oneida well and English partly) applies to the large majority of the people. There is a continuous series from Oneida monolinguals through different grades of bilinguals to English monolinguals. The present state of the community is the interim manifestation passing from a purely Oneida-speaking community to a purely English-speaking community.

The case of a bilingual speech community is quite different from that of the existence of isolated bilingual persons in a community that is essentially monolingual. For if bilingualism affects the speech of a single individual, it probably will go no farther. However, if all or a large part of a speech community is equally affected, it may leave a permanent mark on the language.

PHONETIC EFFECTS OF BILINGUALISM

Bilinguals frequently have occasion to use words of one language in speaking the other. Thus, someone may have occasion to use a technical term he knows only in English while speaking Spanish, or he may be narrating what A said to B and put the quotation in the language it was made in. In such cases he may use English phonetics or he may reform the English words into Spanish phonetics. The many English words used in Mexico are most often pronounced in Spanish fashion: rɪ̃ŋ (ring) is said r̃in, hóm rʌ́n (home run) is said jonr̃ón, klɪp (clip): klíp, bésbɔl (baseball): beisból, etc. Since this bilingualism is mostly literate, it is usual to encounter reading renditions, the English letters read in Spanish fashion; e.g., referee is commonly said r̃éfere. Americans who speak Spanish well usually follow the English phonetics. Mexicans who have mastered English phonetics sometimes use the English sounds but more commonly adapt them in the Spanish context. Sounds that have no close Spanish counterpart are very frequently retained; thus $\check{s}$, z, j (or they may be replaced by roughly similar Spanish phonemes as $\check{c}$, s, y). But e is replaced by ei or Spanish e, o by ou or o, r by $\tilde{r}$ initially and by r otherwise, p, t, k by the corresponding unaspirated stops of Spanish. Bilinguals always differ from monolingual Mexicans in tending to avoid pronunciations based on a Spanish rendition of English orthography.

Yaquis who control both Spanish and Yaqui phonetics usually change the latter when talking Spanish. The changes involved are restricted to the elimination of two phonetic contrasts made in Yaqui: that between simple and geminate vowels (the local Spanish tends to lengthen vowels in accented open penultimate syllables particularly in emphatic speech, but has no contrasting length) and that between presence and absence of ? between vowels. On several occasions I have been told there is no difference between the words for maple and desire; the former is wáta, I was told, and the latter is wáta. The same words spoken by the same individuals in a Yaqui context are wáta and wáata respectively. Sun (táa?a) and know (tá?a), I was told, were both taa (or even ta). The context of dictation for phonetic recording was in part sufficient to educe Yaqui pronunciations, but, on one occasion, in check-ing tómi (money) to decide whether the first vowel was simple or geminate, I had to ask the informant to repeat the word a few times; finally, disturbed at my stupidity, she exclaimed, with a perfect Sonora drawl, "pos tómi!" that is with very long vowel.

Examples involving the omission of glottal stop are gói "two" and gó?i "coyote," both pronounced gói, yóoko "tomorrow" and yó?oko "jaguar" both pronounced yóko, húpa[5] "skunk" and hú?upa "mesquite" both pronounced húpa. In talking to non-Yaquis, these bilinguals like to mention these curious identities which are not identities when they are really speaking their language.

When it comes to using Spanish words in Yaqui contexts, there are two modes of pro-cedure, comparable to those mentioned for English in Spanish. There is the method of partially adapting the Spanish phonetics to the Yaqui, and there is the more thoroughgoing adaptation followed in the old borrowings. The former treats the vowels as long or short according to position and applies the native pattern of speech melody and syllabic division, otherwise making no changes. The latter eliminates initial consonant clusters, unvoices voiced consonants in preconsonantic medial position, changes $\tilde{r}$ to r, $\tilde{n}$ to ny, gu to w. The sound g may be changed to k or w, but the g has already been established as a new phoneme of the language; similarly d and f may or may not be changed to t and p. Examples: láuta "flauta," ringo "gringo," tíiko "trigo," puéplo "official in the political organization" (pueblo), munyéeka "muñeca," pasíhko "Francisco." The substitution of h for s in the last example is not specifically Yaqui, for it likewise characterizes the local Spanish.

[5] The phonemic structure of the words in the strictest kind of Yaqui, is wói and wó?i, the symbol w repre-senting a labioguttural voiced spirant, strongly labial before a, e, i, strongly guttural before o, u. We find the split of g into two phonemes (w before a, e, i; g before o, u) only in forms of the language more profoundly influenced by Spanish: the split results from the introduction of loanwords with g before a, e, i.

It is to be noted that from the phonemic standpoint, the use of sounds in unaccustomed positions involves a new feature; for example, if a Yaqui says puéblo even though pronouncing in Yaqui fashion, with sounds that occur in Yaqui, it is a novelty to have a voiced spirant (b) in syllabic final position. Similarly, bóks "prize fight" in Mexican Spanish introduces a final consonant cluster of a type that does not occur other than in English borrowings. Likewise, the introduction of many words of the other language may involve a change in the relative frequency of sounds.

The few examples cited illustrate phenomena observed many times in various bilingual situations. We may summarize our observations as follows. A relatively perfect bilingual is characterized by a clear conception of the phonetic make-up of the word he is using, while a non-bilingual may have a vague or inaccurate impression, or, if he is literate, may insist on the pronunciation suggested by the spelled form. The bilingual may give a true pronunciation, as it were, imitating the language of the word in the midst of employing another language. However, it is more usual to adapt the word in some degree to the foreign phonetic system. We may differentiate different degrees of adaptation, which may be described as follows:

(a) One may use purely phonemes of the language of the larger utterance, primarily in their usual relations. Mechanical features of intonation and syllabic division are completely adapted. In all cases, the nearest equivalent phoneme of the languages being spoken is substituted, even at the cost of ambiguities that would result in the original language. Unaccustomed sound sequences may be modified to more habitual ones.

(b) One may retain certain phonemes which do not occur in the language being spoken. The ones which have some approximate equivalent are least likely to be kept.

A particularly interesting case is illustrated by the quoting of Tarascan words in Spanish contexts. Usually the Tarascan who also has the mastery of Spanish does not carry the distinction of aspirated and unaspirated stops and affricates into a Spanish context, but pronounces unaspirated ones throughout. This involves the introduction into the Spanish context of ϕ (ts), but words with aspirated ϕ' are pronounced with unaspirated ϕ, which thus serves for two Tarascan phonemes.

This is not the place to enter into a discussion of what determines the degree of adaptation made, but it might be observed in passing that the bilingual community or the bilingual part of a mixed community tends to be consistent in its treatment. It tends to be a cultural pattern rather than an individual matter.

Another problem we do not take up here is the skewing of the phonetic systems of bilinguals. This would include all the phenomena of talking with an accent, of accidental slips, and of subtle peculiarities many of which go unnoticed by other natives.

CONCEPTIONS

The bilingual often gives evidence of not being aware of the phonetic differences between the two languages. There are many cases in the Indian languages of America of words borrowed from the new language. The phonetic form is necessarily different at least to the extent of the minimum adaptation. But always in the case of minimum changes, and often in the case of more extensive changes, the informant will say the word is alike in the two languages. The Nootka will say that keptin is the same as English kǽptʌn (captain) and sometimes that miˑt is the same as English mét (ship's mate). The word ʔalfréedo in a Yaqui context does not sound like Alfrédo in a Spanish context spoken by the same bilingual, but he will insist on their being the same. In a case like Yaqui búrro, Spanish búr̃o or Yaqui munyéeka, Spanish muñeka or manwé, Manuél, he usually will begin by saying they are the same. However, in such cases as these, he will recognize the difference when it is pointed out and after a little experience will learn to look for such differences on his own.

Tarascan has several phonetic manifestations of aspiration or of aspiration-like phenomena. It has an aspirational consonant, written *j*, occurring in prevocalic and preconsonantic medial position, e.g., jiní "there," jájki "hand." It has a series of aspirated stops and affricates, which occur largely in initial position, e.g., čʼéti "tail." It has a mechanical unvoicing of all unaccented phrase-final syllables. A group of twenty bilingual school teachers, already literate in Spanish, had no difficulty in learning to write prevocalic aspiration as *j*, nor in writing the aspirated stops and affricates as *pʼ*, *tʼ*, *ḳʼ*, *ȼʼ*, *čʼ* in contrast to *p*, *t*, *ḳ*, *ȼ*, *č* for the non-aspirates. It cost them an effort to learn to write preconsonantic aspiration, possibly because the aspiration disappears when the word is broken up into syllables. When they learned, almost half of them began by using the diacritic of aspiration‛ instead of the symbol for the aspirational consonant. For the most part these same individuals used the same diacritic to indicate the voicelessness of final syllables, which, as a mechanical feature, is not recognized in the official spelling. These phenomena gave rise to some doubt on the part of the linguists of the project as to the accuracy of their analysis, but after reconsidering the entire system and taking into account the fact that over a half of the subjects had not made this confusion, they concluded that the phonemic analysis was correct and that the manifestation had another cause.

It seems likely that since the subjects were literate in Spanish, the writing of Tarascan amounted to the use of Tarascan in a Spanish context. In this event, even though using the *j* symbol, which corresponds to a weak palatal fricate in the local Spanish, for the aspirational consonant of Tarascan, there was a resistance to using it for a preconsonantic aspiration because *j* does not occur before consonants in Spanish words. The phenomenon remained from the Spanish standpoint an unusual feature and was represented by ‛, a symbol also used to represent what is an unusual feature from the Spanish standpoint. Phrase final unvoicing, while it does not contrast with voiced pronunciation in Tarascan, does contrast with the normal treatment of final syllables in Spanish. From the Spanish standpoint, it had to be specially represented and a logical way to represent it was with the diacritic for aspiration. The fact that final unvoicing is not restricted to syllables with stops or affricates, but occurs also with *m*, *n*, *ŋ*, *l*, *r*, *ɹ*, *s*, *š*, demonstrates that this phenomenon is distinct from the aspirate stops and affricatives in the Tarascan system.

The same situation is involved in the effort it costs some bilingual Yaquis to learn to write double vowels and ?; and the interpretation given here is corroborated by their conversational comments, mentioned above, as to the identity of words like gói and gó?i.

The general conclusion to be drawn from the cases cited is that the bilingual does not ordinarily have a single unified and accurate consciousness of the two phonetic systems he controls. He is, as it were, two phonetic personalities which make use of the same set of speech organs. When he is talking language A, he conceives language B with the prejudices of language A; and in the context of language B, he conceives A from standpoint of the former. His phonemic system in each of the languages may be enlarged as compared with that of monolinguals by virtue of his capacity to introduce certain foreign sounds. Without doubt, cases occur of each system being so extended as to include a phoneme related to each of those of the other system. This gives us two sets of sounds in complementary distribution, which, from the standpoint of phonemic theory, can be regarded as a single system. The tendency of bilinguals to regard similar words in the two languages as identical would indicate that the psychological unification of the two systems in his consciousness is always potentially present.

Instituto Politécnico Nacional
Mexico, D. F.

CULTURE CHANGE AND LANGUAGE: SHIFTS IN THE PIMA VOCABULARY

By GEORGE HERZOG

LANGUAGE is a notoriously flexible instrument, and registers culture changes perhaps more sensitively than does any other phase of culture. Such changes may affect phonetics, vocabulary, or grammar. It is in vocabulary, however, that they can be traced most readily, whether they be conceived as due primarily to developments within the culture or to the effect of external stimuli.

The manner in which the vocabulary of a language adjusts itself to the importation of new objects and ideas is of interest for the study of culture as well as of language. To put it somewhat schematically, there are three methods by which a vocabulary may extend its range and scope to cover such needs. It may take words over bodily from the language which accompanies the impact of another culture, and which to some extent carries it. It may coin new expressions to describe new phenomena. Or old words and formations may be extended in meaning, while the old meanings are either retained or displaced entirely by the new. Obviously, these processes operate side by side, and often more than one of them is active in connection with the same cultural item or expression. At times, however, a language uses one method predominantly, at the expense of the others. Which one it has used is not merely an academic question of concern only to the linguist; a language, for example, that consistently borrows foreign words offers in its vocabulary an important tool for reading the culture history of its speakers. It has been asked, then, what will decide the behavior of the language in this respect.

Linguists have discussed the question mainly under the head of "borrowing," taking examples almost exclusively from Indo-European or Oriental languages. The majority of linguists are inclined to ascribe extensive borrowing, such as English exhibits beginning with the Norman conquest, to the nature of the historical processes involved—which often means; in anthropological parlance, a process of acculturation. Other linguists have emphasized the importance of purely linguistic features, speaking of the character, grammatical structure, type, drift, or "genius" of the language, according to which large-scale borrowing may or may not be feasible.

The latter viewpoint certainly calls for consideration. A language that abounds in descriptive terms for denoting objects, or in which formal methods of word derivation are numerous, will transmute new matter more readily than one in which new constructions are inhibited, grammatical formations are restricted, and the speaker is used to forms which in themselves have little or no descriptive meaning. English is certainly an example of the latter type; many unwritten languages provide examples of the former.

The cultural factors affecting borrowing are apt to show more clearly with languages in which the purely linguistic factors are about evenly balanced for or against borrowing. This is the case with the Pima language in Arizona. Pima is of especial interest because the vocabulary has shifted its behavior radically, and twice, during its known history. Since the grammatical make-up of the language has at the same time remained practically un-changed, and since the shifts coincide with definite changes in the culture, the conclusion follows that the shifts were primarily due to culture changes, and on the whole independent of strictly linguistic factors

Pima belongs to the so-called Uto-Aztecan linguistic stock. The languages of this group are strongly synthetic and would be rated as agglutinative according to the old tripartite classification of isolating, agglutinative, and inflecting languages. Ideas are often expressed in Pima by complex word-constructions, and there are a large number of descriptive terms and phrases. New ideas can be expressed with comparative ease by manipulating the already existing materials of the vocabulary and grammar. On the other hand, most familiar objects of experience are denoted by simple words which in themselves are not at all or not readily amenable to analysis by the native speaker.

A survey of those elements in the vocabulary whose presence, according to cultural or linguistic evidence, must be due to culture contacts with the Western World, shows that they fall into three well defined groups.[1] The largest includes descriptive terms or phrases in idiomatic Pima, well over two hundred, with some words whose meaning has been radically extended or changed. The next comprises words taken over from Spanish, over one hundred and twenty, with minor phonetic modifications. The third consists of words, perhaps fifteen, taken over from English, again with minor phonetic modifications.

The items of the first group may be listed under various headings:[2]

Plants

oats:	"having downward tassels"	June corn (a modern variety from Mexico?):	"big corn"
diverse varieties of wheat:	"having rounded tassels"	dates:	"owl mucus"
	"having whiskered tassels"	lemons:	"very sour"
	"having white tassels"	asparagus:	"looking like a native plant"
	"long-tasseled"	bananas:	"foreskin pulled back" (the vulgar expression)
	"black-tasseled"		
	"reddish tassels"	Bermuda grass:	"grass that grows in all directions"
	"itchy wheat"		
	"very hard"		

[1] Borrowing from Indo-European by North American Indian languages is usually handled as one of the by-products in studying native languages. Part of the material on which this article is based was assembled in similar fashion, in the course of various field trips devoted to the study of Pima. A much larger amount of data was gathered afterward through a systematic canvassing of the vocabulary with native informants in 1935. Acknowledgment is gratefully rendered to the National Research Council whose grant made the latter study possible.

[2] The translations of the Pima equivalents are of necessity only approximate. Unless otherwise indicated, each of the following groups and sub-groups contains all the examples known to me.

Animals
whale: "humped"
camel: "long-necked one" or "hump-backed"
elephant: "wrinkled buttocks"
monkey: "dog person"
greyhound: "slender-in-the-middle dog"
yearling steer: "fattened one"

Foods
chocolate: "climbing" (reference to the muddy color of the swollen and rising river)
pop corn: "blossoming corn"
raisins: "dry grapes"

Diseases
tuberculosis: "coughing"
cholera: "black vomit"

Materials
rubber: "very elastic"
motor-oil: "greasing-thing"
gum: "very sticky"

cement: "ground stone wet-mixture"
lime: "hot stone wet-mixture"

Measures, terms of space and time
a load: "sewed up" (probably reference to a closed sack)
a certain amount (of wood): "a cutting"
cord of wood: "put-standing-up"
half a cord of wood: "stretching-along"
pound: "heavy"
street: "space between parallels"
Tuesday: "two days" (after Sunday)
Wednesday: "three days"
Thursday: "four days"

Place-names
Phoenix: "many houses"
Sacaton: "big house" (from the old agency building)

(There are other examples.)

"Ideological," intellectual or religious expressions are few and far between, chiefly religious terms which are rather laborious:

good deeds: "good deeds"
sin: "not-good deeds"
holy spirit: "life with goodness"
to be saved: "to be led across"
religious faith: "truthfulness"

Protestants: "tables" (from the lack of altars)
leader: "leader"
to be biased: "to hold oneself to the other side"

On the other hand, terms denoting implements or connected with our technology, are abundant; they embrace at least as many words as all the other groups together. A few examples referring to the automobile and electricity may suffice:

automobile: "moves by itself"
the back part: "its anus"
the pistons: "its arms"
the wheels: "its legs"
the fenders: "its ears"
the tires: "its shoes"

the inner tube: "lying inside"
electricity: "lightning"
battery: "lightning box"
plugs: "lightning pots"
battery acid: "lightning liquid"

A considerable number of words for implements and materials are constructed with the suffix -kuṭ which in the old vocabulary denoted primarily place and evidence of activity, and only secondarily the instrument of activity. It has now become a very freely employed suffix for the instrument or sometimes the material with which one performs the act.

A number of words in this first group represent translations from English (good deeds, leader), or extensions of meaning ("truthfulness" for "religious faith"), or restrictions of meaning ("magician" for "medical doctor").

In the vocabulary from the Spanish we have:

Plants: wheat, tomatoes, potatoes, sweet potatoes, barley, peaches, onions, apples, melons, cholla, ocatilla (partly replacing a Pima word).

Animals: horse, mule, goat, donkey, stud, cow, bull, ox, calf, cat.

Foods: sugar, butter, lard, cheese, candy, hominy, comar.

Materials: gold, silver, metal (iron, steel), glass (meaning chiefly bottle and tumbler), paper, soap, muslin.

Measures, terms of space and time: to weigh, gallon, money, cent, nickel (five cents), dollar (peso), to count, number, hundred, thousand, million, minute, hour, week, Monday, Friday, Saturday, Sunday.

Religious terms: padre, god-father, god-mother, fiesta, church, Easter, Catholic, devil, saint, God.

Status terms: governor, boss, servant, twins, soldier, cowboy.

Terms denoting implements or articles connected with Western technology: vest, shirt, cape, drawers, socks, skirt, blouse, pocket, ribbons, drygoods, towel, ring, sword, pistols, armor, lance, lariat, flag, spurs, harp, drum, bells, cup, spoon, jug, table, key, door, sack, barrel, basket, hatchet, pocket-knife, whetstone, blacksmith, machine, ranch, corral, kitchen, medicine.

Amusements: playing-cards, stick dice (quinze), cigar, beer, whiskey.

There are in addition a few personal and national or tribal names, and some miscellaneous terms such as gray, spotted, lame.

In the vocabulary from the English there are few words, but the group is increasing: apricots, oranges, cabbage, tea, coffee, rice, oil, candle (covering also lamp and electric light or light bulb), shoes, window, stirrup, pencil, jack (mechanical), radio, car (for automobile), and a few personal and place names.

Historical evidence indicates that these three groups which have accreted to the Pima vocabulary are related, though roughly, to three distinct periods.

The first was that of contact with Spanish culture, through colonization from Mexico. This contact lasted over 150 years, beginning with the travels of Father Kino and the establishment of missions between 1687 and 1731, and tapering off with the American occupation in 1853. Some words must have come in after this period from Spanish, especially through contact with the Papago. (Papago and Pima are closely related dialects; the Papago, some of whom live across the Mexican border, speak Spanish to a greater extent than the Pima, who have practically given it up.) Also, some of the words, judging from phonological evidence, must have come from Spanish indirectly, through the agency of other

Indian languages (e.g., God and devil), and a few Sonoran words may have entered through Spanish (comar and atole). More pertinent to our discussion is the fact that, as far as can be established, during this period most of the words for new cultural acquisitions were taken over from Spanish; few were coined.

The second period, initiated by the American occupation, is the early reservation period which lasted well into this century. A large number of new words and expressions may be ascribed to it. A few were borrowed from English, such as shoes, axe, stirrups, and candle. That shoes or boots, and the term for them, were well known to the Pima comparatively early—although it is not likely they wore shoes early—is suggested by the curious fact that no words for native footgear survive; sandals are referred to as "stringed shoes." The overwhelming majority of terms to be allocated to this period, however, are Pima descriptive formations.

The third is the modern reservation period, which was hardly under way before the 1920's. Now the Pima began more and more to adopt words bodily from English. This tendency today affects Pima vocabulary and conversation noticeably. The total number of English terms, whether in common usage or optional, may have been near fifty at the time of my last visit to the reservation, in 1935.

Even a cursory comparison of the Spanish and the descriptive word lists substantiates their correlation with distinct historical periods. The Spanish list bears witness that the Pima acquired their contact with Western culture essentially through the Spaniards. It reads like a modest inventory of early rural or colonial life. Plant words from the Spanish designate the domesticated plants and fruits; names for varieties or luxuries found in reservation stores figure in the descriptive list. The domesticated animals in the Spanish group contrast with animals known from hearsay, pictures, or the circus. Store luxuries appear again among the foods on the descriptive list. Status terms occur only on the Spanish list; the American occupation made no attempt to reorient the mode of life or the political organization of the people. The descriptive list is richest when it comes to technological terminology; on the Spanish list this group is represented mainly by simple utensils, articles of clothing, and the like. Telling differences appear throughout, as in connection with the religious terms.

The words introduced from Spanish were fitted to the grammatical patterns of Pima, though as a rule they were not endowed with many grammatical forms. For the new descriptive terms, however, the resources of the language could be utilized smoothly and fully. Many of these new formations follow patterns common in the old Pima vocabulary, such as "the thing that does so and so," "the being that does so and so," or "the thing that has so and so." Forms of this type had fertile ritualistic sources. In songs and formalized speeches the earth, sky, animals, birds, humans, etc., are regularly referred to by some circumlocution that was not current in prose. Some of these locutions consist of the ordinary prose term plus a constant epithet, such as the "flying birds," the "standing trees," etc. Others are special forms like "this that lies spread beneath us" for the earth, "those running about on the earth" for animals. Another source of similar constructs was in dreams. Among the

Pima and Papago, as among the Yuman tribes, dreams played a key part in the culture. Some of the beings which appeared to the dreamers were creatures and objects known in experience, and they appeared more or less in their normal form. But others were beings which had no actual existence and had to be specially described, such as "the upside-down flying bird." The dream content was verbalized chiefly in songs; all significant dreams contained songs and most songs were supposed to be dreamt. Thus both novelty of experience and the poetic conventions fostered imagery. Interestingly enough, it was accepted that in some types of songs, especially those of the girls' puberty ceremony, the happenings mentioned would be frightening, queer, unusual. This too must have been conducive of new imagery; one finds in songs such expressions as "the darkness sounds like metal," "it shakes the darkness," "the morning star descends face downward," etc. Finally, names of children were very often derived from something in a dream of the parent or an older relative at about the time of the birth; they too occasionally display unusual imagery: Stick Rainbow, Moon Fragment, Evening Mourning, Shields-in-Line, Running-Noise.

There was, then, in ritualistic material a process of generating fresh word formations, which fed into the vocabulary a constant stream of descriptive constructions. The patterns employed could readily apply to new phenomena furnished by foreign contacts. Whether objects introduced from white culture were actually invested with a ritualistic tinge is somewhat doubtful.[3] Rather, the ritualistic, poetic, and acculturated elements were expressed through the same linguistic patterns probably because their novelty or their remoteness from every-day life invited analysis and description.

The contrast between the vocabulary of the early and the modern reservation periods is a matter of emphasis and transition. The earlier vocabulary is being gradually displaced. This had already begun to affect the Spanish vocabulary; "wiping thing" was substituted for the Spanish of "towel," "rolled around itself" for "cigar," and "yellow one" or "it sits" (i.e. piled up) for Spanish "centavo." Similarly, in recent years a new English vocabulary has begun to displace some of the Spanish words and more of the descriptive terms of the second period. Younger people use instead Pima-ized versions of English words like car, wheels, whiskey, dollar, penny, pencil, etc., and these are phonetically closer to English than the older borrowings. This results in a curious differentiation in people's vocabulary, depending approximately on the age of the speaker. People of perhaps 55 and over, who often do not speak much English but may know some Spanish, use primarily the Spanish and descriptive terms for modern appliances. Young people more often use the Spanish and English terms. The in-between generation, however, ranging from about 35 to 50, uses terms of both the other generations. To some extent this group draws on a double technical vocabulary for words connected with white modes of life, and employs one or the other depending on the listener. If a man of this generation used many English words in talking to an old person,

[3] Pima ritualists, however, like the biblical fundamentalists, held that everything was foretold and foreordained at the time of the Creation and Origin. Consequently some imported objects were incorporated into the old mythology. When Vulture is about to kill the Culture Hero, he borrows the Sun's "iron bow," that is, gun.

he would appear to pretend to youth, its modernity, license, and identification with White ways. On the other hand, not using English terms in speaking to a young man could stamp him as a premature old fogy, and so he will say English "car" instead of "moves by itself," "radio" for "thing talking in the wind," "pick" for "sharp at both ends," "picture" or "moving picture" for "lightning" (i.e. "electricity, electric light"), "wheel" for "its leg," "Negro" for "very-dark-one," and so forth. A neat balance may be maintained by speakers at public gatherings where the audience is mixed.

The intrusion of English words into the speech of younger people is no doubt facilitated by the fact that the ritualistic material of myths, speeches, songs, and dreams, all packed with descriptive and poetic expression, is practically unknown to them and even to most middle-aged people. However, because the white technological terminology has been cast chiefly in Pima idiom, new expressions for implements and the like are still being coined according to descriptive methods. Yet there is now a tendency to restrict the number of grammatical devices in this extension of the vocabulary; young people who have learned something of English grammar in school begin to complain that their native language is "difficult."[4]

The shifts in the behavior of the Pima vocabulary coincide with significant points of culture change in their history, even though the shifts are to some extent in emphasis only. That the coincidence is by no means fortuitous is suggested by a mere sketch of conditions in the different periods.

The Spanish missionary penetration meant for the Pima the acquisition of new technics, foods, and materials, and also substantial changes in their mode of organization. Trends began toward concentration as against their earlier life in small and scattered settlements, toward a somewhat tighter control by chiefs—they had no true chiefs before—and increased needs and methods of cooperation. How intensive was the pressure exerted upon them we hardly know; it could not have been very stringent. Nothing like the Pueblo rebellion, no sign of resistance, has come down to us. Yet they were subjected to a mode of living supervised and planned for them, and they carried it on after pressure ceased.

During the early reservation period in the nineteenth century the Pima were left largely to their own devices. The territory was of importance to Whites only as mining land and because routes of travel crossed it. Agency administration and efforts at education or hygiene were anything but energetic. Influence seeped in leisurely from the outside rather than coming from administrative centers located within the group, except for missionary activities. The dream-experience, one of the most strategic phases of the culture, continued for quite some time, as did warfare. Technological innovations were gradual.

The contemporary period has brought heightened administrative attention, intensive schooling, familiarity with English, new government policies, and lately relief work activities. There came a more intimate acquaintance with details of technology, a brisker social life centering about the mission churches, more young people going to institutions

---

[4] This complaint, to be sure, often turns out to be merely a symptom of discomfort at unfamiliarity with specialized segments of the old vocabulary, such as the relationship terminology.

like Carlisle, more travel. Better roads, the increase of automobile communication, bus lines, tourist traffic, radio, irrigation projects, all led the Pima to a version of American rural life which could retain little of the old, less of the exotic, if the old people, the language, and the physical type were wiped out.

The question arises then: what did the first and third periods thus briefly surveyed have in common to account for the similarity of linguistic behavior that sets them off from the second? One difference lies in the nature and intensity of the impact of the foreign culture. The Pima, as we have observed, were rather submissive to the slight pressure exerted upon them by the Spanish colonizers. They accepted a cultural domination as they now, notwithstanding the existence of a tribal council, follow completely the lead of modern American culture. This element of submission must be at least one of the causes to which acceptance of foreign words may be ascribed. Yet, striking differences of circumstance between early and late influences must be noted. Today the young Pima are completely dependent on American culture. The old culture is about gone, leaving them nothing with which to build or rebuild. They want to be Americans and are eager to participate as much as is allowed them. We have no evidence of a similarly conditioned receptivity in the Spanish period: it held no threat of acute cultural discontinuity. This disparity, coupled with the irrevocable absence of a more intimate picture of the Spanish period, renders our interpretation of cultural "causes" not fully satisfactory. The fact remains, however, that when, during the early reservation period, pressure was lifted and guidance reduced, the Pima language reasserted its flair for describing in its own terms the new and strange. To put it from another angle, English carries prestige today among the Pima, except for the oldest generation; while in the early colonial days a smattering of Spanish carried probably prestige and certainly material advantages. In the middle period neither language could claim so high a stock.

Linguistic reversals of the type described here are by no means exceptional. In West Africa a large number of native descriptive or analytic terms for foreign technological items were current during the early part of this century. The words are now being replaced by borrowed European equivalents. In West Africa too natives are becoming dependents of Western culture, and aware of it. The exact nature of the forces involved may not always be clear. But if they can produce similar changes in languages quite different in general make-up, then they—rather than linguistic make-up—must account for the moulding of language behavior during the particular period of linguistic and cultural change. Language factors are part, however, of the process of change. No doubt many Indians or West Africans today are more ready to accept English words simply because they are more familiar with the language; this facilitates phonetic acceptance too. The younger generation of the Pima is practically bilingual, and the ease with which English words and forms slip into their conversation reminds one of what happens to the native vocabulary of immigrants in this country. It is not by any means suggested, then, that linguistic factors are irrelevant in culture change, but that if a discussion of borrowing overstresses the importance of either the cultural or the linguistic aspect it fails to do justice to the complex manner in which the two may be intertwined.

Sapir displayed considerable interest in the question.[5] "It is generally assumed that the nature and extent of borrowing depend entirely on the historical facts of culture relation. . . This is . . . not the whole truth. . . . It seems very probable that the psychological attitude of the borrowing language itself towards linguistic material has much to do with its recep-tivity to foreign words." He points out that the languages of the Athapascans of North America, with their speakers' varied culture contacts, have borrowed only an infinitesimal amount. He refers to the difference between Cambodgian and Tibetan; both were strongly influenced by Sanskrit, but while Tibetan, which is more prone to construction by mean-ingful units, has taken over very few Sanskrit loan words, Cambodgian which has many complex words incapable of analysis by the native speaker has absorbed an immense number.

"Psychological attitude" of the language is given concrete meaning in these examples by the exposition of strongly established structural patterns with which extraneous language matter either falls in line or clashes. Another kind of conditioning force is referred to by Sapir in the following: "There are now psychological resistances to borrowing, or rather to new sources of borrowing [fn.: For we still name our new scientific instruments and patent medicines from Greek and Latin], that were not greatly alive in the Middle Ages or during the Renaissance." This type of resistance is not entirely independent of structural forces in language either; yet it is much more intimately tied up with attitudes that have their roots elsewhere and that come to the surface in times of stress and change.

Where a shift of language behavior is observed among non-literate peoples, as in the Pima case, in West Africa, or elsewhere, the linguistic processes involved are largely unconscious. They may become conscious when awareness of language and of the force of words becomes heightened. The history of European languages, especially in central and eastern Europe, is full of periodic purges recurring at times of intense national feeling during which previously imported words were transposed wholesale into the vernacular. It is of some interest to compare the results of these enterprises with the phenomena described here for an Indian tribe. Except that linguistic purists do not always have a good pattern-feeling for their language and produce occasional atrocities, the outcome, on a linguistic level, appears similar. One interesting difference seems to be, however, that in the large literate groups awareness and self-consciousness with regard to language have, at times of stress, resulted in its direct utilization, producing "ideologies" and an excessive crop of highly weighted symbolic word-values. Both seem to be absent under comparable conditions in primitive communities. Such developments sharpen and reveal the picture of what is actually happening, though if taken at face value they merely obscure it. From such considerations emerge further reasons why the study of culture changes and culture processes may benefit greatly by due regard for the tool of language—the medium through which culture becomes perhaps most clearly articulate.

COLUMBIA UNIVERSITY
  NEW YORK CITY

[5] Edward Sapir, *Language* (New York, 1921), pp. 205-10.

THE RELATION OF HABITUAL THOUGHT AND BEHAVIOR TO LANGUAGE

By B. L. WHORF

THERE will probably be general assent to the proposition that an accepted pattern of using words is often prior to certain lines of thinking and forms of behavior, but he who assents often sees in such a statement nothing more than a platitudinous recognition of the hypnotic power of philosophical and learned terminology on the one hand or of catchwords, slogans, and rallying-cries on the other. To see only thus far is to miss the point of one of the important interconnections which Sapir saw between language, culture, and psychology, and succinctly expressed in the introductory quotation. It is not so much in these special uses of language as in its constant ways of arranging data and its most ordinary every-day analysis of phenomena that we need to recognize the influence it has on other activities, cultural and personal.

THE NAME OF THE SITUATION AS AFFECTING BEHAVIOR

I came in touch with an aspect of this problem before I had studied under Dr Sapir, and in a field usually considered remote from linguistics. It was in the course of my professional work for a fire insurance company, in which I undertook the task of analyzing many hundreds of reports of circumstances surrounding the start of fires, and in some cases, of explosions. My analysis was directed toward purely physical conditions, such as defective wiring, presence or lack of air spaces between metal flues and woodwork, etc., and the results were presented in these terms. Indeed it was undertaken with no thought that any other significances would or could be revealed. But in due course it became evident that not only a physical situation *qua* physics, but the meaning of that situation to people, was sometimes a factor, through the behavior of the people, in the start of the fire. And this factor of meaning was clearest when it was a *linguistic meaning*, residing in the name or the linguistic description commonly applied to the situation. Thus around a storage of what are called "gasoline drums" behavior will tend to a certain type, that is, great care will be exercised; while around a storage of what are called "empty gasoline drums" it will tend to be different—careless, with little repression of smoking or of tossing cigarette stubs about. Yet the "empty" drums are perhaps the more dangerous, since they contain explosive vapor. Physically the situation is hazardous, but the linguistic analysis according to regular analogy must employ the word "empty," which inevitably suggests lack of hazard. The word "empty" is used in two linguistic patterns: (1) as a virtual synonym for "null and void, negative, inert," (2) applied in analysis of physical situations without regard to, e.g., vapor, liquid vestiges, or stray rubbish, in the container. The situation is named in one pattern (2) and the name is then "acted out" or "lived up to" in another (1); this being a general formula for the linguistic conditioning of behavior into hazardous forms.

In a wood distillation plant the metal stills were insulated with a composition prepared from limestone and called at the plant "spun limestone." No attempt was made to protect this covering from excessive heat or the contact of flame. After a period of use the fire below one of the stills spread to the "limestone," which to everyone's great surprise burned vigorously. Exposure to acetic acid fumes from the stills had converted part of the lime-stone (calcium carbonate) to calcium acetate. This when heated in a fire decomposes, form-ing inflammable acetone. Behavior that tolerated fire close to the covering was induced by use of the name "limestone," which because it ends in "-stone" implies noncombustibility.

A huge iron kettle of boiling varnish was observed to be overheated, nearing the tem-perature at which it would ignite. The operator moved it off the fire and ran it on its wheels to a distance, but did not cover it. In a minute or so the varnish ignited. Here the linguistic influence is more complex; it is due to the metaphorical objectifying (of which more later) of "cause" as contact or the spatial juxtaposition of "things"—to analyzing the situation as "on" versus "off" the fire. In reality the stage when the external fire was the main factor had passed; the overheating was now an internal process of convection in the varnish from the intensely heated kettle, and still continued when "off" the fire.

An electric glow heater on the wall was little used, and for one workman had the mean-ing of a convenient coat-hanger. At night a watchman entered and snapped a switch, which action he verbalized as "turning on the light." No light appeared, and this result he verbalized as "light is burned out." He could not see the glow of the heater because of the old coat hung on it. Soon the heater ignited the coat, which set fire to the building.

A tannery discharged waste water containing animal matter into an outdoor settling basin partly roofed with wood and partly open. This situation is one that ordinarily would be verbalized as "pool of water." A workman had occasion to light a blow-torch nearby, and threw his match into the water. But the decomposing waste matter was evolving gas under the wood cover, so that the setup was the reverse of "watery." An instant flare of flame ignited the woodwork, and the fire quickly spread into the adjoining building.

A drying room for hides was arranged with a blower at one end to make a current of air along the room and thence outdoors through a vent at the other end. Fire started at a hot bearing on the blower, which blew the flames directly into the hides and fanned them along the room, destroying the entire stock. This hazardous setup followed naturally from the term "blower" with its linguistic equivalence to "that which blows," implying that its function necessarily is to "blow." Also its function is verbalized as "blowing air for drying," overlooking that it can blow other things, e.g., flames and sparks. In reality a blower simply makes a current of air and can exhaust as well as blow. It should have been installed at the vent end to *draw* the air over the hides, then through the hazard (its own casing and bear-ings) and thence outdoors.

Beside a coal-fired melting pot for lead reclaiming was dumped a pile of "scrap lead"—a misleading verbalization, for it consisted of the lead sheets of old radio condensers, which still had paraffin paper between them. Soon the paraffin blazed up and fired the roof, half of which was burned off.

Such examples, which could be greatly multiplied, will suffice to show how the cue to a certain line of behavior is often given by the analogies of the linguistic formula in which the situation is spoken of, and by which to some degree it is analyzed, classified, and allotted its place in that world which is "to a large extent unconsciously built up on the language habits of the group." And we always assume that the linguistic analysis made by our group reflects reality better than it does.

GRAMMATICAL PATTERNS AS INTERPRETATIONS OF EXPERIENCE

The linguistic material in the above examples is limited to single words, phrases, and patterns of limited range. One cannot study the behavioral compulsiveness of such material without suspecting a much more far-reaching compulsion from large-scale patterning of grammatical categories, such as plurality, gender and similar classifications (animate, in-animate, etc.), tenses, voices, and other verb forms, classifications of the type of "parts of speech," and the matter of whether a given experience is denoted by a unit morpheme, an inflected word, or a syntactical combination. A category such as number (singular vs. plural) is an attempted interpretation of a whole large order of experience, virtually of the world or of nature; it attempts to say how experience is to be segmented, what experience is to be called "one" and what "several." But the difficulty of appraising such a far-reaching influence is great because of its background character, because of the difficulty of standing aside from our own language, which is a habit and a cultural *non est disputandum*, and scrutinizing it objectively. And if we take a very dissimilar language, this language becomes a part of nature, and we even do to it what we have already done to nature. We tend to think in our own language in order to examine the exotic language. Or we find the task of unraveling the purely morphological intricacies so gigantic that it seems to absorb all else. Yet the problem, though difficult, is feasible; and the best approach is through an exotic language, for in its study we are at long last pushed willy-nilly out of our ruts. Then we find that the exotic language is a mirror held up to our own.

In my study of the Hopi language, what I now see as an opportunity to work on this problem was first thrust upon me before I was clearly aware of the problem. The seemingly endless task of describing the morphology did finally end. Yet it was evident, especially in the light of Sapir's lectures on Navaho, that the description of the *language* was far from complete. I knew for example the morphological formation of plurals, but not how to use plurals. It was evident that the category of plural in Hopi was not the same thing as in English, French, or German. Certain things that were plural in these languages were singular in Hopi. The phase of investigation which now began consumed nearly two more years.

The work began to assume the character of a comparison between Hopi and western European languages. It also became evident that even the grammar of Hopi bore a relation to Hopi culture, and the grammar of European tongues to our own "Western" or "European" culture. And it appeared that the interrelation brought in those large subsummations of experience by language, such as our own terms "time," "space," "substance," and "matter." Since with respect to the traits compared there is little difference between English, French, German, or other European languages with the *possible* (but doubtful) exception of Balto-Slavic and non-Indo-European, I have lumped these languages into one group called SAE, or "Standard Average European."

That portion of the whole investigation here to be reported may be summed up in two questions: (1) Are our own concepts of "time," "space," and "matter" given in substantially the same form by experience to all men, or are they in part conditioned by the structure of particular languages? (2) Are there traceable affinities between (a) cultural and behavioral norms and (b) large-scale linguistic patterns? (I should be the last to pretend that there is anything so definite as "a correlation" between culture and language, and especially between ethnological rubrics such as "agricultural," "hunting," etc., and linguistic ones like "inflected," "synthetic," or "isolating."[1] When I began the study the problem was by no means so clearly formulated and I had little notion that the answers would turn out as they did.

PLURALITY AND NUMERATION IN SAE AND HOPI

In our language, that is SAE, plurality and cardinal numbers are applied in two ways: to real plurals and imaginary plurals. Or more exactly if less tersely: perceptible spatial aggregates and metaphorical aggregates. We say "ten men" and also "ten days." Ten men either are or could be objectively perceived as ten, ten in one group-perception[2]—ten men on a street corner, for instance. But "ten days" cannot be objectively experienced. We experience only one day, to-day; the other nine (or even all ten) are something conjured up from memory or imagination. If "ten days" be regarded as a group it must be as an "imaginary," mentally constructed group. Whence comes this mental pattern? Just as in the case of the fire-causing errors, from the fact that our language confuses the two different situations, has but one pattern for both. When we speak of ten steps forward, ten strokes on a bell, or any similarly described cyclic sequence, "times" of any sort, we are doing the same thing as with "days." *Cyclicity* brings the response of imaginary plurals. But a likeness of cyclicity to aggregates is not unmistakably given by experience prior to language, or it would be found in all languages, and it is not.

Our *awareness* of time and cyclicity does contain something immediate and subjective— the basic sense of "becoming later and later." But in the habitual thought of us SAE people

---

[1] We have plenty of evidence that this is not the case. Consider only the Hopi and the Ute, with languages that on the overt morphological and lexical level are as similar as, say, English and German. The idea of "correlation" between language and culture, in the generally accepted sense of correlation, is certainly a mistaken one.

[2] As we say, "ten at the *same time*," showing that in our language and thought we restate the fact of group-perception in terms of a concept "time," the large linguistic component of which will appear in the course of this paper.

this is covered under something quite different, which though mental should not be called subjective. I call it *objectified*, or imaginary, because it is patterned on the *outer* world. It is this that reflects our linguistic usage. Our tongue makes no distinction between numbers counted on discrete entities and numbers that are simply counting itself. Habitual thought then assumes that in the latter case the numbers are just as much counted on *something* as in the former. This is objectification. Concepts of time lose contact with the subjective experience of "becoming later" and are objectified as counted *quantities*, especially as lengths, made up of units as a length can be visible marked off into inches. A "length of time" is envisioned as a row of similar units, like a row of bottles.

In Hopi there is a different linguistic situation. Plurals and cardinals are used only for entities that form or can form an objective group. There are no imaginary plurals, but instead ordinals used with singulars. Such an expression as "ten days" is not used. The equivalent statement is an operational one that reaches one day by a suitable count. "They stayed ten days" becomes "they stayed until the eleventh day" or "they left after the tenth day." "Ten days is greater than nine days" becomes "the tenth day is later than the ninth." Our "length of time" is not regarded as a length but as a relation between two events in lateness. Instead of our linguistically promoted objectification of that datum of consciousness we call "time," the Hopi language has not laid down any pattern that would cloak the subjective "becoming later" that is the essence of time.

NOUNS OF PHYSICAL QUANTITY IN SAE AND HOPI

We have two kinds of noun denoting physical things; individual nouns, and mass nouns, e. g., water, milk, wood, granite, sand, flour, meat. Individual nouns denote bodies with definite outlines: a tree, a stick, a man, a hill. Mass nouns denote homogeneous continua without implied boundaries. The distinction is marked by linguistic form; e.g., mass nouns lack plurals,[3] in English drop articles, and in French take the partitive article *du, de la, des*. The distinction is more widespread in language than in the observable appearance of things. Rather few natural occurrences present themselves as unbounded extents; air of course, and often water, rain, snow, sand, rock, dirt, grass. We do not encounter butter, meat, cloth, iron, glass, or most "materials" in such kind of manifestation, but in bodies small or large with definite outlines. The distinction is somewhat forced upon our description of events by an unavoidable pattern in language. It is so inconvenient in a great many cases that we need some way of individualizing the mass noun by further linguistic devices. This is partly done by names of body-types: stick of wood, piece of cloth, pane of glass, cake of soap; also, and even more, by introducing names of containers though their contents be the real issue: glass

---

[3] It is no exception to this rule of lacking a plural that a mass noun may sometimes coincide in lexeme with an individual noun that of course has a plural; e.g., "stone" (no pl.) with "a stone" (pl. "stones"). The plural form denoting varieties, e.g., "wines" is of course a different sort of thing from the true plural; it is a curious outgrowth from the SAE mass nouns, leading to still another sort of imaginary aggregates, which will have to be omitted from this paper.

of water, cup of coffee, dish of food, bag of flour, bottle of beer. These very common con-tainer-formulas, in which "of" has an obvious, visually perceptible meaning ("contents"), influence our feeling about the less obvious type-body formulas: stick of wood, lump of dough, etc. The formulas are very similar: individual noun plus a similar relator (English "of"). In the obvious case this relator denotes contents. In the inobvious one it *suggests* con-tents. Hence the lumps, chunks, blocks, pieces, etc., seem to contain something, a "stuff," "substance," or "matter" that answers to the water, coffee, or flour in the container formu-las. So with SAE people the philosophic "substance" and "matter" are also the naïve idea; they are instantly acceptable, "common sense." It is so through linguistic habit. Our lan-guage patterns often require us to name a physical thing by a binomial that splits the refer-ence into a formless item plus a form.

Hopi is again different. It has a formally distinguished class of nouns. But this class contains no formal sub-class of mass nouns. All nouns have an individual sense and both singular and plural forms. Nouns translating most nearly our mass nouns still refer to vague bodies or vaguely bounded extents. They imply indefiniteness, but not lack, of outline and size. In specific statements "water" means one certain mass or quantity of water, not what we call "the substance water." Generality of statement is conveyed through the verb or predicator, not the noun. Since nouns are individual already they are not individualized either by type-bodies or names of containers, if there is no special need to emphasize shape or container. The noun itself implies a suitable type-body or container. One says, not "a glass of water" but kə·yi "a water," not "a pool of water" but pa·hə,[4] not "a dish of corn-flour" but ŋəmni "a (quantity of) corn-flour," not "a piece of meat" but sikʷi "a meat." The language has neither need for nor analogies on which to build the concept of existence as a duality of formless item and form. It deals with formlessness through other symbols than nouns.

PHASES OF CYCLES IN SAE AND HOPI

Such terms as summer, winter, September, morning, noon, sunset, are with us nouns, and have little formal linguistic difference from other nouns. They can be subjects or objects, and we say "at" sunset or "in" winter just as we say at a corner or in an orchard.[5] They are pluralized and numerated like nouns of physical objects, as we have seen. Our thought about the referents of such words hence becomes objectified. Without objectification it would be a subjective experience of real time, i.e. of the consciousness of "becoming later and later"—simply a cyclic phase similar to an earlier phase in that ever-later-becoming duration. Only by imagination can such a cyclic phase be set beside another and another in

---

[4] Hopi has two words for water-quantities; kə·yi and pa·hə. The difference is something like that between "stone" and "rock" in English, pa·hə implying greater size and "wildness;" flowing water, whether or not out-doors or in nature, is pa·hə, so is "moisture." But unlike "stone" and "rock," the difference is essential, not per-taining to a connotative margin, and the two can hardly ever be interchanged.

[5] To be sure there are a few minor differences from other nouns, in English for instance in the use of the articles.

the manner of a spatial (i.e. visually perceived) configuration. But such is the power of linguistic analogy that we do so objectify cyclic phasing. We do it even by saying "a phase" and "phases" instead of, e.g., "phasing." And the pattern of individual and mass nouns, with the resulting binomial formula of formless item plus form, is so general that it is implicit for all nouns, and hence our very generalized formless items like "substance," "matter," by which we can fill out the binomial for an enormously wide range of nouns. But even these are not quite generalized enough to take in our phase nouns. So for the phase nouns we have made a formless item, "time." We have made it by using "a time," i.e. an occasion or a phase, in the pattern of a mass noun, just as from "a summer" we make "summer" in the pattern of a mass noun. Thus with our binomial formula we can say and think "a moment of time," "a second of time," "a year of time." Let me again point out that the pattern is simply that of "a bottle of milk" or "a piece of cheese." Thus we are assisted to imagine that "a summer" actually contains or consists of such-and-such a quantity of "time."

In Hopi however all phase terms, like summer, morning, etc., are not nouns but a kind of adverb, to use the nearest SAE analogy. They are a formal part of speech by themselves, distinct from nouns, verbs, and even other Hopi "adverbs." Such a word is not a case form or a locative pattern, like "des Abends" or "in the morning." It contains no morpheme like one of "in the house" or "at the tree."[6] It means "when it is morning" or "while morning-phase is occurring." These "temporals" are not used as subjects or objects, or at all like nouns. One does not say "it's a hot summer" or "summer is hot;" summer is not hot, summer is only *when* conditions are hot, *when* heat occurs. One does not say "*this* summer," but "summer now" or "summer recently." There is no objectification, as a region, an extent, a quantity, of the subjective duration-feeling. Nothing is suggested about time except the perpetual "getting later" of it. And so there is no basis here for a formless item answering to our "time."

TEMPORAL FORMS OF VERBS IN SAE AND HOPI

The three-tense system of SAE verbs colors all our thinking about time. This system is amalgamated with that larger scheme of objectification of the subjective experience of duration already noted in other patterns—in the binomial formula applicable to nouns in general, in temporal nouns, in plurality and numeration. This objectification enables us in imagination to "stand time units in a row." Imagination of time as like a row harmonizes with a system of *three* tenses; whereas a system of *two*, an earlier and a later, would seem to correspond better to the feeling of duration as it is experienced. For if we inspect consciousness we find no past, present, future, but a unity embracing complexity. *Everything* is in consciousness, and everything in consciousness *is*, and is together. There is in it a sensuous and a non-sensuous. We may call the sensuous—what we are seeing, hearing,

---

[6] "Year" and certain combinations of "year" with name of season, rarely season names alone, can occur with a locative morpheme "at," but this is exceptional. It appears like historical detritus of an earlier different patterning, or the effect of English analogy, or both.

touching—the "present" while in the non-sensuous the vast image-world of memory is being labelled "the past" and another realm of belief, intuition, and uncertainty "the future;" yet sensation, memory, foresight, all are in consciousness together—one is not "yet to be" nor another "once but no more." Where real time comes in is that all this in consciousness is "getting later," changing certain relations in an irreversible manner. In this "latering" or "durating" there seems to me to be a paramount contrast between the newest, latest instant at the focus of attention and the rest—the earlier. Languages by the score get along well with two tense-like forms answering to this paramount relation of later to earlier. We can of course *construct and contemplate in thought* a system of past, present, future, in the objectified configuration of points on a line. This is what our general objectification tendency leads us to do and our tense system confirms.

In English the present tense seems the one least in harmony with the paramount temporal relation. It is as if pressed into various and not wholly congruous duties. One duty is to stand as objectified middle term between objectified past and objectified future, in narration, discussion, argument, logic, philosophy. Another is to denote inclusion in the sensuous field: "I *see* him." Another is for nomic, i.e. customarily or generally valid, statements: "We *see* with our eyes." These varied uses introduce confusions of thought, of which for the most part we are unaware.

Hopi, as we might expect, is different here too. Verbs have no "tenses" like ours, but have validity-forms ("assertions"), aspects, and clause-linkage forms (modes), that yield even greater precision of speech. The validity-forms denote that the speaker (not the subject) reports the situation (answering to our past and present) or that he expects it (answering to our future)[7] or that he makes a nomic statement (answering to our nomic present). The aspects denote different degrees of duration and different kinds of tendency "during duration." As yet we have noted nothing to indicate whether an event is sooner or later than another when both are *reported*. But need for this does not arise until we have two verbs, i.e. two clauses. In that case the "modes" denote relations between the clauses, including relations of later to earlier and of simultaneity. Then there are many detached words that express similar relations, supplementing the modes and aspects. The duties of our three-tense system and its tripartite linear objectified "time" are distributed among various verb categories, all different from our tenses; and there is no more basis for an objectified time in Hopi verbs than in other Hopi patterns; although this does not in the least hinder the verb forms and other patterns from being closely adjusted to the pertinent realities of actual situations.

----

[7] The expective and reportive assertions contrast according to the "paramount relation." The expective expresses anticipation existing *earlier* than objective fact, and coinciding with objective fact *later* than the status quo of the speaker, this status quo, including all the subsummation of the past therein, being expressed by the reportive. Our notion "future" seems to represent at once the earlier (anticipation) and the later (afterwards, what will be), as Hopi shows. This paradox may hint of how elusive the mystery of real time is, and how artificially it is expressed by a linear relation of past-present-future.

DURATION, INTENSITY, AND TENDENCY IN SAE AND HOPI

To fit discourse to manifold actual situations all languages need to express durations, intensities, and tendencies. It is characteristic of SAE and perhaps of many other language-types to express them metaphorically. The metaphors are those of spatial extension, i.e. of size, number (plurality), position, shape, and motion. We express duration by long, short, great, much, quick, slow, etc.; intensity by large, great, much, heavy, light, high, low, sharp, faint, etc.; tendency by more, increase, grow, turn, get, approach, go, come, rise, fall, stop, smooth, even, rapid, slow, and so on through an almost inexhaustible list of metaphors that we hardly recognize as such since they are virtually the only linguistic media available. The non-metaphorical terms in this field, like early, late, soon, lasting, intense, very, tending, are a mere handful, quite inadequate to the needs.

It is clear how this condition "fits in." It is part of our whole scheme of *objectifying*—imaginatively spatializing qualities and potentials that are quite non-spatial (so far as any spatially-perceptive senses can tell us). Noun-meaning (with us) proceeds from physical bodies to referents of far other sort. Since physical bodies and their outlines in *perceived space* are denoted by size and shape terms and reckoned by cardinal numbers and plurals, these patterns of denotation and reckoning extend to the symbols of non-spatial meanings, and so suggest an *imaginary space*. Physical shapes move, stop, rise, sink, approach, etc., in perceived space; why not these other referents in their imaginary space? This has gone so far that we can hardly refer to the simplest non-spatial situation without constant resort to physical metaphors. I "grasp" the "thread" of another's arguments, but if its "level" is "over my head" my attention may "wander" and "lose touch" with the "drift" of it, so that when he "comes" to his "point" we differ "widely," our "views" being indeed so "far apart" that the "things" he says "appear" "much" too arbitrary, or even "a lot" of nonsense!

The absence of such metaphor from Hopi speech is striking. Use of space terms when there is no space involved is *not there*—as if on it had been laid the taboo teetotal! The reason is clear when we know that Hopi has abundant conjugational and lexical means of expressing duration, intensity, and tendency directly as such, and that major grammatical patterns do not, as with us, provide analogies for an imaginary space. The many verb "aspects" express duration and tendency of manifestations, while some of the "voices" express intensity, tendency, and duration of causes or forces producing manifestations. Then a special part of speech, the "tensors," a huge class of words, denotes only intensity, tendency, duration, and sequence. The function of the tensors is to express intensities, "strengths," and how they continue or vary, their rate-of-change; so that the broad concept of intensity, when considered as necessarily always varying and/or continuing, includes also tendency and duration. Tensors convey distinctions of degree, rate, constancy, repetition, increase and decrease of intensity, immediate sequence, interruption or sequence after an interval, etc., also *qualities* of strengths, such as we should express metaphorically as smooth, even, hard, rough. A striking feature is their lack of resemblance to the terms of real space and move-

ment that to us "mean the same." There is not even more than a trace of apparent derivation from space terms.[8] So while Hopi in its nouns seems highly concrete, here in the tensors
it becomes abstract almost beyond our power to follow.

HABITUAL THOUGHT IN SAE AND HOPI

The comparison now to be made between the habitual thought worlds of SAE and Hopi
speakers is of course incomplete. It is possible only to touch upon certain dominant contrasts
that appear to stem from the linguistic differences already noted. By "habitual thought"
and "thought world" I mean more than simply language, i.e. than the linguistic patterns
themselves. I include all the analogical and suggestive value of the patterns (e.g., our "imaginary space" and its distant implications), and all the give-and-take between language and
the culture as a whole, wherein is a vast amount that is not linguistic yet shows the shaping
influence of language. In brief, this "thought world" is the microcosm that each man carries
about within himself, by which he measures and understands what he can of the macrocosm.

The SAE microcosm has analyzed reality largely in terms of what it calls "things"
(bodies and quasi-bodies) plus modes of extensional but formless existence that it calls
"substances" or "matter." It tends to see existence through a binomial formula that expresses any existent as a spatial form plus a spatial formless continuum related to the form
as contents is related to the outlines of its container. Non-spatial existents are imaginatively
spatialized and charged with similar implications of form and continuum.

The Hopi microcosm seems to have analyzed reality largely in terms of *events* (or better
"eventing"), referred to in two ways, objective and subjective. Objectively, and only if
perceptible physical experience, events are expressed mainly as outlines, colors, movements,
and other perceptive reports. Subjectively, for both the physical and non-physical, events
are considered the expression of invisible intensity-factors, on which depend their stability
and persistence, or their fugitiveness and proclivities. It implies that existents do not "become later and later" all in the same way; but some do so by growing, like plants, some by
diffusing and vanishing, some by a procession of metamorphoses, some by enduring in one
shape till affected by violent forces. In the nature of each existent able to manifest as a
definite whole is the power of its own mode of duration; its growth, decline, stability,
cyclicity, or creativeness. Everything is thus already "prepared" for the way it now manifests by earlier phases, and what it will be later, partly has been, and partly is in act of being
so "prepared." An emphasis and importance rests on this preparing or being prepared
aspect of the world that may to the Hopi correspond to that "quality of reality" that
"matter" or "stuff" has for us.

[8] One such trace is that the tensor "long in duration," while quite different from the adjective "long" of
space, seems to contain the same root as the adjective "large" of space. Another is that "somewhere" of space
used with certain tensors means "at some indefinite time." Possibly however this is not the case and it is only the
tensor that gives the time element, so that "somewhere" still refers to space and that under these conditions
indefinite space means simply general applicability regardless of either time or space. Another trace is that in
the temporal (cycle word) "afternoon" the element meaning "after" is derived from the verb "to separate."
There are other such traces, but they are few and exceptional, and obviously not like our own spatial metaphoriz-
ing.

HABITUAL BEHAVIOR FEATURES OF HOPI CULTURE

Our behavior, and that of Hopi, can be seen to be coordinated in many ways to the linguistically-conditioned microcosm. As in my fire case-book, people act about situations in ways which are like the ways they talk about them. A characteristic of Hopi behavior is the emphasis on preparation. This includes announcing and getting ready for events well beforehand, elaborate precautions to insure persistence of desired conditions, and stress on good will as the preparer of right results. Consider the analogies of the day-counting pattern alone. Time is mainly reckoned "by day" (taʟk, ⸴tala) or "by night" (tok), which words are not nouns but tensors, the first formed on a root "light, day," the second on a root "sleep." The count is by *ordinals*. This is not the pattern of counting a number of different men or things, even though they appear successively, for even then they *could* gather into an assemblage. It is the pattern of counting successive reappearances of the *same* man or thing, incapable of forming an assemblage. The analogy is not to behave about day-cyclicity as to several men ("several days"), which is what *we* tend to do, but to behave as to the successive visits of the *same man*. One does not alter several men by working upon just one, but one can prepare and so alter the later visits of the same man by working to affect the visit he is making now. This is the way the Hopi deal with the future—by working within a present situation which is expected to carry impresses, both obvious and occult, forward into the future event of interest. One might say that Hopi society understands our proverb "Well begun is half done," but not our "To-morrow is another day." This may explain much in Hopi character.

This Hopi preparing behavior may be roughly divided into announcing, outer preparing, inner preparing, covert participation, and persistence. Announcing, or preparative publicity, is an important function in the hands of a special official, the Crier Chief. Outer preparing is preparation involving much visible activity, not all necessarily directly useful within our understanding. It includes ordinary practising, rehearsing, getting ready, introductory formalities, preparing of special food, etc. (all of these to a degree that may seem over-elaborate to us), intensive sustained muscular activity like running, racing, dancing, which is thought to increase the intensity of development of events (such as growth of crops), mimetic and other magic, preparations based on esoteric theory involving perhaps occult instruments like prayer sticks, prayer feathers, and prayer meal, and finally the great cyclic ceremonies and dances, which have the significance of preparing rain and crops. From one of the verbs meaning "prepare" is derived the noun for "harvest" or "crop:" na'twani "the prepared" or the "in preparation."[9]

Inner preparing is use of prayer and meditation, and at lesser intensity good wishes and good will, to further desired results. Hopi attitudes stress the power of desire and thought. With their "microcosm" it is utterly natural that they should. Desire and thought are the earliest, and therefore the most important, most critical and crucial, stage of preparing. Moreover, to the Hopi, one's desires and thoughts influence not only his own actions, but

[9] The Hopi verbs of preparing naturally do not correspond neatly to our "prepare;" so that na'twani could also be rendered "the practised-upon," "the tried-for," and otherwise.

all nature. This too is wholly natural. Consciousness itself is aware of work, of the feel of effort and energy, in desire and thinking. Experience more basic than language tells us that if energy is expended effects are produced. We tend to believe that our bodies can stop up this energy, prevent it from affecting other things until we will our *bodies* to overt action. But this may be only because we have our own linguistic basis for a theory that formless items like "matter" are things in themselves, malleable only by similar things, by more matter, and hence insulated from the powers of life and thought. It is no more unnatural to think that thought contacts everything and pervades the universe than to think, as we all do, that light kindled outdoors does this. And it is not unnatural to suppose that thought, like any other force, leaves everywhere traces of effect. Now when *we* think of a certain actual rose-bush, we do not suppose that our thought goes to that actual bush, and engages with it, like a searchlight turned upon it. What then do we suppose our consciousness is dealing with when we are thinking of that rose-bush? Probably we think it is dealing with a "mental image" which is not the rose-bush but a mental surrogate of it. But why should it be *natural* to think that our thought deals with a surrogate and not with the real rose-bush? Quite possibly because we are dimly aware that we carry about with us a whole imaginary space, full of mental surrogates. To us, mental surrogates are old familiar fare. Along with the images of imaginary space, which we perhaps secretly know to be imaginary only, we tuck the thought-of actually existing rose-bush, which may be quite another story, perhaps just because we have that very convenient "place" for it. The Hopi thought-world has no imaginary space. The corollary to this is that it may not locate thought dealing with real space anywhere but in real space, nor insulate real space from the effects of thought. A Hopi would naturally suppose that his thought (or he himself) traffics with the actual rose-bush—or more likely, corn-plant—that he is thinking about. The thought then should leave some trace of itself with the plant in the field. If it is a good thought, one about health and growth, it is good for the plant; if a bad thought, the reverse.

The Hopi emphasize the intensity-factor of thought. Thought to be most effective should be vivid in consciousness, definite, steady, sustained, charged with strongly-felt good intentions. They render the idea in English as "concentrating," "holding it in your heart," "putting your mind on it," "earnestly hoping." Thought power is the force behind ceremonies, prayer-sticks, ritual smoking, etc. The prayer-pipe is regarded as an aid to "concentrating" (so said my informant). Its name, na'twanpi, means "instrument of preparing."

Covert participation is mental collaboration from people who do not take part in the actual affair, be it a job of work, hunt, race, or ceremony, but direct their thought and good will toward the affair's success. Announcements often seek to enlist the support of such mental helpers as well as of overt participants, and contain exhortations to the people to aid with their active good will.[10] A similarity to our concepts of a sympathetic audience or

[10] See, e.g., Ernest Beaglehole, *Notes on Hopi Economic Life* (Yale University Publications in Anthropology, No. 15, 1937), especially the reference to the announcement of a rabbit hunt, and on p. 30, description of the activities in connection with the cleaning of Toreva Spring—announcing, various preparing activities, and finally, preparing the continuity of the good results already obtained and the continued flow of the spring.

the cheering section at a football game should not obscure the fact that it is primarily the power of directed thought, and not merely sympathy or encouragement, that is expected of covert participants. In fact these latter get in their deadliest work before, not during, the game! A corollary to the power of thought is the power of wrong thought for evil; hence one purpose of covert participation is to obtain the mass force of many good wishers to offset the harmful thought of ill wishers. Such attitudes greatly favor cooperation and community spirit. Not that the Hopi community is not full of rivalries and colliding inter-ests. Against the tendency to social disintegration in such a small, isolated group, the theory of "preparing" by the power of thought, logically leading to the great power of the com-bined, intensified and harmonized thought of the whole community, must help vastly toward the rather remarkable degree of cooperation that in spite of much private bickering the Hopi village displays in all the important cultural activities.

Hopi "preparing" activities again show a result of their linguistic thought background in an emphasis on persistence and constant insistent repetition. A sense of the cumulative value of innumerable small momenta is dulled by an objectified, spatialized view of time like ours, enhanced by a way of thinking close to the subjective awareness of duration, of the ceaseless "latering" of events. To us, for whom time is a motion on a space, unvarying repetition seems to scatter its force along a row of units of that space, and be wasted. To the Hopi, for whom time is not a motion but a "getting later" of everything that has ever been done, unvarying repetition is not wasted but accumulated. It is storing up an invisible change that holds over into later events.[11] As we have seen, it is as if the return of the day were felt as the return of the same person, a little older but with all the impresses of yesterday, not as "another day," i.e. like an entirely different person. This principle joined with that of thought-power and with traits of general Pueblo culture is expressed in the theory of the Hopi ceremonial dance for furthering rain and crops, as well as in its short, piston-like tread, repeated thousands of times, hour after hour.

SOME IMPRESSES OF LINGUISTIC HABIT IN WESTERN CIVILIZATION

It is harder to do justice in few words to the linguistically-conditioned features of our own culture than in the case of the Hopi, because of both vast scope and difficulty of objec-tivity—because of our deeply ingrained familiarity with the attitudes to be analyzed. I wish merely to sketch certain characteristics adjusted to our linguistic binomialism of form plus formless item or "substance," to our metaphoricalness, our imaginary space, and our objectified time. These, as we have seen, are linguistic.

[11] This notion of storing up power, which seems implied by much Hopi behavior, has an analogue in physics, acceleration. It might be said that the linguistic background of Hopi thought equips it to recognize naturally that force manifests not as motion or velocity, but as cumulation or acceleration. Our linguistic background tends to hinder in us this same recognition, for having legitimately conceived force to be that which produces change, we then think of change by our linguistic *metaphorical* analogue, motion, instead of by a pure motionless changingness concept, i.e. accumulation or acceleration. Hence it comes to our naive feeling as a shock to find from physical experiments that it is not possible to define force by motion, that motion and speed, as also "being at rest," are wholly relative, and that force can be measured only by acceleration.

From the form-plus-substance dichotomy the philosophical views most traditionally characteristic of the "Western world" have derived huge support. Here belong materialism, psycho-physical parallelism, physics—at least in its traditional Newtonian form—and dualistic views of the universe in general. Indeed here belongs almost everything that is "hard, practical common sense." Monistic, holistic, and relativistic views of reality appeal to philosophers and some scientists, but they are badly handicapped for appealing to the "common sense" of the Western average man. This is not because nature herself refutes them (if she did, philosophers could have discovered this much) but because they must be talked about in what amounts to a new language. "Common sense," as its name shows, and "practicality" as its name does not show, are largely matters of talking so that one is readily understood. It is sometimes stated that Newtonian space, time, and matter are sensed by everyone intuitively, whereupon relativity is cited as showing how mathematical analysis can prove intuition wrong. This, besides being unfair to intuition, is an attempt to answer offhand question (1) put at the outset of this paper, to answer which this research was under-taken. Presentation of the findings now nears its end, and I think the answer is clear. The offhand answer, laying the blame upon intuition for our slowness in discovering mysteries of the cosmos, such as relativity, is the wrong one The right answer is: Newtonian space, time, and matter are no intuitions. They are recepts from culture and language. That is where Newton got them.

Our objectified view of time is however favorable to historicity and to everything con-nected with the keeping of records, while the Hopi view is unfavorable thereto. The latter is too subtle, complex, and ever-developing, supplying no ready-made answer to the ques-tion of when "one" event ends and "another" begins. When it is implicit that everything that ever happened still is, but is in a necessarily different form from what memory or record reports, there is less incentive to study the past. As for the present, the incentive would be not to record it but to treat it as "preparing." But *our* objectified time puts before imagination something like a ribbon or scroll marked off into equal blank spaces, suggesting that each be filled with an entry. Writing has no doubt helped toward our linguistic treat-ment of time, even as the linguistic treatment has guided the uses of writing. Through this give-and-take between language and the whole culture we get, for instance:

1. Records, diaries, book-keeping, accounting, mathematics stimulated by accounting;
2. Interest in exact sequence, dating, calendars, chronology, clocks, time wages, time graphs, time as used in physics;
3. Annals, histories, the historical attitude, interest in the past, archaeology, attitudes of introjection towards past periods, e.g., classicism, romanticism.

Just as we conceive our objectified time as extending in the future like the way it ex-tends in the past, so we set down our estimates of the future in the same shape as our records of the past, producing programs, schedules, budgets. The formal equality of the space-like units by which we measure and conceive time leads us to consider the "formless item" or "substance" of time to be homogeneous and in ratio to the number of units. Hence our pro-rata allocation of value to time, lending itself to the building up of a commercial structure based on time-prorata values: time wages (time work constantly supersedes piece work), rent, credit, interest, depreciation charges, and insurance premiums. No doubt this vast system once built would continue to run under any sort of linguistic treatment of time; but that it should have been built at all, reaching the magnitude and particular form it has in the Western world, is a fact decidedly in consonance with the patterns of the SAE languages. Whether such a civilization as ours would be possible with widely different linguistic handling of time is a large question—in our civilization our linguistic patterns and the fitting of our behavior to the temporal order are what they are, and they are in accord. We are of course stimulated to use calendars, clocks, and watches, and to try to measure time ever more precisely; this aids science, and science in turn, following these well-worn cultural grooves, gives back to culture an ever-growing store of applications, habits, and values, with which culture again directs science. But what lies outside this spiral? Science is begin-ning to find that there is something in the cosmos that is not in accord with the concepts we have formed in mounting the spiral. It is trying to frame a *new language* by which to adjust itself to a wider universe.

It is clear how the emphasis on "saving time" which goes with all the above, and is very obvious objectification of time, leads to a high valuation of "speed," which shows itself a great deal in our behavior.

Still another behavioral effect is that the character of monotony and regularity possessed by our image of time as an evenly scaled limitless tape measure persuades us to behave as if that monotony were more true of events than it really is. That is, it helps to routinize us. We tend to select and favor whatever bears out this view, to "play up to" the routine aspects of existence. One phase of this is behavior evincing a false sense of security or an assumption that all will always go smoothly, and a lack in foreseeing and protecting our-selves against hazards. Our technique of harnessing energy does well in routine performance, and it is along routine lines that we chiefly strive to improve it—we are, for example, rela-tively uninterested in stopping the energy from causing accidents, fires, and explosions, which it is doing constantly and on a wide scale. Such indifference to the unexpectedness of life would be disastrous to a society as small, isolated, and precariously poised as the Hopi society is, or rather once was.

Thus our linguistically-determined thought world not only collaborates with our cul-tural idols and ideals, but engages even our unconscious personal reactions in its patterns and gives them certain typical characters. One such character, as we have seen, is *careless-ness*, as in reckless driving or throwing cigarette stubs into waste paper. Another of different sort is *gesturing* when we talk. Very many of the gestures made by English-speaking people at least, and probably by all SAE speakers, serve to illustrate by a movement in space, not a real spatial reference but one of the non-spatial references that our language handles by metaphors of imaginary space. That is, we are more apt to make a grasping gesture when we speak of grasping an elusive idea than when we speak of grasping a doorknob. The gesture seeks to make a metaphorical and hence somewhat unclear reference more clear. But if a language refers to non-spatials without implying a spatial analogy, the reference is not made any clearer by gesture. The Hopi gesture very little, perhaps not at all in the sense we understand as gesture.

It would seem as if kinesthesia, or the sensing of muscular movement, though arising prior to language, should be made more highly conscious by linguistic use of imaginary space and metaphorical images of motion. Kinesthesia is marked in two facets of European culture: art and sport. European sculpture, an art in which Europe excels, is strongly kinesthetic, conveying great sense of the body's motions; European painting likewise. The dance in our culture expresses delight in motion rather than symbolism or ceremonial, and our music is greatly influenced by our dance forms. Our sports are strongly imbued with this element of the "poetry of motion." Hopi races and games seem to emphasize rather the virtues of endurance and sustained intensity. Hopi dancing is highly symbolic and is performed with great intensity and earnestness, but has not much movement or swing.

Synesthesia, or suggestion by certain sense receptions of characters belonging to another sense, as of light and color by sounds and *vice versa*, should be made more conscious by a linguistic metaphorical system that refers to non-spatial experiences by terms for spatial ones, though undoubtedly it arises from a deeper source. Probably in the first instance metaphor arises from synesthesia and not the reverse, yet metaphor need not become firmly rooted in linguistic pattern, as Hopi shows. Non-spatial experience has one well-organized sense, *hearing*—for smell and taste are but little organized. Non-spatial consciousness is a realm chiefly of thought, feeling, and *sound*. Spatial consciousness is a realm of light, color, sight, and touch, and presents shapes and dimensions. Our metaphorical system, by naming non-spatial experiences after spatial ones, imputes to sounds, smells, tastes, emotions, and thoughts qualities like the colors, luminosities, shapes, angles, textures, and motions of spatial experience. And to some extent the reverse transference occurs; for after much talking about tones as high, low, sharp, dull, heavy, brilliant, slow, the talker finds it easy to think of some factors in spatial experience as like factors of tone. Thus we speak of "tones" of color, a gray "monotone," a "loud" necktie, a "taste" in dress: all spatial metaphor in reverse. Now European art is distinctive in the way it seeks deliberately to play with synesthesia. Music tries to suggest scenes, color, movement, geometric design; painting and sculpture are often consciously guided by the analogies of music's rhythm; colors are conjoined with feeling for the analogy to concords and discords. The European theatre and opera seek a synthesis of many arts. It may be that in this way our metaphorical language that is in some sense a confusion of thought is producing, through art, a result of far-reaching value—a deeper esthetic sense leading toward a more direct apprehension of underlying unity behind the phenomena so variously reported by our sense channels.

HISTORICAL IMPLICATIONS

How does such a network of language, culture, and behavior come about historically? Which was first, the language patterns or the cultural norms? In main they have grown up together, constantly influencing each other. But in this partnership the nature of the language is the factor that limits free plasticity and rigidifies channels of development in the more autocratic way. This is because a language is a system, not just an assemblage of norms. Large systemic outlines can change to something really new only very slowly, while many other cultural innovations are made with comparative quickness. Language thus represents the mass mind; it is affected by inventions and innovations, but affected little and slowly, whereas *to* inventors and innovators it legislates with the decree immediate.

The growth of the SAE language-culture complex dates from ancient times. Much of its metaphorical reference to the non-spatial by the spatial was already fixed in the ancient tongues, and more especially in Latin. It is indeed a marked trait of Latin. If we compare, say Hebrew, we find that while Hebrew has some allusion to not-space as space, Latin has more. Latin terms for non-spatials, like *educo, religio, principia, comprehendo,* are usually metaphorized physical references: lead out, tying back, etc. This is not true of all languages —it is quite untrue of Hopi. The fact that in Latin the direction of development happened to be from spatial to non-spatial (partly because of secondary stimulation to abstract thinking when the intellectually crude Romans encountered Greek culture) and that later tongues were strongly stimulated to mimic Latin, seems a likely reason for a belief which still lingers on among linguists that this is the natural direction of semantic change in all languages, and for the persistent notion in Western learned circles (in strong contrast to Eastern ones) that objective experience is prior to subjective. Philosophies make out a weighty case for the reverse, and certainly the direction of development is sometimes the reverse. Thus the Hopi word for "heart" can be shown to be a late formation within Hopi from a root meaning think or remember. Or consider what has happened to the word "radio" in such a sentence as "he bought a new radio," as compared to its prior meaning "science of wireless telephony."

In the middle ages the patterns already formed in Latin began to interweave with the increased mechanical invention, industry, trade, and scholastic and scientific thought. The need for measurement in industry and trade, the stores and bulks of "stuffs" in various containers, the type-bodies in which various goods were handled, standardizing of measure and weight units, invention of clocks and measurement of "time," keeping of records, accounts, chronicles, histories, growth of mathematics and the partnership of mathematics and science, all cooperated to bring our thought and language world into its present form.

In Hopi history, could we read it, we should find a different type of language and a different set of cultural and environmental influences working together. A peaceful agricultural society isolated by geographic features and nomad enemies in a land of scanty rainfall, arid agriculture that could be made successful only by the utmost perseverance (hence the value of persistence and repetition), necessity for collaboration (hence emphasis on the psychology of teamwork and on mental factors in general), corn and rain as primary criteria of value, need of extensive *preparations* and precautions to assure crops in the poor soil and precarious climate, keen realization of dependence upon nature favoring prayer and a religious attitude toward the forces of nature, especially prayer and religion directed toward the ever-needed blessing, rain—these things interacted with Hopi linguistic patterns to mold them, to be molded again by them, and so little by little to shape the Hopi world-out-look.

To sum up the matter, our first question asked in the beginning (p. 78) is answered thus: Concepts of "time" and "matter" are not given in substantially the same form by experi-ence to all men but depend upon the nature of the language or languages through the use of which they have been developed. They do not depend so much upon *any one system* (e.g., tense, or nouns) within the grammar as upon the ways of analyzing and reporting experi-ence which have become fixed in the language as integrated "fashions of speaking" and which cut across the typical grammatical classifications, so that such a "fashion" may include lexical, morphological, syntactic, and otherwise systemically diverse means coordinated in a certain frame of consistency. Our own "time" differs markedly from Hopi "duration." It is conceived as like a space of strictly limited dimensions, or sometimes as like a motion upon such a space, and employed as an intellectual tool accordingly. Hopi "duration" seems to be inconceivable in terms of space or motion, being the mode in which life differs from form, and consciousness *in toto* from the spatial elements of consciousness. Certain ideas born of our own time-concept, such as that of absolute simultaneity, would be either very difficult to express or impossible and devoid of meaning under the Hopi conception, and would be replaced by operational concepts. Our "matter" is the physical sub-type of "substance" or "stuff," which is conceived as the formless extensional item that must be joined with form before there can be real existence. In Hopi there seems to be nothing corresponding to it; there are no formless extensional items; existence may or may not have form, but what it also has, with or without form, is intensity and duration, these being non-extensional and at bottom the same.

But what about our concept of "space," which was also included in our first question? There is no such striking difference between Hopi and SAE about space as about time, and probably the apprehension of space is given in substantially the same form by experience irrespective of language. The experiments of the Gestalt psychologists with visual percep-tion appear to establish this as a fact. But the *concept of space* will vary somewhat with language, because as an intellectual tool[12] it is so closely linked with the concomitant em-ployment of other intellectual tools, of the order of "time" and "matter," which are lin-guistically conditioned. We see things with our eyes in the same space forms as the Hopi, but our idea of space has also the property of acting as a surrogate of non-spatial relation-ships like time, intensity, tendency, and as a void to be filled with imagined formless items, one of which may even be called "space." Space as sensed by the Hopi would not be con-

[12] Here belong "Newtonian" and "Euclidean" space, etc.

nected mentally with such surrogates, but would be comparatively "pure," unmixed with extraneous notions.

As for our second question (p. 78): There are connections but not correlations or diagnostic correspondences between cultural norms and linguistic patterns. Although it would be impossible to infer the existence of Crier Chiefs from the lack of tenses in Hopi, or vice versa, there is a relation between a language and the rest of the culture of the society which uses it. There are cases where the "fashions of speaking" are closely integrated with the whole general culture, whether or not this be universally true, and there are connections within this integration, between the kind of linguistic analyses employed and various behavioral reactions and also the shapes taken by various cultural developments. Thus the importance of Crier Chiefs does have a connection, not with tenselessness itself, but with a system of thought in which categories different from our tenses are natural. These connections are to be found not so much by focusing attention on the typical rubrics of linguistic, ethnographic, or sociological description as by examining the culture and the language (always and only when the two have been together historically for a considerable time) as a whole in which concatenations that run across these departmental lines may be expected to exist, and if they do exist, eventually to be discoverable by study.

WETHERSFIELD, CONNECTICUT

BEHAVIOR PATTERNS IN LINGUISTIC STRUCTURE: A CASE STUDY

By STANLEY S. NEWMAN

I

THOSE who have not been initiated into the somewhat esoteric concepts and methods of linguistics frequently express their incredulity at the picture of language presented by linguists. They find it very strange, for example, that a grammatical description can get along without any reference to the persons using the language, for obviously a grammar must be based upon the existence of speakers or writers of the language. As naive observers, they see language as it takes place in the context of human behavior, where it is merely one of the expressive and communicative activities of human beings in their everyday business of living.[1] But the linguist seems to regard language as a huge autonomic mechanism and the language-using person as a passive thing coerced by the relentless operations of phonemic patterns, morphological processes, syntactic configurations, conceptual categories, and all the other paraphernalia of linguistic systems.

This is not the place to enter into a discussion of the validity of linguistic descriptions. For the purposes of this paper it need only be pointed out that the linguist focuses his attention upon those selected aspects of language which, he believes, his methodological equipment gives him the authority to investigate. He does not attempt to study the totality of language phenomena. He is interested in tonal intensities and contours, for example, only insofar as they are structuralized within the formal and functional system of the language; tonal phenomena that do not belong to this system can occur in the language, but they may be omitted from a strictly linguistic description. Consequently, such a description cannot be given the status of a fully rounded picture of language. It is a highly selective and abstract part-picture, which omits a great deal of the language process as it takes place in the speech and writing of human beings.

If this omitted material, this language evidence that is peripheral to a strictly linguistic frame of reference, were merely an area of casual speculative interest, it could be easily dismissed as of no very serious concern. But there is no need for speculating about it. The material is available for sober study, and, as will be pointed out below, it occasionally forces itself upon the linguist's unwilling attention. A study of this peripheral language material

---

[1] Critical appraisals of linguistics are not confined to the sort of informal comments that every linguist has probably heard on many occasions from his friends and colleagues outside of linguistics. As examples of the more systematic criticisms made by a psychologist and by an anthropologist, see J. R. Kantor, *An Objective Psychology of Grammar* (Bloomington, Indiana, 1936) and Bronislaw Malinowski, *Coral Gardens and their Magic* (2 vols., London, 1935), Vol. 2: "The Language of Magic and Gardening."

offers the linguist an opportunity to broaden the scope of his science into a less schematic and more realistic approach to language phenomena, and to discover relations between linguistics and other sciences that could result in a mutual exchange of contributions and insights. The sharp separation which exists between linguistics and other disciplines is, at best, an arbitrary one, based upon the development of an isolated methodology and not upon any empirical division of subject matter.

In addition to its potential theoretical value, the peripheral data of language has a more immediate and practical relevance to linguistic work. Most linguists have undoubtedly had the disturbing experience of coming upon language patterns in their material, only to find them in conflict with the more consistent patterns of the linguistic system. The writer can illustrate from his own experience. After making a study of the tonal prosodemes of English, he had occasion to analyze phonograph recordings of the speech of a large number of English-speaking individuals. Though the purpose of the second project was not linguistic, the analysis brought out certain tonal phenomena which contradicted the previous formulation of English tonal prosodemes. For example, some of these individuals had the habit of using a long shallow rising pitch at the end of their sentences, regardless of whether the sentences were interrogations or declarative statements. Other individuals indulged in what can best be referred to as a prosodic "fade-out" toward the end of responses or sentences: here the utterance would gradually slow down in speed, the articulatory force would diminish to a whisper and disappear into inaudibility, and the tone would drop and likewise disappear with the loss of audibility.

Language phenomena such as this raise a serious dilemma for the linguist. If—to give the linguistic formulation—declarative statements in English are marked by a falling intonation located on the last heavy-stressed syllable of a sentence, how is he to square this with the slightly rising intonation which some English speakers inhabitually employ at the end of declarative statements? In the light of his schematic description of English prosodemes, how is he to explain the curious fade-out phenomena of quantity, stress, and tone?

To dispose of these prosodic fade-outs and rising intonations by labeling them as "idiosyncratic" features or perhaps as special "dialect" variations is merely a terminological device for evading the problem. These are language phenomena that undeniably intrude themselves upon the formal structure of English, and they are therefore within the province and responsibility of the linguist, even in his most restricted capacity as a student of formal linguistic structures.

It should be made clear that these phenomena are not suggested as a source for studying the way in which individuals affect the collective linguistic system. For attacking this crucial problem, we would need to know a great deal more than we do about the conditions under which language deviations are spread from individual to individual within the family and the community, until they attain the status of collective norms in the dialect and, finally, in the larger linguistic unit. We are able to document certain linguistic changes as they become distributed from one group to another, but we cannot trace the inception of these changes in the processes of individual selection which stimulate or inhibit the spread of new linguistic forms.

Nevertheless, there are other strictly linguistic problems which are raised by the phenomena of language deviations. On the descriptive level, the linguist will find that English speech containing prosodic fade-outs, for example, deviates from the structural norm in several respects: because of the fade-out toward the end of a sentence, the presumably normal sentence accent on the last heavy-stressed syllable will not be actualized, and the sentence intonation will be absent or at least obscured; stress will be lowered in end-stressed words and exaggerated in fore-stressed words; vowels will be progressively lengthened throughout the sentence. In short, position in the sentence will function as a major conditioning factor in affecting the presence of certain accents and intonations and in determining the distribution of stresses and quantities. On the historical level, too, there are linguistic problems involved in such phenomena. It is not unlikely that historical trends give rise to some sporadic deviations as well as to deviations which in time become stabilized and leave their impress upon the linguistic system. It may be that the prosodic fade-out is a somewhat eccentric reflex of the historic drift in English toward the development of fore-stressed words, words whose end-stress has faded out. Linguistic evidence bearing on this problem could be obtained by determining whether the prosodic fade-out also occurs as a sporadic deviation in modern French where, in contrast to English, the drift toward fore-stressing has not taken place and where a differentiated stress and accent system has not developed.

Too much importance, however, should not be placed upon the fact that the linguistic structure may manifest deviant forms, here and there, in the language patterns of individuals. When they break through the linguistic structure itself as conflicting phenomena, this is merely an especially dramatic manifestation of the presence of these language patterns which are ignored—even studiously ignored—in linguistic descriptions. But, if the linguist is to gain a fuller understanding of how language operates, he must be willing to examine such patterns when they reveal themselves in a less dramatic manner. They need not necessarily conflict with the linguistic system, as ordinarily conceived by the linguist. The native speaker may find plenty of elbow-room for his individual language patterns within the confines of the collective linguistic system and in conformity with it; his personal mode of expression is, at any rate, conditioned by the structural demands of the particular language which he is using. Because of the tonal demands set up by Chinese, the speaker of this language is more narrowly limited in using pitch for expressive purposes than the speaker of English, but perhaps, as part of the same conditioning process, Chinese permits a greater range of variation than English in other categories of phonetic expression. Though our ignorance of this process is nothing short of magnificent, the conditioning and possible limiting influence of language systems upon individual patterns of verbal expression is a problem of linguistic form. And put in these terms, the problem lies within the field of the linguist.

The internal consistencies, or patterns, that an individual reveals in his language are also within the field of the psychologist, for they are the verbal manifestations of an individual's total behavior and must be studied in the light of his non-verbal modes of functioning. Whether the individual speaks Chinese or English, he is bound to develop his own manner of expression through the network of channels provided by his language.

The student of human behavior would focus his attention upon the functional role of language in the behavior system of the individual. The student of linguistic structures, on the other hand, would be primarily interested in the formal characteristics through which an individual expresses this functioning in each language. But it should be of significance to both the psychologist and the linguist that their two hypothetical systems—the behavioral and the structural—overlap in the process that takes place when an individual uses language.

This paper is an attempt to explore the overlapping area of linguistics and individual psychology by a description of the language behavior of a specific person. Methods for this type of investigation are admittedly exploratory at present, but greater precision and clarity in the use of appropriate methods can be developed only through further inductive study and critical treatment of the manifold ways in which individuals use their language.

II

The subject of this investigation is Paul, an eighteen year old boy, whose speech was studied during his last year of high school.[2] It should be made clear at the outset that Paul was not selected because of any outstanding peculiarities in his language or behavior. There are no bizarre characteristics in his speech, nor does his behavior as a whole show any abnormal departures from the behavior of his age-mates. He is merely a member of a high school class which was one of the groups studied as a representative sample of individuals who might be expected to manifest the typical problems of adolescent adjustment. Paul's speech was chosen primarily because of methodological considerations: a special psychological investigation had been made of his case, and the results of this provided a means of checking the speech study.[3]

On the level of articulation, Paul's speech organs display a good deal of energetic motor movement. His consonantic closures are tightly formed, and the consonants are released

[2] The material presented in this paper was collected under the auspices of the Commission on Secondary School Curriculum, Progressive Education Association. The speech analysis is based upon two sources of data: observations conducted during several visits to Paul's classroom; and a more concentrated study of his speech from a dictaphone recording of a student-teacher conference.

[3] I am indebted to Dr Peter Blos, a fellow-investigator of the Commission on Secondary School Curriculum, who made a detailed psychological study of Paul, based on the evidence in his case history, his interviews with a psychologist in the school, his school records and teachers' reports, and the content of his written compositions. Though, as a matter of procedure, my interpretation of the psychological mechanisms revealed in Paul's speech was first formulated without consulting the fuller interpretation made by Dr Blos from his more extensive data, I have drawn freely from his material in the present paper.

with considerable vigor. In the articulatory habits of English-speaking individuals, a wide range of phonetic variation can be observed, and a better notion of the characteristics of Paul's speech will be gained if they are considered in relation to the practices of other speakers. Variations are particularly noticeable in the qualities of closure and release employed in the articulation of stop consonants. Some speakers of English, for example, pronounce their alveolar stops (d and t) with an incomplete closure and with a partially rubbed release, resulting in a phonetic complex that is very similar to a single-trilled alveolar r, voiced or voiceless. In its most extreme form this lax type of articulation can be heard in speech of fatigued individuals, and it has also been found in the speech of persons suffering from the depressive phase of the manic-depressive psychosis.[4] At the opposite extreme, a vigorously explosive articulation of stop consonants may also be heard in English speech. A manic patient observed by the writer pronounced his initial alveolar stops with such vehemence that in purely phonetic terms these sounds could be accurately described as glottalized consonants. But mentally disturbed patients are not the only people who manifest extreme varieties of lax or energetic articulation. Different degrees of articulative vigor are found in the normal population. As a matter of fact, a vigorously articulated style of speech is consciously sought by many individuals, for this is a characteristic of cultivated diction, approved generally as a cultural ideal and recommended by teachers of speech.

Individual elaborations in the realm of tonal phenomena include a number of variables. The tonal patterns of English define only the direction of pitch changes (e.g., rising, falling, falling-rising), though even these few directional patterns of tone, as was pointed out above, may be swamped out and replaced by the tonal practices of individual speakers. Within the limits of the tone patterns demanded by English, however, the speaker is left free to actualize his own range of pitch. The absolute difference between the highest and lowest register of a given tone pattern, and the relative difference in pitch range between one tone pattern and another are individual characteristics, not determined by the linguistically defined tones of English. An English-speaking person may therefore employ a wide or a narrow pitch range: the tonally colorful speech of the manic and the flat voice of the depressive are clear-cut examples of differences in the absolute range of pitch, for they represent extreme forms of the common pitch variations—though "musical" speech, like vigorously articulated speech, enjoys a favored status in our culture and is by no means rare outside of mental hospitals. As an accompanying characteristic, an individual may also show either variability or sameness of relative range in his use of tone patterns.

In addition to these factors of pitch range, there are other tonal characteristics that identify an individual's speech. His manner of changing registers may be either step-wise, with level tones separated by steep drops and rises, or gliding, with gradually sloping changes of pitch from one register to another. He may distribute these changes of pitch frequently or sparsely in his speech. And the contours of his pitch changes may be varied or stereotyped in character.

[4] Stanley Newman and Vera G. Mather, *Analysis of Spoken Language of Patients with Affective Disorders* American Journal of Psychiatry, Vol. 94, pp. 913–42, 1938), pp. 917–23, 941.

In terms of the tonal variables just discussed, Paul's speech can be described as having a wide pitch range, which recurs with a fairly unvaried high and low register for the different tonal patterns. Pitch changes appear frequently in his speech, and they have a distinctively gliding character. These pitch glides give Paul's speech a drawling quality, for he has the habit of beginning a pitch change with a relatively rapid glide followed by a flattened and drawn-out rise or fall. Because of the frequent recurrence of these characteristic pitch contours, his speech is marked by a stereotyped tonal expression.

English stress and accent place certain limitations upon the individual speaker's manner of employing volume or, to translate this acoustic reference into physiological terms, upon his use of articulatory force and pressure. These linguistic limitations, however, are very broad. The English stress system merely defines the relative weight of syllables, and the acoustic components of stress include the factors of pitch and quantity as well as volume.[5] The stress system does not determine the inherent volume of any given stress phoneme, nor the articulatory force of English speech. Individual voices differ considerably in their volume potentialities and in the degree of articulatory pressure used in actualizing the stress phonemes. Even within the speech of one person, the volume of a stress phoneme does not remain constant, for modulations of volume occur throughout discourse, within wide margins in some cases, within narrow margins in others. Individual styles of volume modulation and the impressive individual differences in volume energy have made the empirical study of stress—stress as it occurs in discourse, not in artificially isolated words—one of the mostly delicate and elusive tasks in linguistics.

Though they operate independently of the stress system, the types of emphatic accent in English also involve the components of volume, pitch, and quantity. The most common types are the contrastive and the rhetorical accents. In the contrastive type, an increment of volume is added to the stress of the word receiving the emphasis, and the sentence intonation is displaced to the emphasized word: e.g., if a contrastive accent is given to green in the green chalk was missing (that is, not the blue chalk), this word is spoken with a heightened volume, and it takes the intonation, in this case the falling tone, that would otherwise appear on the last word of the sentence. The rhetorical accent is characterized mainly by a protracted length in the vowel of the accented word and by a somewhat augmented volume: e.g., a rhetorical accent placed on loud in a loud noise was heard (that is, a very loud noise) would lengthen the word and add to its volume, but it would not displace the sentence intonation. This type of accent will be recognized as a conventional feature of children's language, and it can be encountered most frequently in the speech of adults addressing small children or reading to them.

The description of an individual's speech with regard to the variables of volume will cover such factors as the inherent volume potentialities of his voice in speech, the extent of volume modulations, recurrent patterns of modulation—if any occur, the frequency of emphatic accents, and the type of accent that is favored. It is also important to describe the

[5] Wilbur L. Schramm, The Acoustical Nature of Accent in American Speech (American Speech, Vol. 12, pp. 49–56, 1937).

way in which the use of volume is integrated with pitch and quantity, for in the dynamics of an individual's speech these three elements are often closely associated.

Paul's speech illustrates how an individual's habits of using quantity are manifested in his accentual and intonational practices, in which volume and pitch are the predominant features linguistically. Emphatic accents are distributed generously throughout his speech. But he shows a marked preference for the rhetorical type of accent, in spite of the fact that all of his speech collected for study was addressed to adults and fellow-students. Though the frequent rhetorical accents give his speech an unduly childlike character, their protracted quantity is consistent with his drawling pitch glides and with the slow tempo of his speech. In terms of the linguistic structure of English, the accents and the pitch intonations represent separate patterns, and speech tempo is generally regarded as not relevant to the structure of the language; but in terms of an individual's speech habits, the components of accent, intonation, and tempo tend to be integrated into a more or less consistent style.

The volume of Paul's speech is potentially very loud. When several students are talking at the same time during an excited discussion, Paul can be easily heard above the others. But he modulates his voice over a wide volume range, from extreme loudness to a somewhat breathy softness that is scarcely audible, and these changes of volume take place gradually, rather than suddenly, in his responses.

The individual is permitted even more latitude in quantity and tempo than in volume. In addition to the special quantitative feature of the rhetorical accent, referred to above, quantity phenomena in English are conditioned by phonemic and pausal factors. The relative lengths of consonants and vowels, particularly the latter, are determined by the inherent character of the phoneme (e.g., i is longer than ι) and by the position of the phoneme (e.g., i is longer in *sid*, "seed," than in *sit*, "seat"); pauses or retardations of speed function as phrase markers, associated with some of the intonational prosodemes of English. But, as in the case of volume, there are wide individual differences in the use of quantity and tempo. Some people speak rapidly and others slowly: i will be longer in one person's speech than in another's. Some speakers talk at a fairly even tempo, with only slight variations in speed, and others change their speed over a broad quantitative range. As with volume, too, modulations of speed cut across the linguistically defined quantities: the i's will become progressively shorter as a speaker accelerates the speed of his discourse, and they will be maximally long at his points of slowest speed.

Pausal phenomena are so highly variable in English that they are generally ignored in linguistic descriptions. Pauses occur most commonly in conjunction with the sentence intonations—the rising interrogative tone and the falling declarative tone—and with the "comma dip"—the falling-rising tone which separates a subordinate from a superordinate predication and appears with other types of sub-sentence units. But many people speak in a continuous stream, with only slight retardations of speed taking the place of pausal divisions. Others break up their discourse into short word-groups, with intervening pauses. The nature of these word-groups is of particular significance. In the speech of some individuals the pauses are prosodic: sentences are divided into prosodic word-groups, each of which constitutes a syntactic unit. But, in contrast to this deliberative pause style, some speakers use pauses as points of hesitation: sentences are broken into word-group segments without any regard for syntactic relations. Prosodic pauses occur, for example, between the subject and predicate of a sentence. Pauses of hesitation, on the other hand, may be injected between an article and its noun.

Paul's stream of speech is very uneven in its tempo. It is interrupted by frequent pauses of hesitation, often with a vocalized "er-er," and he has a habit of breaking off a sentence before he has completed it and continuing his response in another direction. Long quantities predominate in his speech. He talks at a slow pace, and he tends to drawl his vowel sounds. Modulations of speed are infrequent. Sudden accelerations, with brief passages of rapid articulation, are occasionally introduced into the slow movement of his speech.

Even in the phonetic features of speech, then, which are regarded as maximally defined by impersonal linguistic regulations, there is considerable room for the play of individual expression. There is still more room for individual selection to manifest itself in a speaker's use of vocabulary and syntax, and in his characteristic habits of verbal response.

An examination of Paul's speech reveals a mixture of two vocabulary levels. As compared with the speech of his fellow-students, he makes use of a rather extreme and violent type of slang: he addresses the instructor with the attention-calling "Say!" and he uses "See?" to finish off some of his remarks to the instructor. On the other hand, he employs terms that belong to a cultivated level of style: he is fond, for example, of using the polite intensive, "quite," but its stylistic connotation does not prevent him from placing it in a slang context, such as, "Say! You know you pulled quite a boner yesterday . . . ," when speaking to the instructor. Evidently Paul can respond to the stylistic effect of individual words and phrases, but he is unable to blend the two vocabulary levels—the cultivated and the slang—into an integrated style of speech.

Paul uses numerous intensive terms, such as "really," "quite," "completely," "particularly," which are usually accompanied by an emphatic accent. These terms and certain tag phrases, such as "I mean," recur at short intervals in his speech; and during a class discussion he sometimes repeats remarks that he has made previously.

Repetition and stereotypy is also characteristic of Paul's use of syntax. A large proportion of his sentences begin with such qualifying predications as "I think that . . . ," "I mean I think that . . . ," "You know that . . . ," "Did you realize that . . . ?" "I was going to say that. . . ." His responses are primarily composed of a sequence of independent predications, with little syntactic elaboration. Except for constructions containing "that," subordinate predications are rare in his speech.

Coherence is very loosely observed in Paul's responses. Syntactic progression and continuity is frequently broken, not only by pauses of hesitation, but also by overlapping predications, in which one predication is begun before the previous one is completed. In a series of completed statements the syntactic relationship between one predication and another is seldom made explicit, and the content shows even less continuity than his syntactic habits might suggest. When he does attempt to use the techniques of logical organization, he is unable to carry them through consistently as a means of organizing the content of his speech. One of his responses in a recorded group conference, for example, begins with "First of all . . . ," which would lead the listener to expect an enumerative sequence; but the first point that he wishes to make is not clearly discernible, and he fails to reach any second point. In this response, as in most of his longer responses, Paul develops his topics with a good deal of circularity: when he is mid-way in a response, he is apt to continue by returning to his initial statements, repeating one and rephrasing another.

In spite of his confused development of topics, Paul is able to begin a response with spontaneity and clarity. He initiates his responses rapidly, without the fumbling for words that characterizes his subsequent remarks, and there is a close and sometimes an explicitly stated relationship in content between his opening predication and the previous discussion of other speakers. It is only as he continues with his response that the threads of his discourse become tangled.

III

The presentation up to this point has been one of analyzing and defining the elements of Paul's speech in terms of linguistic variables. In order to use these speech clues as psychological evidence, it will be necessary to bring together the arbitrarily separated elements and to examine them as a patterned system of behavior.

Two methodological criteria can be employed in assessing the reliability of psychological interpretations based on behavioral data: one of these is the weight of evidence in favor of a given conclusion; the other is the consistency with which a conclusion fits into the total picture of an individual's behavior. When the material is limited to a segment of behavior, such as speech, the second criterion of consistency, or congruence, must be applied with caution, for the complex dynamics of behavior are often obscured by the incompleteness and skewness of the restricted data. Consequently, the internal evidence of speech, in spite of its richness, gives results of varying degrees of reliability. Because of the weight of evidence, certain conclusions can be made with justification; for example, indications of energetic motor movement, of blocking and hesitation are sufficiently numerous in Paul's speech to be accepted as clear and unambiguous evidence of these characteristics in his behavior. Other conclusions, such as those based on the apparent childish manifestations in his treatment of emphatic accents, are supported by so little speech evidence that they must be made tentatively, to be later verified or rejected in the light of external evidence. Furthermore, an individual's speech is apt to contain elements that seem to be mutually contradictory, for, like any other portion of his behavior, it reflects the compensatory trends, conflicts, and ambivalences that are recognized attributes of human adjustment. Frequently these seeming contradictions cannot be resolved into an underlying consistency from the internal speech evidence alone. Thus, external case material is needed to explain Paul's ability to control his volume by gradual modulations, for this characteristic seems to be inconsistent with his wide range and frequent changes of pitch and with other character-istics indicating an energetic but unevenly controlled flow of speech.

Like other types of behavior involving overt muscular activity, speech provides evi-dence that has direct psychosomatic bearing. Paul's vigorous manner of articulation, his wide range of pitch, his frequent use of long pitch glides, his potentially loud voice, his tendency to employ numerous emphatic accents and intensives reveal a highly energetic pattern of motor movement. In Paul's case, however, this movement does not result in a smooth and relaxed flow of speech. There are many evidences of blocking and constraint, such as pauses of hesitation, jerky tempo (slow speech with sudden accelerations), broken sentences, and overlapping predications. The presence of blocking, in conjunction with his vigorous motor energy, indicates the hyperactive quality of Paul's behavior and the jerky character of its expression.

An examination of Paul's health history shows that there are specifically somatic factors involved in his behavioral habits. Because of difficulties in nourishment and the resulting physiological deprivations, Paul's infancy and early childhood were marked by passivity and a low fund of energy. But after the age of four his passive adjustment was replaced by a new pattern of behavior; Paul began to show signs of over-activity, impetuousness, and hypersensitivity to nervous stimuli. Two insidious attacks of these symptoms led to a diagnosis of chorea. This condition diminished in intensity during Paul's middle childhood, but it reappeared when he reached the age of fourteen, three or four years before the present study of his speech was made. Throughout his high school records there are many references to his boisterousness and hyperactivity. The physical education teacher and the school physician also point out the jerkiness of Paul's movements and his lack of coordination in muscular activities.

The emotional concomitants of Paul's hyperactivity and blocking can be more readily discerned in relation to other features of his speech, though these motor symptoms them-selves are manifestations of affective tendencies. Dispersion as well as blocking of affect is shown by the uncertain hesitations, the confused syntax, and the circularity and incon-clusiveness with which Paul develops the content of his discussions. The strong affective pressure of his speech is not only uneven and broken in its flow, it is also diffuse and uncer-tain in its direction. As a means of counteracting this uncertainty, Paul uses the common compensatory device of repetitious activity: stereotyped tonal patterns, stereotyped syn-tactic patterns, repetition of words, phrases, and remarks exemplify a behavioral technique by means of which Paul attempts to achieve a measure of regularity and certainty in the face of emotional forces that threaten to get out of hand.

Another method of compensation is represented by the cultivated vocabulary that Paul superimposes on his speech. This is essentially an attempt to acquire certain conventional standards of propriety, but in Paul's speech the cultivated terms and phrases stand out in sharp contrast to the dominant tone of aggressive and even violent slang. In his writing, where he is able to exercise more deliberation and conscious control of his verbal expression, the compensatory tendencies are much more in evidence: his written vocabulary is cultivated and formal to the point of stiffness; his phrasing and syntax are repetitious; he is extremely meticulous about the mechanics of punctuation, spelling, and sentence structure; and, in direct contrast to his speech, he organizes the content of his compositions with painstaking care. Paul's use of language illustrates how widely different are the roles that speech and writing may play in the psychic economy of an individual. In writing, his language functions primarily as a de-emotionalized and guarded form of verbal expression. But in his speech, where verbalization takes place more spontaneously in face-to-face contact with other persons, he cannot so easily escape from the diffuse emotionality of his behavior.

The school records provide additional evidence concerning Paul's behavior. It is significant that his voice and speech receive a considerable amount of comment in both the elementary and the secondary school. From the third grade onward frequent mention is made of his "loud" and "raucous" voice, and it is even suggested by some of his teachers that he be given speech training to help him control his offensively strong volume. There can be no doubt that Paul himself was made aware of these continuous complaints from his teachers, and his response to adult criticism concerning his loud voice is characteristic of his reaction to authoritarian standards in general. As his present speech habits show, he has succeeded in curbing and modulating his volume to such a degree that this feature of his speech is out of line with the many characteristics indicating a vigorous and unevenly controlled use of his voice. In other areas of behavior as well, Paul shows himself to be a boy who has an ardent desire to please adults and to receive their approval; he tries to fulfill their expectations by meeting their demands and by measuring up to the more general standards of propriety which represent adult authority.

His teachers also complain that Paul talks too much, that he often disturbs class procedure by vehement arguments, in which he generally takes the opposition. He is inclined to make cutting remarks and to give the impression of being an intensely aggressive talker, but he is surprised and deeply contrite when he gives offense. The school records make no specific reference to the slanginess of his vocabulary, and it is impossible to determine how much this habit, if indeed it is an old habit with Paul, contributed to the teachers' impression of contentious aggressiveness in Paul's speech. But the impression itself suggests that, behind Paul's present slanginess, there is a long-standing tendency toward aggressive speech. The school records mention repeatedly that Paul's verbal aggression is not directed toward any particular person or situation. It is a diffuse and impulsive aggression, which the teachers find especially difficult to understand and to deal with, because, as they state again and again, Paul is an obviously cheerful and good-natured boy who is always eager to please.

Two opposing trends can be formulated from the direct speech material and from the information about Paul's speech contained in the school records. There are, on the one hand, many indications of vigorous motor tendencies and strong emotional pressures, which are apt to become aggressive and uncontrollable. Repetitive behavior and submission to authority standards, on the other hand, are evidence of Paul's attempt to control his dangerously impulsive emotionality. As a result of these highly charged and conflicting trends, uncertainty and confusion become pervasive features of Paul's behavior.

The same trends are manifested in Paul's social relationships and in his academic work. On the social level Paul is a friendly boy who seeks the companionship of his classmates. They, in turn, like and respect him. Yet, he has no personal friends. If he makes a potentially fruitful contact with another student, he invariably retreats from the personal implications of the relationship by keeping the conversation to discussions and arguments about abstract intellectual topics, such as the relative merits of Greek and Latin. In these attempts to demonstrate his adequacy, he is of course unsuccessful with his fellow-students, and their unresponsiveness to his friendly approaches merely adds to his perplexity and confusion. As part of his social habits, Paul shows a tendency in his manner of dress that corresponds to the stereotypy in his speech. Though he is meticulously neat about his clothes, he wears the same green sweater, the same brown oxfords, the same trousers during an entire year of school. In this he differs conspicuously from most of his peers. Other boys of his age and class level are inclined to give a good deal of attention to personal grooming, and in Paul's school this interest among the older boys takes the form of a studied carelessness in working out new, but not too conspicuous, combinations of clothes.

Paul is an excellent student in his school work. His academic interests lie in such subjects as mathematics, the physical sciences, and foreign languages. He shows ability and even talent in fields that demand methodical and systematic work with abstract analysis. His teachers comment on his keen delight in words and in their formal operations, but this interest in grammatical forms and processes is coupled with a curious insensitivity to the overtones of words in context. In English composition he receives lower grades than in any other subject; he is precise in the use of isolated forms, but he is unable to combine words effectively. In spite of his obvious intellectual attainments, Paul frequently surprises his teachers by the gross irrelevancy and stupidity of his remarks in class, and he himself is troubled by his uncontrollable tendency to say "silly things," as he expresses it.

Paul's academic activities and his social activities, like his speech and writing, are mutually related aspects of his behavior, and the nature of their relationship is indicated by the changes they have undergone throughout his high school career. As his difficulties on the social level increase, he becomes more and more absorbed in academic work. But in his last year of high school, as he begins to form more intimate friendships with some of his classmates, there is considerably less strain toward academic achievement. This shift in the distribution of his energies and gratifications would suggest that his intellectual interests play a compensatory role in relation to his social adjustments.

The basic difficulty underlying Paul's contradictory behavior can be traced to a conflict over maturation. Like any other normal adolescent, Paul wishes to push ahead with his growth toward maturity and to assert himself against interference and authority. On the other hand, he retreats from the responsibilities and dangers implied in maturation; in particular, he clings to a strong emotional dependence upon his parents, upon his father as well as his mother, and he is consequently unable to strike out for himself in exploring personal relationships with boys and girls and with adults outside the home. An ambivalent attitude toward maturation is present in some form, with varying degrees of mildness or severity, in every growing adolescent. In Paul's case, his strong parental attachment makes this conflict a powerful source of anxiety and gives it a central position in his adjustment.[6]

IV

It has been the purpose of this paper to demonstrate, through the concrete data of a case study, that speech phenomena represent a pooling of individual behavior patterns and collective linguistic patterns. Paul's speech shows psychological characteristics that are manifested in other areas of behavior as well, characteristics such as his vigorous motor and affective tendencies, his impulsive aggressiveness, his repression of emotionality through such compensatory outlets as repetitive activity and compliance with adult-imposed standards, and his blocking and confusion. But his speech, for all its uniqueness, is also structuralized in the forms provided by the particular linguistic system that he uses. The stop consonants of English, for example, must necessarily be contained in his speech, though these phonemes are pronounced by him in an energetically and vigorously articulated manner. In the same way, Paul's behavior influences the manner in which he selects and actualizes any of the other structural forms of English. These forms are firm and distinct enough to carry the burden of culturally-given linguistic patterns, but they are at the same time flexible enough to permit the expression of strictly individual patterns of behavior.

NEW YORK CITY

[6] The psychological evidence leading to this conclusion cannot be taken up in this paper. A detailed analysis of Paul's case is presented in Peter Blos, *The Adolescent Personality; a Study of Individual Behavior* (New York, 1941), pp. 113–219; see reference footnote 3, above.

THE DEVELOPMENT OF CULTURE PATTERNS

"Systems of ideas grow up in endless ways, both within a so-called uniform culture and through the blending of various aspects of so-called distinct cultures, and very different symbolisms and value emphases necessarily arise in the endless sub-cultures or private symbol organizations of the different members of a group."
Cultural Anthropology and Psychiatry

PATTERNING AS EXEMPLIFIED IN NAVAHO CULTURE

By CLYDE KLUCKHOHN

ALL CULTURAL BEHAVIOR is patterned. This is merely a way of saying that many things which an individual does and thinks and feels may be looked upon not merely from the standpoint of the forms of behavior that are proper to himself as a biological organism but from the standpoint of a generalized mode of conduct that is imputed to society rather than to the individual . . . ."[1] "Pattern" is a very popular word with contemporary American anthropologists. Unfortunately it has come to be used with considerable looseness of reference. In particular, confusion has resulted from the circumstance that "pattern" has been used to designate both (a) specific modalities of ideals and behavior, and (b) generalized configurations which structure widely varying contexts of culture content. Professor Sapir hinted on more than one occasion[1a] that "pattern" and "configuration" were concepts of a different order of abstraction, and put forward other terminological suggestions toward the more precise description of various types of patterning. The purpose of this essay is to follow out and elaborate systematically the leads given by Sapir. In view of the present confusion let us begin *de novo* with two examples.[2]

INTRODUCTORY

In my field notes are the reports of one or more interviews with 46 different Navaho informants on the subject of witchcraft. In all save 3 cases it is recorded that before the informant for the first time actually gave me some anecdote or bit of the cultural theory on witchcraft he or she remarked "I don't know—I just heard about it." The fact that 43 out of 46 informants uttered the same form of words (translated in precisely the same way —except for pronouns—by 8 different interpreters) makes it clear that we are here dealing with what Professor Sapir has called a "generalized mode of conduct" (in this case linguistic conduct, of course). So striking is the trend to uniformity that we are likely to label the response a "verbal reaction *pattern*." The content of the statement is (approximately) a disavowal of participation in witchcraft and even of direct observation of it. Clearly this content could have been expressed by a variety of linguistic symbols, arranged in a variety of ways. The remarkable fact is that only one of the wide range of potentialities is actualized. The content which the informant communicates is *patterned* in its expression.

[1] Sapir, *Unconscious Patterning of Behavior*, pp. 118–19.

[1a] Sapir, *Emergence of the Concept of Personality*, p. 411; *Personality* (p. 85), " . . . embodies countless cultural patterns in a unique configuration."

[2] This paper has had the benefit of helpful criticisms from G. Herzog, R. Linton, L. Spier, and L. C. Wyman. The contributions of Florence Kluckhohn to this essay are so extensive that she really ought, in all justice, to be listed as co-author.

Walter Dyk's *Son of Old Man Hat* has for me an overpowering imaginative reality. For me it utterly lacks that necrotic aroma which I find pervasive in the disembodied accounts of most ethnological publications (including my own!). When I read *Son of Old Man Hat* it is as if I were actually hearing living Navahos talk. Now let me leave this slightly romantic exultation in the material to ask coldbloodedly the question: what are the concrete stimuli which provoke in me this extraordinary sense of authenticity? Undoubtedly *one* source is the circumstance that Dyk's interpreter used exactly the same clichés in translating Navaho into English as have numerous interpreters of mine. For example, when the sense is that a person ought to avoid persons, animals, or objects, the preferred English verb is "bother." "Don't bother your wife " (Usually with the meaning: don't have sexual intercourse with your wife). Similarly: "Young boys shouldn't bother the girls." When a helper in a chant was being sent out to gather materials used in the bath a part of the instructions given him was translated, "Then bring it right back to me—don't bother horses, sheep, or herders on the way."[3] Now "avoid" is admittedly far too literary a word to expect as a translation of the Navaho verb in question, but "keep away from," "don't go near," "stay away from," and other words and circumlocutions would be distinctly congruent with the vocabulary of these interpreters. Indeed those I have mentioned are also heard but, in my experience, they are most significantly rarer than "bother." Since the interpreters come from widely separated areas of the Navaho country, went to different schools or learned their English from different whites for whom they worked, the tendency to prefer the term "bother" cannot be set down simply to emulation of a European model. It is evident that here again we have to do with a *patterning* of linguistic expression.

Indeed I was astonished to discover that—with very occasional and trivial substitutions—I could parallel whole groups of sentences as recorded by Dyk with sentences dealing with the same topic as translated by my interpreters.[4] All linguistic material appears to be rich in illustrations of patterning. Conceptions of patterning used in anthropology seem to have been much influenced by linguistics.

LINGUISTIC CONCEPTS IN ANTHROPOLOGY

In a period when even some natural scientists considered the systematic study of humanity as fruitless because of the complexities involved or actually denounced it as contravening the conception of God-given free will, the success of comparative philology, perhaps more than any other single fact, encouraged students of man to seek for regularities in human behavior. As Bloomfield[5] says:

These correspondences [Grimm's law] are a matter of historical detail, but their significance was

---

[3] Cf. Kluckhohn and Wyman, *Introduction*, p. 90.

[4] Some such striking correspondences are pointed out and documented in a paper of mine entitled "The Life Story of a Navaho Indian" which is to be published in 1941 in a volume edited by L. J. Henderson.

[5] Bloomfield, *Language*, p. 14.

overwhelming, since they showed that human action, in the mass, is not altogether haphazard, but may proceed with regularity even in so unimportant a matter as the manner of pronouncing the individual sounds within the flow of speech.

Even today, though the dialect geographers in Germany and the United States have challenged the *Ausnahmslösigkeitsprinzip* of Brugmann and the rest, the uniformities of phonetic change remain, I think, one of the most striking of human phenomena, the astonishing nature of which we now tend to overlook because the facts are so familiar and accepted.

Equally exciting, if one can look at them with at all fresh eyes, are the implications of phonemes, the principle of phonemic configuration, and Zipf's[6] establishment of the "k constant." These discoveries further demonstrate that at least linguistic human behavior is structured to the point where prediction (minimally, in a statistical sense) is possible. Thus, in Navaho, so soon as a single voiceless lenis stop was identified the betting odds became enormous that other sounds in the stop series would turn out to conform to this pattern. Navaho speech organs are physically capable of producing sounds of "b" type as voiceless lenis consonants, sounds of "d" type as voiceless fortis, sounds of "g" type as sonants, etc. But such random actualization of the physical possibilities is just simply not characteristic of actual phonetic systems.

Professor Sapir[7] very early drew explicit attention to the applicability of "prediction in terms of pattern" to nonlinguistic aspects of culture:

. . . The value to social sciences of such comparative study of languages . . . is that it emphasizes the extraordinary persistence in certain cases of complex patterns. It is in virtue of pattern conservatism that it is often possible to foretell the exact form of a specific cultural phenomenon.

Undoubtedly it is awareness of "pattern" (often subliminal) which sometimes enables the field worker to "know" how his natives will react to a set of circumstances before he observes the reaction. Familiarity with the Navaho "pattern" of generalized economic reciprocity between clansmen justifies my anticipation that, if a Navaho journeys into a portion of the Navaho Reservation which he has not visited before and where he has no acquaintances, he will seek out a hogan belonging to someone in his (or occasionally his father's) clan and there obtain lodging and food. Observation shows that this is factually the course of action followed in 13 cases out of 15. In one case, however, a man elected to camp alone; in another he looked for a family of whom a friend had told him. Statistically, the prediction was validated. The student of Navaho ceremonialism similarly can attend a chant which he has never before witnessed and have a relatively concrete idea of what is coming next at any given point.[8]

A number of Sapir's articles, but particularly his *Unconscious Patterning of Behavior in Society* and *The Concept of Phonetic Law*, indicated how the concept of "pattern" might be transferred from linguistics to anthropology. An example where the data are primarily verbal but where the reference goes beyond the narrowly linguistic will bring out par-

---

[6] Zipf, *Psychobiology of Language.*   [7] Sapir, *Concept of Phonetic Law*, p. 306.

[8] Cf. Kluckhohn and Wyman, *Introduction*, p. 105.

ticularly clearly what is involved. The Navaho have been shown to possess unequivocally the sensory capacity for distinguishing between "blue" and "green." It is also true that when the occasion arises they will distinguish (by compound phrases) between the two. However, the basic fact remains that in general they refer to colors which we would designate as "blue" and "green" by a single Navaho word. This seems to me strictly analo-gous with a linguistic example of Sapir's:[9] " . . . the naive Frenchman confounds the two sounds 's' of 'sick' and 'th' of 'thick' in a single pattern point—not because he is really unable to hear the difference, but because the setting up of such a difference disturbs his feeling for the necessary configuration of linguistic sounds." Just as the Frenchman fails normally to distinguish what are to us two sounds (though he can do so), so the Navaho normally fails to distinguish what are to us two colors (although once again he can do so).

THE NUCLEAR CONCEPTION OF PATTERN

What is the conceptual core of the category of patterning? The key is the characteristic which Sapir[10] has predicated of speech and culture in general: "inhibition of the random-ness of instinctive behavior." So far as organic potentialities are concerned a given act can be carried out, an idea stated, or a specific artifact made in a number of different ways. But in all societies the same mode of disposing of many situations is repeated over and over. There is, precisely, "inhibition of the randomness of instinctive behavior." A determinate organization prevails.

Structure, therefore, is the foremost constituent in the nuclear idea of pattern. The reference is predominantly to form, not content. But a cultural pattern is not merely a structure—it is a structure to which there is some degree of conformance on the part of a number of persons. "Pattern" preserves what is probably historically its dominant meaning "something to be copied." Pattern, then, in its most general meaning is *a structural regularity*. Such conceptions are necessarily conscious constructs, abstractions.

While the conceptual nucleus of "pattern" is clear enough, the serviceability of the term is impaired at present by usage in a variety of disparate ways, by being made, in general, to cover too wide a range of phenomena. Sapir[11] has well described the situation:

> There are certain terms that have a peculiar property. Ostensibly, they mark off specific con-cepts, concepts that lay claim to a rigorously objective validity. In practice, they label vague terrains of thought that shift or widen with the point of view of whoso makes use of them, embracing within their gamut of significances conceptions that not only do not harmonize but are in part contradictory.

To escape the imprecisions and contradictions inherent in describing the phenomena unsys-tematically we need a whole hierarchy of concepts. It is convenient, however, to have one word which will designate in inclusive fashion the existence of structuralization (to which there is some degree of conformance in word, or deed, or both) in a range of data. It is

---

[9] Sapir, *Unconscious Patterning of Behavior*, p. 136.
[10] Sapir, *Language*, p. 47, fn. 2. We need not quarrel here over Sapir's use of the word "instinctive," for his meaning for our purposes is clear enough.   [11] Sapir, *Culture, Genuine and Spurious*, pp. 401–402.

suggested that *patterning* is an appropriate designation for this broadest category. We might, for instance, have occasion to speak of "the patterning which exists in Navaho ceremonialism." This is, to be sure, a somewhat loose usage. No distinction is made between the patterning observed in the overt culture and that which is inferred in the covert culture; the ideal and the behavioral is merged; levels of abstraction are not differentiated. But there are context in which these finer discriminations are unnecessary. It may, for example, be only pertinent to point out that the Navaho chant system is not quite so stupendously complex as the very large number of named chants would imply. In this connection it is quite sufficient to draw attention to the omnipresence of *patterning* in the system.[12]

But if this broad basic concept is to be usable with a minimum of confusion and with something approaching precision, its territory must for some purposes be divided up among a number of related auxiliary concepts, the terrain of each of which is roughly staked out with reference to general level of abstraction and other differentiae. To accomplish that end without creating further confusion we must first specify certain delimitations of our interest. The behavior of one individual is often demonstrably distinguished from that of another individual (even one who occupies approximately the same ascribed and achieved statuses) in the same society by "patterns" which are characteristic of him as a personality. It might be well, as Sapir[13] has hinted, to reserve the term "personal habit system" for this class of patterning, but in any case we shall deal only with what Hallowell[14] has called "cultural variables" (as opposed to "individual variables"). Hence we shall also not consider the effects of cultural patterning upon the "psychology" of the individual, a question which Goldenweiser[15] has briefly discussed. We shall likewise disregard the part which patterning plays in cultural dynamics and the historical and psychological origin of "patterns." In short, we limit ourselves to the task of providing definitions and classifications suitable to describing phenomena of patterning *statically*.

American anthropologists with their strongly factual predilections have tended toward inadequate conceptualization of their data. A phase of this is a somewhat exaggerated suspicion of any proposed expansion of the technical terminology and a comparative indifference to the rigorous use of terminology already established (consider "shamanism," for example). While clearly terminology should not be proliferated beyond the point where it would be usable within the degree of specialization to which a science has attained at a given time, I agree heartily with Linton[16] when he writes: "Definitions and classifications are among the most valuable tools of the research worker, and anthropology is still sadly lacking in both." It would be in accord with general anthropological usage to say that planting a field in the form of a helix is an old Navaho "pattern" and equally so to describe the broad stylizations conforming to the principles of "imitative and contagious magic" which pervade Navaho ceremonialism. Now the first of these "patterns" is quite concrete, the second rep-

[12] Cf. Kluckhohn and Wyman, *Introduction*, p. 13.

[13] Sapir, *Contribution of Psychiatry*, p. 865.   [14] Hallowell, *Fear and Anxiety*.

[15] Goldenweiser, *Loose Ends of Theory*.   [16] Linton, *Study of Man*, p. 400.

resents a very high degree of abstraction. It is a truism of general scientific methodology that a term which is to be used in a rather precise and technical sense must not cover too much ground. If a term be applied with widely varying degrees of abstraction, communication will be faulty. Specifically, the fallacy of misplaced concreteness[17] will threaten the structure of such reasoning.

From the point of view of level of abstraction the most basic distinction in phenomena of patterning is between specific modalities of ideals and behavior (such as the helical design of planted fields) and generalized configurations which structure widely varying contexts of culture content (such as the principles of "imitative and contagious magic"). These are conceptually such different orders of phenomena that if we were to insist on designating both as "patterns" we ought to follow Korzybski[18] and speak of Pattern$_1$ and Pattern$_2$ respectively. Pattern$_1$ is a determinate relationship of various highly concrete pattern-parts. It is inevitably tied to a particular culture content. It is a regularity (a mode) in the structuring of that content in that culture and as such is a portion of the *overt* culture (to borrow a useful conception from Linton). Pattern$_2$ is not tied to only one bit of culture content. It approaches the polarity "concept of pure structure." Of phenomena of Pattern$_2$ there is minimal *articulate* awareness on the part of the culture carriers. These are the "patterns" of the *covert* culture and, to avoid confusion, we shall call them *configurations*. Patterns are specifically oriented; *configurations* have a more generalized orientation. A *configuration* is reducible to a "principle" which is, so to speak, "behind" the structural regularities of the overt culture, which "accounts for" two or more specific patterns.

PATTERNING OF OVERT CULTURE: PATTERNS

It is suggested, then, that the technical term *pattern* be rigorously restricted to phenomena of patterning of the *overt* culture. This conforms to the usage which is older and more firmly established in anthropology where the reference has more frequently been to rather concrete and specific modalities of stylization. We can further delimit the concept *pattern* in an oblique way: by contrasting it with other technical terms used in anthropology. The imminent anthropological critic would, at this point in our discussion, be perfectly justified in objecting: "You say that 'pattern' is 'a generalization of behavior or of ideals for behavior.' Well, so is a 'custom' and so, often, is a 'trait.' I can think of certain concrete examples which could be equally well called 'customs,' 'traits,' or 'patterns.' Aren't these all just synonyms?"

The distinctions are not perfectly clear-cut and satisfactory from an existential or philosophic point of view. That is, the same set of facts of behavior could *in certain cases* justifiably be symbolized by any one of the three words. The *empirical* definition (as opposed to definition from the point of view of traditional philosophy) of concepts rests fundamentally on the use for which they are purposed. When one calls a given set of facts a

[17] See Whitehead, *Science and the Modern World*, p. 75; also Parsons, *Structure of Social Action*, pp. 29, 294, 476–77, 589, 704.   [18] Korzybski, *General Semantics*, esp. pp. 23 ff.

pattern one is looking at the facts from a different point of view than when one calls the same set of facts a "custom" or a "trait"—one is purposing a different sort of analysis.

We can properly say "According to Navaho custom one shakes hands less frequently than in our society." There is no doubt that the behavioral reference is to acts and statements which also constitute a pattern of great interest. It is equally true that both "pattern" and "custom" imply some degree of social restraint tending to produce some conformance on the part of culture carriers. But "custom" accentuates the habitual angle, the "givenness" of the phenomena; pattern the interrelationship of pattern-parts, the fact that one part of the pattern presupposes the others. "Custom" indicates that our attention is upon the usualness, the repetitiveness; is, so to speak, merely upon the *regularity;* while "pattern" implies that our interest is in the *structural* regularity. Sapir[19] has pointed out another subtlety of differentiation. The term "custom" is not altogether "purely denotative and objective;" it "has a slightly affective quality indicated by the fact that one uses it more easily to refer to geographically remote, to primitive or bygone societies than to one's own."

As for "trait" and "pattern" there is again unquestionably some overlap between the two concepts. "Pattern" looks more to structure, "trait" more to content. When we talk of "patterns" our question is not primarily: what observable features, what items, traits, and trait complexes[20] appear in this culture? The focus of our question is: what is the arrangement of discrete bits of cultural content? This is, however, not an "all or none" distinction. Indeed we have expressly reserved an entirely different term for the concept which embraces those aspects of patterning which approach the *purely* structural. The difference here is once again primarily that of emphasis. When one speaks of "matrilocal residence" as a trait of Navaho culture, one is mainly interested in the existential import of the various items into which the trait may be decomposed. That is, we are concerned about a discrete set of facts: married daughters with their children remain at the home of their mother; each married daughter (except sometimes in the case of sororal polygyny) usually has her own house, etc. The interrelationships of these isolable facts are secondary from the point of view of the anthropologist who is operating with traits and items. To the anthropologist who is operating with patterns, however, the item is (to paraphrase Sapir) conceived not as a separable unit but as a point in a pattern. When one speaks of matrilocal residence as a pattern one is singling out the circumstance that the parts of the pattern bear a determinate, not a haphazard relationship to one another.

Moreover—not perhaps as a matter of theory, but demonstrably as a matter of practice—the central meaning which is communicated by "trait of matrilocal residence" tends to be limited to only a very few of the items into which the trait could be resolved. Some Berkeley anthropologists have used "traits" in cultural analysis more intensively than any group of anthropologists working in the United States at the present time. In one of their recent publications[21] I find the trait "patrilocal residence" is broken up into only the fol-

---

[19] Sapir, *Custom*, p. 658.   [20] See Linton, *Study of Man*, pp. 397–401.
[21] Driver, *Culture Element Distributions*, p. 346.

lowing items: first residence patrilocal, final (permanent) residence patrilocal, husband's parents' house, own house. To the anthropologist dealing in patterns a much more extensive analysis is obligatory. "The Navaho pattern of matrilocal residence" is indeed a highly elliptical way of referring to a whole network involving such things as the presence of a kinship terminology where a distinction is made between mother's and father's relatives, nursing and care of each other's children by sisters, economic cooperation.

On a trait list "matrilocal residence" among the Navaho and among the Hopi appears as an equivalent. As soon, however, as "pattern" comes into the picture one is careful to differentiate between "the Navaho pattern of matrilocal residence" and "the Hopi pattern of matrilocal residence." Nor can "trait" and "pattern" be reduced to synonyms on the basis that if the decomposition into items proceeded far enough we should have everything which was present in a complete statement of the pattern. The interest would still be in the discrete items as such, not in their phrasing. Besides, in some cases one can show that exactly the same items of content enter into two different patterns. The order in which the items appear in action may be different; the same item may have a different time duration in the two instances; the same item may in the one case be typically associated with manifestations of affect which are lacking in the other or there may be some other differentiating emphasis.

"Pattern" is today almost invariably restricted to describing the relations between persons or between persons and things. Material culture entities are referred to only as "traits." An arrow is never a "pattern." Actually the arrangement of items in a Navaho arrow is patterned. Navaho arrows bear the imprint of patterning which distinguishes them from Hopi arrows as much as the various patterns which structuralize Navaho dances, in which impersonators of supernaturals participate, distinguishes them from the corresponding Hopi dances. But it is significant that it is a terminological convention to call the one and not the other a "pattern." That is, it is preferred to keep the localization of pattern manifestation in persons, not things.

IDEAL AND BEHAVIORAL PATTERNS

Do "patterns" refer to cultural theory or to cultural practice? If I speak simply of "the Navaho pattern that helpers at chants are from the patient's family or clan" it is quite likely that this will be interpreted in two importantly different ways. One group of readers will infer that this is an expected form, enjoined by the ideals of Navaho culture. As a matter of fact, this is not the case. More than 30 informants stated the ideal pattern as "anyone can help."[22] Another group of readers will infer merely that this pattern is the statement of a behavioral modality. In this instance this happens to be factually the correct interpretation. When confronted with concrete facts, 11 informants showed that they recognized the behavioral tendency but made their feeling plain that this "generalized mode of conduct" was not culturally prescribed but arose out of geographical circumstances and other factors of convenience.

[22] See Kluckhohn, *Some Personal and Social Aspects*, pp. 77–80.

On the one hand, a trend toward uniformity in the cultural conception of how a person *ought* to behave in a given situation may be evidenced by regularities of statement and/or manifestations of approval by word and deed. On the other hand, the structural regularity may be of the indicative rather than of the optative or imperative modes—Sapir's "generalized mode of conduct" conceived not as a thematic way in which the culture carriers are *supposed* to respond but as a thematic way in which they do behave in fact. The differential of *ideal pattern* is that one is trying to describe what people would do or say in a defined situation if they conformed completely to ideals accepted in the culture. For purposes of statement of the ideal pattern the degree to which the actual relevant behaviors deviate from the ideal does not matter. On the other hand, in a behavioral pattern the focus of attention is precisely upon some mode of what people do in fact do. A *behavioral pattern* is nothing more not less than a stylized set of behaviors observed as one modal way of meeting a specified situation. The center of interest here is not upon a standard to be achieved but rather upon a central tendency in a range of behavioral dispersion. It is true, of course, that each conception is to some extent dependent upon the other. As I have heard Professor Linton point out, an ideal pattern which (in a non-literate culture) failed for a long period to serve in any sense as a model for actual behavior would almost inevitably sooner or later cease to be a part of the culture (unless perhaps perpetuated through ritualized verbalization). Similarly, behavioral patterns imply standards of selectivity in most cases. Nevertheless the necessity for a distinction is not just for the sake of conceptual neatness. If an anthropological writer refers to a "pattern" (meaning but not specifying an *ideal pattern*) and certain of those who use his material operate as if he had been talking about a behavioral pattern, inferences are drawn which are more than casually misleading.

Much of the criticism which has been directed against Ruth Benedict's *Patterns of Culture* is based upon the premise that she is talking about behavioral patterns. It is said that she has not counted cases to establish the statistical norms of behavior; that she has in some cases neglected anecdotal and other material in the literature which does not fit her leading ideas, and so forth. But close study of her work makes it fairly plain that she is not so much interested in an inductive analysis of how the Zuñi, for example, do in fact behave as in suggesting a relationship between accepted standards of behavior in Zuñi ("*ideal patterns*") and cultural *configurations* of which the Zuñi are largely unconscious. The "selected detail of behavior"[23] is presented not toward an inductive demonstration of behavioral pattern but only as the behavioral counterpart of an ideal pattern or as an exemplification of the influence of configuration. It seems unfortunate that this is not explicit in her text.

IDEA AND ACTION PATTERNS

The dichotomy between ideal patterns and behavioral patterns is partly analogous to that Sapir[24] has made between "idea patterns" and "action patterns." There is, however, a nuance of difference which appears to me important and which leads me to prefer Linton's

[23] Benedict, *Patterns of Culture*, p. 49.   [24] Sapir, *Emergence of the Concept of Personality*, p. 411.

terms as major categories. "Idea" and "action" suggest that the one class of patterns is manifested only in words, the other only in deeds. The distinction between linguistic and other types of behavior is of course one of which the social scientist should never lose sight. But some recent thinkers have given to this distinction an emphasis which seems exaggerated and calculated to obscure the fact that linguistic *behavior* is inescapably a form of behavior. If one Navaho calls another "son of a coyote" and the epithet is obviously not bestowed in friendly jest, this bit of linguistic behavior is quite likely to find a place in a chain of events similar to that which would be initiated by a physical blow. The first patterns to which we called attention were patterns of linguistic behavior. It is sometimes enlightening to contrast such patterns with patterns observed in non-linguistic action. But in our basic terminology the contrast to be underlined is the contrast between those patterns which are "morally" given high value by the culture carriers and the corresponding thematic regularities of behavior (whether in word or in deed).

That the ideal patterns are not arrived at by abstraction from verbal behavior only is shown by the fact that a shake of the head, a disapproving look, a sudden departure are often essential elements in the observer's building up his conception of the ideal pattern. Conversely, an example will show that *idealized* and *ideological* patterns are not necessarily coterminous. Navaho informants agree that uninitiated children *ought* to believe that the masked impersonators are actually the supernaturals themselves. This is the ideal pattern. But of the 23 Navaho children to whom I have talked on the subject only 5 failed to manifest awareness of the impersonation. Most of these had never seen a chant in which masked men take part. But their "idea," their "belief" was: the dancers in Night Way, etc., are just men wearing masks. This is a structural regularity in the realm of ideas—an idea pattern. But it is unmistakably not the same thing as what Navaho children are *supposed* to believe in this connection. There are approved ideas as well as approved deeds. Hence an idea pattern may be either an ideal pattern or a behavioral pattern.

Awareness of Patterns

It is well to remind ourselves of the wide variation in awareness of patterns as such on the part of both the culture carriers and observers. As Sapir[25] has said: "Forms and significances which seem obvious to an outsider will be denied outright by those who carry out the patterns; outlines and implications that are perfectly clear to these may be absent to the eye of the onlooker."

In some cases informants will give quite articulate verbal statements of both types of pattern. The incidence of discrepancy between ideal and behavioral patterns is very high in Navaho culture at the present time—as in most rapidly changing cultures. The conflict between old and new ideas, between traditional and altering modalities of action, tends to bring the contrast of ideal and behavioral patterns into full consciousness for the culture carriers. If you ask an informant who is presenting the ideal pattern of our last example,

[25] Sapir, *Unconscious Patterning of Behavior*, p. 120.

"Well, do the children really believe this?", almost all of the replies are of the type: "Not many do any more;" "Very few do these days." In fact many informants will volunteer remarks of this kind (as a commentary upon the "degeneracy" of the times) without being specifically questioned. The same thing, however, is true of some instances which need not be connected with acculturation. While the ideal pattern prescribes that a man's wife should not (except in certain defined circumstances) object to his taking a second wife, the observer soon realizes that the Navaho are quite aware that resistance and quarreling bulk very prominently in the apposite behavioral pattern. In other words, in these cases the ethnographer could get from interview material not only statements of the ideal patterns but also descriptions of the behavioral patterns which would not differ markedly from that which he would get by abstracting in an inductive analysis of the relevant behaviors.

To take the other extreme, there are instances where neither the ideal nor the behavioral patterns are likely to be discovered merely by direct questioning. A nice example appears in Dyk's book.[26] When Old Man Hat returned home to find that his wife had entertained guests in his absence he required of his son a minute description of the positions which all in the hogan had occupied and of the manner in which the spoon was handed about. He whipped his wife—obviously because of lack of conformance between the ideal pattern and the behavior. And yet in all the other published material on the Navaho and in my own extensive field notes I can nowhere find so much as an explicit hint of such patterns. The trouble is that the ethnographer has a limited time in the field. He can not see everything. Hence he takes to posing questions in the hypothetical mode, "What would the Navaho do in such and such a situation?" This is all very well except that the ethnographer seldom brings up situations which are not formalized in his own culture or other cultures with which he happens to be familiar.

In yet other cases neither extensive questioning alone nor extensive observation alone will suffice. This is illustrated by the gift-giving which goes on at Enemy Way performances between individuals who are not necessarily members of the families of those who are being treated. When the observer first notices one man (apparently rather casually) presenting another with a side of mutton or even a heifer or a horse, the temptation may be to infer that this is a relatively spontaneous act, or that it is at most the repayment of an obligation or the return of a gift and that this only happens to occur at an Enemy Way because this is an occasion when Navaho meet. Experience shows that ethnographers can observe and take careful notes at many Enemy Ways without becoming aware that they are seeing patterned behaviors in this connection. Finally, however, it is likely to strike one that this phenomenon occurs at Enemy Way with far greater regularity and frequency than it does at the comparably large gatherings for Night Way and Mountain Top Way. When one specifically asks Navaho about the practice it is immediately evident that in the concrete they know exactly (within the range of their friends) who is expected to give a gift to whom at a particular Enemy Way. I have never yet, however, found an informant who could give

[26] Dyk, Son of Old Man Hat, pp. 18–19.

me a fully articulate statement of the ideal pattern nor the generalization which is the behavioral pattern. From statements *and* analysis of cases I now know that the ideal pattern centers around an exchange of gifts (in four alternate years) between the blackener and the person whom he has blackened in a previous Enemy Way.

By definition, the culture carriers must have some sort of awareness of an ideal pattern. But this does not imply that the ideal pattern will always be stated in an articulate, abstract form. In some realms of culture this polarity is indeed consistently approached. In fact—particularly in the case of ethnographers who have worked with but a few informants—it is almost exclusively the ideal patterns which make up our accounts of some cultures. With respect to some patterns this may matter practically very little, for the goodness of fit between ideal and behavioral pattern is in certain instances almost perfect. In Navaho culture the ideal patterns for mother-in-law avoidance and avoidance of physical contact on the part of siblings of opposite sex (as stated by informants) and the behavioral patterns (as abstracted from observation) are almost identical among Navaho who are little acculturated. But much depends on the extent to which patterns of both types are formalized. The degree of consciousness ranges widely and is indicated by the extent to which one or more highly concrete features of the action are singled out as "right" or "wrong" or, on the other hand, by the extent to which an unspecific indignation or a vague uncomfortableness is manifested toward the action in general.

It will be instructive, I think, to follow out in some detail how a specific assemblage of data illustrates contrasts between ideal and behavioral patterns and the range of variation in consciousness of both. I have the statements of 53 informants on the ideal patterns for marriage limitation. I shall deal here only with those features which relate to "social organization" in the narrow sense, neglecting cultural predilections for one type of individual as opposed to another ("a girl should always marry a man who is a good worker" and the like). The major mode of statement (39 informants) comes down to this: "You have got to marry outside your own clan." In the minor mode of statement something of this sort was added: "It is best to marry someone from the clan of either your paternal or maternal grandfather." When the attention of a sample of 20 informants from the first group was called to this, all but 3 agreed, remarking, "That's right" or "Yes, I forgot that." In short, while there is some slight disagreement as to the ideal pattern, the principal fact which emerges is that only part of this ideal pattern was immediately present to consciousness. There are, of course, great differences between informants in this respect. When the ethnographer asks a general question in the abstract or phrases a hypothetical situation, some informants characteristically answer very briefly, presenting only the pattern-parts which doubtless seem most central to them, while other informants will, without further prodding, elaborate in considerable detail.

Now let us turn to the behavioral patterns. In the discussion of "marriage and social organization" with these Navaho, 30 of them expressly volunteered information which, scientifically expressed, amounts to "there are a very large number of marriages of pairs of

siblings." These informants were, in effect, making the distinction between the ideal patterns *for* behavior and the actual patterns *of* behavior. They showed their awareness of
the strong tendency for two or more siblings to marry into the same family (or clan),[27] but
they did not put this into their replies to the question, "Whom is a Navaho supposed to
marry?" because the practice is not enjoined by the culture.

To another very important component of the marriage limitation pattern, observers
in the Ramah and Pueblo Alto regions did not have their attention drawn on *either* the
ideal or behavioral levels by the culture carriers. No Navaho told Carr, Spencer, Woolley,
or me that there was a prohibition against marriage into the father's clan or that Navaho
simply did not marry into the father's clan. And yet the figures show that in the Pueblo
Alto area[28] there were only 2 such marriages out of 241 and in the Ramah area only 2 out
of more than 400. When confronted with these figures 8 out of 10 Ramah informants admitted such an element in the ideal pattern, but it is important to note that the pattern
would have been arrived at only by abstraction and inference from the facts analyzed. In
sum, the operations by which *patterns* of both classes are arrived at consist in abstraction
and extrapolation from either the regularities of observed acts or statements or both.

SUBSIDIARY CONCEPTS

Informants who are discussing the behavior proper to a singer during a chant make it
clear that the singer is expected to maintain one of several stylized positions while singing.[29]
All of these are ideal patterns within the ceremonial ideology. It is recognized that a given
singer tends to follow the pattern which his teacher follows but all have equal value status
in the cultural ideology. They are *alternative* ideal patterns. In other words, one must not
confuse *ideal patterns* with "preferred patterns." For some behavioral networks the Navaho
seem to recognize but a single ideal pattern. At the ideal level the pattern is regarded as
compulsory and therefore we well may speak of a *compulsory* ideal pattern. In many other
cases a number of different traditional solutions are approved. Thus the following ideal
patterns prevail with respect to sex: sororal polygyny, non-sororal polygyny, monogamy,
transvestite homosexuality. On the whole, the evidence indicates that sororal polygyny was
in a sense a *preferred ideal pattern*, but all of the patterns were certainly part of the system
of ideal patterns. In cases where one ideal pattern is simply the ideal most frequently expressed (without there being any implication that it is singled out as the object of idealized
preference) *typical ideal pattern* suggests itself as an appropriate designation. Hill's[30] data
and mine both indicate that transvestite homosexuality was considered a proper solution
for some individuals only, and hence it would perhaps be well to call such a pattern a
restricted ideal pattern.

Ideal patterns, then, may be subdivided into *compulsory*, *preferred*, *typical*, *alternative*,
and *restricted* when the context demands such a precise specificity. Always, however, care

---

[27] Cf. Carr, Spencer, and Woolley, *Navaho Clans*, pp. 253–54.   [28] *Ibid.*, p. 254.
[29] Cf. Kluckhohn and Wyman, *Introduction*, p. 15.   [30] Hill, *Status of the Hermaphrodite*.

must be exercised to speak of *the* ideal pattern only when one is either contrasting a particular ideal pattern with the corresponding behavioral pattern or when one unequivocally means a compulsory ideal pattern. Since there is often more than a single locus around which the data relating to culturally idealized ways of handling a situation pile up, the word "mode" was designedly used in discussing the evidence on the ideal patterns of marriage limitation. For in attempting to define both ideal and behavioral patterns, one's conception is operationally much closer to "mode" than to "mean" or "median."

If we were to attempt to obtain a mean average from the facts and state *the* ideal pattern, we should often have either to accept a form of statement which was cumbersome and imprecise or to neglect the minor mode or modes entirely and, with calm disregard of quite a number of facts, consider the major mode as *the* ideal pattern. While the major mode is likely to be the most representative single value in such material, most cultures (since their historical and biological origins have been highly heterogeneous) will strongly tend to give bi-modal or multi-modal distributions with respect to many of their ideals and behaviors. And a single mode is a notoriously unsatisfactory description of any unsymmetrical curve. If the trend of the distributions were pronouncedly regular in the direction of flatness (in which case the mean would doubtless be the most representative value) this fact would in itself signify unpatterned ideals or behaviors.

It is convenient to distinguish the behavioral patterns by names which are different from those used to categorize the ideal patterns. "Compulsory," for instance, plainly refers to a standard of value and only in the case of an extraordinarily well integrated culture or a culture where the external sanctions were uncommonly efficiently enforced could behavioral patterns empirically be characterized as "compulsory." Conversely, one hardly expects the ideal pattern system to encompass patterns which are *disapproved* or *prohibited.*[31] There can be cognizance of such patterns in the *idea* patterns of the culture but not in the *ideal* patterns. Disapproved and prohibited patterns are inevitably behavioral patterns. For example, adultery is not recognized in the ideal patterns of Navaho culture. Behaviorally, however, adultery is common and the carrying out of adulterous acts is most distinctly patterned in ways of which Navaho are rather explicitly aware. Prostitution has likewise (at least at some times and places) been a disapproved pattern of Navaho culture.

Where the anthropologist is interested only in the behavioral patterns or where he has insufficient knowledge of the ideal patterns, the behavioral patterns may be described simply as modalities without in any way begging the question of conformance to the corresponding ideal patterns. *Major behavioral* pattern will serve as a label for a behavioral mode which is unequivocally the major mode of a set of correlative patterns. *Minor behavioral pattern* is suggested for those modes which are definitely minor. When the interest is in conformance and the necessary information is available, *conformant* and *deviant* behavioral patterns may be distinguished. The two sets of terms must not be regarded as synonyms, for in a changing culture it will be found very frequently that the deviant patterns are also the major behavioral patterns.

[31] Many of these terms I have selected from Murdock and Others, *Outline of Cultural Materials*, p. 9.

Pattern Assemblages and Sub-Patterns

We have now proposed an horizontal dichotomy (with possible internal subdivisions) of the patterns of the overt culture. This classification was based upon what I believe to be the conceptually central distinction of ideal and behavioral patterns. It remains to set forth a vertical sub-classification which applies equally well to both ideal and behavioral patterns, but is designed to assist in keeping our levels of abstraction straight. For this purpose I propose using Sapir's[32] terms *pattern assemblage* (to designate a complex of patterns associated with a major cultural function) and *sub-pattern* (to isolate the more concrete patterns within a broader, more general pattern).

In the *pattern assemblage* which centers on marriage there are, on both the ideal and behavioral levels, a host of patterns which interact with each other in a complex state of mutual interdependence. A few of these, labeled according to the outstanding feature of content, are: limitation of choice by clan exogamy, etc.; economic and other qualifications of prospective spouses; role of the relatives in arranging the marriage; the actual marriage ceremony; polygyny; interference of biological and clan relatives in the married life of the couple; mother-in-law avoidance. All of these save the last-named and perhaps "marriage ceremony" can be broken down into various *sub-patterns*.

For example, "qualification of spouses" includes a sub-pattern relating to the virginity of a girl at marriage. On the ideal level this sub-pattern is made up of (at least) the following *pattern-parts*: (1) a girl should be a virgin at her first marriage; (2) a young man's first wife should be a virgin; (3) if a girl is known not to be a virgin, this rightly affects her prospects in general; (4) the gifts of the groom's family may properly be less valuable where the girl has lost her virginity; (5) if a groom finds that his bride is not a virgin (and this is her first marriage) he is justified in returning her to her parents and demanding a return of the marriage gifts; (6) the marriage ceremony ought to be held only over a girl who is a virgin. On the behavioral level the "role of relatives" pattern encompasses such sub-patterns as consulting or informing various relatives, arrangement of economic exchanges between the two families, a particular relative acting as a go-between. (Here, for brevity, I have again used "labels" rather than specifying pattern-parts in detail.) The pattern of polygyny may be resolved into the sub-patterns of sororal polygyny, non-sororal polygyny, mother-daughter (by another marriage, of course) polygyny.

In each of these cases a particular behavioral sub-pattern tends to be (in one locality at a given time) the major one. Among the corresponding ideal sub-patterns *preferred, alternative,* and other forms are distinguishable. Thus the preferred ideal sub-pattern is that the mother's brother (now among some groups the father) should be the go-between; "any relative" is, however, an alternative ideal sub-pattern. It is also to be noted that the same sub-pattern may appear in more than one pattern and the same pattern in more than one pattern assemblage. Thus the pattern of clan exogamy and preference is a component of the pattern assemblage structuralizing the marriage activity and also of the pattern assemblage clustering around the role which clan plays in Navaho culture. And into the assemblage

---

[32] Sapir, *Emergence of the Concept of Personality*, p. 414.

which defines the status of "singer" in Navaho culture enter a number of sub-patterns and patterns which are familiar in other pattern assemblages.

DISCUSSION

The terminology for classifying and describing structural features of overt culture shows crude correspondence with Linton's terminology for the content of culture. Thus *item* and *pattern-part*, *sub-pattern* and *trait*, *pattern* and *trait-complex*, *pattern-assemblage* and *activity* tend in a very general way to be correlative conceptual hierarchies suited to describing approximately the same behavioral phenomena *from different angles of interest*. The parallelism must not be pushed too far or interpreted too rigidly. Thus, from the point of view of logical coherence one *could* distinguish sub-patterns within "arrangement of economic exchanges." Moreover, whether one treats "marriage ceremony" as "pattern" or breaks it up into "sub-patterns" or again whether one considers mother-daughter polygyny an independent sub-pattern or merely a set of pattern-parts in the non-sororal polygyny sub-pattern is altogether a matter of empirical convenience.

The choice therefore must not be phrased as being between "no classification" and "a classification which works in every concrete instance without a hitch." It is a question of having a terminology which affords an ordering of the data roughly consistent with the factual range of levels of abstraction and which permits a classification as coarse or as fine as the purpose in hand suggests. In certain rather general discussions or in treatments where patterning is of only incidental interest the anthropologist might justifiably utilize only a few of the conceptual differentiations which have been made here. On the other hand, an intensive analysis of all the structural details of a body of cultural material would require all of the concepts and perhaps others. For example, in a complete description the degree of flexibility of particular patterns would need to be specified.

PATTERNING OF COVERT CULTURE: CONFIGURATIONS

To phenomena of patterning in the *covert* culture it is proposed to apply the term *configuration* as a master concept comparable to "pattern" in the overt culture. The contrast between these two master concepts can best be seen through a consideration of concrete data from which examples of both can be abstracted. At a time when I was naive enough to suppose that I could get substantial bodies of anecdotal material on witchcraft from Navaho who knew me only casually, I approached 11 persons independently with the request that they tell me what they knew about witchcraft. In 7 cases the first verbal response which I received to my preliminary remarks was "Who told you that I knew about witchcraft?" Here plainly is a trend toward a structural uniformity. The presentation of the stimulus, "Tell me what you know about witchcraft," is not followed by a random assortment of responses: "I don't know anything about it;" "Why do you want to find out about witchcraft?" "That is a very dangerous thing to talk about; I can't do it;" "How much will you pay me if I tell you about witchcraft?" This past summer (with no expectation of learning anything substantial about witchcraft as such, but purely for purposes of this experiment)

I repeated the question—with a standardized technique of presentation—to 25 informants. In 16 cases almost identical verbal responses were manifested. They varied only in this fashion: "Who told you to talk to me about witchcraft?" "Who said I knew anything about witchcraft," and "Why do you come to me to ask about this—who told you I knew about it?" Here we have a behavioral pattern of the overt culture, for the structure consists in a determinate interdigitation of linguistic symbols as a response to a verbal (and situational) stimulus.

Suppose now, however, that we juxtapose this and other behavioral patterns which have no extrinsic interconnection. Unacculturated Navaho are uniformly careful to hide their fæces and to see to it that no other person obtains possession of their hair, nails, sputum, or any other bodily part or product. They are likewise characteristically secretive about their personal names. All three of these patterns (as well as many others which might be mentioned) are manifestations of an abstracted *configuration* which may be intellectualized as "fear of the malevolent intentions of other persons." Only most exceptionally would a Navaho make this abstract generalization, saying, in effect, "These are all ways of showing our anxiety about the activities of others." Nevertheless, this principle does order all sorts of concrete Navaho behaviors and, although *covert*, is as much a part of Navaho culture as the overt pattern of verbal symbols. Similarly, I have never heard "distrust of extremes" verbalized as an overt part of Navaho ideology. In terms of this covert configuration, however, one can understand such patterns as the Navaho tendency to project accusations of witchcraft against persons who are either very poor or very rich. One more example: if any one of the concrete pattern-parts of the "spirit outlet" (a break in design found in weaving, pottery, basketry, etc.) is missing or "wrong" in any respect, Navaho are sensitive to the pattern transgression. But of the configuration as such there is minimal awareness. Configurations are Sapir's "unconscious system of meanings," Benedict's "unconscious canons of choice."

Possibly *sub-configuration* would serve to designate the more specific entities into which a configuration may sometimes be resolved. I have noticed that the replies which an ethnographer receives when he asks questions about various ceremonial subjects which the Navaho show reluctance to discuss are not *verbally* patterned as are those in the case of questions about witchcraft. The responses seemed to take such a wide variety of verbal forms that even an experienced observer could hardly hope to predict in any significant way. I tried this experimentally the past season (using the same 25 informants as in my experiment on witchcraft). While 6 of the 10 arrangements of words which entered into my predictions did occur (in approximately the same form) one or more times in the answers, 5 replies which had not appeared at all in my predictions were given, and in only 2 cases out of 25 did a particular informant make the response predicted specifically of him. While no *verbal pattern* was manifested, there was nevertheless a consistency in the "intent" of the replies, for all showed a disposition to "hedge," to make excuses for not directly answering my questions. It was put as a matter of other engagements, of insufficient pay, of doubt as to my motives, etc. This negativistic pattern may be associated with behavioral patterns toward strangers who travel in the Navaho country and with other behavioral patterns. The principle configurating these patterns may be phrased as "suspicion of any outsider." This, however, is surely but a special instance, a sub-configuration, of the configuration "anxiety as to the activities of others," of which "distrust of extremes" would seem to be another sub-configuration.

A pattern is a generalization *of* behavior or of ideals for behavior. A configuration is a generalization *from* behavior. Both patterns and configurations are thus abstractions. They are not the actual behaviors. For, as Sapir so tenaciously insisted, culture is not behavior— it is an abstraction from behavior. Thus when we abstract the behavioral pattern "sibling-of-opposite sex avoidance" we pay attention to things of this sort in our field notes: "X did not hand the cup directly to his sister, Y. He put it on the ground between them." "Whenever I could hear the conversations at the 'squaw dance' I noted that each man who asked a girl to dance inquired her clan first." We neglect for operations of arriving at the behavioral pattern many details of the specific situations in which the actual behaviors in all their concreteness are imbedded in everyday life. We disregard the observation in our notes that at the moment when the brother put the cup on the ground the sister was wearing a turquoise necklace, the brother had a cold, etc. But when we abstract a configuration we depart even further from the actual behaviors. The recurrent form of words "I don't know—I just heard about it," constitutes a pattern in arriving at which, to be sure, we take each such statement out of its total context and overlook small differences in pronouns, etc. But implicit in these data and others which could be related to it is the *configuration* "Navaho tend to be scrupulous about differentiating what they have themselves seen or done from what they know merely by verbal report." Here it is plain that we are remote from even a generalized statement of the verbal behaviors from which the *pattern* was abstracted.

Any *cultural* conception is an abstraction. It is of cardinal importance that these abstractions should be based upon adequate data. Descriptions of actual behaviors (in more than anecdotal proportions) should find a place in our ethnographies and the ethnographer should provide quantitative materials in terms of which his abstractions can be controlled by the reader. But the point I wish to make here is that a configuration is a conception at a much higher level of abstraction than a pattern. Likewise, inference predominates much more in the operations of deriving configurations. To a considerable extent patterns are arrived at by simple abstraction from trends toward uniformity in statement and deed. Inference enters principally where it is a case of interpreting approval or disapproval. Configurations, on the other hand tend to be purely inferential constructs. Configuration looks to an *inner* coherence in terms of the large structuralizing principles which prevail in the *covert* culture. Patterns are forms; configurations are, so to speak, interrelationships between forms.

It is for such reasons that the term "configuration" seems appropriate. "Configuration" as a technical term in psychology carries with it the implication that "the whole is more than the sum of its parts." A pattern, however, can be defined by listing the pattern-parts in a determinate sequence (and perhaps indicating the duration or accentuation of each). A *configuration* states the principle "behind" a group of patterns—it is only implicit in them and must be inferred out. A pattern is a generalization of what people do or should do; a configuration is in a sense a generalization of "why" they do or should do certain things. Configurations are the abstract principles in terms of which patterns are themselves configurated.

It was, I think, because anthropologists have long realized that there was more to culture than its overt content that Sapir's transfer to configurational principles from linguistics was seized upon so avidly. Examples of this sort[33] confirmed suspicions of the limitations of functional analysis:

> If the plural were to be understood functionally alone, we should find it difficult to explain why we use plural forms with numerals and other words that in themselves imply plurality. "Five man" or "several house" would be just as adequate as "five men" or "several houses."

The substantive aspects of a culture may alter in important features, but to the observer with experience of that culture even the new overt content somehow has a familiar tone. The same holds in a synchronic plane for different sectors of the same culture. One may be attending the Navaho chant "Beauty Way" for the first time, but if one has had a fairly rich experience of other chants one feels quite at home. The sandpaintings may be quite new to one, various articles of ceremonial equipment different, many of the patterns different, yet one has a sense that—to borrow Demoulin's phrase—"*plus ça change, plus c'est la même chose.*"

It is to these perdurable cultural features, the configurations (which are not dissimilar to Pareto's "residues") that Ruth Benedict has given her major attention. To follow out some of the major misunderstandings which appear to have arisen with regard to her work will further clarify our conception of configuration. Many of her critics have been guilty of the fallacy of misplaced concreteness. They have tacitly assumed that she was talking of behavioral patterns, whereas even ideal patterns enter into her schema far less than configurations. Configurations, as we have suggested, come nearer to dealing with the "whyness" than the "whatness" of a culture. We find Dr Benedict writing of "characteristic purposes" and of "the motives, and emotions and values that are institutionalized in that culture."[34] To some anthropologists Dr Benedict has appeared to treat "pattern" as the equivalent of "the outstanding emotional principle of a culture." One hears objections of a sort which may be generalized and paraphrased as follows: "Benedict calls the dominant affects of a culture its patterns. This is a confusing procedure, for culture is, by definition, affect-less. Individuals have affect, yes—but not a culture. Culture is an abstraction from the behavior of individuals. It is illogical to impute emotion to an abstraction. Emotional expression on the part of individuals is usually patterned, but patterns are not emotions." But Benedict is not really

---

[33] Sapir, *Unconscious Patterning of Behavior*, pp. 125-26.   [34] Benedict, *Patterns of Culture*, pp. 46, 49.

identifying her "patterns of culture" with affects. She is attempting to describe what Talcott Parsons[35] has called "ultimate value-attitudes." From the point of view *of the observer* configurations do constitute (largely unconscious) "motivations" for the culture carriers. The locus of emotion remains in the individual, of course, but "pattern" and "configuration" are very useful conceptual tools in attempting to dissect out the emotional structure of a society. For the behavior of individuals with respect to pattern or configuration, conformance on their own part or that of others is, typically, affective. One may generally expect neutral attitudes only toward those areas of behavior where patterning does not prevail. Hence the emotions which are most frequently expressed by the individuals of a particular society or which are characteristic manifestations in certain situations assuredly do bear a determinate relationship to pattern assemblages and configurations. It is for this reason that one finds such a pronounced association between the language of emotion and configurations in Dr Benedict's writings.

That remarkable convergence (which Professor Parsons has so magnificently documented) in social theory upon conceptions of the order of "residue," "value-attitude," and "configuration" suggests that Dr Benedict has raised for anthropologists a series of problems of the greatest significance to their science. But when she designates both types of "pattern" and more than one type of "configuration" by the same term she invites confusion. Sometimes she is talking of different principles of the covert culture; at other times she seems to have in mind a single over-summative principle: "Order is due to the circumstance that in these societies a principle has been set up according to which the assembled cultural material is made over into consistent patterns. . . ."[36] Would it not be well to designate this broadest type of configuration by a special term, say, *integration*? Even though we recognize that "integration" is a polar concept which is seldom if ever fully realized in any culture it is a useful conception just as "health" is useful, although few higher organisms are completely normal. If there be an *integrating principle* in Navaho culture it is, I suspect, subsumed under the root *hóžǫ́—*. But this is only a highly provisional suggestion. The question needs intensive and extensive examination if a determination is to be arrived at inductively rather than by a kind of synthetic apperception.

CONCLUSION

Someone has said "The primary task of science is the detection and description of uniform modes of relationships between things." It is only in the hope that it may be an aid in this task that a somewhat involved terminology (summarized in the accompanying chart) has been set forth. But a science of human behavior could not be content with even the most perfect statement of patterns and configurations. There are too many meaningful descriptions of observable behavior which do not get into such statements. For example, one individual manifests affect in actualizing a pattern; another carrier of the same culture does not.

[35] Parsons, *Structure of Social Action*, pp. 255, 260, 267, 271, 297.
[36] Benedict, *Configurations of Culture*, p. 3.

But Professor Sapir[37] has too brilliantly urged the necessity for studying actual behavior as well as patterns and configurations for the point to need elaboration in this volume.

SUMMARY

PATTERNING—a structural regularity
- A. PATTERN—structural regularity in overt culture
    - 1. IDEAL PATTERN—optative and imperative mode
        - a. Compulsory ideal pattern—one only recognized
        - b. Preferred ideal pattern—one usually selected
        - c. Typical ideal pattern—one most frequently expressed
        - d. Alternative ideal pattern—one which may be selected
        - e. Restricted ideal pattern—proper for some individuals only
    - 2. BEHAVIORAL PATTERN—indicative mode
        - a. Major behavioral pattern—major mode of a set
        - b. Minor behavioral pattern—minor mode of a set
            - aa. Conformant behavioral pattern—conforms with ideal pattern
            - bb. Deviant behavioral pattern—does not conform with ideal pattern
- AA. PATTERN ASSEMBLAGE—complex of patterns (activity)
    - AA[1]. PATTERN (trait complex)
    - AA[2]. SUB-PATTERN (trait)
    - AA[3]. PATTERN-PART (item)
- B. CONFIGURATION—a structural regularity in covert culture
    - a. SUB-CONFIGURATION—part of a configuration
- BB. INTEGRATION—guiding principle of configurations

"Idea pattern"—manifest in words—may be either ideal or behavioral.
"Action pattern"—manifest in deeds—may be either ideal or behavioral.
"Custom"—emphasis on regularity (rather than structural regularity).
"Trait"—emphasis on content rather than structure (things as well as persons).
"Personal habit system"—patterns characteristic of individual as a personality.
Configuration roughly correlative with "residue," "value-attitude," "unconscious canon of choice."

BIBLIOGRAPHY

BENEDICT, RUTH *Configurations of Culture in North America* (American Anthropologist, Vol. 34, pp. 1–27, 1932).
Patterns of Culture (New York, 1934).
BLOOMFIELD, L. *Language* (New York, 1933).
CARR, M., K. SPENCER, and D. WOOLLEY *Navaho Clans and Marriage at Pueblo Alto* (American Anthropologist, Vol. 41, pp. 245–58, 1939).
DRIVER, H. E. *Culture Element Distributions: X. Northwest California* (Anthropological Records, Vol. 1, No. 6, Berkeley, 1939).
DYK, WALTER *Son of Old Man Hat* (New York, 1938).

[37] See especially *Emergence of the Concept of Personality* and *Contribution of Psychiatry*.

GOLDENWEISER, A. A. *Loose Ends of Theory on the Individual, Pattern, and Involution in Primitive Society* (In *Essays in Anthropology Presented to A. L. Kroeber*, R. H. Lowie, ed., pp. 99–104, Berkeley, 1936).

HALLOWELL, A. I. *Fear and Anxiety as Cultural and Individual Variables in a Primitive Society* (Journal of Social Psychology, Vol. 8, pp. 25–47, 1939).

HILL, W. W. *The Status of the Hermaphrodite and Transvestite in Navaho Culture* (American Anthropologist, Vol. 37, pp. 273–79, 1935).

KLUCKHOHN, CLYDE *Some Personal and Social Aspects of Navaho Ceremonial Practice* (Harvard Theological Review, Vol. 32, pp. 52–82, 1939).

KLUCKHOHN, CLYDE, and LELAND C. WYMAN *An Introduction to Navaho Chant Practice* (Memoirs, American Anthropological Association, No. 53, 1940).

KORZYBSKI, ALFRED *General Semantics* (Olivet, Michigan, 1937).

LINTON, RALPH *The Study of Man* (New York, 1936).

MURDOCK, G. P., and OTHERS *Outline of Cultural Materials* (New Haven, 1938).

PARSONS, TALCOTT *The Structure of Social Action* (New York, 1937).

SAPIR, EDWARD *The Concept of Phonetic Law as Tested in Primitive Languages by Leonard Bloomfield* (In *Methods in Social Science*, S. A. Rice, ed., pp. 297–307, Chicago, 1931).

The Contribution of Psychiatry to an Understanding of Behavior in Society (American Journal of Sociology, Vol. 42, pp. 862–71, 1937).

Culture, Genuine and Spurious (American Journal of Sociology, Vol. 29, pp. 401–30, 1924).

Custom (In *Encyclopaedia of the Social Sciences*, Vol. 4, pp. 658–62, 1931).

The Emergence of the Concept of Personality in a Study of Cultures (Journal of Social Psychology, Vol. 5, pp. 408–15, 1934).

Language, an Introduction to the Study of Speech (New York, 1921).

Personality (In *Encyclopaedia of the Social Sciences*, Vol. 12, pp. 85–87, 1934).

The Unconscious Patterning of Behavior in Society (In *The Unconscious: a Symposium*, E. S. Dummer, ed., pp. 114–42, Chicago, 1927).

WHITEHEAD, A. N. *Science and the Modern World* (New York, 1925).

ZIPF, G. K. *The Psychobiology of Language* (Boston, 1935).

HARVARD UNIVERSITY
CAMBRIDGE, MASSACHUSETTS

THE THEORY OF ACCENTUAL SYSTEMS

By GEORGE L. TRAGER

THE ESSENCE of the correct scientific apprehension and description of language as a whole and of all subsidiary linguistic phenomena is that language is a *system*, and that this system consists of an organized series of sub-systems.

To describe such a system or any of its sub-systems is to describe the *relations* between the constituent parts. In such description, it is sufficient to deal with those relations which are not entirely conditioned, that is, to describe the *functions* of the parts of the system.[1]

The validity of this approach has been recognized for a long time in dealing with those phonological phenomena of language that are concerned with the sounds known as vowels and consonants, and with their patterning and arrangement.

In his epoch-making "Sound Patterns in Language,"[2] Edward Sapir pointed out the essential difference between speech-sounds and other non-linguistic but similar sounds, by comparing the sound of the initial *wh* of *when* as currently pronounced by most Americans with the sound made in blowing out a candle. Further examples of this kind may be found in comparing the child's word *choo-choo* with the actual sound of a locomotive; no matter how alike or how different the sounds may be, the two phenomena are utterly distinct. The latter is one of a countless number of sounds being made in the world around us; the former is part of a linguistic system: it consists of two of the English phonemic entities, *č* and *uw* (whether *uw* is a unit phoneme or a cluster of the kind indicated by the orthography here chosen, is not in point), repeated in the order consonant-vowel, consonant-vowel, with loud stress on the first set and medial stress on the second, with pause of the kind found between words separating the first and second sets; further, the two-syllable reduplicating compound is one of a series of such words constituting a pattern of English word-formation, and the relation of the word to other preceding and following words is according to the established patterns of English morphemics and syntax. The point need not be labored with additional examples.

When we come to dealing with those phonological phenomena that involve elements of relative loudness or stress, relative pitch, relative quantity, and similar manifestations—phenomena which are not part of the one-by-one succession of vowels and consonants, but which are something superposed on such a succession—then we find that the usual approach is entirely forgetful of the principles just laid down.

For example, descriptions of the intonations of a language are most likely to be made in

---

[1] Cf. L. Hjelmslev, La *structure morphologique (types de système)* (Rapports, Cinquième Congrès international de linguistes, Deuxième publication, pp. 66–93, Bruges, 1939), especially pp. 66 and 67.

[2] Language, Vol. 1, pp. 37–51, 1925.

terms of musical notation, and with a complete carrying over to language of the quite in-appropriate considerations of music. In the case of stress, all the emphasis is laid on physical considerations of loudness, and of the supposed "logical" consequences of such physical phenomena. And in describing length the attention is nearly always concentrated on exact measurements of elapsed time, with, often, dramatic announcements of the sort which say that some "short" vowels are really longer than some "long" vowels, with the obvious im-plication that the linguist is "wrong" and the technician is "right."

If the linguist will remember that all of language is subject to the same basic principles, and that all *linguistic* phenomena are parts of a system, he will not be troubled by the en-tirely extraneous conclusions of such approaches as those just mentioned. We know that stress, tone, quantity, and the like, are part of language, we conclude that we can deal with them, on a linguistic plane, as parts of systems, and we then proceed to treat them not as physical or musical or emotional phenomena but as linguistic ones. This is not to say that the linguist may not draw on the data of auxiliary sciences in the formulation of his basic postulates; but once he has reached that stage, he must stay rigidly within the confines of his system.

With these preliminary considerations in mind, we proceed to the exposition of a sys-tem of description of the phenomena subsumed under the term *accent* (which must be de-fined).

The entities known as vowels and consonants may be referred to on the phonetic level as *successive sounds*, on the phonemic level as *segmental phonemes;* vowels are nuclear and consonants marginal. On the other hand, the entities of the type of stress, pitch, and quanti-ty will be termed *exponential sounds* and *prosodic phonemes* or *prosodemes*.

Those prosodemes on the first level of analysis, namely, those affecting the syllable and the word (phonemically defined in each language by reference to the syllable), can be called *accents*. All prosodic phenomena, then, of the word and the syllable as part of a word, will be referred to as *accentual*. The prosodemes on the next or super-verbal level, those affecting groups of words—phrases and sentences—can be called *intonations*, and the phenomena in-volved are *intonational*.

The main subject of this paper is the whole of the phenomena of accent as here defined. But the procedure outlined can, it is believed, be extended also to intonations.

In much of the recent literature on phonological (in the broadest sense) phenomena, it has been assumed that the observation of sounds—phonetics, is on a non-linguistic or pre-linguistic level, and that only when we come to phonemes do we have language (*la langue*) as opposed to speech (*la parole*). This is not the place to go into a discussion of the definition of speech as opposed to language. Suffice it to say that observation of a great amount of lin-guistic material from a purely phonetic point of view has convinced the author that such phenomena also fall into systems, and that there is no doubt that the phonetic level is also part of *la langue* and legitimately a subject of linguistic discussion.

Accordingly, we begin our exposition with some phonetic considerations.

The exponential sounds of a language, or of language in general, can be systematically treated from two main points of view. One involves a static description, that of the amount of the particular exponential present, the concentration, as it were; this can be called its *intensity*. The second approach views the exponential kinetically, describing the movement in shape of the exponential in terms of changes of intensity; this is the *contour*.

In describing intensity, it is necessary to have as reference points the two extremes— greatest and least, and include all that lies between the two extremes as medial; these three "points" are enough, interested as we are in relations (see above) and not in non-linguistic and therefore irrelevant details. We shall use the three terms *maximal, medial, minimal* in describing intensity.

In a similar manner, three types are sufficient in describing contour. It is necessary to know whether the intensity changes from lesser to greater—rising, or from greater to lesser —falling, or remains unchanged—level. For these three the terms *crescent, minuent, constant* are proposed.

The treatment of pitch or tonal phenomena on the two levels of intensity and contour is most familiar, and we shall take them up first.

Intensity of tone is manifested as relative height of pitch: maximal intensity is *high* tone, minimal intensity is *low* tone, medial intensity is *middle* tone. In specific descriptions, it may be necessary to subdivide middle tone into several types—higher middle, lower middle, etc.

Tone contour is described thus: crescent contour is *rising* tone, minuent contour is *falling* tone, constant contour is *level* tone.

The basic intensities and contours may be combined in several ways. Combinations of intensities give the following six possibilities: high to middle, high to low, middle to low— falling contours; middle to high, low to middle, low to high—rising contours. Combinations of contours are also six: rising-level, rising-falling, level-falling, level-rising, falling-level, falling-rising. The combinations of contour and intensity are nine: high rising, high level, high falling; middle rising, middle level, middle falling; low rising, low level, low falling. Combinations of more than two elements are also possible.

Turning now to stress, we note that from the point of view of intensity the usual descriptions are fairly adequate. Stress intensity is manifested as relative loudness. Maximal intensity is *loud* stress, medial intensity may be called *medium* stress, or the term *quiet* may be used, and minimal intensity is *soft* stress; if the last two terms are thought to be too much alike to prevent confusion, *quiet* should be the one left out. The usual terminology, which calls loud stress the main stress, quiet stress the secondary one, and soft stress a lack of stress, is objectionable first because it evaluates instead of merely describing, and second because of the negative character of the term *unstressed*. So far, so good.

But what of stress contour? Indeed, is there such a thing? A moment's consideration will show that there are certainly no theoretical reasons why there should not be. A stress that varies in intensity from loud to soft is minuent, one that goes from soft to loud is crescent, one that remains unchanged in loudness is constant. Such stress types are certainly describable on the phonetic level; and the recognition of their existence leads to the possibility of correct phonemic description of phenomena otherwise very confusing and confused (see below). It is possible to supply a special set of terms for stress contours, such as *levant*, *cadent*, *sustained;* but, while it may be theoretically desirable to have these terms, so that it may be instantly apparent that one is speaking of stress, on the practical plane it is perfectly possible to get along without them, and to use the terms rising, falling, level for stress as well as tone.

Combinations of stress intensity and stress contour are possible, and theoretically there will be sets exactly parallel to those for tone, namely: loud to quiet, loud to soft, quiet to loud, quiet to soft, soft to loud, soft to quiet; rising-level, rising-falling, level-falling, level-rising, falling-level, falling-rising; loud-rising, loud-level, loud-falling, quiet-rising, quiet-level, quiet-falling, soft-rising, soft-level, soft-falling.

This brings us to the third type of exponential entity, length or quantity. It is customary to deal with length as a characteristic of successive sounds; a consideration of the matter, however, leads to the conclusion that the length of a successive sound is something exponential to it in the same way as its pitch or its loudness. Thus quantity is at least in this respect parallel to the other two types of exponentials.

Maximal intensity of quantity may be labeled *long;* minimal intensity is *short*. Medial intensity should be provided with a special term, as has been done for tone and stress. I suggest *centric*, but realize that there is no tradition whatsoever for such a term; *medial*, *medium*, or *middle* might any one of them be used, the following word *quantity* being sufficient to avoid all ambiguity.

The next point in our exposition should be a consideration of quantity contours. Quantity involves the passage of time, and the question immediately arises whether the passage of time can have varying contours. The objective answer may be no, time passes at a uniform rate; subjectively, we all know that time may appear to pass slowly or rapidly. But it seems to me that neither of these answers, non-linguistic as they are, has any bearing on our problem. What we are concerned with is not only the elapsed time during which a linguistic entity, a successive sound, is pronounced, but also the rate of speed with which a given amount of such entity may be uttered. The elapsed time is what we have described as the intensity of quantity. The rate of speed and its change or stability seems then to be the contour of quantity. Here it must be emphasized that we are dealing with a linguistic systematization; a linguistically long sound may be pronounced very rapidly or very slowly; in the first case the contour is rising—the intensity increases, so as to get to the end rapidly, as it were; in the second, the contour is falling, intensity decreases, there is no hurry. I suggest the term *staccato* for "rising" quantity, *normal* for "level" quantity, and *drawling* for "falling" quantity. In any case, whatever may be thought of the accuracy of such description on a phonetic level, there is no doubt that phonemically there are quantitative phenomena that function as contours; they can best be discussed below.

Quantity, then, seems to be exactly parallel to stress and tone as a linguistic system,

but the manifestations of its contour, because of the medium of measurement, may be difficult to seize accurately.

It appears from the descriptive data available for some languages that besides the phenomena described there are others which may systematize as exponential. On the phonetic
level, it is hard to say just how one can consider glottalization, let us say, as exponential
rather than successive, when it is manifested as a clear glottal stop; but when it is rather a
glottal affection of a syllable or some part of it, then we can indeed see that it may be exponential. It is suggested that any secondary phonetic character—such as glottalization,
nasalization, labialization, retroflexion, "throatiness," "weight," etc.—may conceivably
function as an exponential in a given language. But it seems most likely that such functioning can become truly apparent only on the phonemic level, and we may leave consideration
of it until later.

To return to our three clear types of exponentials, it must be emphasized that linguistically relevant are the descriptions of their intensities and contours and the possible combinations of these, in terms of the types listed. Nothing else is linguistically important. In
the description of a given language on the phonetic level, it would appear that all three types
of exponentials are present, whatever the language; in English, we may describe a word such
as *bead* as having a long vowel in contrast with *beat*, and may list all the vowels as long, or
short, or of several intermediate quantities; we may say that *blacker* has loud stress on the
first syllable and soft stress on the second, while *blackbird* has loud on the first but quiet
on the second, and the third syllables of both *dormitory* and *dormer window* have two different kinds of quiet or medium stress, and so on to describe all the stresses as loud or soft or
quiet; and then we may note that *protest* as a noun is pronounced (in isolation) with falling
pitch, while the corresponding verb has rising pitch, there being in each word a higher tone
on the loud-stressed syllable than on the soft-stressed one. In all such descriptions, the statement that, as for instance in Navaho, there are no marked differences in stress (i.e., all
stresses are level), is just as important as the recording of the differences in English; and
the same holds for quantity and tone.

We are now ready to consider the phonemic analysis of accents as defined above, on the
basis of the phonetic set-up given on p. 133 ff. The lack of a good theoretical approach to
accentuation has been one of the greatest drawbacks to sound phonemic description of
languages. For it is often impossible to arrive at a correct phonemic analysis of the segmental
phonemes without first correctly describing the accents. Indeed, it seems theoretically desirable to describe the syllabic theory and the prosodemes first in all cases, before proceeding
to the segmental phonemes.

In dealing with the phenomena of tone, stress, and quantity, it is on the phonemic level
that the value of the approach on the basis of linguistic systematization is most evident.
It is the question of how a particular exponential phenomenon functions that needs to be
answered; and it is only by a consideration of system that the prosodic character of certain
phonological entities can be recognized.

Analysis begins with the recording of the distribution of the several kinds of exponentials found to occur with the syllables of the language; in many cases it will be found that an element smaller than the phonetic syllable functions as the accentual or prosodic unit; this unit may be called, following current practise, the mora. But it is suggested that the phonetic and phonemic syllables need not be the same at all, and that the phonemic syllable may be defined as containing one nuclear phoneme; in that case, a "long vowel" or "diph-thong" which is phonemically composed of two nuclear phonemes (vowels) is distributed over two phonemic syllables, and the prosodic system, if any, is described in terms of the unit phonemic syllable, and not of the non-unitary phonetic syllable. The term *mora*, how-ever, is useful in avoiding confusion, even if it should turn out to mean merely phonemic syllable.

The presence of a tone system is disclosed by the fact that the phonetic differences of tone, recorded on the basis of the analysis given above, cannot be shown to depend *entirely* on other factors; even if a partial dependence can be shown, tone must be described as phonemic if any occurrences—no matter how few—are non-conditioned.

The description must state whether the tone system is based on differences of intensity (register differences) or on differences of contour, or on both. An intensity system of tone may have two registers, which are then, for that system, high and low; or there may be three—high, middle, low; if there are more than three, the highest is high, the lowest low, the others various types of middle tone. In an intensity tone system, there are very often subsidiary differences of contour, but these are most likely to be due to juxtaposition of moras with different tone levels. Thus in Navaho[3] there are two basic tones, high and low; these occur with "short" vowels, "long" vowels, and "diphthongs;" but long vowels and diphthongs may also have rising (low-high) and falling (high-low) tones; it is clear that these phonetic long vowels and diphthongs are phonemically composed of two units, that each such unit is a mora (or phonemic syllable), and that the correct statement for Navaho is that there are only two tones, which are two intensities, and that when two vowels adjoin each other in the allowable vowel clusters each may have its own tone, resulting in a compound tone over the cluster as a whole. Systems of the Navaho type, with two or three registers, seem to be widespread.

A tone system may, however, consist of differences in contour, with or without sub-sidiary register differences. The Mandarin Chinese tone system is one of contours: high rising, low rising with accompanying length, falling, level; the high and low rising differ in register, it is true, but they differ chiefly in contour, the low being really a falling-rising tone. In the Chekiang Dang-si dialect[4] there are four tones: if the syllable begins with a consonant of a certain kind (voiceless stop and spirant, palatal semivowel, and certain clus-ters of these) the tones are all on the high register—rising, falling, level, and "checked" (a short, jerky utterance with final glottal stop); syllables with initial nasal, liquid, and labial semivowel may have only level and falling tones, but also on the high register; syllables with

---

[3] Data from Edward Sapir, in a seminar on Navaho attended in 1936–37.

[4] Data from G. A. Kennedy of Yale University.

initial voiced stop or initial sonorant with pharyngalization (these initials are probably phonemically consonant clusters) have tones on the low register, there being only the rising, falling, and checked contours; in this system, as apparently in most Chinese dialects, the register is entirely conditioned, and the contour is basic; one of the tones, also, the checked, involves another phonetic element than tone; see below.

In many intensity systems with more than three registers, or in contour systems with more than the three basic contours, the tones other than those describable by the basic formulas are likely to involve some other, non-tonal entity which functions in the total pattern as a tone: it may be quantity, or stress, or "weight" and "throatiness;"[5] cf. below.

A stress system is present when the variations in stress of syllables cannot be explained by limiting conditions. Thus in Spanish there are noted generally differences in pitch; but it is found that while usually the loud-stressed syllables have a higher pitch than others, this high pitch is not constant or essential, whereas the loud stress in contrast to soft stress is phonemic (*canto* "I sing" versus *cantó* "he sang").

In the description of stress systems the data for loud and soft stresses are usually fairly clear and can be simply stated; but it is important to emphasize that the "unstressed" syllables should be described by one of the terms of a contrast and not negatively; further, it is necessary to look for the possibility of soft stress occurring by itself, as it should be able to do theoretically if it is parallel to low tone; some speakers of English pronounce the adverb *just* with the vowel of the second syllable of *calloused* even when the word is stressed with heavy sentence stress, in contrast with the adjective *just*, and it seems more correct to say that the adverb always has soft stress than to posit two separate vowel phonemes. English may also furnish examples of words with two loud stresses; such may be the *-teen* numerals, one of the two loud stresses being phonetically actualized as a sort of middle stress depending on sentence sandhi.

More difficult problems arise, however, in the case of quiet (secondary) stresses. The situation in English is instructive (I use my own dialect, that of northern New Jersey): in compounds such as *blackbird*, the quiet stress on the second syllable is easily recognizable as phonemic (cf. *black bird*, two loud stresses); in *dormitory* the quiet stress on the third syllable (which is minimally quiet in comparison with the maximally quiet one of *blackbird*) is apparently conditioned by the presence of loud stress two syllables earlier. An examination of the distribution of the two kinds of quiet stress shows these facts: the maximal variety occurs only on those syllables of the subsidiary elements of compounds which are loud-stressed when the elements are used independently, and between the two or more elements of a compound there are always the same phonetic phenomena as between two independent words; the minimal quiet stress occurs only in unit words, on syllables containing the same kinds of vowels as occur with loud stress. The phonemic analysis is: the kind of sandhi found between words occurs in compounds also, but compounds are units

[5] This seems to be the case in Jabo (formerly called Gweabo); cf. Edward Sapir, *Notes on the Gweabo Language of Liberia* (Language, Vol. 7, pp. 30–41, 1931).

(super-words, perhaps, phonemically speaking) because of the accompanying stress change; there is one kind of quiet stress: it is actualized as maximal in the originally loud-stressed syllables of secondary elements of compounds, and as minimal in those cases where it occurs within unit words (in these cases being in part conditioned by the segmental phonemes and by distance from the loud stress); thus, *blackbird* is phonemically a super-word composed of two words with compounding sandhi, and differs in its stresses from *black bird; contents* is a unit word, stressed loud/quiet; *sand-content* is a compound of two elements, stressed loud-quiet/quiet, the two quiets being phonetically different, but this difference being conditioned by their position.[5a] An analysis of this kind is appropriate also to German and the other Germanic languages. In Spanish and Italian compounds are stressed like unit words of the same length, and there are no quiet stresses phonemically. In Russian there are five vowels that occur with loud stress, but only three with soft stress; in certain long (and somewhat learned) compounds and in a few really common words, also compounds, however, all of the five vowels may appear in a phonetically soft-stressed syllable, with the phonetic actualization found in loud-stressed syllables; these cases can be explained only by postulating a quiet or secondary stress in compounds, of the kind found in English, but actualized not as significantly louder stress than have soft-stressed syllables, but with full quality of the vowel.

The systems hitherto considered are based on stress intensity. Let us take up cases of stress contour. In literary Serbocroatian we find, in words of more than one syllable, these phonetic stress-phonemena: falling loud stress, on long or short vowel, limited to the first syllable of a word (monosyllables in isolation have the same kind of stress); level or (level-) rising loud stress on the penult or antepenult, with long or short vowel; soft stress always on the final syllable and on all other syllables not having one of the two kinds of loud stress, but in two varieties—level-falling following a level-rising loud, otherwise falling. There are pitch differences usually accompanying these stress differences, but they are not essential, and may vary greatly, while the stresses are determining and non-conditioned by pitch, length, or other factors. The phonemic stress system is obviously based on contour, with intensity secondary and conditioned, and is analyzed thus: a level or level-rising stress exists, actualized as loud, limited to penult or antepenult (thus not found in monosyllables); in contrast with this is a falling stress, which may occur on any syllable, and is actualized as loud on a monosyllable and on a first syllable if there is no rising stress in the word, and as soft on all syllables following the first if there is no rising stress and if there is a rising stress on all other syllables than that one. The usual descriptions of this system, calling the stresses "tones" and "intonations," miss the point that the element involved is stress, because they do not recognize the possibility of the existence of stress contours. Serbocroatian may also

---

[5a] Since this was written (1939) I have come to the conclusion that the reduced loud stress of subsidiary elements of compounds and the secondary stress here called minimally quiet must be regarded as separate phonemes, giving English a system of four stress intensities: loud, reduced loud, medial, weak. The proof of this must be left to another occasion.

have a quiet stress in compounds, but my material on that point is not extensive enough to be conclusive.[5b]

In Lithuanian on the phonetic level there is a falling loud stress that occurs on short and long vowels and diphthongs, a level-rising loud that does not occur with short vowels, and a soft that occurs only with short vowels (in the Kaunas pronunciation of literary Lithua-nian). But it is found on examination that the long vowels and diphthongs consist of two elements phonemically, so that the phonemic stress system is very simple: a loud stress that may occur on any vowel—whether alone, or the first or the second of a vowel cluster, or followed by a sonorant in the same syllable—and on a sonorant following a vowel in the same syllable; and a soft stress on all vowels in a word not having loud stress. This parallels the Navaho situation for tone, and is an intensity system, the contours being due to juxta-position.

In Norwegian and Swedish there is loud stress, quiet stress (as in English or German) and soft stress. Loud stress is of two kinds: rising, with accompanying low rising pitch, and falling, with accompanying falling-rising pitch; soft and quiet stresses have accompanying high pitch. The pitches are here very important, but the whole mechanism of the word is determined primarily by the distribution of stress, so that this is a stress system, with two contours of loud stress.

The phonemic analysis of quantity systems is more difficult than that of tone or stress systems.

First we must eliminate those cases where quantity is entirely conditioned by stress, tone, or the quality of the segmental phonemes. In standard French there is a long vowel, occurring in such words as tête, bête, and the like, which is phonemically different from the corresponding short vowel, occurring in il tette, dette, etc.; but the phonemic differences between all other French vowels are differences of quality, and other quantity differences are conditioned by position before certain final consonants; accordingly French has no prosodeme of quantity and the difference between the vowels of tette and tête is a segmental difference, though actualized principally as a length difference. In Spanish, Italian, Russian, and other languages, a loud-stressed vowel is longer than a soft-stressed one, but this is automatic; and, in these languages, and especially in Italian, a loud-stressed vowel in a free (open) syllable is longer than one in a checked (closed) syllable. In many languages certain vowels are regularly longer than others, regardless of position. In English, vowels are longest in free syllables, shorter before voiced consonants and voiceless spirants in checked syllables, and shortest before voiceless stops in checked syllables. In Taos[6] vowels are longer with low tone and shorter with high tone than they are with normal tone (see below, p. 143, for further details of this system).

Second, we must eliminate from our consideration most, if not all, cases of consonant

[5b] See now my article Serbo-Croatian Accents and Quantities (Language, Vol. 16, pp. 29–32, 1940).

[6] A Tanoan (Tiwa sub-family) language spoken by the Indians of Taos Pueblo, New Mexico; data gathered by me in field work during 1935–36 and the summer of 1937.

length. The consonants usually are not involved in prosodic functioning except as they de-limit the syllable or word, as the prosodeme is attached to the nuclear element (usually a vowel). Swadesh has described the various phonemic possibilities when long consonants are present.[7]

Let us now take up the several possibilities in connection with long vowels. If there are certain vowels that are long and others that are short, but there is no pattern correspondence between them as groups, then it would seem that there is no prosodeme of quantity, but merely differences between segmental phonemes; such is the case illustrated by French, above. The most common situation, however, is to have a set of short vowels paralleled by the same vowel qualities with long quantity; even if the parallelism is not complete, there is usually enough of it to establish the pattern. In these cases it is necessary to begin with the total prosodic situation before we can determine whether there is a prosodeme of quantity. If vowel clusters are found in the language, then it is likely that long vowels are simply geminate clusters; this is the case in Finnish and Estonian: Finnish has eight short vowel phonemes, and these occur in groups of two in all the clusters not excluded by the laws of vocalic harmony; the eight long vowels occur under the same conditions as other clusters, and are clearly geminates; Estonian has nine vowels, with the same freedom of combination. When there is a prosodic system of tone or stress that functions with long vowels as it does with diphthongs or other two-element groups, then it follows that the long vowels are also composed of two elements, and are either geminates or diphthongs of some kind; this is the case in Lithuanian (stress) or Navaho (tone).

When there is no indication in the general patterning that long vowels are either gemi-nates or diphthongs on the one hand, or simply inherently long segmental phonemes on the other, then we have prosodemes of quantity. In Serbocroatian both long and short vowels occur with both kinds of accents (falling, rising) and in any position in the word, except that long vowels may not occur before the rising stress; there is no possibility of regarding the long vowels as geminates, there being no other vowel clusters and no warrant for it in the stress system; nor does the pattern suggest ten independent vowel phonemes; there is then in Serbocroatian a prosodic system of two quantities, long and short, functioning inde-pendently from the other prosodic system of stress, though partially limited by it. In Nootka[8] there are five long vowels and five corresponding short vowels; there are no vowel clusters, and no other prosodic system, and the correct interpretation seems to be that there are five vowel phonemes with two quantities forming a prosodic system.

On the theoretical basis that we have been following, there seems to be no reason why there should not exist three phonemic intensities of quantity, just as such cases are found

[7] M. Swadesh, *The Phonemic Interpretation of Long Consonants* (Language, Vol. 13, pp. 1–10, 1937).

[8] Cf. Edward Sapir and Morris Swadesh, *Nootka Texts: Tales and Ethnological Narratives, with Grammatical Notes and Lexical Materials* (William Dwight Whitney Linguistic Series, Yale University, 1939), pp. 12–13.

for stress and tone. Hopi[9] seems to be an example, having phonemically distinct vowels that are short, medium, and long; the quantities cannot be explained by the intersecting stress system nor by segmental conditions.

It was stated above that contours of quantity exist, and that their existence is made clear by phonemic analysis. An example is Latvian (Lettish): here we find short vowels, three kinds of long vowels, and similarly three kinds of diphthongs; the short vowels have no prosodically outstanding characteristics phonetically, except that when initial they bear a loud stress; this loud stress, which is also found with initial long vowels and diphthongs, is non-phonemic. The three kinds of long vowels and diphthongs are currently described as having three "intonations," the falling, the prolonged (*Dehnton*), and the interrupted (*Stoßton*).[10] Phonetic observation of a large amount of Latvian material leads me to the conclusion that in these three "intonations" there are involved neither stress nor tone differences, but that the essence of them is quantity; phonetically, a long "falling" vowel is slightly pulsated (reduplicated), about this way, [aᵃ]; a vowel with the "prolonged intonation" is pulsated evenly, [aa]; an "interrupted" vowel is pulsated with a glottal catch after a relatively short beginning, [ă'a]; a diphthong like *ie* is, with the three "intonations," [iě], [ie·], [ĭ'e], and one like *al* is [al], [al·], [a'l]. Phonetically I should explain and describe the situation thus: a long or diphthongal syllabic nucleus may have, respectively, rising quantity (speed increasing, "staccato," at the end), or falling quantity (speed decreasing, "drawling," at the end), or rising-falling quantity (rapid speed at the beginning, interruption, resumption with falling quantity); only in terms of contours of quantity can a satisfactory description be made even phonetically. Phonemically the situation is simpler: it appears from the presence of diphthongs that the long vowels must also be two-element groups (geminate clusters in this case), and the total pattern bears this out; we must then set up two quantity contours, rising or staccato and falling or drawling; all "short" vowels have rising quantity (this is probable because of their clear-cut, clipped quality); "long" vowels and "diphthongs" are two-element groups with these quantity combinations: "falling" is falling quantity followed by rising; "prolonged" is two falling quantities; "interrupted" is rising followed by falling; the combination rising-rising does not occur. In other words, rising quantity appears on a vowel alone, on a vowel when followed by another vowel (including an identical vowel) or by a sonorant, and on a vowel or sonorant following a vowel with falling quantity; falling quantity occurs on a vowel followed by another vowel (including an identical vowel) or by a sonorant in the same syllable, the second element having either rising or falling quantity.

In Estonian[11] there appears to be a similar situation, except that falling quantity may appear on any consonant following a vowel in the same syllable, and the phonetic actualizations are not exactly the same.

---

[9] Data from B. L. Whorf.   [10] Cf. J. Endzelin, *Lettische Grammatik* (Riga, 1922), pp. 22 ff.

[11] Data from P. Ariste of the Archives of the Estonian Language in Tartu.

These two cases suggest that where there are prosodic entities that are not clearly tonal or stress qualities, but partake of the nature of quantities, the description is to be sought in terms of quantity contours.

Besides systems of tones, stresses, and quantities, there seem to be in some languages prosodic systems based on other phonological contrasts and relations. The character of the entities involved can usually be recognized as prosodic on the basis of the total patterning and by consideration of the characteristics of true prosodic systems.

A well-known example is Danish: there are in Danish loud-stressed, quiet-stressed, and soft-stressed syllables, as in other Germanic languages, and, as in Norwegian and Swedish, the loud-stressed are of two kinds; but the difference depends not on stress contour and accompanying pitch differences, but on the difference between syllables with glottalization and those without it. The glottalization is actualized as a glottal stop at some point in the syllable (according to the segmental phonemes involved); thus what is at first glance a seg-mental phoneme is found to function as a prosodeme because its patterning is like that of the other prosodic features and not like that of any other consonant.

A similar situation is found in Mixteco;[12] here there is a system of tone intensity, with three registers—high, middle, low; the tones of the two-syllable (two-mora) word-units are subject to a complex system of sandhi. Certain first syllables of a two-syllable group ap-pear with glottal stop following the vowel, and two-mora groups without medial conso-nants (i.e., those with a "long" vowel) may have glottal affection of the whole of the syl-labic nucleus. The glottal stop may appear before a medial consonant only when it is a voiced consonant, but voiced consonants also appear directly after a vowel. So far the glottal stop appears to be merely a segmental phoneme of a peculiar type; but examination of the tone-sandhi behavior of elements containing it shows that it functions as a special prosodic type. The conclusion is that Mixteco has a second prosodic system having glottalization versus non-glottalization as its contrasting features; this system is distributionally more limited than the tone system.

From Sapir's description of Jabo (above) it appears that beside the tone system Jabo has another prosodic system involving relative "weight" and "throatiness" of a syllable, with four or perhaps even five degrees.

In the Chinese Dang-si dialect mentioned, one of the four entities in the prosodic system is actually not a tone, as are the others, but involves glottalization; here there is only one prosodic system, but not all its elements are phonetically of the same type.

It is suggested that other languages with peculiar phonetic features that seem to apply to syllables as wholes be examined in the light of the prosodic theories here offered. The noting of other kinds of prosodemes than those involving tone, stress, and quantity may help to test the correctness of the theories and of the analyses based on them.

After the examination of the general basis of linguistic analysis, and the specific types of patterning involved in the analysis of accentual systems, we can proceed to certain generalizations.

[12] Spoken in southern Oaxaca, Mexico; data from Kenneth L. Pike.

The first generalization is that it appears certain that prosodic systems, on both the phonetic and phonemic levels, are configurational patterns of the same kind as all other linguistic systems.

Further, it appears that at least the three kinds of prosodic systems known as tone, stress, and quantity systems are exactly parallel not only in the general outline of their functioning but also in the very detail of the pattern. This is a very important thing to know, as it definitely unites the prosodemes of a language into one system or series of systems, and it removes the analysis of prosodic entities from non-linguistic fields into the realm of configurational linguistics. Beyond the three main types of prosodemes, it appears that others may exist and function in the same way. We may have here the outlines of the basic pattern of all prosodemes as opposed to segmental phonemes.

It has already been shown from the material above that on the phonetic level all three main types of exponentials may be recorded and analyzed as existing together. Phonemically, one type of prosodeme is usually predominant, but some of the examples cited show two prosodic systems. The question arises as to how many prosodic systems a language may have.

A few examples will be given before answering. In the Taos language, there are two systems: a tone system with three registers, high, middle ("normal" in the economy of the Taos system), and low; then there is an intercrossing system of stress—loud, quiet, and soft. The combinations possible result in seven kinds of syllables: loud high, loud middle, loud low; quiet high, quiet middle, quiet low; and soft middle, the quiet syllables of all three types occur in subsidiary elements of compounds according to complicated rules not yet entirely worked out; each word has one loud syllable, which may be on any tone, any number of quiet syllables (though rarely more than two), and any number of soft syllables (though rarely for a total of more than eight syllables in a word, with few of more than four). The two systems are clearly separate, and the tone system is subordinate to the stress system.

In Norwegian and Swedish there may be two accentual systems. The stress system has been described. Besides this there may be a quantity system: the nucleus of a loud- or quiet-stressed syllable is either long or short; but the total length of the syllable is always the same, so that if the nucleus is short there must be a following consonant, which is phonetically long, and if the nucleus is long the following consonant, if any, is phonetically short. This quantity system is found also in Danish. In all three languages the nucleus may contain a diphthong of a limited number of types. The presence of these more or less anomalous diphthongs suggests the possibility that the seemingly long vowels may really be clusters, in which case there would be no quantity system, but only a stress system.[12a]

Many languages can be named with one accentual system: English, Spanish, Italian, Russian, have stress systems; standard Chinese, Navaho, and many other American Indian

[12a] At present (1941) I believe that the Scandinavian languages have indeed no quantity system, the "long" vowels being short vowels plus a semivowel which is a segmental phoneme. A similar analysis can be made for English, German, and Dutch. I intend to publish elsewhere the material bearing on this.

languages, have tone systems; Latin, Nootka, Czech, Hungarian, have quantity systems.

Besides the examples already given, there are many languages with two prosodic systems: German possibly with stress and quantity (but here, as for Scandinavian, the "long" vowels are probably clusters, leaving only one system), Serbocroatian with stress and quantity, Jabo with tone and "weight."

Many languages have no prosodic system of accents: French, Polish, Turkish are examples.

But of all the languages known to the author or his colleagues with whom he has discussed the matter there is none which has three or more accentual systems; in Swedish, for instance, stress and pitch form only one system, with quantity, if it exists, as a second. This leads to the following generalization, which may be accepted as a working hypothesis until and unless contrary evidence is adduced:

A language may have phonemically no or one accentual system, of any type, or it may have two accentual systems, of any two types and intercrossing in every possible way, but it may not have more than two such systems.

The problem of intonations or the prosodic-like phenomena of phrases and sentences cannot be taken up here, for lack of space and because there is very little trustworthy evidence on the subject. It is believed, however, that a technique similar to that proposed for accents can be used, and that the essential differences will not be great.

In English a sentence may show as many as five or six degrees of stress. It is suggested that these be looked upon as superposed on and separate from the three word stresses; and it is not unlikely that they can be reduced to a few clear types of relations to the word stresses. English also uses tones for sentence distinctions, and even perhaps quantities. The data must be carefully gathered before generalizations can be made. But it is beyond any doubt that intonations will be found to configurate just as do all other parts of linguistic systems.

One problem posed by the kind of techniques and analyses here presented is that of terminology. The general terms proposed are not the first which came to mind, nor are all of them even now considered wholly satisfactory. I may mention specifically the terms *centric*, *staccato*, *normal*, *drawling*, as applied to quantity, and the general term *intensity;* for the latter *concentration* might be a substitute. But even when an entirely acceptable and accepted terminology exists in one language, there is still the problem of translation into other languages. The author has submitted partial lists of translations of the terms here used into French, German, Spanish, Italian, and Russian to various colleagues; the criticism has been generous and has been such as to indicate that with the collaboration of linguists to whom those, and other, languages are native the creation of a standardized vocabulary for the technique of prosodic description, as well as other linguistic tasks, is not at all hopeless or impossible. It may be noted here that translations for *stress* and for *pattern* are the hardest to find. Beyond this we cannot go now, except to hope that others will be stimulated to take up the task.

And in conclusion it is my hope that the testing of the theories and techniques here pro-pounded may be soon undertaken by many colleagues and for many languages.[13]

YALE UNIVERSITY
NEW HAVEN, CONNECTICUT

[13] This paper is based upon many sources. The factual data, where not specifically acknowledged and identi-fied as to source, come from printed works, my own linguistic experience, and conversations and discussions with many colleagues. The theories are my own, and I assume all responsibility for them, but they have grown, of course, out of all the linguistic contacts I have had, including many discussions by correspondence and in con-versation. I wish specifically to mention a few who have been helpful directly or indirectly in this work: Edward Sapir before his death, Morris Swadesh, Mary Haas, Charles Hockett, John Kepke, B. L. Whorf, Bernard Bloch, Hans Vogt; and to thank them and all others who have at any time discussed linguistic problems with me.

THREE TYPES OF VARIATION AND THEIR RELATION TO CULTURE CHANGE

By MORRIS EDWARD OPLER

EDWARD SAPIR knew that the size of the canvas was not the only criterion of a painter's merit. It was his peculiar ability to demonstrate a theoretical point within a limited frame of reference so deftly and aptly that many of his shorter papers became the gateway to inspiration and research for others. To draw upon his method is not to command his gifts and his magic. Yet in a book dedicated to his memory I have felt emboldened to attempt an expression within the modest dimensions of a problem in mythology of those techniques and interests which he so vividly impressed upon me—the comparison of materials, the determination of the meanings of variations, the dynamic significance of the individual human personality.

The most important single myth of the Chiricahua Apache Indians is the one which has to do with the birth and the exploits of the culture hero, Child of the Water.[1] During the period 1930–35 this myth was recorded in whole or in part no less than eight times from seven different Chiricahua informants.[2] The first of these versions was told to Dr Harry Hoijer in the summer of 1930 while he was engaged in linguistic research at Mescalero, New Mexico. This text and translation have already been published.[3] Between the years 1931 and 1935 I obtained three variants, two of which are to be published in a forthcoming volume of Chiricahua mythology. The remaining four versions have been contributed by members of the 1931 summer field party of the Laboratory of Anthropology of Santa Fé which worked at Mescalero under the direction of Dr Ruth F. Benedict.

The gathering of so many examples of the same story may seem an unnecessary duplication of time and effort. To a degree the duplication was intentional and dictated by an ethnological problem. The Chiricahua were divided into three well-defined bands. One of them differed from the others in some traits of material culture. It became important to determine whether band differences were likewise present in regard to non-material elements; therefore, test cases in the realm of mythology, social organization, etc., were set up. Except for the few modifications in material culture, evidently recent, the tribe was found to be a unit.

---

[1] The field work which provided the material for this study was carried on under the auspices of the Laboratory of Anthropology of Santa Fé, the Southwest Society, the University of Chicago, the Social Science Research Council, the National Research Council, and the Council for Research in the Social Sciences of Columbia University. Supplementary materials were provided by Dr Jules Henry, Dr John Gillin, and Dr Regina Flannery.

[2] The myth was obtained twice from the same man by two different field workers. These two recordings parallel each other in order of events and in details, suggesting a consistent rendition for any one informant.

[3] Harry Hoijer, *Chiricahua and Mescalero Apache Texts* (University of Chicago Publications in Anthropology, Linguistic Series, 1938), pp. 5–14.

But the ease with which such a series of overlapping accounts of the culture hero story has been assembled derives from other circumstances as well. Not all Chiricahua myths may be told by any person at any time. Many Chiricahua fear to talk freely about certain mountain-dwelling supernaturals. They feel that the myths which have to do with these beings are best recounted by those who have obtained power and ceremony from them. The story which explains the coming of daylight may be recited only during the winter and at night. The same is true of the coyote trickster cycle.

In spite of its significance and in contrast to these other legends, the narrative of the culture hero may be told at any time of the year and by any competent adult without fear of untoward consequences. Since many customs, observances, and possessions are rationalized in terms of this myth, discussion of the origin or import of these ethnographic elements is likely to result in an offer to relate this particular account. When a number of field workers are in touch with different informants, it is not difficult to see how accumulations at this point are likely to arise.

Because I continued field work among the Chiricahua Apache after my companions of the 1931 field party had turned their attention to other specialized tasks, the results of their work have been passed on to me for use in a general statement concerning Chiricahua culture now in preparation. A close examination of the combined information relating to the hero myth thus made available indicates that one basic pattern is involved. It also shows, however, that the versions of no two informants are precisely alike. There are differences of detail and emphasis, differences even in the numbers and attributes of the protagonists.

It is by no means unusual in the annals of anthropology for a field worker or several of them to obtain multiple examples of a single story. Ordinarily, when this happens, the best (which usually means the most detailed) of the versions is published and others are used for footnote data or are laid aside. Sometimes variants are appended without much comment. But by the time the task of organizing the mythology fell to me, a prolonged stay among the Chiricahua had made possible a closer acquaintance with a number of the narrators of these culture hero stories. As a result of work with them, autobiographical accounts from them, the testimony of others concerning them, and from such observations of their respective roles in family and tribal life as could be made, a rather vivid impression of the personalities and interests of most of these informants emerged.

Accordingly, when I came to compare the several versions of the story in the light of more comprehensive knowledge of the culture and of the individuals involved, I found that I could not dismiss the variations in the recitals as so many examples of chance divergence. The pictures of the informants, their roles in the society, and their conceptions of themselves were ever before me, and I was overwhelmed time and again by the feeling that these factors were not unrelated to the differentiations of the myths. As a result of this uneasiness and this challenge for a less superficial survey I have analyzed the set of myths further, with greater attention to the nature of the variations. It would take too much space to reproduce all of the myths and to force the reader to retrace with me all the steps of the examination.

All that can be offered in a short article are some of the examples that particularly stimulated the train of thought and a statement of the conclusions and theoretical position to which they have led.

It appears that the variations in the hero myths when they are viewed comparatively are not all of the same kind. The differences fall, in terms of the forces by which they are determined or stimulated, into three main types. There are those modifications which do not seem to derive from the necessities or history of the culture or from idiosyncrasies of the raconteur. These may, therefore, be considered, at least until evidence to the contrary is forthcoming, to be chance or fortuitous variations. Secondly, there are those deviations which may be interpreted as a response to culture change and the pressures exerted upon the culture. Finally, there are those divergences which are apparently induced by the predominating interests and personality of the narrator himself and which are, in a last analysis, explicable in no other way.

That the constant repetition of an exoteric tale over a sufficiently long period of time may lead to variation has been long recognized. That culture change and culture history may be reflected in mythology has likewise been accepted for many years; as a matter of fact, it is an approach which has more than once been abused. It is the evidence for the correlation of personality differences with the myth variations that seems of particular moment, for scant attention has been paid, so far as I am aware, to this extremely interesting and theoretically important facet.

The legend of the birth and adventures of the culture hero is a tribal tradition. It is not, as so many Chiricahua tales are, connected with the personal supernatural power or prerogatives of any individual. It is not more intimately associated with one family or segment of the tribe than another. In short, it is the common property of all tribesmen equally. Theoretically there are no "versions" of the myth. The myth ideally represents an authentic and indisputable account of events which occurred "in the beginning" and concerning which there is no room for conflicting viewpoints.

In outline the myth is reasonably similar in all versions. In the beginning destructive monsters exist in the world and prevent human beings from increasing. White Painted Woman, the culture heroine, allows herself to be impregnated by water during a thunder storm, and a boy named Child of the Water is born to her. She secretes him in a hole under the fire place and thus saves him from Giant, the first of the monsters to appear. When he is grown enough, Child of the Water goes out hunting with Killer of Enemies, a mythological figure whose unsettled position in the stories will receive attention later. In the course of the hunt a deer is slain and the pair make ready to butcher the kill and prepare some of the meat. No sooner has some meat been broiled than Giant arrives and snatches it. Child of the Water retrieves it, angry words and finally a challenge to battle pass between the monster and the hero. The monster shoots four enormous arrows at the hero, who escapes unscathed. The hero then sends his four arrows at Giant, each time piercing a coat of flint and inflicting a fatal wound with the final missile. The giant falls over four ridges and his flint armor is scattered over the area. During the contest Killer of Enemies, who has been terror-ized by Giant during previous hunting expeditions, remains inactive and frightened. After the victory the two return to White Painted Woman who sings and dances with joy at the news.

The next monster which Child of the Water seeks to destroy is a great bull who lies out in an open plain where no one can come near him with impunity. With the aid of Gopher, who digs four tunnels to the beast, the hero is able to approach and shoot this creature through the heart.

Now follows the adventure with the monster eagles. Child of the Water wraps the blood-filled entrails of the slain bull about him and ventures out to a place where he knows the eagles will sight him. One of them sweeps down, lifts him up, and carries him to the high rock on which the nest is built. The eagle assumes that the blood which gushes from the torn bull entrails is a proof that its victim is fatally wounded. The monster urges the eaglets to dine on the kill and leaves. From the little ones Child of the Water learns when the parent birds usually return to the nest and where they sit. He lies in wait and strikes and kills the monster birds when they appear. Then he treats all but the youngest child in similar fashion. He rides to the ground on the back of this eaglet. From the feathers of the eagles he creates the birds of today.

There is less unanimity concerning the identity of the next monster which Child of the Water dispatches. In most versions it is a monster antelope which the culture hero now challenges. This enemy stands out in an open place and looks for smoke or signs of humanity. When it sights a human being it runs to that place and destroys him. Child of the Water shoots arrows to each of the cardinal points in clockwise order, and appropriately colored smoke arises at the spot where each arrow falls. Each time the smoke is seen, the monster runs toward it to determine the cause. By the end of the fourth run it is so exhausted that it is easily conquered by the hero.

Some versions substitute a contest with an animal or evil man who kills with his eyes for the episode of the antelope. In other accounts both of these incidents are retained. When it is an animal that is named as the monster that kills with its eyes, it is the prairie-dog that is designated. Again the problem of the hero is to approach this monster with impunity. This time it is Lizard who assists Child of the Water by lending him his earth-colored coat so that he can advance without detection. The culture hero follows this foe into his hole or home and finds a family of these creatures around the fire. He bids them gaze into the fire and throws salt into the flames. They are blinded by the ensuing explosion and the hero either destroys their power for evil or slays them.

The outline just concluded is the essential core of the story as it emerges in most ver-sions. What then are the variations to which reference has been made and what are their implications? The first series of variations to which I would call attention is that which I have labeled chance or fortuitous. For the most part they are modifications which do not add much to, or subtract much from, the more common version, though they may take the form of an elaboration of some theme previously announced. They grow from the handling and rehandling of the materials of the myth itself, and not from some deep-seated necessity inherent in the culture or in the personality set of the narrator.

Very often variations of this type are little more than a substitution of roughly equivalent elements. Thus, according to most versions, White Painted Woman is impregnated when water enters her vagina. In a single variant, the water is said to enter her navel, however. The difference in mode of impregnation does not seem to be important for the events which follow in the respective stories, and, although some psychiatrists might not be satisfied with the equivalence, I consider these to be, for the purpose of the mythology, comparable methods of catapulting the culture hero into the world.

When the culture hero returns from his first and subsequent triumphs, his mother greets him with dancing and song. In a number of versions the words which she utters are given, and they are different in each case. "What a happy day it is to be bringing in such good news, my grandson," is one form that the song is supposed to have taken. "I am happy now. You have done me a great favor," is the rendition of another informant. Still another interpretation has White Painted Woman chant, "My son, that is good." We are little perturbed by these differences. These expressions of pleasure are alike enough in spirit and import to preserve the essential unity of the episode.

Another of these equivalent substitutions occurs in a variant of the killing of the last monster (the prairie-dog or man who kills with his eyes). In most of the accounts Lizard makes possible the undetected advance and victory by the loan of his coat to the hero. In one version, however, the lizard accompanies Child of the Water and falls flat upon him every time the monster is about to sight him. This is the kind of ingenious change which may well result from playing with a theme without taking drastic liberties in respect to it. The essential ideas of help from the lizard and the utilization of his coat for concealment are retained. The shift from one formal device for employing the help of the lizard to another makes no great difference in the flow of action and conception.

Another kind of variation which belongs essentially to the same type is that which results from a mechanical adjustment of the parts of the story. In most of the myths the bull is slain before the monster eagles. This permits the entrails of the bull to be used in the eagle episode as described in the story outline. But in one version the hero dispatches the eagles before the contest with the bull. Consequently, in order to obtain entrails with which to deceive the eagle, a special deer hunt has to be interpolated.

Still another technique which might well be expected as a natural consequence of the repetition of common mythic material is the greater emphasis of themes already enunciated. Thus, in one version and one only, the hero, when it is Giant's turn to stand and await the arrows of his opponent, bids him fall on his hands and knees that he may better aim at his heart. This is simply a reminder of a point made before, the enormous size of the monster. Again, after the return of Child of the Water from his victory over the monster eagles, White Painted Woman, it is recounted in one narrative only, holds her son on her lap as an expression of joy. This too is but the stressing of a theme which is otherwise indicated in all versions—the extreme youth and small size of the hero in comparison with his gigantic and adult foes.

Many modifications which can be viewed as a consequence of continual preoccupation with the same basic material and therefore fall under our first rubric of chance or fortuitous variation are a matter of elaboration. A good instance of how a theme will be carried along in terms of elaboration is the deception of the giant by the hero's mother. In all the versions the infant Child of the Water is hidden under a hearth in order to confound the suspicious and watchful giant. In three versions the giant discovers a baby's tracks around the camp and is only mollified when White Painted Woman convinces him that she has been lonely for a child and has made the tracks herself (with the side of her hand and her fingers.) Two accounts add to these others a further strategem of the mother. When the giant sees some brown matter which he rightly interprets as a child's excrement, the woman assures him it is nothing more than wild honey from the sotol stalk. One informant referred to all these other devices for shielding the boy and told, in addition, how White Painted Woman saves her child when the giant arrives in time to hear him cry. She persuades the monster that she herself has been imitating the wailing of a baby because of her loneliness and desire to have a child.

Another instance of such elaboration occurs in connection with the episode which ends in the death of the monster bull. In all versions but one it is Gopher alone who helps the hero slay this monster. In these more typical presentations Lizard figures only in a later adventure, usually in connection with the slaying of the prairie-dog or man who kills with his eyes. But in the one variant which is atypical in this regard, both Lizard and Gopher act to help the hero subdue the bull. The lizard lends his coat and helps the hero gain a position near the monster; the gopher digs the tunnels that make possible the fatal wound and the escape. It is clear that the introduction of the lizard at this point is an elaboration based on the analogy with the later episode. It is important to remember that this, too, is merely the greater elaboration of materials already given in the myth and does not express a novel or truly creative development.

A refinement with which an informant embellished the account of the fate of the bull is of much the same character. In this account the bull falls over four hills, and the white flint which covered him is said to be visible today where he fell. It is not difficult to recognize in this a repetition in a second context of elements we have already noted in connection with the destruction of the giant.

Another further elaboration has to do with the blinding of the last monsters of some of the versions, the prairie-dogs or people who kill with their eyes. Wherever this event is included, the monsters are blinded when the hero throws salt into the fire around which they are clustering. In a single variant, however, a pan of blood is tossed into the flames with the salt. We may guess that this addition was inspired by the observation that the juices of broiling meat, as they fall into the fire, cause a sputtering and flaring not unlike that induced by salt in the flames. Here also, then, the elaboration is suggested by an extension of elements and ideas already present in the myth.

Not all change of this first type is in the interests of greater elaboration. The reassembling of the given materials may lead to condensation as well. An example of such variation through condensation marks one myth version, which includes an encounter with the monster antelope but which lacks any episode involving a fifth monster, the prairie-dog or one who kills with his eyes. Yet, in the story, we do find a telescoping of the elements ordinarily found in both of these incidents. The usual device of running the antelope to exhaustion by shooting "smoke arrows" is retained, but it is Lizard, whose assistance is ordinarily limited to the prairie-dog incident, who steals forward to shoot the arrows, because he is brown like the ground and invisible to the monster.

To sum up our impressions of variations of this first type we may say that they include those departures which result, as far as can be determined, from a re-shuffling of elements which are already given in the myth or which are a logical extension, reduplication, or condensation of such elements. To effect such modifications the narrator does not have to draw heavily from his own proclivities or from the reservoir of subsidiary concepts and materials which his culture provides. The processes by which these modifications are brought about permit the raconteur to be different without being drastically original. They vary the content of the story without significantly changing its direction.

A second group of divergences from the norm in the recounting of this myth by the several informants appears to be stimulated, not by any statistical necessity arising from the manipulation of elements already a part of the myth, nor by any preoccupation with the building blocks which are a recognized part of the legend, but by the dynamic and surging background of culture which seeks expression and affirmation. The classical exposition of the tale is studded with such culturally induced or rationalizing bits. For instance, in all complete versions of the story, the culture hero is provided with arrows of grama grass for his duel with the giant. Thus is explained the origin of the widespread ceremonial use of grama grass. This element of the ritual complex, we may say, has been thoroughly rationalized and socialized in the myth.

A number of variations show a straining after these same ends. According to one storyteller, Child of the Water, during his contest with Giant, turned sunwise to another direction each time the monster directed an arrow at him. From the hero's procedure the informant derives the clockwise circuit of the Chiricahua. No other version includes this particular act or this rationalization. Yet it is not difficult to see how an alteration such as this, so well supported by general usage and so congenial to the sensibilities of the listener, might gain currency and become an established and conventional part of the myth, finally appearing in all or almost all versions.

Another provocative instance of the same mechanism at work has to do with the greeting accorded the hero by his mother upon his return from the battle with the giant. All versions have her singing and dancing for joy; in addition one variant describes a long, high-pitched call of pleasure and applause which she utters. This, it is said by the informant, is the first time the cry is sounded on earth, and it provides the prototype for a similar utterance of women today. From a cultural point of view this cry is as valid an expression of rejoicing as the other reactions described. Certainly this must have been the feeling of the narrator who inserted it in his version. To date the contribution has not become current and may never become so, but the tapping of the cultural forms for this addition is an arresting example of a process which must have left its mark upon the mythology many times.

If the background of culture constantly knocks at the gate of the mythology, seeking greater recognition and admission, we may expect that changes in culture and the most significant perplexities of culture will likewise be registered in the legends. The treatment of the mythological figure, Killer of Enemies, is a case in point. For most Apachean[4] speaking tribes of the Southwest he is the culture hero and is credited with the accomplishments which the Chiricahua attribute to Child of the Water. All of the Chiricahua narrators have made the adjustment to the changed point of view, at least in the large; in all versions Child of the Water has become the heroic personage and Killer of Enemies is decidedly secondary and subordinate. But the exact status and role of Killer of Enemies is anything but uniform and certain. While the tendency is to view him as an older brother of the hero, in one version or another he is named an uncle (mother's brother), a terminological father, and a terminological grandfather of Child of the Water. In one account it is he who plans the hunt during which the giant is met; in another he comes along reluctantly at the bidding of Child of the Water. One story has him making the bow and arrows for the culture hero; other versions attribute their manufacture to different characters. In one account Killer of Enemies kills the deer over which the giant and Child of the Water quarrel; in others the feat is that of his companion. The various degrees to which Killer of Enemies is associated with the white man will be developed below. It is abundantly clear that a shift in one of the basic traditions of the culture has stimulated a series of adjustments in the mythology and given rise to variations which have not yet been rubbed down to reasonable uniformity.

The most momentous change to which Chiricahua culture has had to accommodate itself in recent years is the victorious march of the white man. It is interesting to observe what repercussions this event has caused in the hero myth, which is, basically, a rationalization of Chiricahua triumph and supremacy.

One of the problems is to account for the white man and his culture at all. This issue is not always met in the hero myth; sometimes a separate story deals with it. But in the myth versions now under discussion three story-tellers did insert a section to cope with the white intruder and his ways. One informant, unflatteringly, creates the white man from the last monster which the hero kills. Instead of a prairie-dog, a monstrous human-shaped being who kills with his eyes is substituted in this episode. After the monster and his family are subdued by the salt and blood thrown into the fire, the hero kills all but one small boy. He tells

---

[4] The use of this term as a substitute for Southern Athapaskan-speaking has been suggested to me by Dr Harry Hoijer, who intends henceforth to use it in his own writings.

this one to remain small, to work for a living, and to cultivate his food. He explains that he is going to make Indians who shall gather wild foods, and that the two kinds of people must help each other.

Another narrator associates Killer of Enemies with the white man and his culture and thus disposes of two vexing questions at once. In his version, before their separation, Child of the Water and Killer of Enemies are given their choice of the plants of the earth by the Creator. Killer of Enemies, who "is the white people," obtains the corn after Child of the Water chooses the wild fruits. Killer of Enemies goes to the east and becomes rich as a result of the cultivation of the corn.

In the third deviant the opposition and contrast between Child of the Water and Killer of Enemies is retained. (This has become a familiar theme both within and without the hero story.) An Indian man and woman and a white man and woman are fashioned from clay. Possessions are chosen for them by Child of the Water and Killer of Enemies respectively. The former selects the bow and wild food products for his charges; the latter accepts the gun and a barren mountain for those whom he sponsors. The mountain separates and from it come mules, cattle, sheep, swine, and chickens. In this version the white men and Indians are told that they will live on opposite sides of the ocean and that they will fight whenever they see each other.

What classifies all three changes together, despite the greater or less difference in detail, is that every one can be accepted as an attempt to rationalize and come to grips with an up-heaval of greatest import to the people and the culture.

The last type of variation which I have tried to isolate is at once the most elusive and most provocative of the three. It demands more interest in and knowledge of the individuals who provide us with varying accounts and differing interpretations than most of us can muster at present. I am persuaded that the contributions of those informants who furnish us with examples of variations of this type are too often brushed aside as meaningless pre-cocity or aberrancy. An example will indicate the type of variation which is meant.

In one version from a certain informant there is considerable emphasis upon the deer hunt which precedes the encounter with Giant. Killer of Enemies prepares to go hunting. Child of the Water wishes to go. Killer of Enemies considers the hero too young for the rigors of the journey and seeks to discourage him. Child of the Water insists on going, how-ever, and the two start out. When a deer is sighted Killer of Enemies dons a deer-head mask and, with the aid of a stick, crawls toward the animal, imitating its movements. Child of the Water, being unused to the ways of the hunt, calls to Killer of Enemies to shoot and nearly frightens away the deer. Nevertheless Killer of Enemies manages to dispatch the animal.

While the hunt is mentioned in all the versions, this narrator is alone in introducing the use of an animal mask and in minutely describing the progress of the hunt and the hero's part in it. What is the function and meaning of this emphasis and elaboration? Possibly the hero's mistake is expected to call attention to his youth and inexperience and provide contrast for the mighty and miraculous deeds he is soon to perform. It might be a temptation to view the rest as an interesting bit of exuberant play on a theme, and thereupon dismiss it, if it were not for another factor which comes to mind. I worked rather closely with this particular informant and know that he is more than ordinarily interested in the methods and rituals of the hunt. He is a decidedly unwarlike individual who, though predominately concerned with industrial pursuits, became involved, through the accidents of history, in the Chiricahua Indian Wars ending in 1886. The enlargement on the episode of the hunt, it seems to me, can be best understood in terms of his own interests and personality.

A direct antithesis to the case just cited may, perhaps, illuminate the principle more clearly. In the account of a second informant the deer hunt is reduced to a sentence. But included is a long section which appears in no other version, the details of an invulnerability ritual which the culture hero performs before finally facing the giant in battle. No other part of the tale receives as loving and extended treatment as this. It would be an over-simplification to allow this variation to pass as a chance intrusion and elaboration. This particular man is one of the famous Indian scouts in the annals of the West. That he went through bloody wars and arduous campaigns unscathed is attributed to the protective force of a ritual much like the one described in his version of the hero myth. It is to him that I was sent when I inquired about an informant who would acquaint me with the details of war-path usage and ceremonies. That he inserts this item and, indeed, subordinates other more generalized aspects of the legend to it is doubtless a reflection of his own temperament and values.

The shooting contest between Child of the Water and Giant provides another setting in which the influence upon variations of the narrator's attitude or interests may be tested. Three informants specifically mentioned that when the giant aimed his huge arrows at the hero, lightning flashed or thunder (which is an aspect of the same force to the Chiricahua mind) sounded. To one of these narrators this "looked as if Giant was helped by the thunder." The second commentator observes that the missile of the monster breaks to pieces at the flash "as if struck by lightning." Here, while it is not specifically stated that the flash has been responsible for the destruction of the giant's arrow, lightning is plainly considered to be on the side of the hero. In the third version the speaker explicitly asserts that lightning strikes and shatters the giant's arrows each time they are shot.

Are these gradations in attitude concerning the protective function of lightning simply chance variations, or do they have more intimate and revealing correlates? I happen to have worked for generous periods with all three of these informants and have some idea of the personalities and religious outlooks they represent.

Let us take the case of the first man. He consistently disclaims any power experience ending in the acquisition of a ceremony and guardian spirit. He therefore lacks the supernatural protection that most of his tribesmen enjoy. To those who do not possess protection of this kind, one of the most fearsome of forces, since it can cause a serious illness, is lightning. I have ample evidence that this man deeply fears lightning and considers it a malevolent force. This unpleasant connotation is carried over into his version of the hero myth, where he takes the minority position that the sounding of thunder during the battle is an ill omen for the hero.

The second of our informants takes a contrasting but still moderate position in regard to this episode. This is not surprising to one who knows him. He is well aware of the ravages of "lightning sickness" and of the fear and respect which the Chiricahua owe to this phenomenon. But he has not cut himself off, as has the first man, from the protective rituals of his people. He is well enough guarded by amulets and supernatural lore so that he can dwell with composure upon forces often capricious and inimical to the Chiricahua. It is entirely reasonable to him that Lightning, associated with the birth of the culture hero (since White Painted Woman was impregnated by water as the result of a thunder storm) should act to aid the valiant youth.

The unqualified partisanship of the third raconteur is also explicable. This was the man who confessed to the possession of a ceremony derived from a supernatural experience with the personification of lightning and who finally explained to me the details of his rite. To this man lightning is the most beneficent, healing, and revealing force in the universe. His interest in the good deeds to be accomplished through the advice and aid of Lightning colors all the information I obtained from him into which he could conceivably inject this view. It is inevitable that he interprets the appearance of lightning at the time of this contest in the most flattering manner. Actually he goes much farther. If we were to examine the entire version of this hero myth in comparison with others we would note that he has projected his deep commitment to the lightning ritual into it at a number of other points. Thus he tells us, and he is the only informant of this series who does, that the hero's four arrows were imbued with power from Lightning, that they were tipped with "thunder stones" (elongated points of flint or obsidian said to have been shot to earth by the Thunder People) and could be shot like lightning. Later in his story, in the incident of the slaying of the monster antelope, the arrows shot to the directions are said to bring forth black, blue, white, and yellow smoke in turn. In traditional stories the last two colors of the circuit are usually the reverse of what he gives. From whence, then, comes this atypical order? We may suspect the influence of a personal rite, for Chiricahua shamans, in their individualized practices, take liberties with the customary color-directional symbolism. A glance at the record of this man's lightning ceremony reveals what he has done; he has utilized the color scheme of this rite for his recital of the story of the slaying of the monsters!

I do not claim air-tight and mutual exclusiveness for the types of variation I have defined. Obviously there is some overlapping and interpenetration. It must have occurred to everyone that variation by elaboration, which I have subsumed under the first type, is not completely dissociated from mutations growing out of personality differences, the third type. Certainly it takes a particular kind of individual as well as the inspiration of certain kinds of materials to produce elaboration. Despite the artificiality which the definition of any set of logical categories imposes, the types that have been described seem to me to be valid, directing attention as they do to the principal source from which the impulse for modifica-tion and the material for the variation come.

It is necessary to emphasize too, that what I have been analyzing is not change, but the variations which are the basis and the raw material of change. To be considered a cultural change rather than an individual expression, such a variation would have to draw interest, win acceptance, and become the dominant or at least a prevalent form. It is the hope that a preliminary analysis such as this will lead to careful analyses of situations of flux in an effort to determine why particular variations or types of variations become socialized and dominant.

Of particular interest to the social thought of our times and to social scientists should be the variations of the third type, those which spring initially from the personality differ-ences of individuals. It is challenging to find evidences that here, in the most traditional and stylized of settings, the human spirit time and again rises above stultification and routine imitation. If I read the record aright it means that those who would obtain long-term uni-formity in loyalty and response of whole populations by the seizure of institutional controls and the manipulation of internal and external pressures, reckon without the most human of traits, diversity of personality.

This analysis of variation and the basis of change has proceeded within the framework of a problem in mythology. I should be very much surprised if whatever has come out of the treatment is not applicable to a wider context. There is no reason to believe that mythology, an integral part of culture, demonstrates a different basis of reaction from other aspects of human endeavor. It would be instructive to determine whether the types of variation which characterize the round of hero myths are discernible in other areas of the social scene as well.

CLAREMONT COLLEGES
CLAREMONT, CALIFORNIA

LANGUAGE AND SOCIAL FORMS: A STUDY OF TODA KINSHIP TERMS AND DUAL DESCENT

By M. B. EMENEAU

THAT THE DATA obtained by linguistic investigation of any community is of indispensable value for the ethnographer studying that community has long been axiomatic for the anthropological school of which Sapir was a brilliant member. His statement of the point in *The Status of Linguistics as a Science* deserves to be quoted:

> Language is becoming increasingly valuable as a guide to the scientific study of a given culture. In a sense, the network of cultural patterns of a civilization is indexed in the language which expresses that civilization. It is an illusion to think that we can understand the significant outlines of a culture through sheer observation and without the guide of the linguistic symbolism which makes these outlines significant and intelligible to society. Some day the attempt to master a primitive culture without the help of the language of its society will seem as amateurish as the labors of a historian who cannot handle the original documents of the civilization which he is describing.[1]

To go a little further and say that the culminating item of value that the linguistic student can give to ethnology is the study of a community's most highly verbalized cultural manifestations would be what Sapir would and undoubtedly did hold. It is here, in their verbal art-forms, stories, songs, oratory, or the like, that the members of the culture give the most overt and self-conscious expression to the patterns which they follow or profess to follow in their life. Linguistic study, if it is confined to its primary object of recording and analyzing the forms of utterances and never goes beyond that, can offer little to ethnology. It must, with that analysis as a basis, go on to a strict philological analysis of well-recorded and fully guaranteed texts in the forms most highly esteemed by the culture, and the results of such study should provide then "the linguistic symbolism which makes these outlines [of a culture gained through sheer observation] significant and intelligible."

The following study presents the kinship system of the Todas of the Nilgiris in South India. In a previous paper on *Toda Marriage Regulations and Taboos*, the existence was reported of a complete division of the Todas into matrilineal sibs alongside of the previously known complete division into patrilineal sibs. In this paper I present, following on the kinship system, the material on the functions of the two sib-systems as against one another. In these sections an attempt has been made to use the evidence provided by the Toda art-form of highest prestige, the songs. Discussion based on this evidence is found on pp. 160–161 on the use of "friend" terms beside kinship terms, on p. 165 on the special kinship term used by a woman for the wife of her husband's brother by the same father, and throughout the Appendix, which presents the kinship terms; and again on pp. 169–172, where the data on the

---

[1] Edward Sapir, *The Status of Linguistics as a Science* (Language, Vol. 5, pp. 207–14, 1929), p. 209.

emotional attitude of the Todas towards their matrilineal sib-system is presented. It is thought that in this use of song material the "amateurish" methodology against which Sapir protested has been avoided, and some light has been thrown upon Toda institutions in a way which he would have approved. The study ends with some discussion of the bearing of the Todas' dual descent system on the historical question of their "origin," which has engaged the attention of most of those who have studied them.

Rivers' account of the kinship system of the Todas is essentially correct.[2] Linguistic research with this tribe has added little but detail to our knowledge of this department of the tribal institutions, except in the important matter of dual descent, which escaped Rivers' meticulous investigations.[3] In this paper I shall present the kinship terms in correct linguistic shape, and shall make the few factual corrections that are necessary. The main body of the paper will be devoted to a discussion of the dual descent system.

The most important factual correction in Rivers' account relates to the age distinctions made in the kinship system. He records three age-groups in EGO's generation based on age relative to that of EGO.[4] In fact, the system makes only two distinctions. There is a dichotomy on the basis of age relative to EGO. An elder brother or male parallel cousin in either patrilineal or matrilineal sib or outside them (son of EGO's mother's clan-sister) is oṇ in reference, oṇaɪ in address; an elder sister or female parallel cousin related in the same ways is okn in reference, okaɪ in address. A younger sibling or parallel cousin related in the same ways, without distinction of sex, is ·ǔɯɾ-fed in reference, with the appropriate pronominal form preceding, and endaɪ in address. En ǔɯɾ-fed is "my younger sibling," literally "one who was born with, or after, me;" nɯn-ǔɯɾ-fed "your younger sibling," an-ǔɯɾ-fed (or an-dan-ǔɯɾ-fed) "his or her younger sibling," om-ǔɯɾ-fed "our (inclusive) younger sibling," em-ǔɯɾ-fed "our (exclusive) younger sibling," nɯm-ǔɯɾ-fed "your (plural) younger sibling;" "their younger sibling" is the same as "his or her" or aθaɪn-ǔɯɾ-fed. If the sex of the person referred to must be indicated, ·mox added to any of the forms signifies a male, ·xuɪx (=kuɪx) a female.[5]

[2] W. H. R. Rivers, The Todas (London, 1906), pp. 483–501 for the kinship terms. The volume is referred to in this paper as Rivers. In mentioning members of the tribe by name a number is frequently added in brackets after the name; this refers to the corresponding genealogical table in Rivers.

[3] See M. B. Emeneau, Toda Marriage Regulations and Taboos (American Anthropologist, Vol. 39, pp. 103–12, 1937) for a detailed account of the matrilineal sibs which are found within the moieties and cut across the well-known division into patrilineal sibs. In the present paper I employ the same system of phonemic writing that was used in that paper, with the corrections made in my later paper Personal Names of the Todas (American Anthropologist, Vol. 40, pp. 205–23, 1938), p. 205 fn. 1. In this paper I use š, ž for palatalized alveolar sibilants, c, ʒ for post-dental affricates and č, ž for palatalized post-dental affricates; ɯ is a high, back, unrounded vowel. Acknowledgments are due again to the American Council of Learned Societies for aid in my field-work in 1935–36 and to the American Philosophical Society (Penrose Fund) for aid in 1936–38.

[4] Pp. 486 bottom, 487, and passim.

[5] Rivers, p. 487, said: "I do not know whether the children of two women of the same generation in [a patrilineal sib] would call one another brother and sister." The terms are extended to all children of women whom EGO would refer to as mother, whether they are in his patrilineal or matrilineal sib, or outside them. The term

Besides these Rivers distinguished a relative of this type who is of the same age as EGO. This distinction is in fact impossible, both in the strict temporal sense, and in the Toda cultural pattern. It is always known how the persons in question stand to one another in the matter of relative time of birth, and in such cultural contexts as formal greetings[6] no room is left by the pattern for a class of the same age as EGO. For example, at a gathering each new male arrival must salute all the males already present with the proper formal term of address, and among these all classificatory elder brothers must be greeted. If any of those present is neglected, the offender is reprimanded and if necessary fined for the neglect. The pattern in its strict application makes a clean dichotomy and in practically all circumstances the dichotomy is rigidly enforced. The word given by Rivers for his third class is koːɬ "friend," occurring chiefly with pronominal forms preceding, egoːɬ or en-goːɬ "my friend" (in address -es is added), nɯn-goːɬ "your friend," an-goːɬ or tan-goːɬ "his or her friend," etc. These terms are normally used between or with reference to close friends of the same age-level who are not related to one another (e.g., typically between two persons who belong to different moieties). They may also be used where formality is not enforced by the pattern; I have no certain information as to whether they could be used between siblings, but there is some slight evidence to be discussed below which would indicate that it is possible. It is to be noted however that this is only permissive and that the term does not designate any kinship class or even any relationship that is highly formalized in the culture.[7]

When two persons sing together, certain subjects allow or require that vocatives be used at the beginning, the end, and important division-points of the songs. In most of the texts that I have recorded the proper kinship terms are used in such songs. Ten songs use the conventional song-words for "friend (vocative)," enbocxoːɬjaː, eningoːɬjaː.[8] Three situations may be divided off. In the first (three songs) the two singers are of different moieties and presumably no "lover-mistress" relationship would require kinship terms.[9] In a second class (four songs) membership of the same moiety might very well involve a relationship where kinship terms should be used, but I do not know of any such relationship; two of the songs were sung by the same pair of singers and were dictated to me at a sufficient interval of time so that the use of "friend" terms is guaranteed. In a third class (three songs) there was certainly relationship between the singers, but as dictated the "friend" terms were used. These songs were dictated rather early in my field-work before I realized all the implications of the

---

in address is the simple vocative (distinguished by sex and relative age); in reference the simple brother-sister terms might be used or, where more exact reference is necessary, descriptive terms. In the case of address to cross-cousins of the same sex as EGO the brother-sister terms are used (see note 7 below).

[6] Rivers, pp. 496-98.

[7] In the case also of address to cross-cousins of the same sex as the speaker there is no room for Rivers' third classification (p. 488 bottom); only age older or younger than that of EGO is taken into account in determining the kinship term to be used.

[8] For the nature of the song-words, see my paper The Songs of the Todas (Proceedings, American Philosophical Society, Vol. 77, pp. 543-60, 1937), especially pp. 545-49.

[9] For this relationship, see Rivers, pp. 526-29.

DIAGRAM I. GENEALOGY OF TERMS (MAN SPEAKING).
Capitals indicate reference terms of a classificatory nature, numerals reference terms of a descriptive nature, and small letters address terms. (See Appendix.)

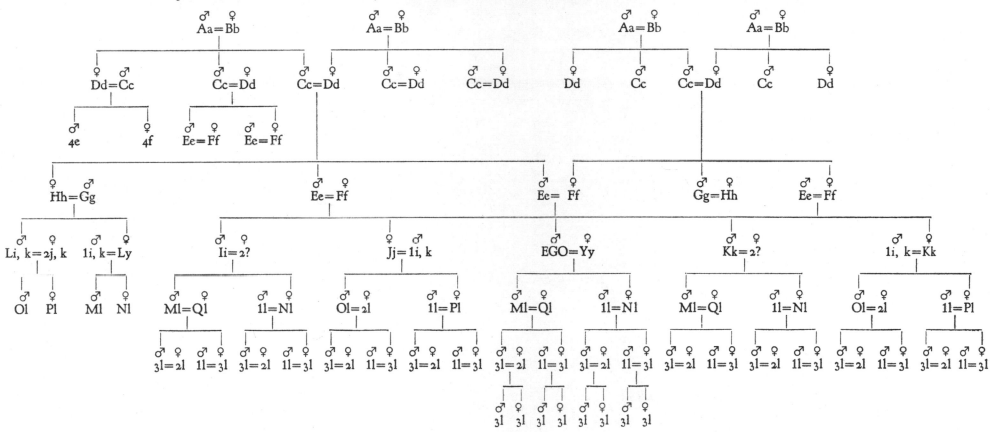

song-language, and it is possible that the informants, who happened to be in no case the singers, dictated incorrectly. In one song piḷjaɪr (Piliar, 52) and meṟṉɯs (Mudriners, 57) sang; these men were of the same patrilineal sib and used "brother" terms to one another. In another sindɯrp (Sintharap), wife of kŭɯɪsjaḷf (Kuriolv, 52), and koɪsɑr (Kosar, 57) sang; these women would certainly have used "sister" terms to one another. In the third song, which was dreamed, two men recently dead were singing: tæɪθjxæɪn, son of sirjaɪr (Siriar, 20), and töŭθŭɯɪ, son of toɪkɑs (Tokas) and pɯnɯr (Puner, 23); they belonged to the same patrilineal sib and the former called the latter ejaɪ "father." Other dreamed songs in which dead persons sang used the correct kinship terms. It is difficult to interpret this small minority of songs in which relationship was neglected. It may be possible that relationship can be neglected; I prefer to suspect mistakes in the record until further field work can clear the matter up.

The kinship system is of the type known as the Dakota-Iroquois system (see accompanying diagrams and Appendix). The salient points of the system are those stressed by Rivers— the obligatory indication of age-distinctions in EGO's generation (with the qualification made in the preceding discussion) and the permissive indication in the first ascending generation (see p. 163 below); the obligatory distinction in the first ascending generation between father's brothers and male parallel cousins and mother's sisters and female parallel cousins on the one hand, and father's sisters and female parallel cousins and mother's brothers and male parallel cousins on the other, and in EGO's generation between the children of these two groups. A clear distinction is made between terms used in reference and those used in address. The reference terms are built about a core of simplex classificatory terms with a large number of phrasal and frequently *ad hoc* terms to indicate those to whom the simplex terms do not apply. Permissively, the simplex terms also may be replaced by phrasal terms when very exact reference is needed, e.g., mɑn-mox "son of sibling of sex opposed to that of EGO" (itself phrasal, but in connotation a simplex) and mɑn-guɪx "daughter, etc." may be replaced by en-okng-fæɪdfoj-mox "son who was born to my elder sister (male speaking)," en-ŭɯr-fed-moxk-fæɪdfoj-xuɪx "daughter who was born to my younger brother (female speaking)," etc. The terms of address, on the other hand, are all simplex classificatory terms and, being extended very widely, neglect a number of the reference classifications, indicated either by simplex or by phrasal terms. A summary of the system follows:

There is no self-reciprocating terminology in address. In reference močiṇj "cross-cousin" is self-reciprocating, since it does not distinguish sex or relative age; when a permissively added word indicates the sex, the self-reciprocating nature of the term is destroyed. In EGO's generation his siblings and classificatory parallel cousins are referred to and addressed by terms which distinguish age older than himself and younger than himself respectively and sex is distinguished in the case of those older than himself.

Sex is specified in referring to and addressing members of the ascending generations, except in referring to the cross-cousins of one's parents and of one's parents' siblings and parallel cousins (en-in-močiṇj "my father's cross-cousin," en-af-močiṇj "my mother's cross-

DIAGRAM 2. GENEALOGY OF TERMS (WOMAN SPEAKING).

Only the section is given where female usage differs from male.

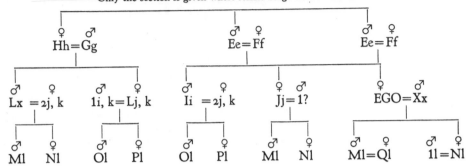

DIAGRAM 3. GENEALOGY OF TERMS FOR WIFE'S RELATIVES.

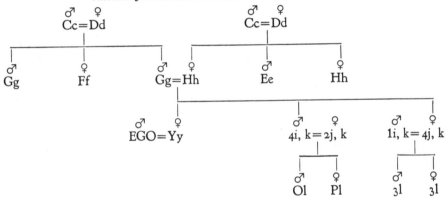

DIAGRAM 4. GENEALOGY OF TERMS FOR HUSBAND'S RELATIVES.

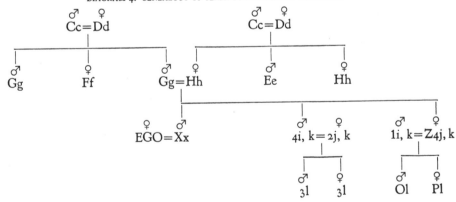

cousin;" sex may however be indicated by the addition of the respective sex-denoting words). In EGO's generation sex is specified in referring to and addressing his siblings and parallel cousins older than himself, and in addressing cross-cousins, but not in referring to and addressing siblings and parallel cousins younger than himself or in referring to cross-cousins; in reference in the latter cases an optional reference is allowed. In descending generations sex is specified in reference but not in address.

In EGO's generation a dichotomy is made in classification on the basis of age older or younger than his own (see above), in the case of siblings and parallel cousins when referred to or addressed, and in the case of cross-cousins of the same sex as EGO when addressed. In the first ascending generation EGO's father's male siblings and parallel cousins are permissively dichotomized on the basis of age elder or younger than the father's, and EGO's mother's female siblings and parallel cousins on the basis of age elder or younger than the mother's, in both cases by prefixing per-ŭɯḍ "big-who is" and kɯr-ŭɯḍ "small-who is" to the classificatory terms, either of reference or address.

The father is not distinguished in address or reference from his brothers and male parallel cousins, nor in address from his male cross-cousins; the mother is not distinguished in address or reference from her sisters and female parallel cousins, nor in address from her female cross-cousins. A step-parent is not distinguished in reference or address from a parent.

In EGO's generation siblings by the same father are not distinguished in reference or address from children of the father's brothers or from children of the mother's sisters. There is a permissively used special term of reference for a man's brother who is a son of the same father, oṇtafn; e.g., aθ en-oṇtafn-ɯji "he is my brother, the son of the same father as myself," oṇtafn-mox faɹjoṭi "do not seize the wife of (your) brother by the same father (i.e. do not carry her off as you may do with other men's wives and then have compensation [ter] arranged by the tribal council)."[10] When special exactness is needed, descriptive phrases may be used.

In the first ascending generation there is a special term, both in reference and address, for the father's sisters and female parallel cousins, and this is also used for the mother's male siblings' and male parallel cousins' wives, and for EGO's mother-in-law and her female siblings. Similarly, there is a special term for the mother's brothers and male parallel cousins, and this is used also for the father's female siblings' and female parallel cousins' husbands, and for EGO's father-in-law and the latter's male siblings. In EGO's generation the classification of cross-cousin applies to all the children of those in the first ascending generation who are classed according to the preceding two sentences, except those who are affines; a spouse's siblings are not classed as EGO's cross-cousins, unless they are really so. In the first descending generation a distinction is made in reference between two groups: (a) the children of one's siblings or parallel cousins of the same sex as oneself and of one's cross-cousins of the opposite sex from oneself (these are all descriptively distinguished, e.g., on-mox "elder brother's son," en-ŭɯr-fed-moxn-mox "my younger brother's son," močiṇj-xuɪxn-mox "female cross-

---

[10] Rivers, pp. 523-25. It is possible that oṇtafn is the word meant by Rivers (p. 484), *annatam*.

cousin's son," male speaking in all three cases), and (b) the children of one's siblings or paral-lel cousins of the opposite sex from oneself and of one's cross-cousins of the same sex as oneself (these are all mɑn-mox [male],[11] mɑn-guːx [female], or may be distinguished descrip-tively, e.g., okn-mox "elder sister's son," en-ŭɯ̟-fed-xuːxn-mox "my younger sister's son," močiɲj-moxn-mox "male cross-cousin's son," male speaking in all cases). The terms mɑn-mox, mɑn-guːx are used also of the children of one's spouse's sibling of the opposite sex to that of one's spouse. Members of (a) are cross-cousins to members of (b). In address members of (a) and members of (b) are not distinguished. It will be noted that the sex of the speaker must be regarded in (a) and (b), as in the last paragraph on this page.

The terms of address that would apply to EGO's spouse's relatives if the spouse were a cross-cousin apply also to those relatives when the spouse is not a cross-cousin. That is, the basic equation for terms for affines is: cross-cousin = spouse. The only violation of the equa-tion is found in that, man speaking, wife's sister is not equated with the daughter of father's sister or of mother's brother, and, woman speaking, husband's brother is not equated with the son of father's sister or of mother's brother. The basic equation also works with terms of reference in the ascending generations and in class (b) of the preceding paragraph for the first descending generation. In the spouse's own generation and in class (a) of that para-graph in the first descending generation descriptive terms of reference are used; e.g., en(k)-koːtfojn-dan-oṇ "elder brother of my wife," en(k)-koːtfojn-dan-okn-mox "son of my wife's elder sister," en-oːɬn-dan-okn "my husband's elder sister," etc. A woman may refer to her husband's female siblings, real or classificatory within his patrilineal sib (mod), as mod-okn, apparently irrespective of their relative ages; in address ordinary "sister" terms are used. This word, though itself a phrasal term, is in connotation a simplex, like mɑn-mox and mɑn-guːx (cf. pp. 161 and this page above).

Two classes in the first ascending generation yield one class only in the second ascending generation, divided in terminology on the basis of sex, both in reference and address. Like-wise, in the third and preceding ascending generations, though occasions for address are comparatively rare. Frequently, when no more exact reference is necessary, the terms for the second ascending generation are used for all preceding generations. In the second and suc-ceeding descending generations no distinctions are made in address, and the same term is used as in the first descending generation (cf. p. 163). In reference descriptive terms are used, distinguishing the sex of the individual and the reference status of the individual's links with EGO as in the second paragraph above, (a) and (b); e.g., moːt-mox or moxk-fæːdfoj-mox "son's son," moːt-xuːx or moxk-fæːdfoj-xuːx "son's daughter," kuːxn-mox or kuːxk-fæːdfoj-mox "daughter's son," moːt-mox-mox "son's son's son," močiɲj-moxn-moːt-mox "son's son of male cross-cousin."

"Husband" is oːɬ in reference, oːɬjaː in address; "wife" is tozmox in reference, tozmoxjaː or kuːxjaː in address. When EGO is male, he addresses a female cross-cousin, even if she is

---

[11] Rivers, p. 488, queried whether mɑn-mox denotes also a son-in-law who is not a sister's son. It is not used of him; he is pojoɬ (see p. 165); when exactness is required kuːxn-oːɬ "daughter's husband."

not his wife, by the same terms that he uses for his wife; similarly, when EGO is female, she addresses a male cross-cousin, even if he is not her husband, by the same term that she uses for her husband.

Affines are referred to collectively as pojoɪʃ; the same term includes also female affines. When the term refers to an individual, it may denote either male or female.

There is a special reference term for the wife of one's son (own son or the son of one's own brother), if she is not one's sister's daughter, viz. moɪt-fiʃθ (moɪt- as in moɪt-mox = "son's;" -fiʃθ [i.e. piʃθ] is not otherwise found).

There is a special reference term used by a woman for the wife of her husband's brother by the same father (or fathers in a polyandrous marriage), viz. ŭɯrxitj. It may also be used of the woman in reference to this type of relationship. In address these women use to one another "sister" terms. The word is frequently combined with oṇtɑfn (cf. p. 163 above) in songs. When a woman laments her husband's death, if her husband had several brothers each married to a separate wife, she may sing:

oɪr-oṇtɑfn   oɪjɯθsɯk
oɪr-ŭɯrxitj   kɯsɯθsɯk (or, ɯṣtjɯθsɯk)

"You (plural) were six (=an indefinite number) sons of one father; you (plural) made (or, caused to sit) six sisters-in-law (wives of brothers)." This may also be said in the words shouted during the dancing at a man's funeral.[12] When a man laments his brother, if he had several brothers each of whom had a separate wife, he may sing:

oɪr-oṇtɑfn   oɪjɯθuk
oɪr-ŭɯrxitj   oɪjɯθuk

"We (inclusive) were six (=an indefinite number) sons of one father: we (inclusive) were (having) six wives." When a man laments his wife under the same circumstances, he may sing:

oɪr-oṇtɑfn   oɪjθemɯn
oɪr-ŭɯrxitj   oɪjθiɯn

"We (exclusive) were six (=an indefinite number) sons of one father; you were one of six wives of the brothers."

The system is essentially classificatory, as is shown especially by the terms of address. It is used in this way by the Todas. Each member of a person's patrilineal sib is addressed by the appropriate classificatory vocative. It will be remembered from Rivers' treatment[13] that the classification is made even when the various families of a sib are unrelated so far as the Todas' genealogical knowledge goes; the correlation of generations is handed down by adaptation and frequent use, and even when the links of a pedigree have been lost to memory, the correct terminology based on the lost pedigree is maintained. Each male and female born to the sib is addressed with the appropriate term by every other member of the sib, and the persons related by marriage to and descent from the sib members are also addressed with

[12] See *The Songs of the Todas*, pp. 556–57.   [13] Pp. 490–92.

the appropriate terms. Similarly, the members of a matrilineal sib use the appropriate terms to one another, assigning the appropriate terms between any two individuals in the same way that it is done within the patrilineal sib, even when knowledge of the pedigree has been lost. An example may be given of the usage between members of matrilineal sibs. Tisjoɩn, son of tæɩgŭɯɩɽ of the noɩş patrilineal sib (Teigudr, 4) and his wife uɩaɩɽ (Uwer), is related to kaɳfɯsodj of the kaɩs patrilineal sib (Kunpuradi, 14) as nephew to maternal uncle, addresses him with the vocative mumaɩ, and is addressed as enaɩ. Kaɳfɯsodj addresses uɩaɩɽ as elder sister (okaɩ), since his mother addressed her as daughter (enaɩ); they are members of the same matrilineal sib but the pedigree is not known to the Todas.

Within each moiety of the tribe, the Todas may be related, when they are related, as members of the same patrilineal sib, as members of the same matrilineal sib, or by marriage. Frequently, between the same two individuals there is not only one relationship, but two or even three. The question arises as to which relationship takes precedence in determining the use of kinship terms. When this matter was investigated, it was found that the informants were quite articulate on the subject and gave an answer in general terms. Relationship within a matrilineal sib overrides any other relationship; of the other two, relationship by marriage overrides relationship within a patrilineal sib. Relationship by marriage may involve two marriage links, i.e. it is necessary for a Toda to address with the correct terms his wife's relations by another marriage in her family. If the wife has a choice of terminology for any of her relations by marriage, once she has determined the correct term, her husband adopts an appropriate term on the basis of his wife's usage, provided that he is not himself related to the person involved as co-member of a matrilineal sib, this relationship overriding all others. This statement also applies *mutatis mutandis* between a woman and her relations by marriage. The general statement given by the informants is borne out by usage. A few examples will suffice.

Kæɩnoẓ (Keinodz, 21) calls töŭθuxn (Teitukhen, 23) father (ejaɩ) since they are members of the same patrilineal sib and related thus by generations. He should then by this relationship call the latter's son moɩɽonɯs younger brother (endaɩ). But nafab (Navob), mother of moɩɽonɯs, calls kæɩnoẓ elder brother (oɳaɩ) by an untraceable relationship within a matrilineal sib. Consequently, moɩɽonɯs calls kæɩnoẓ maternal uncle (mumaɩ).

Kaɳfɯsodj (Kunpuradi, 14) and pɯnog (Punog, 14) are brothers' sons within the same family, and the former should call the latter elder brother (oɳaɩ). But kaɳfɯsodj's mother piɫjθoḍfiɫj (Pathudveli) called pɯnog's mother kupiɩẓfiɫj (Kupizveli) grandmother (piafaɩ) by an untraceable relationship within a matrilineal sib. Hence kaɳfɯsodj calls pɯnog grandfather (piaɩ).

Kalginɯs (Kalgeners, 15) is by relationship in the same patrilineal sib elder brother to kaɳfɯsodj. The former's son tɯɩɽxuḍ should then be called by kaɳfɯsodj son (enaɩ). But the mother of tɯɩɽxuḍ, košɯl (Kuzil, 27), is by an untraceable relationship within a matrilineal sib grandmother to kaɳfɯsodj, i.e. mother to his mother. Hence he calls her son maternal uncle (mumaɩ).

Piːldjnɯs (Püldenir, 21) is by relationship within a patrilineal sib grandson to panɯs (Paners, 23). By an untraceable relationship in a matrilineal sib the latter is maternal uncle to the former and is called by him mumaː. The wives of these men were sinmiːr (Sinmir) married to piːldjnɯs, and pæːrgfiḷj (Pergveli) married to panɯs. If the men's relationship within a patrilineal sib had determined the terminology, sinmiːr would have called pæːrgfiḷj grandmother (piafaː). Since this relationship was overridden for the men, it was overridden for their wives also; following the terms used by the men, sinmiːr should have called pæːrg-fiḷj mimjaː (here indicating husband's maternal uncle's wife). Actually, sinmiːr's mother ocefiḷj (Achaveli, 43) was sister to pæːrgfiḷj, both being daughters of the same mother pɯnbuːf. Consequently, by this relationship in a matrilineal sib, sinmiːr called pæːrgfiḷj mother (afaː).

DIAGRAM 5

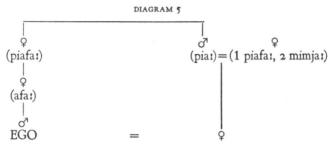

In a hypothetical case, a man married the daughter of his mother's mother's brother. Previous to the marriage he called this man grandfather (piaː) because of relationship within the same matrilineal sib; after the marriage he retained the term, this relationship overriding in terminology the new relationship of father-in-law (mumaː). The older man's wife was called, prior to the marriage, grandmother (piafaː), even if she had been of the same patrilineal sib as the younger man (affinal relationship overriding relationship in the same patrilineal sib). After the marriage she is called by the younger man mother-in-law (mimjaː) even if she had been of the same patrilineal sib. In this case one relationship by marriage has preference over another, apparently the nearer marriage overriding the more distant. Unfortunately, this matter was not investigated further.

One of the functions of the matrilineal sibs has appeared in this discussion of the kinship terminology. The primary function was shown in a previous paper[14] to be that of regulating marriage; no Toda may marry a person who is a co-member of a matrilineal sib. In another cultural context matrilineal sibs are of importance. This is in the matter of mourning for a dead person. This in general was treated by Rivers;[15] an account of the rules regulating

[14] *Toda Marriage Regulations and Taboos.*

[15] Pp. 367-71. One slight correction should be made in his account of the manner of wearing the hair (p. 369). Rivers there says that the hair must be tied in a knot in front. The real rule is that the hair must not be cut during the period of pollution. It grows long and is usually tied up in a knot in front so that it will not obscure the sight.

dancing will add somewhat to the treatment. Dancing takes place at weddings[16] and at such
religious ceremonies as the giving of salt to the buffaloes (up·otjt), the rethatching of a dairy
(poḷj·ful·fæːst), and the prayer-ceremony at a chief mund[17] (mod·fartjt), as well as at such
unusual social occasions as the reception of an important European visitor, the celebration
under the patronage of the Governor of Madras by all the inhabitants of the Nilgiris of a
Jubilee in the British royal family, large Badaga ceremonies which many Todas attend, etc.
At such dances men from both moieties participate in the same dance. Men who may not
dance are those who are mourning a death. (a) If the first funeral has not yet taken place,
dancing is prohibited to those who are mourning the death of a man of the same patrilineal
sib, of the same matrilineal sib, or of one who is called pojoːḷ, i.e., wife's father or brother,
wife's father's brother, and conversely, daughter's husband, sister's husband, brother's
daughter's husband (cf. p. 165). If the dead person is a woman, the prohibition affects, besides
members of her matrilineal sib and her pojoːḷ, only those members of her father's patrilineal
sib who belong to her immediate family. (b) If the first funeral has taken place, but mourning
still obtains until the second funeral shall have been performed, no one may dance who is
related to the dead person by relationship within the matrilineal sib, by the closest relationship within the patrilineal sib, i.e. by membership in the immediate family of the dead person, or by pojoːḷ relationship as in (a). In both (a) and (b), when a man is dead, dancing is
prohibited for the husband and sons of the woman in the opposite moiety with whom he
has had sexual relations of the "lover-mistress" type;[18] when a woman is dead, dancing is
prohibited for the man in the opposite moiety with whom she has had "lover-mistress"
relations, and for his sons.

Dancing also takes place at funerals, whether first or second. Normally only men are
allowed to dance who belong to the other moiety than the one to which the dead person
belonged. Here again the prohibitions indicated in the preceding paragraph hold with regard
to people in the "lover-mistress" relationship to the dead person. And, of course, no person
may dance who is mourning any other death. The rule permitting only men of the opposite
moiety to dance is sometimes broken. At the funeral of some relatively unimportant person
there may not be enough men of the opposite moiety present to dance, or at the funeral of
a member of the ɯṇkitj, nirj, and pɯrgoːr sibs of the toːrθas moiety, since the munds of
these sibs are far from any munds of the töüfiḷj moiety. In this case members of the same
moiety as the dead person will be permitted to dance, but no one who is mourning the dead

---

[16] There is no dancing at the ceremony when a man gives the toy bow and arrow to his wife during her
pregnancy to legitimize the child (pɯs·ɯṭt). At a ceremony of this kind which I attended with Mr C. P. Skrine,
Agent of the Madras States and author of *Chinese Central Asia* (London, 1926), the men danced so that he should
be able to see how it is done. The words composed during the dance were about myself and the ceremony was
mentioned only as one in a list of ceremonies that I had seen.

[17] A mund (Toda word mod) is, throughout this paper, a dairy institution plus a dwelling place. The significance of "chief mund" (ɯt·ŭɯḍ·mod) as opposed to other munds (mɑx·mod) has been explained in my paper *Toda
Culture Thirty-five Years After* (Annals, Bhandarkar Oriental Research Institute, Vol. 19, pp. 101–21, 1938), pp.
113–15.   [18] See reference in note 9 above.

person because of relationship in the same matrilineal sib, in the same patrilineal sib, or by pojoːḷ relationship may be permitted to dance.[19] Or, it may happen that, although there are enough members of the proper moiety to dance, there is no one present of the proper moiety who knows how to compose dance-words.[20] In this case if a composer of the moiety of the dead person is present, he may be permitted to dance and compose words. It may happen that all the composers of both moieties will be prevented from dancing by the mourning rules; in this case one of them will be allowed to dance and compose words.

It will be seen from the manner in which the rules are relaxed between situations (a) and (b) for a man, and within the situation (a) as between a man and a woman, that no one may ever dance who is related by co-membership in the same matrilineal sib to any dead person, either of whose funerals is outstanding. In both cases however when the rules are relaxed, i.e. when a man's second funeral only is outstanding and when a woman's first or second funeral is outstanding, the only co-members of the patrilineal sib who are forbidden to dance are those within the immediate family. We may conclude from these rules and from the universally overriding force of relationship within the same matrilineal sib in the application of kinship terms, that in these social spheres the matrilineal sib has greater importance than the patrilineal.[21] Rivers' description has of course made clear the overwhelming importance of the patrilineal sibs in the economic, religious, and social spheres. A man belongs to the patrilineal sib of his father and inherits his property and all his ownership rights and duties in the sacred herds of buffaloes, the dairies at which they are tended, the pastures, etc. This is the pivot of Toda life and in it the matrilineal sibs do not figure at all. In the matter of marriage patrilineal and matrilineal sibs are of equal value; no Toda may marry a person belonging to his own sib of either type. In the matters treated in this paper, however, though both types of sib play a part, the matrilineal sib relationship has greater weight than the other.

A hint of the attitude of a Toda towards the members of his matrilineal sib is provided by the words of the songs. The attitude is identified by the work noːškj which was translated as "shame," and refers to the sensation of shrinking felt when one is confronted with an embarrasing situation. We shall first examine a prose account of the expedition of kajniːr (Kainir, 3) to the points of interest on the path over the hills followed by the dead on their way to the afterworld. His daughter ɑrliːẕ had married piːḷkoṛ (Pilkòdr, 16) of the möːr patrilineal sib, whose mund pɑn is very near the point where the path starts southwestward into the Kundah hills. She assured her father of the interest that such an expedition would have and he with several companions made it successfully. One of the points is

---

[19] A person who cannot dance on any occasion because of mourning is called köːṭ(k)-koːṭpoːḷ "person who is waiting for a funeral."   [20] See reference in note 12 above.

[21] Another place where relationship in the matrilineal sib counts is in the salutations performed at various ceremonies, as e.g., at the pɯs-ɯṭṭ or bow-giving ceremony. There the wife salutes all the male and female members of her father's patrilineal sib and her own matrilineal sib, and those of her husband's patrilineal sib who are older than herself. Likewise the husband salutes all the male and female members of his patrilineal sib, his matrilineal sib, and his wife's patrilineal sib without respect to relative ages. So correct Rivers, p. 320.

paɽmaxθɯɽ,[22] a swamp reached shortly after the path is entered. When kɑjniːr asked what it was he was told: il-θon-ɯji pɯːrotj-noːj yst "It is just here that the pɯːrotj-noːj [a tiger that looks like a dog] chases people." The text proceeds: 'æːd' ɯd fintjn. 'poɬjoːɬ-xuːrjfojoːɬ ŭɯd-mortk-fæːdfoj-xuːrjfojoːɬn̩ pɯːrotj-noːj ysti; poɬjoːɬ n̩oːn̩jti; oːtoːɬ xɑrsti' ɯdng. "He asked: 'Why?' They said: 'The pɯːrotj-noːj chases a man who has had sexual intercourse with one of his matrilineal sib or who has had sexual intercourse with one of his patrilineal sib; his poɬjoːɬ feel shame; the oːtoːɬ laugh.' " The word poɬjoːɬ was said to mean his relations, and the word oːtoːɬ those not related to him. The latter word is quite obscure, is never used except in songs and in this passage quoted, and only the use in this passage as explained by the narrator gives any clue to its meaning. If poɬjoːɬ means all relations, and not merely members of the same matrilineal sib, it is the only place, where its meaning can be determined, in which it has such an extended meaning. It is very possible that the two phrases used here are derived from the song-language; the use of oːtoːɬ, otherwise only a song-word, is rather good evidence that this is so. Such use of song-phrases in the telling of stories would not be unusual. If so, we need not force poɬjoːɬ into the extended meaning required in the story. It refers literally to members of the matrilineal sib only, but by the implications of the context to members of the patrilineal sib as well.

If we now examine the cases where poɬjoːɬ occurs in the songs, we find that it is in all but one case joined with the word noːškj (cf. the verb noːn̩jti "are ashamed" in the prose above). In one case three sons of a man of the toːroːr patrilineal sib wanted to make a two-day funeral for their father, and their sib approved and joined in making preparations. These included getting a permit from the Government authorities to slaughter more than the normally permitted two buffaloes. One important man of the kɑːs patrilineal sib was overlooked in the distribution of gratuities and from spite blocked the issue of the permit. In her lament for her husband, the widow says:

pɯlkŭɯːrθoːr	poɬjoːɬ-noːškj	oːjxŭɯθɯn
pæːθoːr	oːtoːɬ-n̩oːn̩	oːjxŭɯθɯn
	noːd̩oːɬk-noːškj	oːjxŭɯθɯn
	siːmjoːɬk-sig	oːjxŭɯθɯn

"The toːroːr patrilineal sib became ashamed before the poɬjoːɬ, the oːtoːɬ, the people of the country (noːd̩oːɬ), the people of the district (siːmjoːɬ; district = country)." It is apparent here that the poɬjoːɬ and the oːtoːɬ together make up the Todas, and that the shame is that of one patrilineal sib when thwarted in an honorable undertaking by another. The words poɬjoːɬ and oːtoːɬ have no real pertinence in this context; they are the conventional words in song-language when speaking of shame.

---

[22] One account given to me placed this near the beginning of the path, another (perhaps the more trust-worthy) where it is placed in Rivers' account of the path (Padrmukhteir; pp. 398–400); his account is in general incomplete.

In another passage a man carried off the wife of another man, but she was recovered by her husband with the help of other men, and the abductor says:

poļjoːɭ-noːškj	æːfꞷnen
oːtoːɭ-foṇt	æːfꞷnen
noːroːɭ-noːškj	æːfꞷnen
siːmjoːɭ-sig	æːfꞷnen

"I have become ashamed before the poļjoːɭ; I have become a word [i.e. a subject for ridicule] before the oːtoːɭ; I have become ashamed before the people of the country, I have become ashamed before the people of the district." Here again, though the use of pont "word" with oːtoːɭ seems to suggest a dichotomy of the tribe similar to that in the prose passage above, so that the man's poļjoːɭ would be ashamed along with him, the two final sentences imply an interpretation like that of the passage just discussed. The poļjoːɭ and the oːtoːɭ together are the Todas before whom he is ashamed, and are of no pertinence here except in their conventional connection with feelings of shame.

In two other passages we seem at first sight to get nearer to literal meanings. A woman laments her daughter, who died an untimely death before she had borne children. She says:

poļjoːɭk-noːškj	æːfꞷnen
oːtoːɭk-foṇt	æːfꞷnen

"I have become ashamed before the poļjoːɭ; I have become a subject for ridicule before the oːtoːɭ." It was explained that the lamenting woman now has no daughter and is considered unlucky by the people. This explanation need imply no more than that all the people, indicated with no special pertinence by poļjoːɭ and oːtoːɭ, think her unlucky and that she has feelings of shame before them on this account. Dare we read in the interpretation that the woman and her daughter belonged to one matrilineal sib and their branch of it is now going to fail, so that the woman feels shame before her matrilineal sib on that account? The Todas certainly seem not to interpret in this way.

Again, a woman bore a daughter to her husband, but no sons. He began negotiations to divorce her and take another wife. In despair she sings, with her child in her arms:

poļjoːɭ-noːškj	æːfꞷnum
oːtoːɭ-foṇt	æːfꞷnum

"We have become ashamed before the poļjoːɭ, we have become a subject for ridicule before the oːtoːɭ." Previously she has said that her father is to be told that the girl child was rejected as an unsuitable offspring and she, the wife, as an unsuitable wife, and all the Todas (by furthering the divorce) have come to be against her. So their treatment has caused them shame before all the Todas. Again, poļjoːɭ and oːtoːɭ seem to have no pertinence except as referring to the whole tribe conventionally when shame is to be spoken of. And again we feel that the poļjoːɭ relation between mother and daughter is perhaps in point, though the Todas do not make such an interpretation and the context is decidedly against it.

The remaining passage in a song about my investigations is as follows:

naḻkanɯsk	sydj-mil-sydj	pɯṭɯθik		
poḻjoɪḻ-xoɪrjm	oɪtoɪḻ-foṇt	öštjɯḍoɪ	ɯdɯθik	
oɪn arjen	enk öštoθ	sotj-moɪḍkin	ɯdɯθɯng	noɪrṇɯsfɯn

"You sent message after message to the mund omgaɪs. You said: 'Tell me without fail the nature of the poḻjoɪḻ.' Noɪrṇɯs (Nòdrners, 67) said: 'I do not know; I was not told; I swear an oath.'" The pair poḻjoɪḻ, oɪtoɪḻ is used as demanded by convention, as is also poṇt "word," but to fit the pertinent word poḻjoɪḻ (which I was enquiring about) into the context, the conventional noɪškj was replaced by koɪrjm,[23] primarily "ceremony, ritual detail," here "details in general, nature." The song-phrases have been violently torn from their usual contexts and oɪtoɪḻ-foṇt, necessary by convention, is here quite meaningless. (Incidentally, noɪrṇɯs was the only Toda who ever refused information about matters that he certainly knew thoroughly.) The relationship within a matrilineal sib is essentially surrounded by shame, embarrassment (noɪškj), and should not be talked about to outsiders. This was undoubtedly Rivers' experience, and so his failure to find out about the matrilineal sibs, even though he got the word poḻjoɪḻ, is to be explained.

On the whole, then, examination of the song-passages where matrilineal sibs are mentioned convinces me that the key-passage to an understanding of the conventional song-pair poḻjoɪḻ, oɪtoɪḻ did not turn up in the many texts that I recorded. This was my frequent experience in recording songs and interpreting the song-language. In many cases a pair can have originated in one context only and was then transferred, sometimes violently, to other contexts where it did not quite fit. If it did not fit but was used only in an allusive manner, it was usually impossible to get at a literal meaning. Occasionally the original context would be found in a song only after dozens of instances had occurred in which the words were badly fitted. In the case of the phrase under discussion the original context has not turned up. We may suspect that an account in a song of the path of the dead might contain the key-passage, and yet such accounts occur in the material to the number of half a dozen, none containing the desired passage. Moreover, as has been seen above in the discussion of the prose passage, the pair poḻjoɪḻ, oɪtoɪḻ may have been imported into it from the songs and certainly is not a good fit in its context.

It is clear however from the song-passages, the prose passage, and the refusal of noɪrṇɯs to give information that the essential element in the attitude of the Todas to the matrilineal sibs is one of shame and embarrassment. And yet we are not much further in our understanding of the psychology of the matter. The best guess on the reason for the difference of attitude towards the patrilineal sibs and the matrilineal sibs is that, while incestuous relations are forbidden within both types of sibs, the latter, as the one containing one's mother and sisters, is the one where incest comes closest home. In Toda culture the crucial relations are part of a larger division which is worked intimately into the entire social structure of the

---

[23] This word is borrowed ultimately from Sanskrit kārya-.

tribe, and probably the shame feeling towards mother and sisters has been extended from these few relationships through the whole matrilineal sib, and then from the single sib as such to the entire matrilineal sib structure.

Where an attitude of disapproval is strongly verbalized, as is that of the Todas towards incestuous sexual intercourse, we may expect to find that there are infractions of the rules. Certainly this is the case with this rule among the Todas. As a tribe, they are vigorously and adventurously sexual, as might be expected from the number of socialized channels provided for sexual activity. Ordinary marriage within the moiety and the freedom allowed in changing mates, and the toːtjfoj ("lover-mistress") institution providing for sexual unions overstepping the boundary between the moieties[24] give evidence of a high degree of sexual activity. But these do not exhaust the possibilities. There are many more irregular liaisons, not provided for by overt institutions, and indeed punishable by fines if discovered, but well attested in the verbal content of the songs. In none of the songs did I find any evidence that the restrictions on incestuous intercourse were infringed. But chance allusions by my informants and interpreters provided sufficient evidence that sexual adventuresomeness extended to such relations, and one case was specifically alluded to. It is rumored that sirjaːr (Siriar, 20) at one time had sexual intercourse occasionally with his sister eʒag (Edjog). Such relations, if they were discovered, would be punished by a heavy fine, and there is of course also a deterrent in the fear that misfortune to the people involved or to their buffaloes would follow such offences as evidence of the anger of the gods. This deterring pattern, though strong enough elsewhere in the culture, tends to yield when it conflicts with the pattern of sexual adventurousness. The impression gained is that cases of incest, as defined by Toda patterns, are frequent enough.

While the origin of the structure of matrilineal sibs among the Todas cannot with much profit be discussed without reference to the origin of the whole Toda culture, it seems that something should be attempted. We are not likely ever to reach certainty on the larger question. The Todas were already in the Nilgiris in A.D. 1117,[25] and for how long before is anybody's guess. Certainly their traditions give no help in the matter, since they claim to have been created in the Nilgiris along with the Kotas and Kurumbas. But, since they

---

[24] An interesting point arises in the case of a woman's child, whose biological father is the woman's toːtjfoj-oːl. It is well known that there are many such children but no socialized attention is paid to the biological fact. It is, however, felt to be disgraceful if such a child should resemble facially its biological father. Makniːr (Makner), wife of tuškiːθj of the noːṣ patrilineal sib (Tuskeidi, 3), had six children, all born during her husband's lifetime. The eldest of these, töüfaːɯ (Tevò), looked like his mother's toːtjfoj-oːl, nobɯs of the piːṭoːl patrilineal sib (Naburs, 64), also called kɯtj (he reared the children after tuškiːθj died). In a quarrel töüfaːɯ might be abused (it is very insulting abuse) as: nobɯs-mox "son of nobɯs" or kɯtj-mox "son of kɯtj," or as nobɯs or kɯtj.

[25] B. Lewis Rice, *Epigraphia Carnatica* (Bangalore, 1898), Vol. 4, Inscription 83 in Châmarâjnagar Taluq of Mysore State. The inscription, in the Kannaḍa language and mostly in verse, describes the campaigns of a general, Puṇisa Daṇḍanāyaka, of the Hoysala king Viṣṇuvardhana (Biṭṭiga Hoysala Dēvaru). This general invaded the Nilgiris and "frightened the Toda" (the singular probably because of metrical requirements). No other Nilgiri tribes are mentioned, and the item occurring in a list of communities in the Coimbatore and Salem districts, Conjeevaram, and Malabar, gives no ethnological information. The date is quite certain.

speak a Dravidian language, closely allied with Kannaḍa and Tamil, and more closely, as I judge provisionally, with Kannaḍa, it seems profitable to look to a generalized South Indian background as a basis for the highly specialized and aberrant Toda culture forms. We find at once that the generalized South Indian culture background includes exogamous patrilineal sibs with marriage forbidden also within the matrilineal line to degrees that vary from community to community.[26] There is no record of fully developed exogamous matrilineal sibs in the large area until we reach the Malabar region on the southwest coast of India. There we find in some caste-communities matrilineal descent to the exclusion of patrilineal. Rivers was inclined on a number of grounds to uphold the hypothesis that the Todas in very early times migrated to the Nilgiris from Malabar.[27] Practically all of his pieces of evidence prove invalid.

It was a wild guess that the Toda language is closely related to Malayalam, and the fact that some of the diviners of the Todas undoubtedly do speak a very fragmentary Malayalam during their performances is irrelevant. The diviners speak the language of the god by whom they are possessed; the god who inspires most of the Toda diviners has his temple in the Wynaad among a Malayalam-speaking population. It was suggested[28] that the model house or dairy used in the uɪr-fott ceremony, and called poɪl-poʃj (Rivers' pülpali), has some connection with the tamarind juice used in a Nair ceremony. Linguistically this is impossible; the Toda word for tamarind (pyʃj) has no possible connection.

Toda polyandry was connected with the various types of polyandry formerly, and in some castes still, practised in Malabar. Much more investigation is needed in Malabar before comparison can be made safely between the institutions. It has been the experience of ethnologists in India that no summary accounts of communities hitherto published can be trusted. Even the best of them, such as the various *Castes and Tribes* volumes, are highly untrustworthy. Since in Malabar, polyandry is combined with matrilineal descent, the situation is undoubtedly oriented differently from that of the Todas, and a study of the total configuration in Malabar castes should be made before comparisons are entered upon. Furthermore, Toda polyandry needs to be reexamined in the light of the fact that the Kotas of the Nilgiris have been found to practise a special type of fraternal polyandry.[29]

The toɪtjfoj or "lover-mistress" institution (Rivers' mokhthoditi) is on the whole so unlike the marriages between the younger sons of Nambutiri Brahmans and Nair women that use of the superficial and strained resemblance is highly unprofitable.

---

[26] I base this statement partly on the literature (not all the pertinent facts are to be found there), partly on my own investigations (which were thorough among the Coorgs, an account of whose regulations will be found in my paper *Kinship and Marriage among the Coorgs* [Journal, Royal Asiatic Society of Bengal, Letters, Vol. 4, pp. 123–47, 1938]; sketchy enquiries were made on several other communities). The point, I think, is of more fundamental importance for the understanding of South Indian ethnology than that about cross-cousin marriage, which Rivers treated in *The Marriage of Cousins in India* (Journal, Royal Asiatic Society, pp. 611–40, 1907).   [27] Pp. 693–718, especially pp. 698 ff.   [28] Rivers, p. 702.

[29] D. G. Mandelbaum, *Polyandry in Kota Society* (American Anthropologist, Vol. 40, pp. 574–83, 1938).

The giving of cloths in various Toda ceremonies was compared with cloth-giving ceremonies in Malabar. It will be found, however, as Rivers recognized,[30] that giving of cloths, both in marriage ceremonies and otherwise, is very general throughout India. No stress should be laid on this detail until and unless further investigations of other Indian communities warrant it. So also with the breaking of pots at funerals; it is not confined to the Todas and the Malabar coast.

The use of poles and boxes at funerals, of cowries, and of leaf-umbrellas, all of these being obtained from Malabar, is hardly more than the use of trade-objects, and is probably to be regarded as an example of diffusion of comparatively unessential material objects. The place of origin does not matter in the case of the cowries and the umbrellas; they have now been replaced by glass beads and European-type umbrellas respectively. It is doubtful whether the place of origin has any significance in the case of the other objects.

The Toda munds at Gudalur are well known in tradition as recent foundations; they have now been abandoned. The origin of some sacred buffaloes in the Wynaad, i.e. the same general area between the Nilgiris and Malabar, is paralleled by the origin of other sacred buffaloes on the Coimbatore, i.e. the Tamilian, plains on the other side of the Nilgiris.

It is evident then that the Malabar origin for the Todas and their customs favored by Rivers is untenable.[31] The Toda matrilineal sibs, which were unknown to Rivers, could have been used by him to bolster up his hypothesis, but it would have proved to be of no more value than his other evidence. It is clear that the general South Indian situation sketched above provides a sufficient basis for the Toda developments. The South Indian exogamous patrilineal sib has retained full vigor among the Todas. The exogamous tendencies of the matrilineal line which work in varying degrees in all South Indian communities have been developed among the Todas into full-fledged exogamous matrilineal sibs, probably on the model of the patrilineal sibs and facilitated by the small size of the tribe. We have here nothing more than an isolated local development, easily derivable from a general cultural feature of South India. The resemblance to the Malabar matrilineal communities is only superficial, for there the patrilineal units, if they originally existed, have been entirely superseded by the matrilineal units.

[30] Rivers, p. 700.

[31] Rivers also toyed with Coorg as a source for Toda customs, basing this partly on linguistic, partly on ethnological grounds. It may be mentioned here that the polyandry alleged for the Coorgs, if it ever existed, seems to have left no trace either verbally or in relic-institutions, so far as I was able to discover in eight months of linguistic work in Coorg. The linguistic grounds given by Rivers (p. 114) for Toda knowledge of the Coorgs are incorrect. The Todas call the plains at the foot of the Nilgiris, i.e. to the south, east, and northeast, kǔɯg. This is etymologically connected with Kota koŋg in the same meaning, Tamil koŋku "the Tamil country comprising the districts of Coimbatore, Salem, and a portion of Mysore," in effect the same area as that meant by the Toda and Kota words, Kannaḍa koŋgu with the same meaning as the Tamil word, Malayalam koŋŋu (no dictionary is accessible for the meaning). Rivers understood at least one instance of the Toda word as being equivalent to the English word Coorg. This is impossible. "Coorg" represents the Kannaḍa koḍagu, which cannot be connected with Toda kǔɯg and its cognates. The Todas have no knowledge of the Coorg country or of its inhabitants.

APPENDIX

Reference terms, classificatory

A peꞔiin

B peꞔiaf; members of preceding generations may be referred to exactly as muːd-tal-ꞔiin, muːd-tal-ꞔiaf (great-great-grandparents), noːn-tal-ꞔiin, noːn-tal-ꞔiaf (great-great-great-grandparents), or they and the great-grandparents may all be referred to by grandparent terms.

C piin

D piaf

E in, ejiː ⎫
F af, afuf ⎮ The second entries are reduplicated forms which do not differ from
G mun, mumum ⎮ the simplex forms in denotation; they are in connotation somewhat
H mimj, mimimj ⎮ less formal, and no trace of them has been found in the song-language
I on̯, on̯on̯ ⎮ or in the address terms, formal or otherwise. For a preliminary discus-
J okn, okok ⎭ sion of the linguistic structure of the forms, see my paper *Echo-words in Toda* (New Indian Antiquary, Vol. 1, pp. 109–17, 1938), p. 112.

K -ŭɯɽ-fed (-mox, -xuːx; see p. 159)

L močiṇj (-oːļ̣ or -mox, -θoƶmox or -xuːx)

M mox

N kuːx

O man-mox ⎫ (see pp. 161, 164)
P man-guːx ⎭

Q moːt-ꞔiļ̣θ (see p. 165)

X oːļ̣

Y toƶmox

Z mod-okn (see p. 164)

Reference terms, descriptive

1. The husband of a female relative is referred to by -n-oːļ̣ suffixed to the term by which she is referred to; e.g., okn(n)-oːļ̣ "elder sister's husband," en-ŭɯɽ-fedn-oːļ̣ or en-ŭɯɽ-fed-xuːxn-oːļ̣ "younger sister's husband" (in both cases if the husband is not EGO's cross-cousin, and permissively if he is), močiṇj-xuːxn-oːļ̣ "female cross-cousin's husband" (if he is not EGO's brother), kuːxn-oːļ̣ "daughter's husband" (otherwise pojoːļ̣), man-guːxn-oːļ̣ "sister's daughter's husband (man speaking), brother's daughter's husband (woman speaking)" (unless he is EGO's son), moːt-xuːxn-oːļ̣ "son's daughter's husband," kuːxn-guːxn-oːļ̣ or kuːxk-fæːdfoj-xuːxn-oːļ̣ "daughter's daughter's husband," en(k)-koːtfojn-dan-okn-oːļ̣ "my wife's elder sister's husband," en-oːļ̣n-dan-okn-oːļ̣ "my husband's elder sister's husband" (see 4 below for discussion of -dan- = tan), etc. In most cases explicit description could be carried further, as okng-fæːdfoj-xuːxn-oːļ̣ "elder sister's daughter's husband."

2. The wife of a male relative is referred to by -(k)-koːtfoj (or -(g)-goːtfoj, depending on certain grammatical rules) suffixed to the term by which he is referred to; e.g., on̯(g)-goːtfoj "elder brother's wife," en-ŭɯɽ-fed(k)-koːtfoj or en-ŭɯɽ-fed-mox(k)-koːtfoj "my younger

brother's wife" (in both cases if the wife is not EGO's cross-cousin, and permissively if she is), močinj-mox(k)-koːtfoj "male cross-cousin's wife" (if she is not EGO's sister), man-mox(k)-koːtfoj "sister's son's wife (man speaking), brother's son's wife (woman speaking)" (unless she is EGO's daughter), moːt-mox(k)-koːtfoj "son's son's wife," kuːxn-mox(k)-koːtfoj or kuːxk-fæːdfoj-mox(k)-koːtfoj "daughter's son's wife," en(k)-koːtfojn-dan-oṇ(g)-goːtfoj "my wife's elder brother's wife," en-oːḷn-dan-oṇ(g)-goːtfoj "my husband's elder brother's wife," etc. Explicit reference can be carried further, as okng-fæːdfoj-mox(k)-koːtfoj "elder sister's son's wife."

3. The son or daughter of a relative is referred to (a) by suffixing -n-mox or -n-guːx (-n- need not be found) respectively to the term for the relative, or (b) by suffixing -k-fæːdfoj-mox or -k-fæːdfoj-xuːx respectively (-k- may be replaced by -g- depending on certain grammatical rules as in 2); e.g., oŋ-mox or oŋg-fæːdfoj-mox "elder brother's son," oŋ-guːx or oŋg-fæːdfoj-xuːx "elder brother's daughter," en-ŭwɾ-fedn-mox or en-ŭwɾ-fedk-fæːdfoj-mox "my younger sibling's son," kuːx[n]-mox or kuːxk-fæːdfoj-mox "daughter's son," man-mox[n]-mox or man-moxk-fæːdfoj-mox "sister's son's son (man speaking), brother's son's son (woman speaking)," en(k)-koːtfojn-dan-okn(n)-mox or en(k)-koːtfojn-dan-okng-fæːdfoj-mox "my wife's elder sister's son," etc. Permissively for explicit reference we may find, e.g., en-okn(n)-mox or en-okng-fæːdfoj-mox "my elder sister's son." A son's son is moːt-mox (moːt- = moxn; cf. p. 165), a son's daughter moːt-xuːx; a son's son's son is moːt-mox-mox.

4. Other relatives of relatives may be referred to by suffixing -n- (which need not be found) plus the appropriate term. Most frequently -dan- or -θan- (= tan; the variation depends on grammatical rules) is inserted after -n- or after the member which may end in -n-; e.g., en(k)-koːtfojn-dan-on "my wife's elder brother," en(k)-koːtfojn-[dan]-ŭwɾ-fed "my wife's younger sibling," en-in-[dan]-močinj "my father's cross-cousin." This tan is originally the reflexive pronoun of the 3rd person; it is used often enough in this sense, but more often with kinship terms as in the examples just given without any meaning that I have been able to discover (never, however, when a 1st or 2nd personal pronoun form would immediately precede it). Though it might mean in these uses "(his) own" there are some contexts where no question of the persons being "own" brothers or the like can arise. The reflexive force seems to have been lost in this use with kinship terms, and one is tempted to think that kinship terms are on the way to a grammatical state in which they will not occur without a pronominal reference, i.e. inalienable possession (in reference only, not in address). The reduplicated forms of E-J do not occur with tan preceding. A few other examples may be given: kŭætæːn-dan-af "kŭætæːn's mother," piḷjaːr-θan-biin "piḷjaːr's grandfather," i-oːḷ-θan-man-mox "this man's sister's son," iθaːn-dan-mun "the maternal uncle of these men," in-dan-mun-öŭ-m "all the seven maternal uncles of this man," an-dan-oːḷ "her husband," e(m)-muːd-om tan-oṇaːm-oːfemi "we (exclusive) three are brothers," iθ-æːd-m tan-oṇ-m tan-ŭwɾ-fed-m-wk-oč wcwn "these two were living like brother and sister;" in one passage a snake's coming is referred to and the snake, not referred to previously, is called tan-a(f)-foːb "the mother snake" and later on tan-in-foːb "the father snake" comes. Cf. for other examples 1–3 above and pp. 159, 164.

Terms of address

	Ordinary	Formal	
		Used by men	Used by women
a	pefiaː ⎫ ⎰piaː ⎱		
b	pefiafaː ⎭ or ⎱piafaː ⎰	a and b same as for c and d	
c	piaː	timbjeː?	(e)tjfia?
d	piafaː	timbiafa?	(e)tjfiafa?
e	ejaː	tjɛː?, tįː?	(e)tjeja?
f	afaː	tjafa?	(e)tjafa?
g	mumaː	tjųː?	(e)tjmuma?
h	mimjaː	tjmimja?	(e)tjmimja?
i	oņaː	tjǫː?	(e)tjoņa?
j	okaː	tjoka?	(e)tjoka?
k	endaː		
l	enaː		
x	oːḻjaː		
y	toʒmoxjaː, kuːxjaː		

(The formal terms contain extra-phonemic phonetic material, the glottal stop, nasalized vowels, and initial consonant groups.)

In formal address a man, to a man whom he calls endaː or enaː, uses the latter's name plus -es; e.g., kŭaɽoːnes.

A man who is addressed formally by another man with the salutation timbjeː?, tjɛː?, or tjųː?, answers tæːm.

Older man or woman to younger woman when putting feet to the latter's forehead in salutation, i.e. in formal address: (e)tjfɯne?.

Woman to younger male related to her within a patrilineal or matrilineal sib, by marriage or by "lover-mistress" relation, says, if he is of:

töŭfiḻj moiety	(e)tjfɑke?
toːrθas moiety	
melgaːs patrilineal sib	(e)tjfɑke?
kaːs patrilineal sib	(e)tjxena?
noːṣ, möːɽ patrilineal sibs	(e)tjŭɯːθe?
toːroːɽ, köːroːɽ, niɽj, ɯņkitj,	
kerɯɽ, pɯrgoːɽ patrilineal sibs	(e)tjxŭɯțe?

Corresponding to these salutations, in a lament for her husband a woman uses the vocatives: ɯsafakaː, ɯsafakaː, ɯsaxenaː, ɯsaθŭɯːθaː, ɯsaxŭɯțaː; cf. with these terms the Badaga classification of the Todas given by Rivers, pp. 541–42. A man in a lament for his wife uses the vocative ɯsafanaː; cf. the salutation (e)tjfɯne? used by older man or woman to younger woman.

Formal salutations are not used by a man to his female cross-cousins, or to any woman not related to him in a patrilineal or matrilineal sib, by marriage, or by a "lover-mistress" relation; nor by a woman to her male cross-cousins, or to any man not related to her in a patrilineal or matrilineal sib, by marriage, or by a "lover-mistress" relation.

There is an unfortunate omission in my material; it is not known how a man addresses his brother's wife and how a woman addresses her sister's husband. Husband-wife terms seem more probable than brother-sister terms, but the point needs to be investigated.

A further note should be added on the words mox and kuɪx. It will be seen that in reference the simplex terms mox = "son" (sometimes extended in a collective sense "children") and kuɪx = "daughter," and that as final members of terms they denote "male" and "female" respectively, but that in address neither is used in this sense, while kuɪxjaɪ in address = "wife." Further, tozmox "wife" is a combination of toz-, not otherwise found, and mox (the first element must be descriptive of the second, i.e. it is the wife who is some kind of mox). Kuɪx is used in texts often to mean "young woman." In the songs a wife is addressed, usually when a husband laments her death, with the vocative ɯsaxuɪxjaɪ, containing kuɪx; a husband, usually when a wife laments his death, with a vocative ɯsamoxjaɪ, containing mox. Any child is addressed in songs with the pair: enmoxubaɪ, enmarjubaɪ, containing mox in the meaning "child" and, equated with it, marj which in prose means "offspring of animal (except buffalo) or bird." From a Toda point of view the basic meaning of kuɪx is probably "female" or perhaps "young female," all the other meanings developing from that. Mox is much more intractable, though the meaning "child, especially male child" may possibly be basic. The term ɯsamoxjaɪ "husband!" could possibly have been derived from a practise whereby the wife adopted her mother-in-law's usage, but the conditions certainly do not exist in present-day usage, and on the whole such an explanation is dubious. Tozmox would still be unexplained and will remain so until the prior element is explained.

UNIVERSITY OF CALIFORNIA
BERKELEY, CALIFORNIA

CULTURE SUCCESSION IN THE GREAT BASIN

By WILLARD Z. PARK

INTRODUCTION

MORE than twenty years ago Sapir pointed out the chronological problems in the culture area concept. With other American ethnologists he recognized that the familiar areas in native American culture are little more than devices for the descriptive classification of cultural data. At the same time Sapir sought to go beyond this limitation and view the cultural areas from an historical standpoint. His stimulating suggestion of a small number of primary cultures, historically underlying the development of the specializations that differentiate the ethnologists' culture areas, has not, unfortunately, been put to sufficient empirical test. However, the importance of giving different historical weighting to various elements, institutions, and complexes must be the starting point for the reconstruction of New World history.[1]

Americanists generally are agreed that some features of native culture are old whereas others are specialized forms. Further, there is general recognition that the several culture areas represent different historical levels; that some areas arose from a regrouping and a specialized development of elements of the older culture. The problem then is one of an historical analysis of the cultures in various areas in order to uncover the different chronologic levels.

It is of course essential that all cultural provinces should be rigorously examined in the light of the materials from both ethnography and archaeology. Progress has been made in this direction, notably in the Southwest and in the Plains, and in each instance the picture of the type culture has had to be sharply revised.[2] Too little attention, however, has been directed to those areas of less pronounced cultural growth. In part this oversight has been due to the lack of substantial ethnographic data from such areas but at the same time a noticeable feeling that such areas as the Great Basin or the Plateau are of a different (and lesser) order has discouraged a definitive examination of the position that the more undifferentiated areas of culture hold in the total New World picture. A reexamination of some of the generalized or simple cultures would profitably shift the emphasis from their dependence on other regions to the more fundamental problem of the sequences in development that tie them to the highly specialized areas of culture.

---

[1] Sapir, *Time Perspective in Aboriginal American Culture*, pp. 44–46.

[2] Kroeber has stimulatingly discussed the Southwest from the point of view of historical problems in New World cultures. His conception of the culture area as an historical device harmonizes nicely with Sapir's arguments for primary cultures (*Native Culture of the Southwest*).

Recently Strong has reappraised the validity of one ethnographic culture area, the Plains, in the light of the newly uncovered archaeological materials. A significant realignment of the ethnographic classification is indicated from the prehistoric cultures of the Plains region (*Plains Culture in the Light of Archaeology*).

Some of the data now available from the Great Basin suggest sequences in cultural development locally, and in addition bear directly on the interpretations of differentiation in the more highly specialized cultures in western North America. The present paper will consider some of these data and seek to define their relation to the problem of cultural succession suggested by the historical connections inferred from similarities between the Great Basin and neighboring areas.

The Great Basin has for a number of years had an anomalous position in North American ethnology. In the customary culture area classification this region has frequently been regarded as an adjunct of either one or all of the surrounding areas.[3] On the other hand, largely because little more than an incomplete picture of cultural simplicity in this region has been available in ethnographic literature, Great Basin institutions have often been regarded as the contemporary undifferentiated type culture that formed the substratum of large blocks of native civilizations in western North America. Both the conception of the Great Basin as a hinterland of areas of higher development and the notion of an old undifferentiated culture minimize the succession of culture within the area. At the same time the Great Basin seen from these points of view raises fundamental questions as to the relation of its cultures and those of neighboring regions.

The lack of satisfactorily complete data on the archaeology and ethnography of the Great Basin does not as yet permit a realistic analysis of developments in this area. Problems can be defined and suggestive inferences drawn at least from certain materials now available. Data on the dance complex of the Great Basin indicate a relatively simple aggregate of practises and beliefs, but one that has grown out of historically diverse elements. Moreover, parallels between the dances of the Basin and of neighboring areas raise questions about the historical affiliations of these cultures. Are these dancing practises earlier in neighboring areas than in the Great Basin? Or are they to be assigned to a common substratum, differentiating more or less along specialized lines in each area? A summary of available information may not provide the final answers to these questions, but at least it will help clarify the position of the Great Basin in relation to other North American areas. There is a further possibility of achieving a somewhat more systematic picture of the internal relationships of Great Basin cultures.

The type culture of the Great Basin is not yet clearly defined but it is likely that a fairly high degree of uniformity prevailed throughout the area. It can be assumed for the time being that the Paviotso of Western Nevada afford a reasonably typical example of Great Basin people. Although linguistically and culturally closely related to the Northern Paiute

---

[3] Thus Basin peoples are frequently mentioned in the literature as "Plateau Shoshoneans." Kroeber, on the other hand, regards the Great Basin as a cultural adjunct of central California (*op. cit.*, p. 390; *Handbook of Indians of California*, p. 917). Wissler assigns the eastern part of the Basin to the Plains area, and the western half—made up of the Mono-Paviotso tribes—to central California (*American Indian*, pp. 226–27). A sounder case for alignment of Basin cultures with the Ranchería group of non-pueblo tribes in the Southwest has been made by Spier in his analysis of Havasupai and other Upland Yumans (*Cultural Position of the Havasupai*).

of Surprise and Owens Valleys in California, the Paviotso of Nevada regard themselves as an independent cultural and political unit.[4]

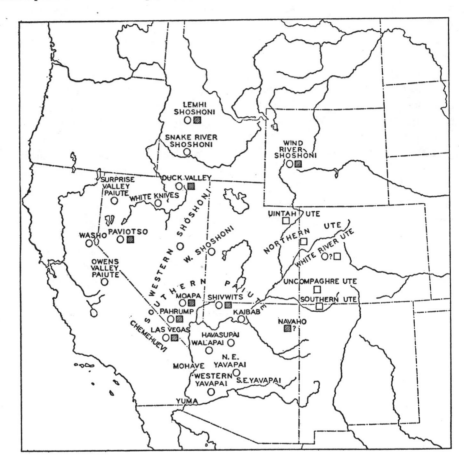

DISTRIBUTION OF THE ROUND AND BEAR DANCES
Circle: Round Dance. Square: Bear Dance. Shaded square indicates the introduction of the Bear Dance in the post-Caucasian period.

In the social life of pre-white times, large gatherings were confined to communal hunts and to the Round Dance. These occasions were relatively infrequent, however, the com-

[4] Locations of the Great Basin tribal groups which are mentioned in this paper are indicated in the accompanying map. Only groups referred to in the present discussion are mapped here. More detailed mappings of Great Basin tribes are to be found in Steward, *Linguistic Distributions and Political Groups;* Ray and Others, *Tribal Distribution in Eastern Oregon;* Park and Others, *Tribal Distribution in Great Basin.*

munal antelope drives usually occurring in the spring and the dances customarily in late spring and early fall.[5] The Round Dances, therefore, bringing together people from far and near with a substantial representation usually from each of the localized bands, loomed large in the social activities of the Paviotoso. The larger affairs seem, moreover, to have transcended the loose band distinctions both in the inter-band participation and in the absence of possessive attitudes toward the dance on the part of the local group. Dances even today are described as being held at a particular place, such as at Pyramid Lake or Walker Lake, but the people of that locality do not give the dance: it is the joint enterprise of all who attend. In this connection it is to be noted that no invitations are issued; all Paviotso who hear news of the approaching affair come. The attitude of tribal solidarity is also evident in the treatment of Northern Paiute from California and Western Shoshoni who occasionally attended Paviotso dances even in pre-reservation days. These people were looked upon as visitors and so treated.

The data now available suggests that throughout the Great Basin dance gatherings were equally important and played similar roles in tribal life. In order to present a concrete picture of this Basin institution the details of the Paviotso dances will first be offered.[6] The Great Basin picture can then be rounded out from other accounts.

THE DANCE COMPLEX IN THE GREAT BASIN

In aboriginal days the Paviotso held dances fairly frequently in the late spring, summer, and early fall. Most informants agreed, however, that the large affairs attended by people from all the bands occurred at two well defined times of the year. In the spring when the kuyui fish in Pyramid Lake went up the Truckee River, food was abundant and people gathered near the mouth of the river to fish. At this time one of the big dances was held. Again in the fall large numbers came together to dance just before the pine nut harvest got under way. Dances are now held on the Fourth of July and at Christmas. The dance witnessed in the summer of 1934 at Pyramid Lake corresponds in most features to the details of earlier practises described by the majority of informants. In the modern version dances lasting only one night are customary, but in the pre-white period dancing continued for five nights. Further indications of decay in the old dance pattern is seen in the tendency in recent years to omit the clownish performances or "fun dances" from the Round Dance repertory.

The account of Paviotso dances given here applies both to the large affairs customarily held semi-annually and to the smaller dances occurring more frequently during the months in which the weather permitted travel and in which a surplus of food was available. The smaller gatherings differed only in that fewer people attended. The frequency as well as the purpose of both large and small dances is indicated by the statement of one informant:

[5] The communal rabbit drives involved smaller groups and less preparation than did the antelope hunts.

[6] The data presented here are from an ethnographic study of the Paviotso now in preparation. Field work was carried on in the summers of 1933, 1934, 1935, and 1939. Ethnographic studies in 1934 and 1935 were financed by grants from the Institute of Human Relations, Yale University.

"In the old days dances were held as often as once a month. People had to pray for things all the time."

The Round Dance (nugab°, meaning simply dance, is the more common term) is held on a flat cleared space 200 to 300 yards in diameter; usually the same dance grounds are used each year. The decision to hold a dance rests with a local group, composed of the people camping more or less temporarily in the neighborhood. This is probably not true of the dances formerly held in the spring in connection with the opening of the spring fishing season at the mouth of the Truckee River and at the beginning of the pine nut harvest in the fall. The precise dates of these two large tribal dances were set by the head men when the fish were about to run or when the pine nuts were ripe. But these gatherings are described as regular annual affairs and aside from the variations from year to year due to the influences of nature, the dances were fixed annual events. Word of a coming dance is carried by people traveling to other localities either in search of game or seeds or on social visits. Formal messengers are not employed to notify other bands or to invite guests but usually the news of a dance is spread widely by the constant inter-band visiting.

On the day appointed for the beginning of the dance, families converge on the dance grounds and erect temporary brush shelters around the space reserved for dancing. Before the dancing starts a pole is set up in the center of the dance ground. People who were familiar with the old life insist that the pole had no other purpose than to provide a point of orientation for the circle of dancers; without the pole, it is thought, the dancers would have difficulty in staying in the center of the dance grounds.

During the day men and women engage in various gambling games which are played on the dance grounds or, in the old days if additional food supplies were needed, hunting and seed gathering expeditions would be sent out. After nightfall fires are built around the dance circles and the dancing starts; the young people, at least, often continuing to dance until morning.

Information is not clear on feasting but it is likely that food was pooled and a big meal was prepared on at least one or two days of the festival. Perhaps if supplies were especially plentiful this was done every day. A simple routine of dancing, gambling, some flirting among the young people, and much gossiping was followed for five nights and on the sixth day the dance grounds were deserted by people returning to the normal business of life.

The most popular dance among the Paviotso is the Round Dance, typical of the Great Basin; it forms in fact the core of the larger dance complex here given the same name. In the post-reservation period other dances are given on several nights of the gathering, and in the earlier days there was at least a clownish performance to relieve occasionally the monotony of the Round Dance. All adults and older children participate in the Round Dance whereas special performers appear in "fun dances that make people laugh and give them a good time." It is significant that religious beliefs and activities are associated only with the Round Dance. Prayers or "talking" for rain, seeds, game, and other blessings do not appear at all in connection with the "fun dances." The Round Dance then is the backbone of the complex and the other parts are supported by it. In the words of one Paviotso: "It is the big dance; it is to pray for good crops and to ask for game. The dance is for a good time, for many seeds and pine nuts; it lasts five nights."

The Round Dance follows the familiar pattern of men and women forming a circle and joining hands with palms together and fingers interlaced or dovetailed. The dancers then shuffle or sidestep in a clockwise direction around the dance grounds. The sole musical accompaniment is provided by singing. A singer, not the leader or head man in charge of the dance, takes his place in the circle and starts a song which is quickly taken up by the other dancers.

The dance witnessed at Pyramid Lake in 1934 exhibited many of these features. Shortly after dark people formed in a large circle about a tall pole erected in the middle of the dance grounds. The man who was to lead the songs took his place in the circle and began to sing. In less than a minute the other people in the circle joined in the singing, and, clasping hands, began to walk clockwise around the pole. They walked nearly three quarters of the distance around the grounds keeping about a half arm's length apart. Then the singer, quickly followed by the others, began to dance with a shuffling or gliding movement to the side. As the dancers changed from a walk to a shuffling movement they closed ranks and, each pressing close to the person on either side, danced shoulder to shoulder. The dance step seen on this occasion was simple: sliding the left foot six or eight inches to the side and slightly forward, the dancer followed with the right foot. The dancers continued this step until the singing stopped. They then dropped hands and stood in the circle for several minutes waiting for the singer to start singing again. Men and women entered and left the dance circle at any time without any apparent ceremony. The number of times the pole was circled in each dance depended on the number of dancers in the circle and the length of the song, both varying considerably from dance to dance. Differences in cadence from song to song were also quite noticeable.

The dance songs, unlike the shamans' songs which are always dreamed, are composed by the singer. Shamans' songs, moreover, are never used in the dance. "You can't foxtrot to a sacred hymn. If people danced to a doctor's song it would be like dancing to religious music." Singers for the Round Dance receive no pay for their services but a good singer, one who has a good voice and knows many songs, is much in demand.

Men and women frequently alternate in the dance circle but there is no rule requiring such an arrangement. At the beginning of the dance men usually form the circle with the women standing behind them. After the circle is in motion the women break in between the men and, joining hands with them, begin to dance. Both men and women enter the dance circle or drop out whenever they wish. Women and girls usually take the initiative in selecting dancing partners, although men who are not already in the dance circle are not customarily invited by the women to dance.[7]

[7] Courtship figures as a part of the dancing pattern here. Girls try to dance with unmarried men who are considered desirable for husbands; often they are encouraged by their parents to make advances. Men also court girls by dancing with them in the circle. The old morality is said to be suffering at the dances that are held in modern times. "Nowadays couples sneak off into the brush, but a long time ago it was not this way. In the old days parents watched girls closely. If a boy was a good hunter and brought in many deer and rabbits, parents told their daughters to dance with him but the girls were carefully watched."

The dance costume does not differ in style from the dress of the workaday world. The best clothes are worn, and the face and exposed parts of the body of both men and women are painted with simple bars and dots in red and white. Painting and other features of the dance costume are said to have no other purpose than to enhance the personal appearance. Men who act as dance chiefs are not distinguished in dress or in decoration from the dancers. Dance leaders, moreover, are not distinguished by badges or other symbols of office, nor are paraphernalia used in the performance of their religious duties. Men and women not taking part are urged to dance by the leader or head man who walks about and calls in a loud voice for everyone to join in the dancing.

In addition to its social and recreational functions, the Round Dance is also an occasion for the performance of simple but important religious rites. The repeated statements of nearly all informants that praying or "talking" is one of the chief reasons for giving the dances indicates something of the importance attached by the Paviotso to this part of the ceremony. These religious practises are simple to an unusual degree, but the dance has clearly the double function of bringing people together for a thoroughgoing good time and for an appeal to vaguely conceived supernatural powers that are thought to control human health and supplies of wild seeds and game. The Paviotso frequently expressed the view that the prayers and "talking for things" are as much a part of the occasion as the dancing. The religious character of these dances is further evidenced by the statement quoted above: "People had to pray for things all the time."

These simple religious observances often have been neglected at the dances given in recent years. The consequences that have followed the failure to observe old practises have been pointed out by several Paviotso. "Nowadays no one asks for pine nuts at the dances. The pine nuts grow but the weather is too hot so they burn on one side. People should talk about pine nuts at the dances as they did in the old days."

Religious expression at the dances is confined to "talking" or praying while the dancers were singing and circling the pole in the Round Dance. A dance leader or head man (sometimes called the dance chief or "boss") selected for the occasion walks around outside the circle of dancers, asking for rain, wild seeds, pine nuts, fish, game, and good health for all. All agree that he is asking aid and blessings from some supernatural force or power. "The chief of the dance talks while the poeple dance. It is just like praying. He talks about the weather. He asks for rain so the people will have plenty of roots and seeds. He wishes for pine nuts and other foods for the coming year. He talks to some kind of spirit." The head man continues his talking for some time; at large dances several men alternate in this role throughout the greater part of the night. One informant described additional ritual acts: as the head man walked around the dance circle he scattered seeds or pine nuts on the ground and over the dancers.[8]

The head men who are entrusted with the duty of praying at the dances are selected

[8] There seems to be no distinction made between the rites and prayers in the spring and those of the dances held to celebrate the pine nut harvests.

for the occasion. Although these head men are influential they need not hold the position of chief, nor are they regularly the leaders in the communal hunts. "They are old men. The old people are better for this; they know the ways from long ago." These dance leaders are not shamans and possession of supernatural power is not a qualification for the position.

An account of the simple rain and fertility ritual in the Paviotso dance has been recorded by Lowie among the Washo. These people told Lowie that they learned of such a dance from the Paviotso. The dance, held early in the spring, is believed to make everything sprout well, to prevent the frost and storm from killing the blossoms, and to encourage the growth of pine nuts. A part of the rite not mentioned by the Paviotso but apparently credited to them by the Washo is the preparation of one burr with "medicine" to insure a plentiful supply of pine nuts.[9]

The supernatural powers supplicated for rain and other blessings are not clearly defined by the Paviotso. Pressed to name or describe the powers addressed, informants several times stated: "It is like talking to the sun in the morning when a man asks for luck in hunting deer, for health, and to have bad dreams taken away." Again it is said that the prayers are addressed to "some kind of spirit."[10]

It is to be noted that praying to the sun was an important part of the pre-white religious pattern. Usually just at sunrise, as the face and hands are washed in cold water, requests for aid in throwing off illness that results from a dream or for success in the hunt are addressed to the sun.

The dance chief or leader also prayed to the sun as he washed in the morning. At this time he asked for rain, for abundant supplies of game and seeds, and for freedom from ill health. The pattern is identical with that of the early morning prayers mentioned above, but a number of informants were far from certain that the "talking" of the dance leader was also addressed to the sun.

The religious beliefs and practises connected with the dance gatherings do not involve relations with the animal spirits, ghosts, and other supernatural beings which are the source of Paviotso shamanistic power.

The Round Dance, and the accompanying rites, may be interrupted during the night for special performances. It is in any event customary to stop for a rest period after several hours of dancing. These intermissions sometimes may be taken up with performances of the so-called "fun dances" which are given for the entertainment of those present. Most of these special dances have been adopted by the Paviotso in the past forty or fifty years and they are still regarded as foreign. Among the dances so acquired are the Bear Dance, said to have come either from the Shoshoni or the Southern Paiute; a war dance learned from

[9] Lowie, *Ethnographic Notes on the Washo*, p. 315.

[10] Hazy or vague conceptions argue neither for recent adoption nor for any measure of antiquity, hence are of little significance in empirically proving succession in cultural growth. Vagueness in these and other beliefs probably only reflects the lack of formalization and explicitness which is so characteristic of the culture. Paviotso conceptions of magic and much of the folklore bear out this impression.

the Bannock; and a so-called "Medicine Man" dance introduced by California Indians. The formations and movements in these dances, as well as the use of the drum and split-stick rattle, are clearly alien to the Paviotso dance pattern.

Addition of these dances to the Paviotso repertory is, of course, an obvious part of cultural growth, but as borrowing occurred in the reservation period, the circumstances surounding their incorporation into Paviotso culture were probably, in terms of the old life, abnormal. An analysis of these recent accretions contributes little to the understanding of earlier developments in the culture and may, therefore, be omitted from the present discussion. Knowledge of these modern changes are not, on the other hand, to be dismissed as of little significance. Data on these recent events are valuable for sociological inquiries into the subject of cultural change. Information on these innovations would have for such studies inestimably greater value than inferential evidence of more remote and hence less definitely ascertainable developments in culture. It may be that the borrowing of dances, almost on a wholesale scale, in the reservation period is consistent with a larger picture of cultural change during this time. The profound alterations wrought by reservation life have not precluded intensification of cultural borrowing from other Indians, for the Paviotso appear to have become more receptive in this period than ever before to influences from other native cultures.

The more recent additions to the Paviotso dance complex are not, however, the only performances offering variety and entertainment at the Round Dance. At least one of the "fun dances," the hump dance (tu'nɔnugabᵉ; tu'nɔ, hump; nugabᵉ, dance), is claimed by the majority of informants to be old among the Paviotso. This is a masked clownish performance regarded as highly amusing and entertaining. The name of the dance is said to be derived from the great lumps or humps on the dancers' backs that give the performers the appearance of grotesque hunchbacks.

The number of men participating in the hump dance is apparently not rigidly fixed by custom, informants reporting anywhere from five to ten dancers and three or four singers. The account given by the present singer at Pyramid Lake also includes women among the dancers, two or three without special costumes or masks dancing with the men. Probably women frequently participate in the performance but men wearing women's clothes and imitating their actions also figure prominently in the dance.

The costumes for the hump dance are designed to give the performers above all a grotesque and ridiculous appearance. Clothing is stuffed with rags (formerly skins) to achieve the effect of lumps on the back and legs or to indicate a large belly. Several dancers may each have a foot bandaged, and others dress as women. Some dancers also wear a coyote tail dangling in the rear and all, or nearly all, are masked. Those who do not have masks paint their faces with streaks and dots of red and white, making themselves look as fantastic as possible.

The masks are made with skin taken from the faces of such animals as the coyote, badger, wildcat, and deer, but coyote masks seem to be more desirable and are perhaps more common. The appearance of the animal face is approximated by stuffing the skin with grass. Information on the care and preservation of these masks is not definite, but it seems that they are given no special attention.

The hump dancers give their performance as a rule once or twice during the Round Dance. Often the clownish performance is given on the second night and may be repeated either on the third or fourth night. Usually the hump dancers perform for one or two hours during the first half of the night. When the clowns are dressed and masked the leader of the Round Dance calls a halt to the dancing and the people gather around the dance circle.

Three or four men who know the songs for this dance act as singers; other musical accompaniment is lacking. One of the singers, who holds the rather vague position of dance leader, usually arranges the details of the performance. The singers are not masked nor do they participate in the dancing. Contrary to the Round Dance practise, the dancers do not join in the singing.

At the time appointed for the dance to begin, the singers seated at one side of the dance grounds start to sing. At once the masked performers come on the dance grounds in single file and, breaking rank, dance and burlesque for the amusement of the spectators. In this performance there is no regular dance formation; the dancers do not stay in line nor do they join hands and move in a circle.

The outstanding feature of the hump dance in the opinion of the Paviotso is the clownish behavior of the performers. This point was made by a number of informants who compared these dancers with the clowns in a circus. The grotesque costumes and masks, the buffoonery, and the mimicry of women and cripples are sources of great merriment. Some performers imitate women carrying baskets, others walk as though they are lame or wounded, and several carry bows and arrows and pretend to shoot at imaginary targets. All actions of the dancers emphasize the foolish and the exaggeratedly awkward, especially in the familiar behavior of men and women. There is in this clownish play no suggestion of the obscene, either in behavior or in jokes.[11]

As the dancers carry on their clownish play they sway their bodies and make quick, short jumps to the side. Part of the time a dancer moves to the left and then turning around he advances with the same short jumps to the right. Although the dancers do not stay in any definite formation, they all move around the dance grounds in a clockwise direction, "because all the dances go that way."

When the singing stops the dancers gather around the singers and wait for the next song. The dance continues in this fashion for an hour or more; sometimes it lasts as long as two hours but never longer. The dancers then file off the dance grounds and remove their costumes. Shortly after the dancers leave, the Round Dance is resumed.

[11] The Paviotso are not lacking in the formal or institutionalized expressions of obscenity. Obscene joking between the sexes is customary when people come together in the evenings for gossip or in other purely social gatherings. The obscene remarks on these occasions are regulated by fairly explicit rules. It is further interesting to note that the nicknames so commonly used by the Paviotso are often derived from the obscene banter that goes on between the sexes at these gatherings.

The description of the hump dance given by Curtis is essentially similar to the details of the foregoing account.[12] His additional information on the dancers' costumes is also of interest. Willow withes are tied to various parts of the body and some dancers wear coyotes' ears. Further, one performer, who is always dressed in an entire coyote skin, runs about snapping and imitating actions of the animal. Curtis also notes that the dance is given for entertainment and is, moreover, one of the few dances indigenous to the Paviotso.

One account of the hump dance is of interest because it suggests a connection between the clownish performances and the Ghost Dance movement. Billy Biscuit, who gave the following statement, was born near Silver City, Nevada. For many years he lived at Lovelock, moving to Pyramid Lake Reservation when he was past middle age. He was probably past seventy when interviewed in 1934.

When I [Billy Biscuit] was a boy the dance [hump dance] was more secret than it is now. When the big dance [the Round Dance] was over for the night the men who were going to hold a hump dance went off to the side to dress. They danced on the regular dance grounds, but people were not allowed to come on the grounds to watch. They [the spectators] had to sneak into the brush shelters that were built around the dance grounds and watch from there. The dancers were supposed to be ghosts. I think this dance was part of the talk about bringing back the dead [the Ghost Dance] and these dancers were the ghosts of the dead, but I am not sure about that. This hump dance started here at Pyramid Lake.

Other accounts of the hump dance as well as several eye witness descriptions of the 1890 Ghost Dance failed to corroborate this statement. Ten or more informants questioned on this point, moreover, insisted that there was no connection between the Ghost Dance and the hump dance. Further, these people were unanimous in denying that the clownish performances had any religious meaning at all.

The Paviotso are not entirely agreed that the hump dance is an old institution among them. The majority opinion held that the dance originated with the Paviotso. Two informants, however, maintained that the dance had been acquired from other Indians, but their statements did not agree. The leader of the hump dance at Pyramid Lake, Johnny Newman, said that the Paviotso learned about the dance from the Northern Paiute at Fort Bidwell. This, he estimated, took place about 1850. Another informant on the same reservation stated that the dance was introduced fifty years later by Northern Paiute visitors from northern California, that is, from the same general area.

Attention again may be called to differences between the hump dance and the other performances for entertainment given at the dance gatherings. Those dances which all informants agree are of recent introduction employ the rasp, split-stick rattle, or the drum, whereas the masked performance conforms to the undoubtedly older pattern of the Round Dance in accompanying the dancing only with singing. It seems highly probable, therefore, that the masked clowns' performance formed a part of the dance complex at least as early as

[12] Curtis, *North American Indian*, Vol. 15, p. 85.

the opening of the reservation period, but no evidence is available to establish its precise antiquity.

The aboriginal Paviotso dance complex is then composed of a relatively small aggregation of simple practises and vague religious beliefs that involve a minimum of ritual observances. The several parts of this complex combine in an integrated institution which has both social and religious functions. Seen in this way the social and religious aspects of the festivals merge as the inseparable purposes of the dances.

A clear picture of the dance complex throughout the Great Basin cannot be formed from the present scanty ethnographic data, but the Round Dance appears to be the basic type of dancing among the greater majority of the tribes. The gliding dance step, clasping hands in a circle, singing accompaniment to dancing, and the absence of musical instruments are characteristic of the Round Dances held by the Northern Paiute in California.[13] The simple religious practise of the Nevada dances are not definitely reported for the Californians, although dancing before the pine nut and after seed harvests suggests that the Owens Valley and Mono Lake people formerly may have sought supernatural blessings of rain and abundant harvests at these festivals. Further, head men among the California Paviotso, like their Nevada neighbors, make speeches while dancing is in progress.[14]

A fragmentary account of a rain dance with performers dressed as antelope and dancers pretending to shoot with bows and arrows comes from the Surprise Valley Paiute.[15] Fuller information would possibly reveal some connection here with the Paviotso hump dance, although the Nevada performance has no rain-fertility implications. The dance of clowns is not reported for the Owens Valley people, but masks, woman impersonation, and mimicry brought by "Paiute from the north" are mentioned for one dance, presumably held in recent years.[16]

A suggestion from Surprise Valley that ghost impersonation figured in the 1890 Ghost Dance movement[17] is of interest because it may have a bearing on the uncorroborated statement of the Paviotso given above. It is possible that these two accounts, both describing a dance at Pyramid Lake, indicate an aberrant performance of the Ghost Dance under the direction of Jack Wilson. Other descriptions of Ghost Dance ceremonies definitely deny that ghost impersonation figured in the rites, but it is just possible that the Surprise Valley and Pyramid Lake accounts picture an unsuccessful attempt to introduce a novel feature into the established pattern of the Ghost Dance. That the innovation failed may be due to the circumstances mentioned by Kelly's informant: after the dance some of the people followed the ghosts and discovered that they were impersonators.

Two groups of the western Shoshoni, the White Knives and the Salmon Eaters, now living on the Duck Valley Reservation in Nevada, formerly held ceremonies several times a year at which as many as four hundred people gathered. Dancing on these occasions is

[13] Steward, *Owens Valley Paiute*, pp. 320–21; Kelly, *Surprise Valley Paiute*, pp. 178–80.
[14] Steward, *op. cit.*, pp. 320, 322.   [15] Kelly, *op. cit.*, p. 179.
[16] Steward, *op. cit.*, p. 321.   [17] Kelly, *op. cit.*, p. 180.

reported to have been closely associated with fertility rites. Here the pattern is similar to that described for the Paviotso: the Round Dance lasting five nights with the head man praying for rain, for an abundance of wild seed and game, and for relief from illness. These western Shoshoni dance leaders also prayed to the sun in the morning. The rain-fertility ritual is here perhaps even more prominent than in the Paviotso dance complex.[18]

The Shoshoni groups elsewhere in the Great Basin appear to have had much the same complex of rain-fertility observances associated with dancing. The meager accounts of dancing and the supernatural beliefs and practises associated with the festivals suggest a fairly uniform pattern. The complex is everywhere simple: dances in connection with harvests of pine nuts and seeds or at communal drives of game held for five days or nights; dance directors who talk or make speeches while the dancing is in progress; exhibition dances with performers, in post-Caucasian times at least, paid for their services; and the belief that the ceremony brings rain, assures a bountiful supply of seeds, game, or fish, and promotes health or general well being. It is also likely that the dominant form of dancing is the familiar circle of men and women moving clockwise with a shuffling step to the accompaniment of singing. Steward's recent survey of the Great Basin Shoshoni suggests that this dance complex prevails from eastern California through Nevada and Utah to central Idaho.[19]

Information from the Lemhi Shoshoni of Idaho indicates that the dance gatherings were, in former days, associated with fertility. The Round Dance was, moreover, the most important Lemhi festival. It was held customarily in the spring and fall for the purpose of assuring an abundance of salmon and berries; apparently it also made the grass grow and brought other blessings, such as health. The dancers interlocked fingers and glided clockwise in a circle, singing as they danced. Leaders or dance directors are reported to have been in charge of these festivals.[20]

The Wind River Shoshoni likewise regard a form of the Round Dance as old. Data on this performance are scanty, but it appears that the dance lasts five nights, causes storms, and is given to bring about the cure of illness. The dancers form a circle, clasp hands with fingers interlocked, and move clockwise to the accompaniment of singing in which the dancers participate.[21]

The Round Dance seems, from the meager information, to hold a less important place in the dance complex of the Ute and Southern Paiute. The typical features of men and women joining hands in a circle and dancing to the accompaniment of singing are reported, but the dance step among the Uintah Ute, at least, is not the familiar shuffling or gliding movement of the Round Dance. The Ute performance is, moreover, reported to have been recently introduced. Further, there is no indication that fertility rites are associated with the Ute

[18] Ray and Others, *Tribal Distribution in Oregon*, p. 409; Harris, *White Knife Shoshoni of Nevada*, p. 53.
[19] Steward, *Basin-Plateau Sociopolitical Groups*, pp. 45, 54, 60–61, 70, 74–76, 90, 98, 106–107, 122–23, 139, 159, 169–70, 193.
[20] Lowie, *Northern Shoshone*, p. 217; Steward, *op. cit.*, p. 193.
[21] Lowie, *Dances and Societies of the Plains Shoshone*, p. 817.

and Southern Paiute Round Dances, although in the ceremony of the latter people a chief makes speeches while dancing is in progress.[22]

Among the several Ute groups the Round Dance is definitely overshadowed by another dancing performance, the Bear Dance, associated with somewhat different religious conceptions. The Bear Dance, held usually in the spring, is believed to conciliate the bear when he comes from hibernation. In addition the ceremony is believed to cure the sick or prevent illness and to bring about changes in the weather; for example, snow is expected to fall during the dance or within a short time after its close.

The Bear Dance differs from the Round Dance in nearly all important details. The ceremony is held in a large circular brush enclosure in contrast to the more or less open space which is the scene of the Round Dance. The dancing formations of the two performances also are significantly different. In the Bear Dance men and women either face one another, forming two lines which approach each other and then move back to the original positions, or they dance in single pairs, dancers holding their partners. Further, the data suggest that impersonation or mimicry of the bear figures in the dance and on the final morning of the ceremony. Musical accompaniment for the dancing is provided by scraping a notched stick or rasp. The dancing comes to an end when a dancer, falling exhausted, is ceremonially revived by one of the musicians or the head man who directs the dance.

In the Bear Dance, as in the Round Dance, women customarily choose dancing partners but the act is ritualized in the former ceremony. Women usually invite men to dance by tapping them on the shoulder with the hand or a stick. Refusal to dance is punished by a whipping at the hands of the dance leader. This practise has not apparently accompanied the Bear Dance in its post-Caucasion diffusion. The Lemhi Shoshoni, however, believe that the refusal of a woman's invitation to dance will result in the injury or death of the offender.[23] Moreover, Paviotso men, fearing the sickness thought to result from declining an invitation to join in the Bear Dance, throw a handful of dust at the woman who has been refused.[24]

From all indications the Bear Dance was the most important pre-Caucasian socio-religious ceremony of the Ute, overshadowing all other festivals of both the Southern and Northern Ute.[25] Under aboriginal conditions, therefore, two distinct dance complexes are discernible in the Great Basin: the Round Dance with its rain-fertility rites as a characteristically Paviotso-Shoshoni performance, and the Bear Dance, involving magico-religious conciliation of the bear. Available data suggest that, at least until the opening of the reservation period, the latter performance was almost entirely limited to the Ute.

[22] Lowie, *Notes on Shoshonean Ethnography*, p. 302; *Dances and Societies of the Plains Shoshone*, p. 832; Steward, *op. cit.*, p. 184.

[23] Lowie, *Northern Shoshone*, pp. 219–20.

[24] This probably is an extension of the belief that throwing dust at a whirlwind will drive away the evil spirit that inhabits it and thereby protect one against the illness believed to result from such an encounter.

[25] Lowie, *Dances and Societies of the Plains Shoshone*, pp. 823–31; Densmore, *Northern Ute Music*, pp. 56–58.

Even wider historical significance attaches to the distribution of the basic religious conceptions of both dance complexes, for these, of course, appear far beyond the limits of the Great Basin. Thus the Ute dance suggests a local recombination in a dance ceremony of the widespread magico-religious beliefs and rites associated with the bear. The rain-fertility belief and ritual of the Paviotso and Shoshoni festivals, on the other hand, suggest a South-western pattern, but one that is unqualifiedly simple. The distinction between the two aggregations of dance practises seems to be fundamental and to have separate historical backgrounds. If such is the case, it might suggest that two streams of development are to be traced in the Great Basin. There is no evidence, however, that this cleavage between Ute and Paviotso-Shoshoni dance customs extends through a substantial part of Basin culture.

The few data on the Bear Dance among other Great Basin tribes indicate that the dance was radically changed as it diffused within the area. The Southern Paiute (at least Moapa and Shivwits), Paviotso, and the Shoshoni (or Paiute) of the Duck Valley Reservation have adopted the Bear Dance within the past forty or fifty years; the Wind River and Lemhi Shoshoni learned it somewhat earlier. In each group the Ute are reported to be the source of the dance. In this new setting the Bear Dance above all has been stripped largely of its religious meaning. In particular, conciliation of the bear did not accompany the spread of the dance formation, the characteristic movements, and the rasp.[26]

The Paviotso and at least two Southern Paiute bands, the Pahrump and Las Vegas, have incorporated the Bear Dance into the familiar pattern of the exhibition dances that are performed during intermissions in the Round Dance.[27] Fuller information from other Great Basin tribes may show that this has been the common fate of the Bear Dance in its recent history.

Still another reorientation of the dance has been observed among the Southern Paiute. The Moapa and Shivwits are reported to have borrowed the Bear Dance from the Ute in the period 1900–1910. Somewhat earlier a public mourning ceremony was introduced from California. The Shivwits, according to Lowie, have combined the two institutions and now the Bear Dance is performed as part of the wailing rites held for the dead. The Moapa also dance during a similar mourning ceremony that continues from one to five nights but here the older pattern of dancing in a circle, as in the Round Dance, prevails.[28]

To what extent this recent introduction of the mourning ceremony is an extension of the influence that Mohave culture has been said to have on other Southern Paiute groups is not clear. The rite is clearly not the anniversary mourning of many Californians but does definitely resemble the Mohave and Yuma performances following cremation. On the other hand, the Mohave-Yuma song cycles, known in part to the Chemehuevi and Kaibab bands of Southern Paiute, are not reported for the Moapa and Shivwits mourning rites although of course singing is a part of the ceremony. Moapa-Shivwits mourning further lacks the

[26] Lowie, *Northern Shoshone*, pp. 219–20; *Notes on Shoshonean Ethnography*, pp. 299, 301–302; *Dances and Societies of the Plains Shoshone*, p. 818.   [27] Steward, *Basin-Plateau Sociopolitical Groups*, p. 184.

[28] Lowie, *Notes on Shoshonean Ethnography*, p. 279.

ritualistic performances of the Mohave and Yuma ceremonies.[29] If the Southern Paiute mourning is to be connected with Mohave and Yuma practises it is clear that not only was the change late in Great Basin cultural history but the influence of the Californians was weak because only an attenuated form of the ceremony reached the Moapa and Shivwits. It is possible that further investigation of Southern Paiute mourning customs would bring to light significant information about the introduction of the California ceremony and the manner in which it has been combined either with the older Round Dance or with the recently borrowed Bear Dance.

As yet there is no definite evidence that the recent spread of the Bear Dance extended beyond the Colorado River. Lowie's Southern Ute interpreter reported that the Navaho and Apache performed this dance in curing the sick, and Spier has related the Havasupai "Mohave Dance," borrowed from the Walapai, to the Bear Dance.[30] Inclusion of the Navaho and Apache in the area covered by the Bear Dance must await more definite evidence but the relation of the Mohave Dance of the Walapai, and more recently of the Havasupai, to the Bear Dance of the Great Basin may be briefly reexamined.

The Walapai dance that was borrowed by the Havasupai is part of the mourning ceremony adopted from the Mohave within the last fifty years. In both the Walapai and the Havasupai versions of the ceremony the dancers form in two lines facing each other. The lines of dancers among the Havasupai move back and forth but the Walapai men run about fifty yards and then return to their original positions, the line of women remaining stationary. The Havasupai dance formation has an analogue in the Bear Dance custom of two lines of dancers, one composed of men and the other of women, moving to and fro.[31]

In addition to the Walapai testimony that the mourning ceremony, including the dance, was borrowed from the Mohave the close correspondence to some of the details in the Mohave and Yuma performances suggests that the Mohave Dance of the Havasupai may be but a simple and somewhat altered form of war mimicry which belongs to the mourning ceremony of the California Yumans. It is to be noted also that dancing lines, one of men and the other of women, occur in Mohave performances which are given primarily for amusement. Further, no evidence of a Bear Dance of the Great Basin type is to be found in the available literature on the Mohave and Yuma.[32]

The difference between the Shivwits and Havasupai-Walapai performances, therefore, is probably fundamental: the Shivwits added to the mourning ceremony a simplified form of the Bear Dance and the Walapai adopted a modified version of an already existing and thoroughly integrated complex of dancing (or a conventionalized representation of warfare) and mourning practises. This latter performance was subsequently adopted, at least

---

[29] Kroeber, Handbook of Indians of California, pp. 599, 750–51, 793.

[30] Lowie, Dances and Societies of the Plains Shoshone, p. 825; Spier, Havasupai Ethnography, pp. 267–68, 272–73. These dances and their distributions have been discussed by Spier (op. cit., pp. 269–74, fig. 53). The material presented here supplements Spier's discussion and mapping.

[31] Spier, op. cit., p. 268; Kniffen and Others, Walapai Ethnography, pp. 150–53.

[32] Kniffen and Others, op. cit., pp. 150–51; Kroeber, Handbook of Indians of California, pp. 750–51, 765, 792.

in part, by the Havasupai, possibly with the dance formation and movements influenced somewhat by the Bear Dance of their Southern Paiute neighbors. The Bear Dance is, there-fore, in development and probably almost entirely in distribution a Great Basin perform-ance.

Great Basin dances are too meagerly described to permit a definitive survey at this time of local or tribal variations. Still, sufficient information is in print to indicate that the Bear Dance complex must have been fairly uniform among the Ute groups where it probably de-veloped in its characteristic form. The far-reaching modifications of the earlier pattern appear usually during the post-reservation history which is largely characterized by decline of religious content and meaning.

The Round Dance complex of the Shoshoni and the Paviotso may have also lacked in aboriginal life marked differentiation from tribe to tribe. Present information indicates a widespread basic pattern: dances lasting five nights; the twofold purpose of social gather-ings and securing rain and abundance of food from supernatural blessings; men and women holding hands and dancing clockwise in a circle; singing by the dancers providing the only musical accompaniment; chiefs or speakers addressing the dancers and praying for bless-ings; and exhibition dances. In the pattern of exhibition dances the masked clownish per-formances of the Paviotso are unique and differ fundamentally from other Basin dances.

Ceremonial clowns, often masked, appear widely in native American cultures, of course. The connection between the Paviotso performances and those of other areas is, however, far from clear. Clowns for example are reported for the neighboring northeastern Maidu and also figure prominently in the Kuksu Cult rituals of other Californians, but only ex-tremely vague similarities with the Paviotso performers are evidenced. On the other hand, the animal impersonation in the cult ceremonial dances may connect the Paviotso dance and its coyote mimicry with California. To mention only one instance: the Miwok clowns who appear in interludes in ceremonies and represent coyotes resemble, at least superficially, some of the hump dance performers.

But dissimilarities in Paviotso and California performances are, at the same time, quite substantial. The clowns of the neighboring Maidu, for example, bear no resemblances in costume or in behavior to the Nevada performers, with little likeness between Paviotso and Maidu mimicry of the coyote and the impersonation of other animals.[33] There is fur-ther a marked dissimilarity in native interpretation of the masked clowns and their per-formances.

If the Paviotso masked clownish play was derived from California the performance has undergone a thoroughgoing revision. Aside from the similarity in coyote mimicry Cali-fornia and Paviotso performances are related largely by an underlying concept of ceremonial clownish play. Certainly such vague relationships do not argue for a very effective domina-tion of California cultures over those in the Great Basin.

[33] Dixon, *Northern Maidu*, pp. 298, 304; Kroeber, *Handbook of Indians of California*, pp. 383, 389, 425, 435-36, 450.

The masks and clownish behavior reported for the public ceremonies of the Northwest Coast and Plains tribes are still further removed, both geographically as well as in a significant array of details, from the simple Paviotso masked performances. Connections with the masked clowns of the Southwest are likewise not apparent. The Havasupai situation perhaps summarizes the lack of immediate relationships between the clowns of the two areas. A masked dance, which was discontinued in recent years, was clearly Pueblo or Navaho in origin.[34] Details of the masks as well as the dance formation definitely distinguish this ceremony from the Paviotso performance.

This uniqueness does not necessarily argue that a masked dance developed in Nevada without stimulation from the clownish performances elsewhere in native America. Geographically California would be, of course, the most obvious source of such influences. The Miwok clowns with their coyote mimicry and the face coverings in some of the Kuksu rituals offer the closest California parallels to Paviotso performers and their masks.[35] Still the somewhat vague evidence of similarities would be overworked if the Nevada performances are to be inferred as deriving directly from California. In all probability the Paviotso received from California some ideas, such as coyote mimicry, perhaps even suggestions of clownish behavior and masks, and out of these developed a performance that bears little resemblance to ceremonial buffoonery in central California.

Final proof of an historical connection in this case rests on determining just how far vagueness in similarities and resemblances in generalized ideas or patterns are acceptable as evidence of diffusion. Steward has suggested that the ceremonial performances of clowns in the several North American aboriginal culture areas are historically related to a single origin either in Mexico or in the Southwestern area. According to this thesis a generalized pattern of an individual—or a group—acting the buffoon in public ceremonies diffused from a single center to be given different contents of behavior and interpretation in various cultures. Accordingly, it would be argued that the Paviotso performance was stimulated by a generalized idea of clownish mimicry spreading into Nevada probably from California, with California in turn receiving the pattern from the Southwest.[36]

That such a vague pattern, devoid of any very specific content of practises and meaning, spread widely over the continent is difficult to reconcile with the realities of diffusion processes. Diffusion studies show beyond question that patterns formed by a particular combination and interpretation of ideas spread over greater or smaller areas. The guardian spirit concept, the bear ceremonial complex of Asia and northern North America, and the cattle complex of east Africa, are defined as much by ideas—including attitudes and beliefs—as by a particular aggregation of practises, and it is the specific content of these patterns that empirically establish their diffusion. The widely divergent practises and meanings manifested in the ceremonial clowning of American Indians suggest that such a continent-wide

[34] Spier, *Havasupai Ethnography*, pp. 266–67
[35] Kroeber, *op. cit.*, p. 450.
[36] Steward, *Ceremonial Buffoon*, pp. 188–89, 200.

"pattern" has little value for inferences of inter-regional historical connections, and thus is probably no more than what Sapir has called "a conceptualistic mirage."[37]

Whatever the historical connections may be between the Nevada masked dance and clownish performances elsewhere in North America, the absence of such an institution in the Great Basin generally has definite implications for the reconstruction of the growth of the Paviotso dance complex. If clownish performances have not been adopted by neighboring peoples, who in all other respects have similar dance festivals, addition of the masked dance to the Paviotso complex would seem to be relatively late, even though the development occurred prior to the reservation period. The Round Dance combined with rain and fertility rites, therefore, forms a complex that in all probability is older than the masked performance among the Paviotso. This latter ceremony, as well as other dances that have been developed or introduced subsequently, were then incorporated into the Round Dance as exhibition performances.

The chronological order in the growth of this basic Paviotso-Shoshoni Round Dance complex cannot now be reconstructed. That it developed independently of the Bear Dance is evidenced by the quite sharp distinction between Ute and Paviotso-Shoshoni ceremonies; a difference that probably existed even before Ute culture began to feel, not long before the beginning of the Caucasian period, the powerful influences coming from the northern Plains. Even more far-reaching implications for the historical interpretation of the Round Dance emerge when several features of the ceremony are considered in their larger inter-areal distributions. As these suggest significant historical connections between the Great Basin and neighboring areas of culture, the data will be summarized here.

CULTURAL RELATIONS AND CULTURAL SUCCESSION

Important similarities between the cultures of the Plateau and the Great Basin are commonplace in ethnological literature but it is significant that there are almost no resemblances in the dance practises of the two areas. The Klamath have the only Plateau parallel to the Round Dance on record but the similarities here are slight indeed. Elsewhere in the Plateau, as for example among the Southern Okanagon, the Round Dance is definitely non-existent; social dances in general also appear to be lacking. Shamanistic winter dances and first fruit and salmon ceremonies are commonly the outstanding Plateau performances, whereas the Basin is singularly deficient in either isolated elements of these rites or in attention to these occasions.[38] It is clear that Plateau and Basin dance institutions are historically unrelated.

The Round Dance festival stands as one of the most important socio-religious events in a large part of the Great Basin. Competition of these ceremonies with other public performances is not severe. Shamanistic curing rites and the communal hunts are the only other occasions for gatherings of people in any numbers.

To the south the closest parallel to the Round Dance complex is to be found among the

---

[37] Sapir, *Time Perspective in Aboriginal American Culture*, pp. 38–39.

[38] Spier, *Klamath Ethnography*, pp. 90–91, 112–15, 148–49, 266–67; Cline and Others, *Sinkaietk or Southern Okanagon*, pp. 32, 77, 146–53.

Havasupai. Here similarities in practises and beliefs are imposing. The Havasupai have the Basin dance formations and steps; dance leaders address moral discourses to the dancers and speeches, which are in part prayers, are made; and the dance is believed to bring rain and prosperity. At only two points are the Havasupai dances to be distinguished from the Basin festivals: the dance customarily lasts only two nights (five nights of dancing is the accepted Basin pattern) and a drum is employed. This complex is probably an old Havasupai institution, at least antedating, according to Spier, the 1870 Ghost Dance movement.[39]

Information on the dances among other Yuman speaking people of the Arizona plateau is unsatisfactorily meager, but the Walapai report indicates that these people had the Havasupai form of the Round Dance as early as 1870 or 1880.[40] There is, further, no suggestion in the available literature that the Walapai ceremony replaced earlier socio-religious performances.

The Northeastern and Western Yavapai have a dance in which a circle of men and women holding hands move clockwise, but these performances are exclusively social in purpose. The Southeastern Yavapai, on the other hand, hold a spring dance to insure bountiful harvests of wild products but the dance formation and movements, resembling somewhat the Bear Dance, are quite unlike the Round Dance pattern.[41]

Dancing, in brief, is almost at a minimum among the Yavapai and probably until recently with the Walapai. This would agree with Gifford's suggestion that the Yavapai-Havasupai-Walapai cultures never developed this activity very far.[42] It may, therefore, be argued that the Havasupai (and Walapai) performance was, in nearly all details, derived from the Great Basin.

The affiliations of the Upland Yumans with Great Basin cultures have already been outlined by Spier.[43] The data offered here calls for a revision of his formulation at only one important point. The rain-fertility purpose of dancing is attributed by him to the influence of Pueblo religion whereas the simple but well-defined pattern closely associated with the Basin Round Dance argues forcefully for the inference that the entire complex came from the latter area.[44]

If this conclusion is valid it implies more than a restatement of the source of a particular Havasupai institution. A reformulation of Great Basin cultural relations with other areas might well be indicated. At any rate the evidence challenges the assumption that holds institutions or other elements of culture vaguely resembling some part of Pueblo civilization must be derived from the more highly specialized center of development. The simplicity of the Basin rain-fertility rites taken with the distributional evidence suggest a somewhat different explanation; that undifferentiated observances to insure an abundance of food are a part of an older stratum of native American culture. Rain-fertility conceptions are not

[39] Spier, *Havasupai Ethnography*, pp. 261–66.
[40] Kniffen and Others, *Walapai Ethnography*, pp. 202–203.
[41] Gifford, *Northeastern and Western Yavapai*, p. 291; *Southeastern Yavapai*, p. 238.
[42] Gifford, *Northeastern and Western Yavapai*, p. 322.
[43] Spier, *Cultural Position of the Havasupai*.   [44] *Ibid.*, p. 216.

limited to the Great Basin and Southwest, for the dances of the Kuksu society in California are thought also to bring rain and insure bountiful harvests of wild foods.[45] The South-western and central Californian fertility ceremonies probably represent, then, particular specializations of earlier undifferentiated and widespread rain-fertility practises. This in-ferential reconstruction cannot, of course, determine the precise form of ancient rites or be-liefs because recent Basin institutions probably are expressions of both local developments and intrusive influences. Certainly the particular combination of magico-religious observ-ances to insure fertility with the Round Dance in the Great Basin cannot with any cer-tainty be assigned to an old cultural stratum of western North America.

The distribution of another feature of the Round Dance complex is significant in the light of the thesis advanced here. The dance leader or chief who orates and prays at the dance festival has a very close parallel in the ceremonial leaders and chiefs of California and the adjacent Southwest. Speeches, often in a stereotyped pattern, are definitely important functions of dance chiefs or other ceremonial directors throughout a large part of Cali-fornia.[46] Similarly oratory, exercised chiefly at dances, is one of the most important functions of the head man in the Basin.[47] The widespread similarity in the basic pattern gives added support to the argument that the Round Dance complex includes institutions which are older than the specializations on which the classification of regional culture types rests.

The inter-areal affiliations at this historical level are of course not peculiar to the dance complex. A sampling of other data indicates relationships of a similar order as well as affili-ations in somewhat different directions.

The brushing of a person or object with feathers or other sacred paraphernalia is a tech-nique widespread in native American religious practise. In the Great Basin this rite appears in connection with shamanistic curing and dancing.[48] Similar practises occur in connection with the dance gatherings. The rasp has been mentioned as being put to this use in the Bear Dance, and the White Knife Shoshoni in the Round Dance brush off "evil, filth and disease" with the hands.[49] The Paviotso report brushing the dancers with sage brush in the Ghost Dance and in shamanistic curing. Similar practises may have been part of the fertility ritual of their Round Dance.

A sampling of the data indicates that brushing as a curing technique, or as a practise in some way related to it, has almost a continuous distribution from the Great Basin through the Owens Valley Paiute, Western Mono, Yokuts, Cahuilla, Cupeño, Chemehuevi, Luiseño, and Diegueño to and including the Gila-Colorado block of cultures defined by Spier's analysis, the Maricopa, Pima, Papago, and Lower Colorado Yumans.[50] Ritualistic

[45] Kroeber, Handbook of Indians of California, pp. 381–82.

[46] Ibid., pp. 210, 252, 389, 750.

[47] Steward, Basin-Plateau Sociopolitical Groups, p. 247.

[48] Shamanistic usages in the Great Basin and surrounding areas have been surveyed in Park, Shamanism in Western North America.

[49] Lowie, Dances and Societies of the Plains Shoshone, p. 829; Harris, White Knife Shoshoni of Nevada, p. 53.

[50] Steward, Owens Valley Paiute, pp. 313, 315, 316; Driver, Culture Element Distributions: Southern Sierra Nevada, pp. 103, 137, 142; Drucker, Culture Element Distributions: Southern California, p. 42; Spier, Gila River and Lower Colorado River Tribes, p. 21.

brushing, of course, also figures prominently in Pueblo ceremonialism and may derive from an older cultural stratum common to this block of relatively unspecialized cultures.

This widespread practise associated with such a variety of meanings and usages adds weight, then, to the argument that resemblances between Great Basin and more highly developed cultures form part of an older, less differentiated, cultural stratum. This view harmonizes with Lowie's suggestive discussion of a basic area west of the Rockies separate from the cultures elsewhere on the continent.[51] The relationships indicated by the evidence discussed here, taken in conjunction with Lowie's survey of such western institutions as kinship, raise historical problems which cannot be met simply with assumption that the similarities are to be ascribed to diffusion from a center of highly differentiated culture. Fuller ethnographic data will doubtless clarify these basic historical relationships.

Not all inter-regional affiliations of Great Basin cultures are with areas to the west. The recent overlay of Plains institutions on the older cultures in the eastern part of the Great Basin obscures older cultural connections. Recently a survey of the shamanistic complex in the Basin indicated that the Plains shared with the Basin a number of well defined practises and concepts.[52] In particular the communal drives of game are significantly similar in the two areas. Data now at hand extend the distribution in the Basin of the shamanistic antelope-drive complex and more clearly define the importance of this institution in Great Basin culture. It is now known that antelope charming at communal drives occurs in the Basin from western Nevada through most of the Shoshoni groups in Nevada and Utah to the Bannock and Shoshoni at Fort Hall, Idaho.[53]

This evidence establishes beyond question that antelope charming is an old Basin institution, with, of course, Plains affiliations. But if Plains archaeology calls for a revision of the historical development of the type culture in that area, Plains-Basin relationships may require reformulation in the light of Strong's characterization of prehistoric Plains cultures.[54]

An historical analysis of a single Great Basin institution can but suggest the existence of an underlying inter-regional culture. More complete data from archaeology and ethnography will not only fill in needed details but will also sharpen the broader outlines of the cultural developments which culminated in the specialized cultures in native western America. The slowly accumulating data at last begin to make evident the need in historical reconstruction of what Sapir called "the synthetic process by elimination" in order to uncover the inter-regional relationships.[55] If such an element as rain-fertility ritual appears in the Great Basin, not from recent Southwestern influence, but from an older culture fundamental to the specialized developments of both central California and the Southwest, significant differences in the historical levels of these areas are established.

A rigorous analysis of Great Basin ethnography and archaeology, when the data are in,

[51] Lowie, *Cultural Connection of California and Plateau Shoshoneans.*
[52] Park, *Shamanism in Western North America*, pp. 62–66, 139–44, 152.
[53] Steward, *Basin-Plateau Sociopolitical Groups*, pp. 34–36, *passim.*
[54] Strong, *Plains Culture in the Light of Archaeology*, pp. 283–86.
[55] Sapir, *Time Perspective in Aboriginal American Culture*, p. 45.

should yield interesting results for the native history of the western portion of the continent. The data available at present at least vaguely outline Basin affiliations with an old basic culture which extended well beyond the boundaries of the familiar culture areas of recent native history. If this historical view of Great Basin antecedents stands the empirical test, the relationships of the Basin with other regional types of culture may be analogous chronologically to the connections, suggested by Sapir, between a general Eastern Woodland culture and the development of specialized Plains forms.[56] It is now at least evident that the historical problems lie in this direction. A realistic examination of them should throw interesting light on native cultural developments and serve to sharpen the methodological tools of ethnology.

BIBLIOGRAPHY

CLINE, WALTER, RACHEL S. COMMONS, MAY MANDELBAUM, RICHARD H. POST, and L. V. W. WALTERS (Leslie Spier, ed.) *The Sinkaietk or Southern Okanagon of Washington* (General Series in Anthropology, No. 6, 1938).

CURTIS, EDWARD S. *The North American Indian* (Vol. 15, Cambridge, 1926).

DENSMORE, FRANCES *Northern Ute Music* (Bulletin, Bureau of American Ethnology, No. 75, 1922).

DIXON, ROLAND B. *The Northern Maidu* (Bulletin, American Museum of Natural History, Vol. 17, Part 3, 1905).

DRIVER, HAROLD E. *Culture Element Distributions: VI. Southern Sierra Nevada* (Anthropological Records, Vol. 1, No. 2, 1937).

DRUCKER, PHILIP *Culture Element Distributions: V. Southern California* (Anthropological Records, Vol. 1, No. 1, 1937).

GIFFORD, E. W. *Northeastern and Western Yavapai* (University of California Publications in American Archaeology and Ethnology, Vol. 34, No. 4, 1936).

The Southeastern Yavapai (University of California Publications in American Archaeology and Ethnology, Vol. 29, No. 3, 1932).

HARRIS, JACK S. *The White Knife Shoshoni of Nevada* (In Acculturation in Seven American Indian Tribes, Ralph Linton, ed., New York, 1940).

KELLY, ISABEL T. *Ethnography of the Surprise Valley Paiute* (University of California Publications in American Archaeology and Ethnology, Vol. 31, No. 3, 1932).

KNIFFEN, FRED, GORDON MACGREGOR, ROBERT MCKENNAN, SCUDDER MEKEEL, and MAURICE MOOK (A. L. Kroeber, ed.) *Walapai Ethnography* (Memoirs, American Anthropological Association, No. 42, 1935).

KROEBER, A. L. *Handbook of the Indians of California* (Bulletin, Bureau of American Ethnology, No. 78, 1925).

Native Culture of the Southwest (University of California Publications in American Archaeology and Ethnology, Vol. 23, No. 9, 1928).

[56] Sapir, *op. cit.*, pp. 44-45.

LOWIE, ROBERT H. *The Cultural Connection of Californian and Plateau Shoshonean Tribes* (University of California Publications in American Archaeology and Ethnology, Vol. 20, pp. 145–56, 1923).

Dances and Societies of the Plains Shoshone (Anthropological Papers, American Museum of Natural History, Vol. 11, Part 10, 1915).

Ethnographic Notes on the Washo (University of California Publications in American Archaeology and Ethnology, Vol. 36, No. 5, 1939).

The Northern Shoshone (Anthropological Papers, American Museum of Natural History, Vol. 2, Part 2, 1909).

Notes on Shoshonean Ethnography (Anthropological Papers, American Museum of Natural History, Vol. 20, Part 3, 1924).

PARK, WILLARD Z. *Shamanism in Western North America* (Northwestern University Studies in the Social Sciences, No. 2, 1938).

PARK, WILLARD Z., and OTHERS *Tribal Distribution in the Great Basin* (American Anthropologist, Vol. 40, pp. 622–38, 1938).

RAY, VERNE F., and OTHERS *Tribal Distribution in Eastern Oregon and Adjacent Regions* (American Anthropologist, Vol. 40, pp. 384–415, 1938).

SAPIR, EDWARD *Time Perspective in Aboriginal American Culture, a Study in Method* (Memoirs, Canada Department of Mines, Geological Survey, No. 90, Anthropological Series, No. 13, 1916).

SPIER, LESLIE *Cultural Relations of the Gila River and Lower Colorado Tribes* (Yale University Publications in Anthropology, No. 3, 1936).

Havasupai Ethnography (Anthropological Papers, American Museum of Natural History, Vol. 29, Part 3, 1928).

Klamath Ethnography (University of California Publications in American Archaeology and Ethnology, Vol. 30, 1930).

Problems Arising from the Cultural Position of the Havasupai (American Anthropologist, Vol. 31, pp. 213–22, 1929).

STEWARD, JULIAN H. *Basin-Plateau Aboriginal Sociopolitical Groups* (Bulletin, Bureau of American Ethnology, No. 120, 1938).

The Ceremonial Buffoon of the American Indian (Papers, Michigan Academy of Science, Arts and Letters, Vol. 14, pp. 187–207, 1931).

Ethnography of the Owens Valley Paiute (University of California Publications in American Archaeology and Ethnology, Vol. 33, No. 3, 1933).

Linguistic Distributions and Political Groups of the Great Basin Shoshoneans (American Anthropologist, Vol. 39, pp. 625–34, 1937).

STRONG, W. D. *The Plains Culture in the Light of Archaeology* (American Anthropologist, Vol. 35, pp. 271–87, 1933).

WISSLER, CLARK *The American Indian* (3rd ed., New York, 1938).

UNIVERSITY OF OKLAHOMA
NORMAN, OKLAHOMA

HISTORIC BACKGROUNDS OF THE CONJURING COMPLEX IN THE PLATEAU AND THE PLAINS

By VERNE F. RAY

CULTURAL ANTHROPOLOGY is more and more rapidly getting to realize itself as a strictly historical science. Its data can not be understood, either in themselves or in their relation to one another, except as the end-points of specific sequences of events reaching back into the remote past."[1]

In pursuance of an historical understanding of ethnographic facts, interpreted by Professor Sapir as the proper ethnological goal, I have at various times analyzed cultural data gathered from the Plateau of northwestern America. One of the most provocative and productive phases of this study has been concerned with religious ceremonialism. Fieldwork in this connection recently brought to light a spectacular ceremony centering around conjuring. This ritual, shared by the Colville of eastern Washington and the Kutenai of British Columbia, exhibits striking parallelism with the djasakid performances of Ojibwa shamans. This was pointed out in a recent paper but the profound historical implications were left for future examination.[2]

Subsequent study of the pertinent literature has revealed other parallels and widened the distribution. The procedure, which I shall designate as the conjuring complex, is found in the Plains area as well as in the Woodlands and the Plateau. As might be anticipated, the complex is shared by those Plains tribes immediately adjacent to the Woodlands. But also among the far distant Cheyenne the ritual is found in typical form. The Cheyenne are not farther removed from the Woodlands than are the Kutenai, it is true, but the practise is thus brought into the heart of the intervening culture area.

In the Plateau itself the ritual is restricted to the two tribes mentioned. However, certain phases of the ceremony are found implanted in the Bluejay complex, a Plateau ritual of wider but definitely restricted distribution. It is altogether certain that the Bluejay performances are not merely wide variants of the conjuring complex. They are structurally and conceptually distinct; they form internally integrated procedures functionally associated with the great midwinter Spirit Dances around which much of Plateau religion revolves.[3]

Indeed, quite another pattern of activity in the Plains shows an even greater affinity with Bluejay ritualism. This is the contrary-behavior complex, a prominent feature of cere-

[1] Sapir, *Time Perspective*, p. 1.

[2] Ray, *Cultural Relations*, pp. 116-19. The Colville ritual was reported by Cline in 1938 (*Southern Okanagon*, p. 152 f.).

[3] Ray, *Bluejay Character;* cf. Ray, *Cultural Relations*, pp. 114-16.

monialism in the Plains. Parallels are impressively numerous, considerably outweighing those shown by the conjuring complex.[4]

The nature of the conjuring ritual and the extent of the similarities in the various regions can only be understood in terms of specific procedure. Consequently a type picture from each area is in order.[5]

The conjurers of the Parry Island Ojibwa (Georgian Bay, Lake Huron) have been described by Jenness.[6] Two classes were recognized, the kusabindugeyu and the djasakid. Procedures differed somewhat and the latter ranked higher than the former. Both received their power through adolescent visions and belonged to the category of shamans, not laymen. The principal spiritual source of power was Thunder; Owl and Whip-poor-will were of secondary importance.

The kusabindugeyu treated illnesses due to sorcery. He removed intrusive objects implanted by the sorcerer by a sucking technique in which several bone tubes were "swallowed," the last protruding from the mouth. With this tube placed against the patient's body he withdrew the disease object and deposited it in a container of clear water, together with the bones which he simultaneously regurgitated. The object removed was sometimes a small feather. He was also capable of retrieving a soul when stolen by a sorcerer; his clairvoyant powers enabled him to seek out the place of hiding. The same talent made it possible for him to discern the innermost thoughts of others.

The public performance involved the calling of spirits by means of singing and the use of a disc rattle. The appearance of each spirt was indicated by a dull thud of audible volume. The spirits did not speak, but merely "opened the seer's eyes so that he might behold the object of his quest."

The djasakid or djiskiu used the "shaking tent" for the performance of his feats. This was a cylindrical lodge about four feet in diameter. The framework of poles and hoops was covered with birch bark or cloth. The ritual, which was held after dark, began when the shaman crawled inside the lodge and started speaking in an indistinguishable voice. Soon a thud was heard and the lodge swayed violently, marking the arrival of a spirit. This was repeated until a number of spirits had assembled. Among the sounds the voice of Turtle was heard; it was he who acted as intermediary between the other spirits and the shaman. At the top of the lodge, "covering it like a lid," was Thunder, and other spirits were perched upon the hoop near the top.

A present of tobacco was sometimes necessary before the spirits would begin their work. This was handed over the top of the lodge and soon tobacco smoke could be seen floating above. Shortly thereafter the spirits were heard conferring and soon one departed to carry out the mission at hand, perhaps to bring back a sorcerer's soul. The departure and subsequent return were marked by violent thuds and the swaying of the lodge. Conversa-

[4] In the near future I shall present a study of the contrary-behavior complex in the Plateau and Plains; the work is now nearing completion.

[5] No attempt is made in this paper to exhaust the distribution of the conjuring complex. This task has been undertaken by Dr A. I. Hallowell, whose analysis is now in progress.   [6] *The Ojibwa*, pp. 60–68.

tion ensued between the spirits and the audience as to the disposal of the captured soul. After the matter was settled the spirits departed, the audience disbanded, and the seance was ended.

The object of the performance was sometimes aid in hunting. The spirits were sent in search of moose and deer in much the same manner as though a soul were being sought. Success in the spiritual quest enabled hunters to find and kill the actual animals without difficulty. Conjurers are reported to have performed, upon occasion, remarkable feats of agility.

A conjurer has taken a man and lifted him high in the air with one hand; has loosened himself, unaided, from a network of ropes that bound him; has destroyed, with the aid of Thunder, evil serpents that preyed on the Indians' camps.

We may now turn to the Ojibwa of Minnesota and summarize the findings of Coleman, Densmore, and Hoffman.[7] Here the power of the conjurer was received in a dream rather than a vision. Thunder played no role; indeed, no specific spirit was segregated except Turtle, who acted as intermediary much in the manner we have seen. The talents of the conjurer included curing, the finding of lost articles and lost persons, the prediction of future events and the performance of strange feats.

The curing power differed considerably from that of the Parry Islanders. Coleman strongly contrasts the conjurer and the medicine man, but Densmore mentions curing and describes an incident in which the djasakid swallowed and regurgitated bone tubes, then placed one against the throat of the patient and blew with great force, causing the congestion to "break." One or more of these bones was worn by the conjurer as a badge of his profession. Prognosis was definitely a field which the conjurer exploited but this was but one aspect of his ability to predict.

In preparation for the seance the "shaking tent" was constructed. The conjurer was bound hand and foot with rope or thongs and placed in the lodge. The appearance of the intermediary, the Turtle, was signalled by a loud whistling sound. The tent swayed violently as the spirits gathered and the voices of animals were heard to the accompaniment of the conjurer's rattle. The spectators were now asked if they wished to question the spirits. The questions put concerned prognosis, future events, and lost articles and persons. The successful conclusion of a search for a lost object or person was made known to the audience by a thud as of a heavy object hitting the ground. At the end of the performance the spirits departed and the conjurer called for a light to be provided. The audience could then see that he was free of his bonds; the ropes were often found entangled in the upper poles of the lodge or at some distant place.

The Cheyenne conjuring complex, as reported by Grinnell,[8] presents now familiar elements in typical arrangement. The talent was spiritually conferred in a dream. Any spirit

---

[7] Coleman, *Religion of the Ojibwa*, pp. 50–53; Densmore, *Chippewa Customs*, p. 45 f.; Densmore, *An Explanation of a Trick*; Hoffman, *Midē'wiwin*, pp. 176–78; cf. idem, pp. 251–55, 276–78; cf. Skinner, *Political Organization*, p. 505; cf. Jones, *Central Algonkin*, p. 145 f.   [8] *Cheyenne Indians*, Vol. 2, pp. 112–17.

might confer this power, it seems, but relatively few persons were recipients. Only the Badger played a special role; he served as intermediary and his identity was made known by his voice. The conjurer was sometimes provided with a whistle and a pipe. Helpers occasionally beat upon parfleches. Usually a single spirit appeared at the seance but at some times many of them assembled; it was then that the intermediary functioned.

The seance was held at night in a dwelling tipi in which many spectators and singers gathered. The performer unwrapped his sacred objects; then the fire was allowed to die.

Before the fire was out, the man who was calling the spirit was tied with four bowstrings. Each finger of each hand was tied separately to the next finger, in a hard knot, and the ends of the bowstrings on each hand were tied together, behind his back, so that his hands were tightly bound there. His feet were tied together in the same way, each toe being tied to the next one in a hard knot, and the feet bound together by the bowstrings. Thus tied, he sat in the back of the lodge, and sometimes he was tied to one of the lodge-poles. At times a little shelter shaped like a sweat-lodge, was built in the middle of the lodge, and the man was put in that.

After the fire had gone out, in some interval of the singing the lodge was shaken as if by a strong wind; the poles creaked, and suddenly in the lodge a strange voice was heard talking to the man. This secret helper was perhaps called to ask where there were buffalo; or where there were enemies; where missing people were; or even where lost horses might be found. Sometimes the secret helper told what was happening at a distance; or perhaps warned the camp of enemies near at hand. After the spirit had gone, and a light had again been made, the man was found to be untied, and the bowstrings were lying in the door, tied in innumerable knots.[9]

A sketch from the Plateau will serve to complete this descriptive survey. The Kutenai of southeastern British Columbia utilized the conjuring seance for the prediction of future events, particularly in wartime, the finding of lost objects, and the like. The performance served to bring the spirits into direct contact with the petitioner, thus making available immediate help and advice. The performer was not necessarily a shaman; anyone possessing a guardian spirit was privileged to attempt the contact. One's particular spirit was the effective agent in establishing the relationship, but that relationship was with the entire spirit world, not merely with the individual spirit. Owl was the central spirit figuring in the seance but did not serve as intermediary.

The performance was conducted in an ordinary tipi. The suppliant blew steadily on a whistle as he slowly disappeared behind a partition formed by a mat or blanket. He soon reappeared with his arms behind him, his thumbs tied to his belt. The knots were untied, he returned, and the same procedure was repeated seven times, or until seven knots were tied. The end of a long rope was then tied around the conjurer's waist. Thereupon he went behind the partition and threw the loose end of the rope over the pole from which the blanket was suspended. Soon the entire rope fell, in full view of the audience, and to the end of it was found tied a small whistle. Thus it was indicated that the performer had been "cut in two" by the rope; the two parts of the body were heard to fall with a thud. But the spirits soon reassembled the halves and the performer appeared, smoked briefly, and re-

[9] *Idem*, p. 113 f.

turned. At this point the Owl spirit carried him away; the flight, as of a bird, was heard by the audience. The sound of a whistle was also audible; with it the conjurer called the spirits to take his place. The whistle used was that attached to the rope.

During these activities the audience drummed and sang spirit songs, and pipes were prepared and smudges lighted. Immediately thereafter the audience conversed with the spirits. One so desiring lighted a pipe and handed it over the partition. The spirits took seven puffs and returned the pipe. If the tobacco were no longer burning misfortune was portended. A second pipe was sometimes requested. The converser inquired directly of the spirits and answers were directly given, but in an unnatural voice. Following the questions the conjurer returned, his thumbs once more tied. The knots were loosed and the seance was concluded.

These sketches have not been selected to indicate extremes of distribution but rather to provide type pictures from the various areas. The western extreme is represented by the Colville of northeastern Washington.[10] The complex extends to the east as far as Labrador.[11]

It is now in order to examine the variations presented by the western examples. The Colville ceremony followed very closely the pattern of the Kutenai. However, only those possessing a specific spirit, that of a certain fish, became conjurers. It is perhaps significant that this spirit was called the director or leader of all other spirits; its place in the ceremony was analogous to that of Owl among the Kutenai. But it also performed the function of intermediary, answering the questions of the audience in a thick, muffled voice. In the questioning much emphasis was placed upon the finding of lost articles and persons. Marking the close of the seance, the spirits returned the conjurer, but he remained unconscious for several hours. He was brought to consciousness by a smudging process.

Cline states that the Colville conjurer was a shaman, but this may be questioned. Apparently no curing of any kind was involved in the seance. Furthermore, the performance was a part of the Winter Spirit Dances in which all persons possessing spirits participated. Cline tends to speak of any performer at the Winter Dance as a shaman. One minor point may be added: the conjurer's compartment was provided with a special aperture opening to the outdoors for the entry of the spirits.[12]

The most significant difference between the performance of the Kutenai and that of the Colville appears to have been the presence of a spirit intermediary among the latter. However, the idea of the intermediary was also present in the Kutenai interpretation. The conjurer played this role so far as members of the audience were concerned. Throughout Kutenai

[10] Cline, *Southern Okanagon*, p. 152 f.

[11] Flannery, *Shaking-Tent Rite*, p. 14.

An excellent description for the Montagnais of James Bay, provided by Regina Flannery (*op. cit.*), indicates close parallelism on almost every point with Ojibwa practise. The most noticeable variation is the substitution of Mistabeo for Turtle as intermediary.

Skinner has recorded brief notes for the Cree and Salteaux (*Notes on the Eastern Cree*, pp. 67, 153); and Rossignol should be consulted (*Religion of the Saskatchewan*).

As noted above, the object here is not to examine the ramifications of the complex in the Woodlands but rather to seek the significance of its presence in the Far West.   [12] Cline, *Southern Okanagon*, p. 152 f.

religious practise one's familiar spirit served to bring him in contact with all spiritual beings and permitted him to receive the benefits of this wider contact. It may be noted that this concept was quite foreign to all other parts of the Plateau but was wholly congenial to Ojibwa thought.[13]

Unique aspects not encountered among others sharing the seance include the bisection of the conjurer's body by the rope encircling him and the flight through the air. The latter was not inconsistent with the pattern of the complex. In all cases the spirits came and left by such a method; in some instances the upper portion of the lodge was left open or some other aperture was provided as an avenue of entrance and exit. The dramatic "cutting in two" appears to have been a local interpretation of the trickery element of the seance. The placing of the cord around the waist possibly was related to the widespread practise in the Plateau and Puget Sound areas of holding a shaman, while engaged in treatment, by a rope similarly placed (so that he would not lose control of his actions while handling spirits).[14] But more probably the linkage was with the wrapping and tying of the conjurer among the Assiniboin and Gros Ventre, to be described later.

The feature most notably absent from the Colville and Kutenai seances was the shaking of the lodge. It is true that the huge Colville dance house was hardly susceptible to swaying but the partition might well have been vibrated. The Kutenai performance was held in a tipi which might quite conceivably have been swayed by one mechanism or another. It will be remembered that the Cheyenne performance sometimes involved the building of a hemispherical hut within the tipi. Several interpretations are possible to account for the absence of the shaking feature. The possibility of diffusion from west to east hardly merits serious consideration in the light of relative distributions and the organization of the complex. But granting east to west diffusion, perhaps the idea spread before the addition of the "shaking tent" feature to the basic conjuring concept. This seems highly improbable since all eastern interpretations, and even that of the Cheyenne, involved shaking, and in most cases this feature was thoroughly integrated. Furthermore, evidence is to be presented below which indicates a recent diffusion. Consequently, the absence of the shaking feature is clearly a case of loss, either loss in the process of diffusion or a conscious discarding of the trait.[15]

The Cheyenne interpretation of the complex presents but few fundamental contrasts with that of the Colville-Kutenai. Any spirit might confer the conjuring power, as among the Kutenai. As in the north, the performer was definitely a layman, not a shaman. The highly specific and complex method of binding the conjurer stands out, but it will be recalled that the Colville-Kutenai method was identical in pattern although less elaborate. The Gros Ventre, too, shared this feature.

The Cheyenne ceremony lacked the involved ritual of exchanging a pipe of tobacco between the spirits and the questioners. Grinnell mentions, however, the presentation of a

---

[13] Cf. Ray, Cultural Relations, pp. 68 ff.
[14] Cf. Ray, Sanpoil and Nespelem, p. 206.
[15] Incidentally, rendering the term "shaking tent" inapplicable to the general complex.

pipe to the conjurer upon a specific occasion.[16] The exchange or presentation of tobacco or a pipe was characteristic of Ojibwa and Montagnais practise, hence it appears to have been a basic feature of the complex. The slight emphasis by the Cheyenne might mark a step in the discarding of the trait, while the Northwest practises would indicate local elaboration.

The Badger intermediary of the Cheyenne was unique. The fish spirit which played this role among the Colville was perhaps an equally independent selection, but a parallel did exist among the far distant Montagnais.[17] Among the Ojibwa the intermediary was invariably Turtle, although the source of the conjurer's power was often Thunder. These are interpretations unknown in the west.

The possession by the Cheyenne of the "shaking tent" phase of the complex has been noted. Historically considered this fact is of utmost significance. It indicates more than any other single feature the intimacy of relationships between the Cheyenne ceremony and that of the Ojibwa. The Colville-Kutenai seance, on the other hand, exhibits its closest affinity with the more eastern form in the wholly typical assemblage of spirits at the call of the conjurer, and, incidentally, the signalling of arrival by a thud or a thumping sound. The "shaking tent" and the spirit assembly must be considered two of the most basic features of the complex. This is not to minimize the importance of the conjuring aspect; conjuring is common to all. Of these two central features the assembly of spirits is clearly the more fundamental. The "shaking tent" element is detachable without loss of identity; witness the Colville-Kutenai. Since the Cheyenne seance seems largely to have revolved around the calling of a single spirit, we might conclude that this gives the Colville-Kutenai affair the greater claim to closeness of relationship with the type ceremony. But this would be to overlook the fact that the Cheyenne conjurer was capable, at least upon occasion, of establishing contact with many spirits through the agency of his own particular spirit.[18] In other words, although the concept was minimized, it was known. This is strong evidence of diffusion as a part of the conjuring complex, since it was not typical of the Plains and was completely alien to the Plateau at large, being found only among the Kutenai and in the Colville seance. Consequently we must look upon the Cheyenne ceremony as bearing closer relationship to the type, since spirit assembly and "shaking tent" were both known, and the Colville-Kutenai complex as being one step farther removed. Although suggestive, this is far from definitive. Further illumination is provided by data on tribal movements to be offered a little later.

Two variants of the conjuring complex as found in the Plains remain to be considered, those of the Assiniboin and the Gros Ventre. The Assiniboin ceremony contrasts with those thus far encountered in the many modifications it exhibits; the Gros Ventre example is a mere fragment.

The Assiniboin ceremony differed not only in detail but in conceptual phrasing as well. Direct quotation from Lowie's informant will make this clear:

[16] *Cheyenne Indians*, Vol. 2, p. 114.   [17] Flannery, *Shaking-Tent Rite*, pp. 12, 14.
[18] Grinnell, *Cheyenne Indians*, Vol. 2, p. 115.

I dreamt of several men who told me I was wanted in a certain tent. . . . An old man was sitting inside. He said "My son, I am the one who has summoned you. I shall give you the painted lodge and teach you how to use it. . . ." Then he told me I was to get the waka$^{n'}$ power to aid the sick. "Thus you will get plenty of horses and abundance of food, besides your family will always be well. When you doctor a patient, you must act as follows: Near the fireplace plant one end of a tree trunk not stripped of its foliage, and stick the other end into the flap-holes; get three or four dressed buffalo skins, and construct a little booth. Allow yourself to be tied hand and foot with buckskin thongs, then have tanned robes wrapped about you and tied from the outside. Have a rock put near the fireplace. It should be painted red and ought to rest on a clean piece of calico. Have a little dog suck-ling cooked and set near the fireplace. Two, or three, drummers are to sit on the right-hand side of the entrance; no one else must be admitted. . . . " [After ritual preparations a spirit would speak.] A noise would be heard in the skies. The visitant was not to be seen, but only heard. He would ask what was the matter. "Then you must ask him for aid. He will first eat the pup. Then he will tell you whether the patient can be cured, and if so, how soon. If a cure is impossible, he will say so. He will disappear, but first he will free you in the twinkle of an eye, and hang your bonds on the tops of the tipi-poles."[19]

Before discussing this remarkable variant, the obviously derivative Gros Ventre remnant may be presented:

There were some medicine-men who, having had their fingers tied, then had their knees fastened together and their hands secured behind their back. After this they were wrapped in a robe and the robe was wound about with a rope. Then such a medicine-man called his spirit. When it appeared, he was loosened instantaneously, and the robe and the rope were thrown at the man that tied him.[20]

The two fundamental conceptual features of the conjuring complex—assembly of spirits and the shaking tent—were clearly absent from the Assiniboin ceremony. However, the binding of the conjurer and subsequent spiritual release were practised. Further, it will be noted that the ropes were discovered exactly as among the Minnesota Ojibwa: at the top of the tipi poles. This highly arbitrary element points clearly to a common source. The wrapping of the conjurer in a blanket, however, is newly encountered and is doubtless a local interpretation. The Gros Ventre presumably borrowed the practise from the Assini-boin.

The fact that the Assiniboin conjurer was a shaman is surely significant. This was uni-form practise to the east but was unknown to the west. However, the talent was conferred in a dream, a typical Plains phrasing. It goes without saying that the ritual flavor of the whole affair was in perfect accord with Plains taste.

Apparently the Assiniboin, in their contacts with the Plains-Ojibwa (or Cree), be-came thoroughly acquainted with the conjuring ritual, adopted the general framework and some of the most spectacular features, dropped the esoteric assembly of spirits, and adapted the whole to their own concept of a properly executed ceremony. Why the "shaking tent" feature was abandoned is uncertain.

[19] Lowie, *The Assiniboine*, p. 49.   [20] Kroeber, *Ethnology of the Gros Ventre*, p. 223.

In comparing the type ceremony of the Ojibwa with the western interpretations generally, two points stand out in bold relief. First, the western distribution is irregular and discordant. The groups discussed above were the only ones possessing the ritual as far as I have been able to ascertain. It seems unlikely that the intensive ethnological work in the Plains left undiscovered any instance of this ceremony; if other Plains tribes shared the seance the references have been overlooked. All tribes of the Plateau except the Spokane (adjacent to the Colville) are sufficiently well known so that the complex could hardly have been overlooked.

Second, in the face of this sporadic distribution and the distances involved, the conformity of the individual variants to the general pattern is strikingly close, excepting only the Assiniboin.

How, then, are we to account for this uniformity of pattern and erratic distribution at one and the same time? I think the answer is to be found in the extensive movements of Algonkin peoples in recent times. It is generally recognized that large scale movements have carried Algonkin groups from their Woodland homes far westward into the Plains. For present purposes, however, we need precise statements, not general phrasings. We have these specific analyses as the result of the work of Strong, Wissler, and others.

That these Algonkin movements have not all occurred in the immediate past is indicated in the conclusions drawn by Strong in his analysis of Plains culture in the light of archaeology:

It is a Woodland culture of northeastern affiliations that occurs on the eastern border as the earliest known occupation of this sort in Nebraska. This was demonstrated by Sterns' discoveries at the Walker Gilmore site; and the fact that Sterns creek culture is apparently related to the "Algonkian" and Lake Michigan cultures of Iowa and Wisconsin is undoubtedly significant. . . .

In the light of the archaeological evidence it appears that the horse culture of historic times spread like a thin and strikingly uniform veneer over the central Plains, bringing with it many traits more typical of the forest hunting regions to the north than of the prehistoric Plains themselves. Given the horse, the Plains with their vast bison herds could not be resisted, and in the course of a century or two a new mode of life developed, involving many peoples that were apparently relative strangers to the region.[21]

It is possible, then, that the conjuring complex was carried westward at either a relatively early date or a very late date. An early diffusion would account for the sporadic distribution: the complex would have had ample time to disappear in intervening areas. But this same lapse of time would undoubtedly have led to a greater modification and differentiation of the western examples, particularly in view of the ideological conflict between the complex and general Plateau religious concepts.

Assuming a late diffusion, we may examine more minutely the recent movements. Wissler summarizes his findings relative to Algonkin migrations as follows:

[The study] reveals successive expansions of groups into the northern Plains largely by Algon-

[21] Strong, Plains Culture, pp. 283, 285.

kin-speaking tribes: Blackfoot, Arapaho, Gros Ventre, Cheyenne, Ojibwa, and Cree. Thus, the repeated expansions in this area seem to have had a common source. The uniformity of this westward movement of Cree-like Algonkin is broken only by the Siouan-speaking Assiniboin. The historical data suggest that the Blackfoot first expanded into the area, followed by the Arapaho-Gros Ventre. The Cheyenne thrust was toward the southwest and to the Missouri. Later the Ojibwa followed on their heels. The Gros Ventre held most of the Saskatchewan area in 1754, but shortly thereafter began to contract their range and to decrease in population. At the same time the Assiniboin were expanding westward into the same area, reaching their maximum population about 1830. Following them, the Cree expanded westward, first along the north Saskatchewan, but gradually took to the plains in which their great expansion began after 1800 and culminated about 1875.[22]

With respect to the Cheyenne migration, Grinnell furnishes highly specific data. He explains that the movement proceeded band by band, with the laggards remaining in their older habitat until after 1800. This habitat was within the woodlands in Minnesota but quite near the prairie. Here they were already separated from their linguistic relatives by an area of Siouan-speaking peoples. After arrival in the west a split occurred, beginning about 1830, which gave rise to the divisions Northern Cheyenne and Southern Cheyenne.[23]

Cheyenne speech is much closer to Central-Eastern Algonkin than is either Blackfoot or Arapaho. It is much more different, however, than it could have become during a separation of only two or three centuries. The purely linguistic inference thus is that the Cheyenne, though recent in the plains, lived, before that, somewhere apart from the Central Algonkins of the woodland; therefore most likely in the prairies.[24]

In the light of this evidence it seems reasonable to assume that the Cheyenne possessed the conjuring complex in their western habitat because they had brought it with them; that groups with whom they were in contact during the progress of their migrations did not take over the idea because those contacts were relatively brief and the concept not overly congenial; that the period of separation from Central Algonkins was sufficiently brief so that the conjuring complex retained its identity but at the same time was of ample duration to permit a waning of emphasis upon congregation of spirits and a shift in the nature of the conjurer from shaman to layman, thus bringing the complex closer into line with ideologies prevailing among the new neighbors.

If this interpretation is correct, the Colville-Kutenai could not have received their ceremony from the Cheyenne either directly or indirectly. Indirect reception would have demanded a wider diffusion; direct borrowing would have required a degree of contact between the two which we know did not exist.

This being the case, how are we to account for features common to the Cheyenne and the Colville-Kutenai, but lacking among the Central Algonkins? We find but two such features: the conjurer was a layman rather than a shaman; and a quite arbitrary method was used in tying him during the seance. The former is easily resolved. As explained above, this

[22] Wissler, *Population Changes*, p. 18.   [23] Grinnell, *Cheyenne Indians*, Vol. 1, pp. 1–46.
[24] Kroeber, *Cultural and Natural Areas*, p. 81.

was simply an adjustment which brought the ceremony into accord with a prominent principle of western religion; that is, the shaman was conceived as one who cured diseases by
spiritual means, and anyone not so gifted was a layman no matter what marvelous supernatural powers of other kinds he possessed.

The second point is more involved. The same method of tying the fingers is suggested
for the Gros Ventre. The Kutenai practise was perhaps closer to that of the Gros Ventre
than the Cheyenne. Definitive comparisons are not possible because of the variant phrasings
in the descriptions. The Kutenai achieved the elaboration of the Cheyenne in quite another
context. The fingers and toes of the pubescent girl, during her isolation, were twined
together so that they could not be separated. According to a superficial rationalization, this
procedure insured against the stiffening of the fingers in later life.[25] It is possible that this
was a somewhat general cultural practise and should be considered as such. Without further
data a satisfying interpretation is elusive or impossible.

Nor could the Northwestern complex have been borrowed from the Assiniboin. The
Kutenai ceremony was more closely related to the parent form than was that of the Assiniboin. This was true of both conception and ritualistic structure. The Assiniboin lacked the
significant congregation of spirits and the intermediary spirit.

Parenthetically it may be noted that a cultural inconsistency appears here. It was the
Colville who emphasized the typical spirit intermediary, not the Kutenai. And yet there
is no question that the former borrowed the complex from the latter. Apparently the Kutenai dropped the feature, at least in its typical form, after transmitting the ceremony to
the Colville. This seems curious, since the Colville cling much more tenaciously to Plateau
ideology than do the Kutenai. Perhaps for the Colville the complex was so markedly foreign
that they reacted to it in an all-or-none fashion. Why both lacked the "shaking tent" is
problematical. The Assiniboin, too, lacked this feature. Possibly the Plains Cree themselves
had given it up in the Far West.

The Plains Cree emerge as donors of the Northwestern complex. This conclusion is
necessarily indirectly reached, since adequate data are unavailable for the Plains Cree.[26]
But recent contacts between the Kutenai and western Cree established an unbroken route
of diffusion from the eastern Algonkins. We are thus provided a satisfying explanation for

[25] Ray, *Cultural Relations*, p. 56.

[26] Mandelbaum's study, *The Plains Cree*, appeared subsequent to the writing of the above. He provides a
full description of the conjuring complex (p. 261 f.), the details of which accord thoroughly with the interpretation here offered. The Plains Cree ritual followed closely the basic pattern of the eastern Algonkin ceremony.
The "shaking tent" feature was present in a form resembling that of the Cheyenne. This suggests that the
Cheyenne variant was linked more immediately with the (central ?) Cree than with the Ojibwa, although a dual
indebtedness is not improbable.

Since the Plains Cree utilized the "shaking tent" it appears that the Kutenai were the first to discard it.
However, Mandelbaum's data may not apply to the westernmost bands.

The Plains Cree, surprisingly, shared the unique method of tying the conjurer's fingers together. Thus they
may have been the originators of this trait. However, the more general context in which this practise appears
among the Kutenai still favors a western point of origin.

the close kinship of eastern and western variants. The conclusion is thoroughly consistent with the positive findings throughout this analysis.

In the above study an attempt has been made to work out certain problems in consonance with Professor Sapir's precept that ethnological data must be treated "historically, that is, in terms of actual happenings, however inferred, that are conceived to have a specific sequence, a specific localization, and specific relations among themselves." The degree to which this effort has been successful is largely attributable to the methodology employed, a methodology interpreted and clarified by Professor Sapir.

The reflection of the teachings of Professor Sapir is apparent in this paper, I trust. But the point deserving emphasis is that an equally profound impression is to be seen in the great bulk of comparable studies, and surely will continue to be seen in the work of the future.

BIBLIOGRAPHY

CLINE, WALTER, and OTHERS *The Sinkaietk or Southern Okanagon of Washington* (General Series in Anthropology, No. 6, 1938).

COLEMAN, BERNARD *The Religion of the Ojibwa of Northern Minnesota* (Primitive Man, Vol. 10, pp. 33–57, 1937).

DENSMORE, FRANCES *Chippewa Customs* (Bulletin, Bureau of American Ethnology, No. 86, 1929).

An Explanation of a Trick Performed by Indian Jugglers (American Anthropologist, Vol. 34, pp. 310–14, 1932).

FLANNERY, REGINA *The Shaking-Tent Rite among the Montagnais of James Bay* (Primitive Man, Vol. 12, pp. 11–16, 1939).

GRINNELL, GEORGE BIRD *The Cheyenne Indians: their History and Ways of Life* (2 vols., New Haven, 1923).

HOFFMAN, W. J. *The Midē'wiwin or "Grand Medicine Society"* (Seventh Annual Report, Bureau of American Ethnology, pp. 143–300, 1891).

JENNESS, DIAMOND *The Ojibwa Indians of Parry Island, their Social and Religious Life* (Bulletin, National Museum of Canada, No. 78, 1935).

JONES, WILLIAM *The Central Algonkin* (Annual Archaeological Report, Toronto, 1905, pp. 136–46, 1906).

KROEBER, A. L. *Cultural and Natural Areas of Native North America* (University of California Publications in American Archaeology and Ethnology, Vol. 38, 1939).

Ethnology of the Gros Ventre (Anthropological Papers, American Museum of Natural History, Vol. 1, pp. 141–281, 1908).

LOWIE, ROBERT H. *The Assiniboine* (Anthropological Papers, American Museum of Natural History, Vol. 4, pp. 1–270, 1909).

MANDELBAUM, DAVID G. *The Plains Cree* (Anthropological Papers, American Museum of Natural History, Vol. 37, pp. 155–316, 1940).

RAY, VERNE F. *The Bluejay Character in the Plateau Spirit Dance* (American Anthropologist, Vol. 39, pp. 593–601, 1937).

  Cultural Relations in the Plateau of Northwestern America (Publications of the Frederick Webb Hodge Anniversary Publication Fund, Vol. 3, 1939).

  The Sanpoil and Nespelem: Salishan Peoples of Northeastern Washington (University of Washington Publications in Anthropology, Vol. 5, 1932).

ROSSIGNOL, M. *The Religion of the Saskatchewan and Western Manitoba Cree* (Primitive Man, Vol. 11, pp. 67–71, 1938).

SAPIR, EDWARD *Time Perspective in Aboriginal American Culture, a Study in Method* (Memoir, Canada Department of Mines, Geological Survey, No. 90; Anthropological Series, No. 13, 1916).

SKINNER, ALANSON *Notes on the Eastern Cree and Northern Salteaux* (Anthropological Papers, American Museum of Natural History, Vol. 9, pp. 1–177, 1911).

  Political Organization, Cults and Ceremonies of the Plains-Ojibway and Plains-Cree Indians (Anthropological Papers, American Museum of Natural History, Vol. 11, pp. 475–542, 1914).

STRONG, W. D. *The Plains Culture in the Light of Archaeology* (American Anthropologist, Vol. 35, pp. 271–87, 1933).

WISSLER, CLARK *Population Changes among the Northern Plains Indians* (Yale University Publications in Anthropology, No. 1, 1936).

UNIVERSITY OF WASHINGTON
SEATTLE, WASHINGTON

CULTURE NORMS AND THE INDIVIDUAL

"Not what the culture consists of or what are the values it seems to point to will be the psychiatrist's concern, but rather how this culture lends itself to the ceaseless need of the individual personality for symbols of expression and communication which can be intelligently read by one's fellow-men on the social plane, but whose relative depth or shallowness of meaning in the individual's total economy of symbols need never be adequately divined either by himself or his neighbor."

The Contribution of Psychiatry to an
Understanding of Behavior in Society

SOCIAL TRENDS AND PERSONAL PRESSURES: THE GROWTH OF A CULTURE PATTERN

By DAVID G. MANDELBAUM

EDWARD SAPIR was much interested in the interplay between culture and personality. He felt that there was an invidious dissociation between the ethnologist's studies of cultural forms and the psychologist's or psychiatrist's studies of individual behavior. In his writings, and especially in his course, *The Impact of Culture on Personality*, Professor Sapir led the way to a field of dynamic ethnology wherein the two approaches to the study of man could be brought together. The problems in that field have to do largely with the meanings for the individual of the patterns which culture recognizes. He called this a bastard field, disowned by the orthodox families of both anthropology and psychology. His influence has had much to do with the increasing awareness of its legitimacy. If he may not be called the father of this realm of research, he is certainly one godfather who stood sponsor for it and steadfastly worked to make its name respectable and its importance recognized. The present paper is an attempt to illustrate some of the principles propounded by Sapir with case examples from a field study which he fostered.

In March of 1924, an epidemic of relapsing fever—a louse borne disease—struck the Kotas of the Nilgiri Hills in South India. Of all the tribe, the village Kolme·l was hardest hit. Within a month almost one fourth of its three hundred inhabitants were dead; before the epidemic burnt itself out in September, well over half the villagers had fallen victims to the disease. During the following years, a new set of gods was adopted by the villagers, shrines built to them, new ceremonies conducted by special officiants consecrated to their worship.

In 1937–38, when the writer was with the tribe, the new religious complex was firmly installed in Kolme·l.[1] Those of the villagers who worship the new gods also fulfill their duties to the ancient deities of the tribe. Some, however, stubbornly refuse to admit the innovation and continue to follow only the older religious forms. The shift of religious allegiance is an event of significance in the historical career of the tribe and is a matter of concern to the individuals involved. Since this bit of culture change is of recent occurrence, the chief participants could be used as informants. It is the purpose of this paper to trace the genesis and development of the new religious idea complex in terms of the pressures, both personal and societal, which affected its growth.

[1] The Kota field work was financed by the National Research Council and by the Institute of Human Relations, Yale University. It was carried on while Dr M. B. Emeneau was conducting researches on the Kota language. I am deeply indebted to him for aid and advice in the field. An interpreter was used with all informants save one, Sulli.

To set the scene for a discussion of the event, we may briefly outline the salient features of Kota culture. The two great mountain ranges which run parallel to the east and west coasts of the Indian peninsula, meet in the south to form the Nilgiri plateau. This high, isolated tract, often capped by mist, is much cooler than the plains which surround it. Rolling grasslands cover the plateau, with scattered groves and thickets in the sheltered valleys and hillsides. The flora and the fauna of the Nilgiris are different from those of the neighboring lowlands, and the aboriginal inhabitants, too, are culturally distinct from the peoples who live below.

Four tribes live on the plateau: Todas, Kotas, Kurumbas, Badagas. The Badagas are agriculturalists, whose staple of diet was and is millet. The Todas are purely a pastoral people whose whole interest—economic, social, religious—revolves about their herds of buffalo. The Kurumbas live on the fringes of the plateau where the jungle creeps up the hillsides. They depend partly on hunting and food gathering, but mostly on the yield of their tribal trade, sorcery. The Kotas are artisans and musicians who live in seven villages which are scattered among the Toda and Badaga settlements.

The long cultural isolation of the Nilgiri tribes may be attributed to the steepness of their hills and to the climate of their highland terrain. They formed a cultural enclave which was unperturbed by the great goings and comings that went on below, not fifty miles away. But when the English came to India, all this was changed. The English sought some refuge from the summer heat of the plains, and about a hundred years ago discovered the Nilgiris. Before long a road was hacked through to the plateau and every summer the provincial government was moved up to the hills. With the Europeans came their servants and an influx of merchants. The cultural solitude of the tribes was broken; they were exposed to the simultaneous impact of two differing cultures, Indian and English.

Although the old patterns of intertribal relations have been weakened, they still are maintained. The tightly integrated Toda culture has been little affected by alien influence; the Kurumbas in their jungles are remote from it; many conservative Badagas still carry on the old relations with the Kotas. At the present time the Kotas still practise their traditional trades and the Kota village functions much as it did a century ago.

In each Kota village there are three exogamous patrilineal sibs, making a total of twenty-one father-sibs for the tribe. There is some cultural differentiation among the villages but all adhere to a general pattern of religious observance. Three deities are worshipped: Aynoˑr, Amnoˑr, Kunaynoˑr—Father God, Mother God, Younger Brother God. Three temples are to be found in every Kota village, one for each deity.

A seasonal cycle of ceremonies is devoted to the worship of the gods. Every village has its own set of religious officiants for the enactment of the ceremonies. The priest leads the people in prayer, makes the offerings, conducts the sequence of ritual observance. In some villages there is but one priest; in others there are two, one to care for the male gods, the other for the female deity. The priest's life is dedicated to the service of the gods and is surrounded with interdictions and taboos. The priest must keep apart from all other men, may not mingle with them too freely.

At specified times during the course of every major ritual, the priest stands aside and the focus of attention rests on another religious officiant, the diviner. Every village has three diviners, one for each god. It is through them that the deities make their voices heard and their desires known to men. When the appropriate time arrives for the presence of the divinity to manifest itself, the priest addresses a special prayer to the god. A spasm of shivering works through the diviner, then another, and his head begins to shake from side to side. The head movements continue with increasing velocity until it seems as though no human vertebræ could stand the strain. The diviner may fall to his knees and beat his palms against the earth with furious tattoo, but the deity does not speak through him until his hair is loosened. The long Kota locks are tied up with a cord which has ritual significance, and this cord must be dislodged by the force of the head motion. When the diviner's hair does fly free about his oscillating head, a strangled sob bursts forth from him—the first articulation of the god speaking through its chosen medium. With jerky, strangulated utterance, the diviner's voice serves as the mouthpiece of the deity. The voice tells the tribesmen wherein they have transgressed, what they must do if the gods are no longer to frown. Questions are asked of the god—why has the south field not yielded a crop; why is my wife barren; why is my child ill—and the queries are answered. The messages imparted, the god withdraws. The diviner's gesticulations come to an abrupt end and he sinks limply to the ground.

The life of the diviner, too, is hedged about with ritual restraints. But these are not as numerous nor as exacting as those which govern the conduct of the priest. A widower may not hold either office. Priest and diviner alike must relinquish his office upon the death of his spouse.

When either office is vacant, the post is filled by divine appointment. During the course of the God Ceremony, the most important on the calendar, all eligible men stand before the temple and a group prayer is addressed to the god who is to choose one of them. If it is a priest that is to be chosen, the diviner becomes possessed and pulls one of the worshipers forward to bow before the entrance to the temple. Later, a consecration ceremony is held to dedicate the nominee to the service of the god. The new priest occupies a special house, is given cattle by the community, and should he be unmarried, may have any woman, be she maid or wife—though not widow—for his own.

When a diviner is to be chosen, the men similarly assemble before the temple. The priest, who never becomes possessed himself, fervently prays for the appointment of a new diviner. One of the assembly begins to shake in the stereotyped manner of diviners, comes forward, touches the front pillar of the temple, and forthwith becomes the new Voice. Sometimes it happens that more than one man will quake and shiver on this occasion. The one who comes forward and touches the pillar first is the choice of the god.

The questions asked of the diviners in their trance have usually to do with misfortunes, personal and communal. And misfortunes usually are the work of Kurumbas. A Kurumba may have been offended by too small a fee and has laid a spell on a child in revenge. Or a fellow villager in envy of his neighbor's fine crop and bonny son has hired a Kurumba to send a blight to both. The only remedy is to secure the services of another Kurumba to practise more powerful sorcery and exorcise the evil.

But exorcism was of little avail in 1924. People were dying so rapidly that the Kurumbas themselves were afraid to come near the village. As the epidemic blazed on, the cremation ceremonies for the dead were not forgotten or stinted. In a few months the scanty village stores of food and fuel were exhausted. Cold and hunger were added to the general misery. Sulli, the schoolmaster, the only Kota who understands English and who has had some edu-cation among the Hindus, counselled the villagers to abandon their customary funeral rituals and bury the bodies with little ado. But the villagers had no desire to abandon this morsel of certitude, this familiar traditional form, in the moment of greatest stress. As is often true for other men, so too for the Kotas. At the time of greatest uncertainty, they clung most desperately to the known, and had least desire to venture out into unknown procedures. Though they knew that the traditional ceremonies for so many dead would sorely deplete their reserves, still they felt that when all seemed uncertain, when life itself was perilously balanced, they must fulfill this ceremony unchanged.

Toward the end of the year the epidemic finally burnt itself out. The daily round of Kota life was reestablished; men tried to carry on with their former ways. A month or so after the "dry funeral" in December the Kotas celebrate the God Ceremony. This is the great event of the ceremonial year. Solemn rituals entail weeks of preparation, extend through days. All that pertains to the gods is renewed or refurbished. If a sacred office is open, a recruit is divinely chosen to join with the old priests and diviners in the performance of the service. But at the God Ceremony in January of 1925, there were no old priests or diviners. To a man, the former officiants had died of the fever. The men eligible for the offices stood before the temples as always. The assembled villagers prayed with deep fervor for the ap-pointment of successors as always. But as had not happened before in the memory of the people, no man was supernaturally propelled to the temple pillar to be diviner, none was seized as priest.

Soon after, another strange occurrence took place. Kusvain became possessed. Kusvain had once been a diviner but had had to give up the office when his wife had died. As an unfrocked diviner, he could not officially be chosen as the vehicle of a deity. Stranger still, the voice that came through him in his possession announced that it was that of Raŋgaynoʾr. This deity was a Hindu god, worshipped at a temple in the hamlet of Karaimadai, near the foot of the plateau. Moreover, the voice of this new deity announced that priests and divin-ers could not be chosen for the old triad until shrines were built for Raŋgaynoʾr and two other deities who were to form a new Trinity.

Now Kusvain is a person of little prestige. Shiftless, irresponsible, he commands small respect. It is understandable then, why the villagers would have none of his revelations and did not heed the injunctions which issued from him. But when a year passed, and the God Ceremony was held once again, and still no priests or diviners were chosen, then the villagers were more disposed to take note and obey. Sulli, especially, advocated the accep-tance of the new revelation and urged the others to heed the new gods.

So when Kusvain became possessed again and the god Raŋgayṇoʿr spoke through him, the people worshipfully saluted and replied that they would take heed. Shaking with the spirit of the deity, Kusvain led the congregation to a pasture near the village and the voice commanded, "Here shall you build me a temple." Some men, Kaʿkn among them, had little enthusiasm for the venture and tried to counter some objections. But in the end the shrines were built, small structures of brick with one side open and roofs of corrugated iron. Kusvain's spirit told of the proper procedure for the service of the new gods. For them coconuts and plantains must be offered on brass platters before a lamp lit within the shrine. The ritual of the old gods included none of these elements. Coconuts and plantains were unobtainable before roads and the railroad were built; temple lamps and ceremonial platters were used in Hindu temples on the plains.

Not long after Kusvain had led the villagers to the site of the shrines, two other men became possessed. One had never been a diviner before. His voice proclaimed him to be the vehicle of Beṭḍamn, a female deity whose worship is known to the plainsmen. The other had once before been diviner, but, like Kusvain, had been relieved of the position by the death of his wife. He became diviner for Raʿmayṇoʿr, the Kota version of the Hindu deity Rama. Kusvain chose a priest for these gods.

Kusvain had prophesied that sacred retainers for the old gods would be chosen after shrines for the new were built, and so it came to pass. When the villagers had made their obeisance to the new trinity, the God Ceremony was resumed. The men of Kolmeʿl stood before the temples, the spirit of the old gods came upon three men and they were the diviners. They seized two men who became the priests.

In the years that followed, the ritual for the service of the new gods became established. In general pattern the worship of the new gods closely parallels the worship of the old. The priest of the keʿrvaʿy gods—so-called from the pasture, keʿrvaʿy, in which the shrines were built—must pray before the shrines at dawn and again at dusk, just as do the other priests for the ancient gods. Kusvain and his fellow diviners of the new dispensation become possessed and speak with the voice of their particular deity. It is noteworthy that the voice of the new gods never advises the abandonment of the worship of the old gods. And the diviners of the orthodox convention never revile the upstart supernaturals.

During the celebration of the ancient ceremonies, the adherents of the new gods go through the traditional ritual and then come to the keʿrvaʿy shrines to make additional offerings and intone more prayers. But the form of the prayers is exactly the same as those repeated before the old temples save that the names of the new gods are substituted for those of the old.

Only one ceremony is celebrated exclusively for the newer divinities. After the traditional God Ceremony is completed, another God Ceremony is staged for the new gods. It is somewhat less elaborate than the first, extends over a much shorter time, but maintains essentially the same ritual procedure. In like manner the whole corpus of taboo and duty toward the new gods is less rigorous than that for the old, but the general pattern of worship is the same for the two.

The names of the new gods have been taken from the Hindu pantheon and lowland traits have been introduced into the new ritual, but apart from these particulars the ke·rva·y complex closely resembles the older religion. For barriers of language and social status separate the Kota villager from any intimate contact with followers of the Hindu deities, hence he cannot obtain fresh ideas concerning the nature of the gods or new concepts about the proper behavior of religionists. A casual Kota observer, peeping into a Hindu temple, can see the use of plantains and coconuts, lamps and platters, incense and camphor, and can easily obtain these things in the bazaar. But he is shut off from any glimpse of the attitudes which surround the use of these material traits. Here as in much of the history of culture change we find that material traits and formalized modes of action are more amenable to diffusion than are the less readily apparent complexes of behavior. The villagers of Kolme·l, no less than other peoples, have integrated the borrowed bits of material culture and formal procedure into a pre-existing larger pattern which remains, in bold outline, but little altered.

At this juncture we can make certain preliminary statements to answer the question—how have the Kota come by this new element of their culture? The evidence of diffusion is clear and simple. Men of the tribe occasionally ride the railroad down to the plains, sometimes visit the temple at Karaimode. There they have learned of a deity called Rangen, as well as of Rama and Beṭdamn. Hindu temples have also been established on the plateau and a Kota can hardly escape observing certain gross features of Hindu ritual. These have been borrowed by the tribesmen and adapted to their tribal usage. Since Kota deities have names ending in the suffix -ayṇ "father," or -ayno·r "father god," the Hindu names Rama and Rangen become Ra·mayṇo·r and Raŋgayno·r. Since the old pattern calls for a trinity, the divine couple of the Karaimadai temple are accompanied by another Hindu deity. Other aspects of the new pattern also demonstrate the process of diffusion and integration.

This piece of historic reconstruction clears the way for an approach to further questions. Why were these new elements introduced precisely at this time? What factors eased the change, what conditions hampered it? What meaning did the new cult have for different individuals within the village? Why has it been embraced by some and rejected by others? The answers to these questions can best be couched in terms of the personalities involved. To establish the fact of diffusion it was possible and advisable to speak of culture complexes and of the diffusion and integration of culture traits. But if we are to make sense of the succeeding problems, reference must be made to the human *dramatis personæ*, the living characters who took part in the event.

The locus of this culture change lies in the fact that Tom and Dick of Kolme·l village began to do certain things they had not done before. Harry did not join them in this new behavior and did his utmost to prevent them from going on with it. If we are to understand why Tom and Dick were impelled toward a certain mode of action while Harry recoiled from it, we must have a look at the personal make-up of Tom, Dick, and Harry. True, it will never be possible to plumb the depths of each personality involved in a social situation, but a good deal of light can be thrown on the dynamics of social interaction by a consideration of key personalities. Three men have played major roles in the action at Kolme·l.

Kusvain appears to be the prime mover in all that went on. A brief account of the oc-currence, such as that above, must give Kusvain the center of the stage. He is the vehicle of the new divinities; their words through him institute the new worship and direct the form of the ritual; he speaks (with the voice of the Gods to be sure) and the people listen and obey. But a closer study of Kusvain's personal history and of his relations within the society must relegate him to a part of considerably less importance.

Kusvain has never been a person of any consequence in the regard of his fellow tribes-men. Men may acquire prestige via several avenues. Able craftsmanship, accumulation of wealth, adeptness in catching buffalo, skillful argumentation in council, all enhance the status of a man and enable him to influence the behavior of others—to be a leader. Kusvain often has to beg for his food, is not a craftsman at all, has never gained particular acclaim in the buffalo chase, does not open his mouth in council. Several informants characterized him as a shiftless ne'er-do-well.

The one way in which he is able to distinguish himself, to win personal victories, is by being a diviner. The diviner, by his very office, commands the accoutrements of prestige and respect. He stands before the assembled congregation during ceremonies; he is accorded a special place when he visits another house; he is respectfully attended by the priest during ceremonies. But despite these symbols of respect, a diviner's prestige status in the group depends on how he measures up to the requirements for prestige which apply to all men. Moreover, the utterances of a diviner in possession may be disregarded if he is known to be a fool in the daily round of life or obeyed to the letter if he is a man of standing. The formal dogma of the religion has it that anything revealed by the diviner during possession is a message from the godhead. Any informant will solemnly and sincerely assert that it is so and marshall many wondrous case examples in which the diviner's prediction came to pass. But an intimate acquaintance with the culture reveals numerous instances in which the prediction went wild. These cases do not shake Kota faith, since the diviner may have been misunderstood or his words misinterpreted. Similarly, an observer can find occasions in which a diviner's message was utterly disregarded. When pressed to account for these, a Kota will answer somewhat in this wise, "Well, sometimes it is an evil spirit that gets into the diviner instead of the God, or else it may be that the God didn't really come to the diviner and he just speaks out of his own mind."

The crux of the matter is that the whole life behavior of the diviner determines the manner in which his supernatural speeches are received. Just as a minister in our society is accorded the show of respect due his office, while his prestige in the society—i.e. his ability to influence behavior—rests on his personal attributes, so among the Kota, the diviner must be treated with deference, but the compulsive force of his messages depends on his status and personality. It must be said that the official significance of this pattern usually coincides with its actual significance; the diviner's words are taken very seriously. But when a diviner is patently an eccentric or a dimwit, then the villagers, by a sort of tacit consent, rarely listen to what he has to say, in possession or out.

Such a person is Kusvain. Sulli scornfully epitomized his behavior:

Kusvain's conduct is very bad. . . . His habit is this. He calls a woman over to him and when she stands before him he begins to shake as though possessed and says, "You have sinned, you have sinned." The poor ignorant woman, what does she know? She fears and says, "O God, O God," and she thinks, "O, the God knows what mistakes I have done." Then he says to her, while shaking, "If you come and lie with me tonight at such and such a place you will be forgiven." The woman promises and goes there. He lies with the woman and comes away. He is not a good worker; he seems just like mad.

Most Kota men have amorous adventures during the greater part of their lives, in which they secretly speak to a woman, cajole or threaten or use force to achieve their purpose. There is a bagful of stereotyped tricks available for these affairs and a man who rings a change on an old trick gains a certain measure of fame. But Kusvain alone resorts to posses-sion for this end and to Kota men it appears as a scurvy trick indeed, a perversion of the sacred state for a very profane purpose. Little wonder it is that Kusvain is generally a per-sonage of no account in the community.

The anecdote brings out a dominant note in Kusvain's personality. His way to personal power and ego satisfaction is attained by exercising his propensities for possession. He used these abilities in culturally approved situations, as when he first became a diviner. He also uses them in situations not sanctioned by his society, as a means of getting women. Though he was officially barred from doing so he used them again during the crisis situation of January 1925, when all were bewildered. He became possessed and revealed a new dispen-sation by which he could continue to follow his own road to personal victories.

A whole set of problems must be glossed over here. The psychological nature of posses-sion among the Kota can be described only briefly and impressionistically. It is my feeling, from observing Kota diviners in possession, that the rapid movements help induce a state of dissociation in which the words which then tumble through the diviner's lips do not rise from a conscious level and are not later recognized by the speaker as products of his conscious thinking. It seems to me a diviner rarely fakes his performance, and that Kusvain himself probably thinks of his possessed states as being of supernatural origin. For lack of controlled data, these observations cannot be adequately documented.

The import of possession for Kusvain is clear enough. It is for him the prime means of self-assertion, of personal dominance. Less clear are the processes whereby the means of per-sonal satisfaction for an aberrant individual came to attain social significance.

The condition which led to this socialization of an individual symbolism is to be found in the general disorientation of established societal values which came with the epidemic. Kota culture, like every other, has a set of basic behavior patterns to meet the exigencies of life. Each of these patterns has a certain potential of energy, so to speak. It may be more or less compelling than another pattern which might be used in the same life situation. When two patterns conflict, the one with the greater dynamic potency is translated into action. For example, when a man's child is ill, the first pattern to follow is that of coddling the child, keeping it warm, administering herbal remedies. If this course of action fails to work, another

SULLI, HIS SON, WIFE, AND VILLAGERS

A GROUP OF KOTA MUSICIANS

[*Facing page 226*]

KUSVAIN AND HIS SON

[*Facing page 227*]

supersedes it. A Kurumba is sent for; he doctors the child magically. Now a powerful maxim of Kota conduct is to have as little as possible to do with Kurumbas. Yet this principle is overridden when a person is gravely ill; the Kurumba sorcerer is invited into the village. Should the child die, or linger in pain, a father may have recourse to yet another socially recognized pattern—that of beating, even killing, the Kurumba thought responsible for the illness. Under ordinary circumstances a Kota will go far out of his way to avoid meeting Kurumbas, but personal fears may give way before the more compelling behavior of personal grief.

In this situation and in the countless number of major and minor crises that characterize the life of any human group, the scale of values is socially calibrated. That is to say, any tribesman knows what values may normally be expected to have highest compulsive power in a familiar situation. Thus he can predict that no man in his senses will ordinarily molest a Kurumba, but a sorrowing father may deliberately pick a fight with one.

In the ordinary round of life, the general hierarchy of values is well known and consistently observed. The culture may be said to be well integrated. Conflict and strife do occur within such a society, but the existence of a recognized scale of values enables men to allay societal friction. The dockets of our legal system are crowded with trials and debates, yet the existence of a calibrated code of behavior, law, enables society to deal effectively with these conflict situations.

But when the scale of values has been undermined, when men are not sure which patterns are most compelling and which less compelling, then such a society is full of stresses which are not relieved. It displays a lack of coordinated action, frequency of continued friction, a general disphoric state.

And the society is disorientated because the individuals within the group are personally disoriented. Kolme·l society was dislocated because each villager had suffered the loss of many relatives and friends. Most men felt that the old set of patterns dealing with illness and death were suddenly inadequate. These patterns and the dynamic value which adhered to them were rarely questioned as long as the usual cycle of life and death prevailed. But when one's kin and companions keel over wholesale, then a man wants to find some new way of coping with death. He is not so sure of the authority of the priests or of the supernatural sanction of the diviners, and these doubts shake his whole scheme of evaluation and response. He is ready to accept some new way of behavior which can be evaluated as more puissant than the old. For the disruption of one's personal and social scale of values is a dreadfully uncomfortable experience. It blasts all security and ease out of the universe. Hence men seek a quick reinstallment of paramount values. Best of all is some fresh pattern of thought and action which will explain away all previous difficulties with one sweeping generalization. In short, many villagers were ripe subjects for conversion.

Just any explanation and new pattern will not do. New ideas may be rejected if they deviate too greatly from established modes or if the proffered pattern conflicts with an old pattern of great compulsive power. The Kolme·l incident affords an example of such rejection. While the villagers were standing before the temples in January 1924—before Kusvain went into his historic spasm of possession—a woman, Niˑĵ, became possessed. She attempted to come forward to the temple pillar, began to speak as diviners do about the sins of the folk and the desires of the deities.

Niˑĵ, like Kusvain, is an aberrant personality. Kota women may not participate directly in the service of the gods. A sacred object touched by a woman becomes profaned; a sacerdotal personage who happens to see a woman during her period of catamenia becomes defiled; of all the phenomena of the universe the object most repugnant to the gods is a menstruating woman. Hence women may not become the vehicles of the gods, although they do become possessed with the spirits of the deceased. Niˑĵ had long been a peˑnbačoˑl, a medium of communication with the beings of the afterworld—who are not as fussy as the gods themselves. But to have a god deliberately choose a defiling vessel was an intolerable concept. It would invalidate the most basic, the most compelling ideas concerning the relation of women to gods and men.

Thus it came about that when Niˑĵ trembled and shook before the temple, stepped into a fire as diviners do, and uttered prophesies, Maˑgaˑly settled the matter. Maˑgaˑly was one of the headmen of the village, an ally of Kaˑkn. Let me quote Sulli again.

That was the first time I ever saw a woman shaking. All were astounded except Maˑgaˑly. He told . . . her to stop. She kept on shaking. He asked her, "If you are a true god tell me what I have in my hand." She didn't speak but kept on shaking. So he took a stick and beat her.

That finished the career of Niˑĵ as a diviner for the gods. No one was disposed to listen to her since the concept of a woman diviner clashed with other concepts at too many strategic points. Maˑgaˑly's action summarily and decisively rejected this new avenue of behavior. It was too great a departure from previous patterns, too great a negation of established concepts.

Yet Kusvain's behavior also departed from previous patterns and established concepts. Some villagers have never become reconciled to his innovations. To say that the villagers were disorganized and ripe for the adoption of a new pattern is hardly a sufficient explanation of the event since some of them proved impervious to the new idea. From the testimony of these men it is apparent that they too were beset by fears, they too had suffered and were not sure of the old values, but still they have refused to accept Kusvain's proposal. The reasons for acceptance by some and rejection by others may be brought out by a consideration of two more personalities, Sulli the advocate of the new and Kaˑkn the defender of the old.

Sulli has already figured in the narrative of the epidemic and its aftermath. He is now a man of about fifty, the teacher of the village school. His manifold energies and unique position make him a powerful influence in the community. He is the only member of the tribe who has learned to speak and write English; he is the only Kota who holds a government post; the only tribesman who has had extensive contacts both with Europeans and with Hindus.

Sulli's command of English—not a very firm command, incidentally—is a potent weapon in his hands. Whenever he is balked by others of the tribe, whenever he seeks to overcome resistance, he can cow his opponents by threatening to submit a petition to the British officials. The advent of the English did not of itself greatly affect Kota political and social organization since their colonial policy refrains from unduly disturbing existing social mechanisms. But it did impose an ultimate authority above the tribal council which previously had been the court of last appeal. Since Sulli possesses something of a monopoly on communications with this higher authority, his words and desires carry weight.

He also fulfills some of the traditional requirements for a leader. From his teacher's salary, his agricultural activity, his trading pursuits, Sulli has acquired more wealth than most of his people, and Kota society accords social recognition to men of wealth. More important, he argues impassionately and fluently. A man who can speak effectively, who can quote an apt proverb at the right time, who can meet and master opponents in debate, is the man who swings the decision of a council. And Sulli is glib beyond most of his tribe.

This is not to say that the tribesmen meekly follow his lead. Despite his strategic social position and personal attributes, his opponents are many and the number of his devoted followers is small. For Sulli is a rebel and a reformer. He is everlastingly advocating change. He wants to alter tribal dress and diet, to abandon old occupations and take up new. He has scant respect for some of the most venerable taboos of the culture, wants to abolish certain phases of social behavior which are now right and proper. Like men the world over, many Kotas resent gratuitous attempts to manipulate the established way of life. Hence they dislike Sulli's propensities for reform and refuse to follow his lead.

Sulli's easy flow of language lent itself well to the compilation of a life history, and the pages of the record of his personal career are many. Through all the material the dominant note of his personality is sounded again and again. He must always seek to deviate from the societal norm, and often attempts to induce others to adhere to his deviation. When he was just a boy, he ran off to a missionary and announced his desire to be converted. No Kota has ever become a Christian and it took a mass raid by villagers to carry him away from the mission compound. This social recognition of his deviation evidently satisfied him, for there was no further talk of being converted. The very fact that he alone has gone through a long and painful process of schooling is another manifestation of his drive to depart from tribal custom.

The genesis of this compelling factor in Sulli's personality cannot be traced here. But it is interesting to note that Sulli's father and grandfather also flouted convention. His grandfather raised a quarrel whose reverberations are still remembered when he was the first to use tile instead of thatch as roofing material. Sulli's father, against strenuous opposition from his fellows, insisted on being the one Kota to own a horse. Roof tiles and a single horse may seem of little moment, but in this area such matters serve as insignia of group status. The adoption of these traits promised to affect intertribal relations. But parental influence alone cannot account for Sulli's perpetual itch to tamper with the setup of his society, because his two brothers who shared the same familial environment do not share his deviant desires.

Sulli's radical notions apply only to a few narrowly circumscribed aspects of Kota cul-ture. He does not question most of the dominant themes of his society, and if they should be questioned by his non-Kota associates, he stoutly defends them. At the time of my stay on the Nilgiris, Sulli was moving heaven and earth in an attempt to keep a young second wife. He has only one son by his first wife, who is now beyond childbearing age. While a Kota with a single son is saved from social ignominy, to be truly a man one must have several sons. The difficulties Sulli encountered in keeping a second wife arose from the disparity between his and the bride's age and even more from the machinations of the senior wife. The troub-lous quest for a second wife was hardly motivated by sensuous considerations, because even when a marriage was contracted the elder saw to it that Sulli had little time for the younger spouse. And the second wife was known to have alliances with other men. These affairs did not disturb Sulli a bit, for he shares the prevailing Kota notion that biological paternity is of slight importance. He knows what store a European or a Hindu sets on being the bio-logical father of his wife's children but regards that view as one of the queer notions of alien peoples. Sulli is content to accept the greater part of the prevailing values of his society.

This in spite of the fact that he is culturally isolated beyond all his tribe. He has par-ticipated in ways of life foreign to Kota society. He has been exposed to cultural influences which have not yet seeped through to any other Kota. Whole complexes of behavior which are significant to present day Kota life—behavior toward Europeans, literacy in English and Tamil—are carried only by him among the tribesmen. But even he does not resist the most pervasive and compelling modes of Kota behavior. He rings no discordant note on the great majority of the dominant themes in Kota life. Most of the ideas and attitudes which have a high rating in the cultural scale of values have also high rank in Sulli's personal scale.

Sulli's desire to deviate, to modify his culture, finds expression in his efforts to get his fellows to cut their hair, to give over the eating of carrion, to abandon music as a tribal voca-tion, to curtail or abolish the menstrual seclusion hut. Around these four issues Sulli's reforming campaigns are currently crystallized. The life history data reveal that each of these issues has a different symbolic meaning for Sulli, and each strikes deep at fundamental precepts of Kota life.

The matter of a hair cut is a serious matter indeed to the tribe. Kota men wear their hair long, tied up in a bun at the nape of the neck. The knot of hair has ceremonial significance and is the hallmark whereby a man can be recognized as a Kota. This is precisely why Sulli wants the Kotas to cut their hair. He sees Kota status among the other tribes as lowly and mean, degrading and distasteful. Their carrion eating habits and tribal occupations make them defiling and repugnant to caste Hindus. Sulli was often refused admittance to tea-shops in the district because his hairdress made him immediately recognizable as a Kota. Only his bun of hair marked him and he long had yearned to lop it off. But no Kota had ever worn short hair and the pressure from within and without the tribe was great enough to keep Sulli from a barber until the end of 1936. In that year Dr M. B. Emeneau began using

Sulli as a linguistic informant. This intimate contact with a member of the white ruling class strengthened his prestige and determination until he mustered enough courage to cut his hair and face the criticism of his tribesmen and Badaga neighbors. Three young men of Kolme·l, egged on by Sulli, followed his example.

For all other Kotas there is nothing particularly mean in the tribal status nor is their chignon a symbol of inferiority. If they may not enter the houses of other peoples, why others may not enter theirs. They go to the weekly market, but feel no urge to enter a tea-shop there where the food is queer and the surroundings uncomfortable and strange. They have not sampled of the extra-Kota world as has Sulli, they have no feeling of being barred from places and associations since they have as yet no desire to seek out strange places and non-Kota associates.

The symbolic significance of long hair for Sulli is quite contrary to its meaning for his group. To him it is an irritating stigma of social inferiority; to them it is a comfortable part of the way of life. A similar differential in symbolic connotation occurs in the other issues on Sulli's agenda of reform. Sulli has learned from his Hindu acquaintances that musicians are lowly and subservient folk. But the other tribesmen tootling away at a Badaga or Toda ceremony feel a justified measure of self importance in their music. They know that without it, the ceremony could not go on. In the matter of meat-eating there is less of a gap between Sulli's evaluation of the custom and that of his people. The strong antipathy to the eaters of flesh and carrion, held by Badagas and Todas as well as caste Hindus, has percolated through to the Kotas and they are not too eager to defend the practise. Sulli's drive to abolish the menstrual hut—at least as a shelter for childbirth— is derived either from some unique personal experience within the village or from the influence of European hygiene. Hindus and tribesmen alike observe menstrual and childbirth seclusion. At any rate, the Kotas recognize no necessity for change in this as well as in the other issues.

These battles of Sulli's may be interpreted as overt manifestations of a trend discernible in his childhood, the drive to deviate from the cultural norm. The desire to deviate, as we have seen above, affects only selected aspects of the culture, but appears in the life history over and again as a theme of high compulsive power. And for Sulli, the advent of the new gods harmonized with this personal motif. They signalized the introduction of new elements to the pattern of Kota life, and since the new gods were Hindu deities, the direction of the change accorded with his own inclinations.

It is understandable then, why Sulli adopted the new dispensation and urged its acceptance in spite of his contempt for Kusvain and his continuing loyalty to the old gods. It was one means of actualizing a goal, social change, that is of great importance to him. To most of the men who have accepted the new trinity, the deed has no such symbolic significance. For them, the new gods were a means of reestablishing the equilibrium of life, of abolishing uncertainty, of coping with new conditions. Fear and panic motivated their conversion. Fear played little part in Sulli's motivation. He had been inoculated against the disease by health officers; he believed firmly in the efficacy of Western medicine. His conduct during an epidemic of bubonic plague in 1937 confirms his relative coolness in an epidemic situation. His continuing efforts to induce all the villagers to take over the new deities are attempts to secure social recognition for a personal symbol.

Since the new religious complex did not bear the same symbolic force to other men as it did to Kusvain and Sulli, some of them abjured the worship of the new gods soon after the shock of the epidemic had passed. A coterie of vigorous older men, of which Ka·kn was one, refused to bow at the new shrines, opposed the new rites. These men see the new complex as a dangerous thing, a symbol of the sinister influences which are attacking the established customs. The meaning of the new dispensation to this group may be gauged by a glimpse of Ka·kn's career.

While the record of Ka·kn's personal history is not as ample or as complete as is Sulli's, there is enough data to indicate the nature of his main avenue to personal satisfactions. Ka·kn is about ten years older than Sulli, bulky, mustachioed, aggressive. He is not a particularly good craftsman or agriculturalist, has never achieved notable successes with women, and though he shouts down opponents in debate by sheer physical vigor, his wit is not keen or subtle enough to win plaudits in council. But when complex funeral rites are to be held, or a ceremony performed, it is Ka·kn who directs the procedure and leads the participants. He has no official role to fulfill, being neither diviner nor priest, but he tells the diviners and priests what to do next. The mastery of ritual and authority in ceremonies constitute for Ka·kn the means to personal ascendancy. His stakes in life cluster around the old ceremonies.

From Ka·kn's recorded remarks it is evident that the introduction of a new ritual meant for him the ultimate displacement of the old and hence the blocking of his road to glory. He made little attempt to secure a dominating position in the service of the new deities, for their acceptance threatened to allow the influx of a host of new elements which would ultimately invalidate his position of competence. His refusal to tolerate the new religious complex can thus be understood as a refusal to tolerate a threat to his personal status.

The single event, the intrusion of a new worship, had opposite meanings for these two Kotas. To one, it was a useful instrument which helped him toward his goal; to the other, it was an inimical weapon which menaced his security. Each gave a different version of the affair, stressed different aspects of the situation, derived different conclusions from the episode both had lived through. The historical outline of the preceding pages has been winnowed from the testimony of a number of informants. But a comparison of Sulli's story with that of Ka·kn reflects their respective attitudes toward the new complex.

Sulli's tale begins with a statement of the epidemic and its severity, and goes on to tell of the council meeting at which he tried to persuade the elders to be inoculated and to bury the dead. His advice was disregarded and on his own initiative Sulli petitioned the health officers to inoculate the villagers. When they arrived, only the younger men submitted to treatment. This narrative describes the ceremony of January 1925 when the congregated villagers prayed for a visitation from the gods.

At once the god came to Kusvain. "Yes, my people, you ask that priests and diviners be chosen as they formerly were. But first you must build three shrines at ke·rva·y [for the new gods] and I will choose three men for that place, and then I will choose your old priests and diviners."

The men asked, "We already have three gods, why should we have three more?"

"Those gods do not know about the modern rules. . . . I am going to leave the ma:mu:l, the old rules. Now I have made pudmu:l, new rules. . . ."

All the men said, "We want only the old ma:mu:l; why do you treat us in this pudmu:l?"

"See my people, in former times you were the only ones living here and you need not get new rules. After a while the Badagas came, but they had the same ceremonies and customs as you. So I let you live together as ma:mu:l. Now I won't let you do as before, for many different people have come from the plains and other places. You mix with other people, and now I want to change the old rule. You must obey me and build three shrines."

Sulli tells how the shrines were finally built, and a ceremony for the new deities per-formed. On this occasion the new god again spoke through Kusvain, saying,

"Why did I come here? I want to change the old customs of the Kotas. You Kotas have been senselessly killing buffaloes for your funerals. Till today you send the women to the te·lul (menstrual hut) for three to six months when they give birth. . . . Stop killing cows and buffaloes. Your an-cestor Kitu·rpayk [the culture hero] tamed these wild animals for your use in milking and plowing. Or you may sell them and in that way become rich."

Sulli's version of Kusvain's speeches goes on at length to give an elaborate rationale for these reforms. Now it is quite certain that Kusvain's words simply commanded the new worship, gave a few details of the new ritual, hinted at general modifications of tribal be-havior. Sulli has apparently amplified these hints to include his pet controversies. Kusvain, in possession or out, is little interested in reform. When Sulli was asked about Kusvain's allegiance, his answer was, "When he has something to eat he is for me; when he needs food he is for the others." It is difficult to visualize Kusvain as being deeply concerned with social amelioration. Yet the main emphasis in Sulli's account of the event is on the long-winded program of reform and the reasons therefor which are cited as the words of the gods. From all the evidence it appears very unlikely that Kusvain ever uttered such harangues, and that the words, their interpretation, the stress laid on them, all stem from Sulli.

Ka·kn's tale, in turn, indicates the focus of his interest and desires. It begins with Kus-vain's possession, does not mention the epidemic. The new god insists that devotions be performed to him, else retainers for the old gods cannot be chosen. This account then goes on to tell how Kusvain became possessed on subsequent occasions. One time he ran through the brush to a swift flowing stream several miles from the village. There he mounted a tree which had fallen across the stream, ran along its length, crossing and recrossing the stream several times. This extremely dangerous procedure was halted when Ka·kn and others, who had followed, pounced on him as soon as they could and brought him back to the village. Then, says Ka·kn,

We waited for a few days. Meanwhile Kusvain was shaking even in his own house. One day

Kusvain went to the smithy . . . and was hammering a piece of iron to make an axe. At that moment he became possessed. I and some others were looking on there. Kusvain grabbed the red hot iron in his hand. "Now if you don't believe me," he said, "you come and grab this iron." Then I agreed to his word.

Although Ka·kn thus accepted the revelation—tentatively—he countered objections at every step. His story continues:

I thought the shrine should be built at ponatgal, farther off, which is more convenient and cleaner than the ke·rva·y place which Kusvain had chosen. But Kusvain said, "I will punish you if you say that." In all other villages the shrines are built on a hill, so I thought that this temple also should be built on a hill. But they wanted the shrine at ke·rva·y and so I agreed.

The two other diviners of the new gods demanded, while possessed, that shrines be built for all three new divinities. Ka·kn thus met this demand.

I refused that entirely and told them, "We can't build a temple to you here. Do you want us to leave our ma:mu:l gods entirely and build temples to you?" Then the Goddess said, "Unless you make three temples to us here, you will not be able to get diviners for the Kamaṭrayṇ [the old] gods." So we were forced to agree, because without diviners we cannot carry on the old ceremonies.

The shrines were built. The ceremony conducted before them followed closely the pattern of the old God Ceremony save for the introduction of coconuts and other lowland ritual traits. One part of the God Ceremony entails the making of new pots in which the ceremonial feast is cooked. When the newly made pots were fired on this occasion, they broke. Ka·kn's account continues:

Then Kusvain became possessed and told us to bring those pots which we use for the ma:mu:l [the old] gods. I refused and told him that those pots cannot be used here. But the young men said, "If you do not like it, go. We are going to use the sacred pots—you know nothing." I told them, "Don't get angry; the ma:mu:l rule is ma:mu:l; don't spoil the sacred pots." So I did not give my sacred pots. Those who were on my side gave other pots, not the sacred ones. Those who were against me gave the sacred pots. . . . While they were preparing the food, a big rain came. All were talking about it. I told them, "This is the punishment for using the sacred pots. If it were a true god, why couldn't the rain be averted?" . . . They were going to prepare the food with salt only [as is done in the traditional God Ceremony], but I told them to mix in curry powder also [as for ordinary foodstuffs]. Because I thought that if they make the food in the same way as they do for the Kamaṭrayṇ gods, then they will honor the new gods the same as the old. . . . They agreed to put curry-stuff in the food. By my talking I defeated those who wanted salt only. Then I thought, by the rain and by my winning in the matter of the salt, I know that the Kamaṭrayṇ gods are the true gods."

The wonders he had witnessed counted for so little to Ka·kn that a heavy rain and a skirmish in argument sufficed to cancel their effect. Kusvain's deeds, he decided, were inspired by evil spirits and not by genuine gods, and so he renounced the new worship. The dominant motif in his personality which impells him to cling to and preserve the ancient ritual led him to discount the force and influence of Kusvain's wondrous acts. Sulli, too, made little of these acts, but for another reason. In his story they are only of marginal inter-

TEMPLE OF THE YOUNGER MALE GOD OF THE OLD TRINITY

TWO MEN BOWING BEFORE THE SHRINE OF THE NEW FEMALE DEITY BETDAMN

[Facing page 234]

est because these new gods are a means toward his goal of social change, and Sulli accepts these means as useful without too searching questions as to their supernatural validity.

One last episode in Kusvain's career may be cited to demonstrate a situation in which both Sulli and Ka·kn share the same attitudes and values. When a priest and a full comple-ment of three diviners had been selected for the new gods, Kusvain's deity again spoke through him. The god commanded the four newly-chosen retainers to bedeck themselves in ceremonial raiment. They were told to go to a certain Badaga village to demand tribute for the Kotas and their gods. The men faithfully dressed in new waistcloths, wore shoulder cloths in the fashion of high caste men, and painted on their foreheads the red and white trident of Vishnu. A sad fate awaited them among the Badagas. The temerity of these Kotas in adopting dress and symbols sacred to the Badagas and coming to levy tribute to boot, so aroused the villagers that a mob intent on trouncing the four soon collected. When the crowd closed in, Kusvain, ever reliant on his single weapon, went into a fit of possession and was allowed to escape. But the other three received a mauling whose marks they still bear.

This debacle might have been a cause for rejoicing by the opponents of the new complex as an additional proof of the impotence of the new revelation. Actually they were highly indignant and took retaliatory measures against the culprits who had hurt their fellow tribes-men. The beating was felt by Ka·kn and his coterie as a blow against themselves as Kotas, and not as a well deserved slap at the followers of the new faith. Their loyalty to their group overrode sentiments of hostility to a faction within the group. They decided to boycott the Badagas until a suitable fine had been paid in expiation. When they were next called to provide music at the Badaga village all the Kolme·l men refused. The hot-blooded younger Badagas now felt that the Kotas were becoming obstreperous beyond all tolerance, and they systematically began to waylay and beat Kotas. The Kolme·l elders then invoked Sulli's aid. A petition was dispatched to the police who put an end to the Badaga campaign of terror. A token fine was paid by a Badaga elder to smooth the ruffled Kota feelings and amicable relations once again prevailed between the Badaga village and Kolme·l.

Manifest in this incident is the operation of a principle which spreads wide through Kota society and through many another society as well. The hostilities which were rife within the group were temporarily abandoned in the face of external aggression. Ka·kn's opposition to the new gods and their followers was subordinated to another impulse. The impulse to defend one's own people against the onslaught of an out-group, the Badagas, was paramount to the urge to discredit a hostile faction within the in-group. Once the Badaga trouble died down, the Kolme·l dispute flared anew.[2]

[2] It is probably safe to say that if the Badaga onslaught had continued, the dissension within Kolme·l would have been suppressed—at least for the duration of the larger conflict. But the inner antagonism would become dominant again when the extra-tribal pressure was raised—as did happen—or if the external hostilities so har-assed the group as to undermine confidence in all established values—as may yet occur. In the latter case, the disintegration of the hierarchy of values would foster strife within the group and then the religious rivalry might well become the focus of civil violence.

Both recorded and reconstructed history are replete with examples of the process noted here. Dissident factions within a group suddenly consolidate when the security of the larger group is menaced. Perhaps the principle may be stated most succinctly as: loyalty to a larger social entity is more demanding than loyalty to a smaller social entity. When the security of the total societal unit is in danger—or is thought to be in danger—then the members of that unit spring to its defense, shelve the antagonisms and narrower allegiances which obtain among the lesser groups than comprise the whole.

Although principles of social behavior need not necessarily have logical basis, there is a measure of logic to this doctrine. For the dissolution of the greater unit would automatically wipe out all within its compass, would cancel both the strife and the solidarity of the lesser unit. Hence the larger group must be defended first. This may well be one of the " . . . culture patterns which tend to be universal, not only in form but in psychological significance. . . . "[3]

Furthermore, the reason for the ubiquity of this pattern among cultures, and the basis for its dominance within a given society, may be attributed to a drive for self-preservation. The collapse of the structure of the larger society means the collapse of every compartment within the general organization, therefore each member must rise to the defense of the whole to preserve his own particular niche. This seems to hold true for all units of society down to the ultimate entity, the individual. The individual too forgets about internal conflict when his general status as a personality is endangered. Ka·kn evidently was just as much in a conflict situation during the epidemic as were the others, but when the new complex began to threaten his personal status, he relinquished any tendency to follow the new way and opposed it with might and main. It looks as though he felt that his whole role in the drama of society would be cut out by the introduction of a new scene into the play. Here again one of Edward Sapir's observations is germane. "Personality organizations, which at last analysis are psychologically comparable with the greatest cultures or idea systems, have as their first law of being their essential self-preservation. . . . "[4]

The life situation that concerns us here includes phenomena we recognize as cultural and—as we have seen—personal, individualized aspects. The two are not mutually exclusive categories nor do they represent irreconcilable points of vantage. An understanding of Ka·kn's personal conflicts and reactions clears the way for an understanding of the behavior of others in his group. Kolme·l village still supported sectarian differences—really a cultural dichotomy—when the Kota field work was terminated at the end of May 1938.

The men belonging to the conservative faction, as Ka·kn's group may be called, are mostly older men. The meaning which the new complex bears for them is generally the same as its meaning to Ka·kn. Like him, they know the old ways, cherish them, feel comfortable within them. Though new circumstances make the old shoe of custom pinch a bit, they would rather keep it than chance a try with new gear. In the personal scale of values of

[3] Edward Sapir, *Cultural Anthropology and Psychiatry* (Journal of Abnormal and Social Psychology, Vol. 27, pp. 229–42, 1932), p. 238.   [4] *Ibid.*, p. 242.

each of these older men, the new complex is similarly rated, and it is no startling discovery to note that this congruence of evaluation and response constitutes cultural behavior.

The similarity of response by these Kota conservatives is, in large measure, a corollary of the similarity of their ages. An old Kota does not have the same value-system as does a young Kota, and the Kota elder does not have the same scale of values he maintained when younger. Age, in itself, brings about a certain kind of shift in the personal dynamics of evaluation of an individual. This process operating in the personal career of each older man is largely responsible for the like response manifested by the members of the Ka·kn faction.

The age-shift is a condition which occurs in the life experience of all individuals (save, perhaps, in some exceptional cases), which transcends the limits of any one society, which operates in all societies. It ensues from the very nature of the human materials which constitute a society. All men grow old. As each individual advances in age, his values change. The exact nature of the shift varies from individual to individual, and the range of the shift must be redefined for every culture, but the juxtaposition of values with advancing years is a process that must be taken into account in any thorough analysis of personal and cultural history.

The common denominator of age is not to be taken as a blanket explanation for the actions of all members of the conservative group. Young men also have repudiated the new complex. For them, any predeliction for the new has been overriden by stronger considerations, such as filial loyalty or private symbolisms discerned in the new triad. Conversely, Sulli is getting on in years but is not a conservative. And Sulli's elder brother belongs to his party simply because he follows his brother wherever Sulli may lead. Behind the façade of this cultural expression there lie multiple personal meanings as well as the uniformity of evaluation and response which comes out of the common age alignment of values.

We may now supply certain answers to the questions asked above. The new complex could gain a foothold after 1924 because the old had lost compulsive value for some individuals. The value of a culture pattern lies in its relative power to be translated into action in a given situation. A pattern has compulsive value when an individual always brings it into play to meet a certain need, when alternative patterns of behavior are never used to meet that need.

A pattern is culturally compulsive if it has compulsive value for most individuals (or all individuals) within a given society. Prior to the epidemic, the way of the old religion was culturally compulsive in Kolme·l. It adequately met and fulfilled at least one basic need, the need for coping with death. After the epidemic, many villagers felt that it no longer met that need satisfactorily. For them, the old pattern lost its compulsive validity and they could admit a supplemental pattern of equal potency into their evaluation system.

The new pattern did not entail the same kind of value displacement for its progenitor, Kusvain. For him it was largely a projection of a unique personal compulsion. Nor did it involve the same displacement for its chief sponsor, Sulli. For him the new worship was merely one pattern which could be nicely adapted to the actualization of a personal goal.

These private meanings of the new pattern were factors which brought about the culture change no less than the general weakening of the old in the scale of values of many villagers. The origin and growth of a culture pattern must ultimately be referred to motivations and reactions within the individual.

The special connotation which the new complex had for Ka·kn and his adherents worked to block the change. Each of these men evidently felt that the new complex took away more than it might add to their personal security. For these individuals, therefore, the old religion still has compulsive value and continues to function as a cultural compulsion within their group. A graduated weighting of patterns, a hierarchy of values, is character-istic of the phenomena we call cultural as well as of the behavior we term personal. The shape of a culture, when we probe into its essential nature, begins to look more and more like the structure of a personality.

University of Minnesota
   Minneapolis, Minnesota

SOCIAL CONTROL AND THE INDIVIDUAL IN EASTERN HAZARA CULTURE

By ALFRED E. HUDSON AND ELIZABETH BACON

INTRODUCTION

IN THIS PAPER we wish to analyze the factors which regulate the relations of the individual to the community among the Hazara tribes of Afghanistan.[1] Our discussion is based largely upon ethnographical rather than psychological data and to a great extent deals with the explicit and semi-formal aspects of group participation rather than with the implicit and unformalized. In his lectures and in conversation Dr Sapir frequently stressed the necessity of such an approach in order to provide an adequate understanding of the cultural milieu before attempting the hazardous interpretation of more tenuous relationships. A profound respect, originally derived to no small extent from Dr Sapir and reenforced by every field experience, for the possible depths and subtleties of even the most obvious and overt cultural behavior makes us reluctant on the basis of present material to go beyond a largely descriptive analysis. We will describe first the formal agencies of social control and their operation, secondly some unformalized aspects of cultural pressure on the individual, and finally suggest certain basic attitudes of mind which appear to underlie them.

Since the literature on the Hazaras is scanty and no descriptive ethnography exists, we will briefly summarize the culture in order that the points which we wish to emphasize may be viewed in proper perspective.

The several tribes known collectively as Hazaras are located chiefly in central Afghanistan, in the region named after its inhabitants, the Hazarajat. This term is applied to the greater part of the country lying between Kabul to the east and Herat to the west, bordered on the north by the Hindu Kush and on the south by the upper Helmand River, an area of some 15,000 square miles. Several Hazara tribes are also to be found north of the Hindu Kush in western Afghanistan, but since no information was obtained on these groups they will not be considered here. The Hazaras of the Hazarajat appear to have no intercourse with them and for the most part deny all relationship.

The average elevation of the Hazarajat is 10,000 feet, with numerous peaks over 15,000 feet, but most permanently inhabited places are in mountain valleys with an elevation of

[1] Field work was made possible by a Research Fellowship in Anthropology from Yale University, grants-in-aid from the Social Science Research Council and the American Council of Learned Societies, and the generosity of Mr Bayard Dominick. Research on the historical background of the Hazaras was made possible by grants-in-aid from the American Philosophical Society and the Social Science Research Council. We are grateful for many courtesies from Afghan officials, especially His Highness Sardar Mohammed Naim Khan, Minister of Public Instruction, and His Excellency Ali Mohammed Khan, Minister of Foreign Affairs.

about 8,000 feet. Such valleys, narrow and winding, hemmed in by steeply rising mountains, are the chief features of the topography, although in the southern and western parts of the region there are extensive high plateaus of open rolling country.

The climate throughout the Hazarajat is extremely severe in the long winter; snow covers the ground to a considerable depth and travel is difficult, with the result that most communities are isolated for several months at a time. The snow melts in April and the

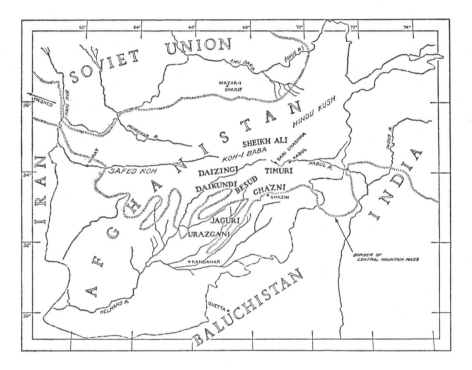

HAZARA TRIBES OF AFGHANISTAN

ensuing heavy floods are augmented by torrential rains for a period of a month or six weeks. From May to September the days are pleasantly warm and generally sunny.

During the brief summer cultivated crops flourish and the mountains are thinly covered with wild plants and grasses. The mountain slopes are devoid of trees except for a few wild almond or other trees in an occasional upper valley. In the valleys poplars and a few fruit trees are planted at the margins of cultivated fields.

The Hazaras are a people of definitely Mongoloid physical type. The inaccessibility of their mountain habitat, combined with marked antipathy between Hazaras and the surrounding tribes, has operated to prevent intermarriage.

"Hazara" is the Persian word for thousand which the Mongols in Persia early came to apply to the military subdivision.[2] The Hazaras do not appear to have entered the territory they now occupy in a single body. Chingis Khan, who actually entered part of what is now the Hazarajat in 1221-1223, ordered each of his four sons to furnish a thousand soldiers to act as permanent frontier garrisons.[3] Some years later Mangu Khan, the grandson of Chingis, sent another thousand men from Mongolia to reinforce these troops.[4] Elias' statement[5] that Khulagu's son Nikudar, who became Ilkhan of the western Mongol empire in 1282,[6] settled garrisons in this region, would appear to be substantiated by references to the Nikudari tribes as of 1318[7] and of 1504.[8] It is probable that garrisons also were left in Afghanistan by later Mongol conquerors and by Timur (1336-1405).[9]

In most cases these military cantonments were peripheral to, rather than within, the boundaries of the present Hazarajat. As the Mongol empire gradually disintegrated and finally collapsed it would appear that these garrisons became isolated from the main armies and were pushed farther and farther back into the high mountains, both from the north and from the south, by each successive group which gained control in the populous lowlands. This process of compression still continues.

We were unable to discover among our informants any tradition free from the suspicion of outside influence which would indicate a consciousness of descent from the Mongol conquerors. Elias, however, cites a group living south of Meshed in 1894 who had a very clear cut and plausible tradition of descent from soldiers of Chingis Khan.[10]

For a period of over five hundred years the Hazaras maintained their practical, if not always their nominal, independence. Shah Abbas of Persia undertook, without evident success, to appoint a chief over all the tribes, and Nadir Shah received their technical submission; neighboring states such as Kandahar and Kabul taxed nearby Hazara tribes when they were able to enforce collection; but nothing in recorded history or tradition indicates that the Hazaras were ever for long either subject to a foreign ruler or united under their own

During the second half of the nineteenth century, however, the amirs of Kabul gradually extended their authority over what is now Afghanistan, and the Hazaras, despite long and violent resistance, were finally subjugated in the 1890's by Abdur Rahman. The

---

[2] For some reason, possibly a phonetic one, the Mongol terms juz (hundred) and ming (thousand) were quickly displaced by the Persian equivalents, sad and hazara, whereas the Mongol tumen (ten thousand) continued to be used.   [3] D'Ohsson, Histoire des Mongols, Vol. 2, p. 280.

[4] D'Ohsson, loc. cit., quoting Vassaf.   [5] Elias and Ross, History of the Moghuls, p. 80, Introduction.

[6] These Nikudari may, however, be descendants of the troops of Nikudar the son (according to Browne, History of Persian Literature, p. 25) or grandson of Chagatai (Howorth, History of the Mongols, Vol. 3, p. 229). This Nikudar was chiefly active in Georgia, but after his disgrace around 1270 his troops, called by Browne the Nikudari, were incorporated into the army of the Ilkhan (Howorth, Vol. 3, p. 240), and may well have been transferred to western Afghanistan.   [7] D'Ohsson, Vol. 4, pp. 617-18.

[8] Beveridge, The Babur-nama in English, Vol. 1, pp. 200, 207, 274.

[9] Petis de la Croix, History of Timur-Bec, Vol. 1, p. 150; Khanikoff, Mémoire, pp. 348-49.

[10] Elias and Ross, p. 494d.

ultimate authority of the Afghan government is now fairly well established, although local administration rests with the Hazaras.

There are no reliable statistics concerning the Hazara population. A rough estimate places the number in Afghanistan at slightly over half a million. There are also at the present time communities in Iran and Baluchistan.

In language and religion the Hazaras have been strongly influenced by Iran. Unlike most Turco-Mongol groups, who show a notable tendency to retain their language no matter how greatly their culture may have been influenced otherwise by non-Turco-Mongol peoples, the various Hazara tribes whom we studied all speak Persian dialects, although the vocabularies contain many Mongol words. The studies of Ramstedt[11] and von der Gabelentz[12] indicate that some of the western Hazaras living north of the Hindu Kush still speak a basically Mongol language, but so far as we know all of the eastern Hazaras, i.e. those living in the Hazarajat, speak Persian.

Like the Persians the Hazaras are firm adherents of the Shiia sect of Islam, an adherence which sets them apart from their Sunni neighbors, the Afghans, Turcomans, Usbegs, and at least some of the western Hazaras. We have as yet found no precise date for the adoption of Islam by the ancestors of the Hazaras. It is quite possible that the Hazaras acquired not only their Persian speech, as Longworth Dames suggests,[13] but their Shiia religion as well from the inhabitants of the mountain kingdom of Ghor whom they displaced.[14] On the other hand it may be that the Hazaras were influenced by the general wave of conversion which swept the Mongols in Persia during the end of the thirteenth and beginning of the fourteenth centuries. Ghazan Khan, who was overlord of Khorasan, which included the Hazarajat, before he became Ilkhan in 1295, is specifically stated to have been a Shiia.[15]

The Hazaras have to a large extent exchanged the nomadic life of the steppe for a sedentary one, but have achieved in their economy a careful balance between agriculture and herding. Practically all available land in the narrow watered valleys is under cultivation; where the valleys are wholly inadequate for the community, dry farming is practised on high mountain meadows. The most important crops are wheat, barley, and various types of field pea. Engulfing the small cultivated areas are steep mountain slopes suitable only for grazing, so that herding continues to play a vital part in Hazara economy. Horses have lost their importance in this mountainous country, being largely displaced by donkeys and cattle, but sheep and goats appear to be as numerous as among the nomads to the north. The Hazara diet is still essentially that of a pastoral people, consisting largely of milk products, with the addition of bread.

Community life centers around the fortified village which is typical of the area extend-

[11] Ramstedt, *Mogholica.*

[12] Von der Gabelentz, *Über die Sprache der Hazaras.* This is based on material presented by Leech in *A Vocabulary of the Language of the Moghal Aimaks.*   [13] Longworth Dames, *Hazara,* p. 297.

[14] We have discovered no specific reference to the religion of the Ghori, but Ebn Haukal, an Arabic traveller of the tenth century, states that some of the country districts and villages to the west and north of the Hazarajat were Shiia. (See Ouseley, *Oriental Geography of Ebn Haukal,* pp. 219-20.)   [15] D'Ohsson, Vol. 4, pp. 141, 540.

ing from Iran to the northwest frontier of India. It consists of a massive walled rectangular enclosure with a gate in the middle of one side and usually with a tower at each of the four corners. The dwellings, which, like the outer walls, are made of sun-baked mud mixed with straw, are built against the inner surface of the wall, thus leaving an open court in the center of the enclosure. Some communities do not take the form of a rectangular fortress but in such cases the houses are built protectively wall to wall, under the shadow of a high watch tower.

Villages are normally situated at a point where the mountain slope meets the valley, so that it is immediately adjacent to cultivable valley land while not encroaching on it. Below the village lie the fields. Above it rise the mountain slopes where the flocks go out each day to graze. During the summer, in some parts of Urazgani and Jaguri (see below) and possibly elsewhere among those who have large flocks of sheep, most of the inhabitants of the village set up summer residences in the pasture lands, leaving a few men behind to irrigate the crops. They returned in autumn for the harvest and to lay in winter fodder. This seasonal shift can scarcely be considered a migration since the summer camping ground was usually very close to the village, indeed sometimes just outside the walls.

The formal pattern of social organization among all the Hazara tribes is in general similar to that of the Turks and Mongols of Central Asia: all the members of a tribe consider themselves descended from some traditional common ancestor. Within this group sub-tribes and further sub-divisions set apart the lineage groups of less remote progenitors. It is impossible to give the exact number of tribes because during the last century some tribes have lost their existence entirely, some have merged with other tribes and assumed the status of sub-tribes, while in other cases groups have split off from the parent tribe and become completely independent. Among the most important tribes historically are the Daizingi, Daikundi, Besud, Jaguri, and Urazgani. The Urazgani lived in the extreme south of the Hazarajat, somewhat northeast of Kandahar, while Jaguri territory lies immediately northeast of Urazgani. Some distance to the northeast of Jaguri is Besud. The Daizingi occupied a large territory extending roughly from north of Jaguri to the Hindu Kush and from Besud on the east to Daikundi, which borders Daizingi on the west. On the eastern border of Besud live the Timuri,[16] a small tribe which forms the last outpost of Hazaras as one approaches Kabul.

These several tribes differ to a certain extent one from another culturally, linguistically, and even, subtly, in physical type. As might be expected the greatest difference appears between the two most widely separated groups, namely Urazgani and Timuri. It is probable also that some of the differences as reflected in our information are due to the various time levels to which it relates.

Our material was gathered from members of the Urazgani, Jaguri, Besud, and Timuri

---

[16] These Timuri have a tradition that their ancestors came to their present territory from Herat. It seems probable that they may be descended from the troops stationed there by Timur in 1396 (Khanikoff, *Mémoire*, pp. 348–49), as their name suggests.

tribes. The Urazgani, formerly a powerful tribe, were to a considerable degree broken up after the war with Abdur Rahman and our informant left Afghanistan in 1902 at the age of thirty-seven. Consequently most of his recollections go back to the period prior to the revolt of 1893, although he has revisited relatives now living in Afghan Turkistan. Our Jaguri informants are middle-aged men who left Afghanistan some twenty years ago, though one at least has returned on visits from time to time. Our scant Besud information was obtained from a man in his thirties who now lives in Kabul, but who returns to Besud at frequent intervals. Our Timuri material was obtained from various informants, mostly from the chief of the tribe and a village headman, while we were living among the Timuri. Thus there is a time spread of some fifty or sixty years between Urazgani and Timuri material which must be considered in weighting the variations between the groups. It may perhaps be well to add that, according to our chief Jaguri informant, who has travelled extensively throughout the whole Hazarajat, the Urazgani were considered the most "backward" of the Hazara tribes, the most warlike, and the least influenced by Islam.

In each of the groups the emphasis given to the social devices which regulate the relations of the individual to the community differ, sometimes slightly, sometimes markedly. In order to give cohesion to this paper it seems advisable for descriptive purposes to adopt as a norm the Jaguri data as far as possible, since it lies midway, both geographically and in time, between the two extremes of Urazgani and Timuri. Deviations from this norm will then be indicated.

CHANNELS OF SOCIAL CONTROL

The village, which ranges in size from a hamlet of four or five families to a town of as many as two or three hundred families, is the basic unit of social organization among all the Hazara tribes, and it is with his village that the individual feels himself most closely identified. A number of villages, from five to as many as three or four hundred, are coordinated under the leadership of a chief who usually bears the title of malik[17] but the group of villages as a whole over which he presides has no generic name. At the present time there are no wider, more inclusive groupings than these, although in former times there were tribal and sub-tribal khans among the Hazaras.

Among the Jaguri and Urazgani the residents of a village or agil[18] are fairly closely related members of a single lineage, part of a whole lineage group which is closely localized in a series of neighboring agil. While there may be present in the village a few families of servants belonging to other lineage groups, even to other tribes, most of the population, and usually all the landowners, belong to the one group, as do the headman and riš safits[19] or elders of the village. Among the Besud and Timuri, on the other hand, several lineage groups may be and often are represented in a single village, and headman or riš safits may be drawn from any of these.

---

[17] An Arabic title used throughout Afghanistan.   [18] Compare with Turkic aul and Mongol ayil.
[19] Literally, white beards. Compare with the Turkic equivalent, aḳ saḳal, white beard.

The agil enjoys a high degree of autonomy, deals with internal affairs in its own way, and requires the services of the malik of the larger group only in matters pertaining to its dealings with the outside world. Affairs involving neighboring villages are usually settled amicably among themselves, the malik being called in only when the chances of agreement appear remote.

The selection of the village headman differs considerably from tribe to tribe. Among the Jaguri he was elected by representatives of all the families in the village, including those not belonging to the prevailing lineage group. In Urazgani[20] there was a tendency to hereditary succession. The people, however, appear to have had some voice in the matter, for if they considered the usual heir, the eldest son, unfit for the position, they might pass him over in favor of another, usually a younger son or a brother of the deceased headman. Among the Timuri on the other hand, and also, it would appear, among the Besud, there is no formally elected headman, no title corresponding to the Urazgani iš fariš, the Jaguri doruga.[21] Nevertheless our observations among the Timuri indicate quite clearly that one man, by reason of his wisdom and dignity, stands out from all the others as leader of the village, although we were assured that he has no formal authority.

It is evident that whatever the mode of selection, the functions and authority of the headman are fairly similar among the different tribes. The Hazaras are an independent folk, unlikely to submit to undue displays of authority. A leader is required to deal with problems outside the scope of the individual or the family, but he is chosen that he may be of service and not to rule autocratically. The Jaguri doruga is elected because of his "good conduct" and his wisdom. The logical heir of the Urazgani iš fariš is passed over if he does not possess the requisite qualities. The Timuri, without formal position and elective machinery, informally acknowledge as their leader the man who is wisest and best among them.

The village headman is consulted as advisor and arbiter in local matters. If a family is unable to agree upon a fair distribution of an inheritance, he may be called upon to suggest a reasonable division. If an orphan girl is without near relatives he will appoint a guardian for her. In those places where the people move out of the villages to the pasture land in the summer, it is the headman who directs the details of departure and the establishment of the camp.

The headman's authority over the village is based upon the confidence which his sagacity and justice inspire in the people. He deals with recalcitrants by "giving them a lecture." He can make a petty thief of the village give up his booty and perhaps pay a fine because the force of public opinion is behind him. This force can as a last resort exclude from the village and drive into exile an individual hopelessly lacking in cooperation and unresponsive to persuasion.

[20] The territory which a tribe occupies has generally taken over the name of that tribe, so that one may speak of Urazgani, Besud, etc., referring to the geographical regions or to the people of the tribes inhabiting them.

[21] A Mongol term used by the conquerors to designate the civil governor of a city or the military governor of a garrison.

The headman acts also as spokesman for the village in dealing with neighboring communities and as intermediary between the villagers and the malik. In minor altercations between residents of two neighboring villages the respective headmen act as arbiters. In more serious affairs it is the headman who carries his villager's case before the malik. If a malik is unpopular, the headman acts as spokesman for his village delegation in the parleys involved in deposing one malik and electing another.

In addition to the headman there are in most villages a number of riš safits or elders. Among the Jaguri they seem to have filled a clearly defined office. Our chief Jaguri informant describes rather large villages which were divided into wards, each with its own riš safit who acted as deputy for the headman among the families in his care. In such a capacity the functions of the riš safits are similar, on a smaller scale, to those of the headman. Individually they advise their people and arbitrate small disputes which at their discretion may be referred to the headman. Collectively they, together with the headman, serve as a village council to consider matters of importance to the group as a whole. If a man wishes to sell land to an outsider, they debate the desirability of the prospective purchaser as a member of the community and grant or withhold permission to sell. In case of general dissatisfaction with the malik, the council of riš safits and the headman represent the interests of their people in the meetings with delegations from other villages to select a successor.

Our Urazgani informant does not mention the riš safit, possibly because he did not wish to detract from the appearance of authority which his father, the iš fariš, enjoyed, possibly because the riš safit was less important in the feudal times of which he speaks. In all events, it will be necessary to omit the Urazgani from consideration for the moment.

Among the Timuri the role of the riš safit, as well as that of the headman, is much less formalized than it appears to be among the Jaguri. The Timuri riš safits are simply the elderly men of the village who enjoy the respect of their neighbors by virtue of their years and experience and who, individually or collectively, may appropriately offer advice and guidance. Inasmuch as among the Timuri neither the village headman nor the riš safits are formally appointed or elected and do not bear any specific titles, the difference between the two offices is tenuous. Usually, however, there is in a Timuri village one riš safit, younger, more competent or assertive than the others, who is the functioning executive of the group though he bears no title corresponding to the Jaguri doruga or Urazgani iš fariš. The extent to which he stands out from the other riš safits varies, of course, from one community to another. It is possible that the unformalized government of Timuri villages may be somewhat related to the smallness of the local groups; the largest in the tribe having only eighty families while the smallest contains but three.

It should be emphasized that among the Hazaras studied, the duties of both the village headman and of the riš safits are carried out, though with dignity, with considerable informality. The headman knows personally every member of the village and, as well, the headmen of neighboring villages. The riš safits are intimately acquainted with, often related to, the people with whom they deal. They are called in as wise friends to settle disputes.

Released by grown sons or servants from the more arduous tasks involved in gaining a livelihood, they have ample opportunity to indulge in the favorite Hazara pastime, conversation. They can stroll about, talking to this person or that, discovering his feelings and opinions; they can sit together, under a tree or at the village gate, where anyone who wishes may join them, discussing among themselves the problems of the community.

The larger administrative unit, under the leadership of the malik, has no special name and corresponds to no particular tribal subdivision. Among the Timuri, which includes altogether no more than twenty villages, there is one malik over the whole tribe; among the Jaguri there was a malik over each sub-tribe. These sub-tribes varied considerably in size. In the Nukroz sub-tribe of Urazgani, there were four maliks, each over some eighty villages. Our Besud material is somewhat uncertain, since the term malik is not used there. The kariador, who is said to correspond to the malik, presides over a hundred or more villages, but the askol, who governs from five to fifty agils, is the real leader who concerns himself with the welfare of the people under him. Since it was not possible to obtain detailed information concerning these two Besud subdivisions we are unable to discuss their leaders in relation to those of the other tribes.

As in the case of the village headman, the position of the malik among the Urazgani tended to be hereditary. But it was quite definitely stated that he was elected by the people, and if the son of the former malik seemed unfit for the position he was passed over in favor of another.

All our evidence suggests that Urazgani political life of fifty years ago was semi-feudal in character and, of the four Hazara tribes studied, approximates most closely that of the medieval Mongols as well as that of the tribes of Turkistan up to the middle of the nineteenth century.[22] The Urazgani constantly engaged in wars, raids and feuds; one sub-tribe against another, one tribe against another, Hazaras against the hostile Afghans to the south. That a malik be wise and just was not sufficient. He must be a forceful leader in war, and command a strong armed personal following with which to protect his people against their enemies. Thus as long as a family retained its commanding wealth and following, the malikship would be entrusted to it, since the chief duty of the malik was to protect the people under him, and at that time their rights might best be protected by force.

To a rather less extent similar qualifications were demanded of a malik throughout the Hazarajat before the Afghan government gained control. A suggestion of this is given in the statement of a Jaguri informant that a man was chosen to be malik "because he was a good man and had 2,000 tents."[23] Thus a strong personal following was considered a valuable adjunct to leadership even thirty years ago. As wars and feuds became rarer under the new regime disputes came more and more to be settled with a consideration for justice and the merits of the case rather than for the respective military strength of the two contestants.

[22] Hudson, *Kazak Social Structure*, pp. 61–67.

[23] It is suggestive that power should be measured in terms of tents, as among the nomads of Turkistan, rather than in terms of houses or families.

During this period for which we have material on the Jaguri, Besud, and Timuri, therefore, the chief qualifications of a malik are that he be a "good" man, i.e. that he be wise, just, endowed with a personality which commands obedience (there was no formal machinery by which he could enforce his rulings), and that he be genuinely concerned with the welfare of the people who had chosen him.

He was retained in office during good behavior, deposed as soon as the people became dissatisfied with him.[24] The taxes paid to him may be considered as a kind of salary. As long as the taxes remained moderate the people more or less willingly paid them, for they did not wish their representative "to go without things he needed." But let the people suspect that their malik was growing wealthy or extravagant on the proceeds of their toil and they were quick to turn against him.

Theoretically every adult male in the group was privileged to vote for the malik. In practise only the riš safts of all the villages, together with the leading mullahs and seyeds (see below) of the group, attended the meetings which decided on the deposition of the old malik and choice of the new. The deposed malik had no recourse but to accept the will of the people and quietly give way to the new leader. During recent years his tenure of office has not been protracted. The Besud counterpart of the malik generally retains office from one to three years. The Timuri, at the time of our visit, had just emerged from a series of terms lasting only a month or two each, though the current incumbent still seemed popular after holding the title for six months.

A major function of the Timuri malik at the present time is as intermediary between the tribe and the central Afghan government. He collects the taxes for the government and distributes any largesse which may be forthcoming from it. He is responsible to the government for the actions of the tribe: he must see that such regulations as may be imposed are carried out.

The malik of the Jaguri also represented the people in its few dealings with the government, but in addition he was closely concerned with the internal administration of the group. Disputes between two villages or the residents of two villages were taken to him for arbitration. He acted as judge in cases of theft. If the thief belonged to another group the malik of the victim's group must attempt to obtain restitution from the malik representing the thief. In former times such negotiations sometimes led to war.

In spite of the considerable variations described above the role of the malik is essentially identical among the various tribes. While the village headman concerns himself with the internal affairs of the basic village unit, the malik is responsible for the external dealings of the people, whether they be inter-village, inter-group, or with the central government.

In addition to the system of civil administration described above, there is also a strong religious control exerted by the mullahs, Moslem priests, and the seyeds, alleged descendants of Mohammed.

[24] The Jaguri have a proverb which says: "The malik is not sent by God."

We have little information concerning their specific role among the Urazgani, but, although we were informed that the influence of Islam was least strong among that group, it is evident that the power of these representatives of religion was considerable. A people loathe to expend their goods in civil taxes willingly paid the mullah his zakot (one-tenth of the year's harvest) and the seyeds their xoms (one-fifth of the year's increase), as did all the other tribes. We know that the mullah was in demand for curing illness attributed to supernatural causes, and that he performed the marriage ceremony. Presumably he had many other functions. The seyed, because of the respect accorded him by all groups, was particularly valuable as an intermediary between belligerent parties in time of war, attempting by his mediation to avoid hostilities, and, if this proved unsuccessful, negotiating for the return of prisoners. The seyed even among the Urazgani appears to have exerted some moral influence over the people, since we know that he was at least occasionally able to persuade an outraged family to accept compensation for the murder of one of its number in lieu of the revenge which they would have preferred and to which they were entitled by customary law.

Our much fuller Jaguri material may possibly exaggerate the influence of the Moslem leaders, since our principal informant was himself a seyed and a very religious man, yet our Besud information, given by a fairly sophisticated young man, tends to confirm it. The kazi (kosi in Besud),[25] the chief mullah of the group, has considerable administrative and judicial powers. Indeed, his word has more weight than that of the malik. As guardian of the sharyat or Quranic law he judges all offenses against it, and administers punishment. Where injuries are to be compounded rather than revenge exacted, the case is brought before the mullah, who consults the Quran and ascertains the correct amount of damages. He grants divorce. The kazi, together with the leading seyed, acts as advisor and arbiter in the proceedings involved in deposing a malik.

Among the Jaguri the zakot, theoretically paid to the mullah, is usually given directly to the poor of the community, but the mullah of each village designates those who are to receive it, and the donors advise him as to the disposal of their tithe. The mullahs perform marriage ceremonies, are called in for serious illnesses and difficult childbirths. If a widow administers her own property and has no near relative to assist her with the manual labor, the mullah appoints a man from the village to cultivate her fields and help with the harvest, and he warns all the village that they must be scrupulously fair in their business dealings with the widow.

The mullah exerts a great moral influence over the people. Music and song, so integral a part of Jaguri life, have been almost completely obliterated by Timuri mullahs, and they appear to be undergoing the same fate in Besud. Under the careful guidance of the mullahs the people observe strictly the ban on alcohol. When it was discovered some twenty years ago that the practise of geophagy had filtered in from Kabul to the women of Besud, the

[25] An Arabic title.

mullahs exerted their influence, suggested that the women nibble on krut, a hard dry cheese, instead of the clay which they had learned to crave, and the custom was shortly stamped out.

The seyeds appear to occupy no official position in the Hazara social structure, although, according to our Jaguri information, they acted with the mullahs as arbiters in certain cases and also might pass judgment on offenders of Quranic law. It is quite clear, however, that they occupied a position of marked honor even among the Urazgani, since they were deemed the only persons who might safely negotiate with the enemy in times of war. They are careful to maintain their prestige by the practise of endogamy. A few observe this in the strictest sense, as is evidenced by their clearly Arab physical type. Others keep intact their precious genealogies but permit an infiltration of Hazara blood through marriage of seyed men with Hazara women.

Even more the seyed maintains his prestige by conducting himself in so exemplary a fashion that his actions serve as a model to those about him. He must be honest and more than just, and he must not indulge in petty quarrels. Where others might cry for revenge his family would be satisfied at most with compensation, and would frequently pardon the offense without asking for restitution. By upholding the honor and dignity of his descent the seyed is held in great respect by the people and exerts a strong moderating influence over them.

Thus we find two more or less formal channels of social control among the Hazaras: that provided by the representatives of Islam and that of the civil administration. But certainly the most powerful factor of all is that of public opinion. Chiefly through conversation public opinion imposes on the individual restrictions which it would refuse to accept from its leaders. Indeed, the authority of leaders depends almost entirely upon the sanction by public opinion of their enactments. The functioning of this force will be considered more in detail in our discussion of the individual in relation to the group.

THE INDIVIDUAL IN RELATION TO THE GROUP

The actual day to day relationships of individuals are usually, of course, regulated not by even such informal institutions as those described above but by custom, which among the Hazaras appears to be rooted in a sense of mutual responsibility enforced by public opinion. Time and again our informants explained that a man would be "ashamed" to do this or not to do that. Men would be ashamed to kill prisoners captured in war. The amount of a girl's dowry was not specified by contract but her father would be ashamed not to give a dowry at least equal in amount to the bride-price and as much more as his wealth would permit. His neighbors would know and be quick to comment on his niggardliness. A man who had frittered away his patrimony would probably leave his village, stealing away secretly at night, because he would be ashamed to admit his incompetence before the people. On the other hand, if he failed to make this ignominious exit, his relatives would, when the time came for him to marry, assist in making up a suitable bride-price, since they would be ashamed to have a permanently impoverished kinsman who had been forced through insufficient funds to marry beneath the economic class of his family. This sense of shame extended to the violation of even the most apparently trivial matters of convention. It was customary to boil milk before using it and no man would drink unboiled milk for fear of the ridicule which such an act would excite.

Such sensitivity to the appropriate and inappropriate action, the honorable and the shameful procedure, is fundamental in regulating the relation of the individual to his family, to other individuals, and to the community as a whole.

It is early impressed upon even the child that his own honor and that of his family is in his keeping. As an example, a child who has appropriated for his own use some small article of his brother receives an awesome but withal affectionate lecture on the sanctity of property, with the clinching argument that if he acquires the habit of taking things belonging to members of his family he may later covet and take the property of an outsider, thus bringing great shame to himself and to the family. At the same time it is significant to note that the individuality and personality, the rights and privileges of the child, are respected by others as are those of an adult. In an isolated mountain village we once saw in a house a pair of child's shoes, extremely worn and battered but distinctive in type. When we asked if we might buy them, we were told that as they were old and worthless we could doubtless have them for nothing but they belonged to a little boy who was herding goats on the mountain and we must await his return to consult him.

All topics of adult conversation seem to be freely discussed in the presence of children who thus quickly acquire the intellectual and moral outlook of their elders as well as their manner of dignified yet courteous reserve. As far as could be ascertained, spanking or other physical punishment is never used to discipline children. In cases of serious misdemeanor, such as lying and stealing, a lecture appears to be adequate, or when the conduct of a small child is merely troublesome to the people about him, a mild temporary ostracism is effectively employed. It should not be stretching a point to assume that the methods employed in dealing with children's misdemeanors and indiscretions is directly related to the dependence on lecture and the general force of public opinion in coping with adult crime, and, more important, to the rarity of crime among the Hazaras.

Crimes listed in the order of their seriousness are: lying, murder, theft, "looking at another man's wife," and drinking alcoholic beverages. Murder was omitted from the first enumeration of crimes by two informants. When questioned, they somewhat hesitatingly placed it second.

Lying appears to be practically unknown among the Hazaras. One informant stated that he had not known what lying was until he left the Hazarajat. While this was probably an exaggeration, it became evident on another occasion that even he, a wily old man who had lived for forty years in countries where falsehood was accepted as a normal part of social and business intercourse, could not bring himself to make the direct lie even though he might have gained money by so doing. Certainly other Hazaras with whom we talked seemed to feel an inner compulsion to answer our questions truthfully, even though on occasion they may have preferred to keep silent. There is no formal punishment for lying other than the supernatural one meted out by Allah to those who swear falsely upon the Quran.

Although the machinery exists for punishing theft, that crime appears to be extremely rare. The rule against "looking at another man's wife," or, as another informant expressed it, "laughing with a woman" outside one's family appears to have been adhered to rigidly. A man had the right to kill a wife or daughter who permitted such familiarity, at least among the Urazgani. No case of adultery was cited by any of our informants. One informant recalled that his father had told him of two instances where girls had indulged in pre-marital intercourse. Their lovers had both been forced, apparently by public opinion, to marry the girls. At another time this same Jaguri informant stated that if a girl wished to marry a man of whom her father disapproved, she had only to threaten elopement to win his permission, so great was the dishonor which would have fallen upon the family as the result of such an act.

Drinking alcoholic liquors, forbidden by the Quran, perhaps acquired its criminal status fairly recently in comparison with the crimes cited above. It is punished by whipping, the only instance of corporal punishment which we have encountered among the Hazaras. The sin would appear to be fairly infrequent, although our most saintly informant smiled as he volunteered the suggestion that if a culprit were not caught in the act he could not be punished. Their Mongol ancestors were extremely fond of alcoholic stimulants and it is conceivable that drinking still goes on *sub rosa* among such Hazaras as can afford the luxury.

It was perhaps not entirely accidental that two informants omitted murder in their enumeration of Hazara crimes. It would seem to have been not infrequent, and to have brought no particular shame either to the murderer or to his family. It has grown less in recent years as blood feuds have decreased.

As the maintenance of family honor is the concern of each individual member, similarly is the welfare of its members the concern of the family as a whole. The family cares for its poorer relatives, for its widows and orphans, and for those who are ill or injured. A widow with small children must be cared for by some relative of her former husband, whether a brother, uncle, or cousin. Sons who have married before their father dies must, if the estate is inadequate for the purpose, contribute to the bride-prices and dowries of their unmarried brothers and sisters.

If any unusual situation arises, the unity of the family is expressed in a family council comprising in general the head of the family, his brothers, paternal uncles, and his grown sons. It is not certain whether women actually participate in the council. If not, they undoubtedly in most cases make their opinions heard through husbands or brothers. In these gatherings all affairs which concern the family as a whole are discussed. For example, although the general rules governing inheritance are prescribed by custom and Islamic law, there are many details to be adjusted, such as the evaluation of all objects included in the estate, and their apportionment among the heirs. Usually the eldest brother acts as guardian for an unmarried orphan sister. If she wishes to live with another brother she may do so, however, and if the first shows reluctance to turn over her property to the newly chosen guardian a family council will be called to enforce the transfer. Our Jaguri informant described an episode in which a man wished to divorce his wife, whom he considered extremely unsatisfactory. While divorce is permitted by Islamic law and is practised by some Hazara tribes, it is heavily frowned upon by Jaguri custom. His family, in united conclave, persuaded him to spare them the shame of a divorce, but permitted him the compromise of taking a second, more agreeable, wife.

All the evidence indicates that the patriarchal form of the family is strongest among the Urazgani and weakest among the Timuri, with Jaguri resembling more nearly Urazgani, and Besud approaching the Timuri in the range between the two extremes. In an Urazgani or Jaguri village all, or nearly all, the inhabitants belonged to one extended family; among the Besud and Timuri several lineage groups are represented. The blood feud was common among the Urazgani, less frequent among Jaguri, and is rare or non-existent among Besud and Timuri. Rights of primogeniture were strong in Urazgani, weaker among the Jaguri, and least evident among the Timuri. Possibly correlated with this patriarchal emphasis is the greater restriction placed on women among the Urazgani. There the husband had the right to kill his wife. Among the Jaguri the right was recognized but not accepted in practise, while among the Timuri it does not exist. The Urazgani husband could divorce his wife but a woman could not divorce her husband. In Besud divorce is fairly common and a woman may divorce her husband. The Jaguri and Timuri look on divorce of any kind as a disgrace. Among the Urazgani the levirate was strictly enforced: a widow, unless she was old enough to have a grown son who could support her, had to marry a relative of her deceased husband. If a Jaguri widow wished to remarry, she necessarily chose a mate from her former husband's family, but she was quite at liberty to remain single and administer her own property if she so desired. A Timuri woman on the other hand is free to remarry outside the family and often does so, although if she chooses a mate from among the relatives of her first husband the rules of the levirate still obligate him to marry her even though he may not wish to do so.

The patriarchal aspect of Urazgani culture results in a rather different type of relationship between individuals within the community. Urazgani social structure was semifeudal in character, as was Jaguri to rather a less degree, while Besud and Timuri community life is essentially democratic. Thus the average man in Urazgani looked for help and protection to the chief of his village, who was also head of the wealthiest and most powerful branch of the extended family which made up the village, as well as being military leader of the group. In return for his help and protection this leader expected service and loyalty. Such a feudal patriarch naturally assumed rights and privileges not consonant with the democratic theory of equal rights and privileges which prevails among the other Hazara groups studied. On the other hand he assumed responsibilities which were distributed over the community as a whole in other tribes. The Urazgani village chief often built summer dwellings for the use of the poorer people of his community. If a rich man felt that his son was a spendthrift, he might make a will asking the headman to act as guardian and administrator of the son and his property.

While the Jaguri retained to some extent the patriarchal system we find a much stronger emphasis on democratic cooperation. Whereas the office of the Urazgani headman was largely hereditary, among the Jaguri it was elective and leadership was shared by the riš safits. People helped each other, rather than looking to the headman for assistance. The poorer people aided one another in building their houses and took turns in herding the sheep. If a stream was to be dammed or an irrigation ditch built, the whole village took part in the enterprise.

Among the Timuri and also, it would appear, among the Besud, patriarchy has been displaced to such an extent that the position of headman has become obscured. In addition there is a tendency toward individualism as evidenced by the fact that pasture land, elsewhere communally owned by the village, is individually owned among the Timuri. This tendency should not be over-emphasized, however, in view of the much stronger emphasis on cooperation as compared to individualism.

Correlated with the feudal tinge of Urazgani society, there appears a feeling for class stratification which in the other groups under consideration is attenuated or manifested indirectly. Among the Urazgani there were three definite economic classes: those who owned no land and therefore must hire out as laborers; those who owned just enough land to support the family, land which could be worked by its members without outside assistance; and those rich enough to employ laborers. The people of the laborer class were in a sense serfs, in that a whole family worked for one employer and could not change to another without obtaining the permission of the first master. The master would assist laborers in need, contribute toward the bride-price when a man wished to marry, and continue to support a laborer too old to work. Intermarriage between classes was very rare.

Class distinctions were weaker among the Jaguri. Thus they say that "we are all descended from Adam," and "all professions are equal before God," but they admit that the "embarrassment" of the poor man tends to keep him apart from the rich one. This embarrassment seems to be due to sensitive pride rather than a feeling of inferiority. While inter-class marriage was infrequent, it did exist among the Jaguri. They adhered strictly to the Moslem rule that a couple should not marry unless both the man and the girl willingly agreed to the match, and if a rich young man happened by chance to see the face of a poor girl and to fall in love with her he could persuade his family to permit the marriage. In such a case his father would furnish not only the bride-price but the dowry as well. A rich girl enamored of a poor man could always force the issue with her family by threatening to elope with him. In such a case the proposal would have to come from the girl's family rather than the man's, and the father of the groom, proud though poor, would insist upon the usual patrilocal residence of the young couple, whereupon the equally proud father of the bride usually made a gift of land and animals to the groom's father so that he might not be shamed by having poor relatives while he himself remained rich.

We were unable to obtain much specific information on class consciousness among the Timuri. Our observations would indicate, however, that while obvious economic dif-ferences were recognized, especially by the poor people, they were not stressed.

The same factors of pride and mutual responsibility which so strongly influence family and individual relationships prevail also in the relations of the individual and the com-munity as a whole. In many places, especially in Urazgani, the community to a great ex-tent coincides with the extended family, and there the concerns of all individual members of the group are focussed in the head of the family as its patron and protector. Of course even among the Urazgani there was a distinction between the responsibilities of the im-mediate family and those of the extended family or village group.

Where the community is composed of several family groups, as among the Timuri, the feeling of communal responsibility appears to be so deeply ingrained that it operates almost automatically without the directive agencies which the Urazgani and Jaguri have in the headman and the mullah. As an example we may cite the zakot, the tithe which Moslems pay for the support of the poor and needy. Among the Urazgani and Jaguri, the zakot was either collected by the mullah and apportioned among the poor, or a man paid the money or goods directly to those who had been previously designated by the mullah to receive them. Among the Timuri assistance is given as required without the medium of a third party. That this system actually works is indicated by the case of one of our informants. The house which her husband had inherited from his father was destroyed during a minor revolution a few years ago. The man had no family in the village, the woman's brother was already giving shelter to his mother and two unmarried brothers, and could not ac-commodate the couple. For a time they lived with another family, but as the quarters were not very good they were invited to share the house of a second family in the village who were neither relatives nor particularly close friends. No rent was paid. The owner of the house simply happened to have an extra room and as a matter of course suggested that the homeless family move in.

Of course it is frequently difficult to distinguish between such spontaneous individual actions and what might be called organized community effort. Our material indicates that while people directly assist unfortunate members of the community as best they can, the local leaders may coordinate activities, as when the mullah designates some individual to cultivate the land of a widow if she has no family to help her.

The aid freely given by the community to those of its members who are in need seems to be looked upon not as charity but as a manifestation of the group's deep set sense of responsibility, pride in its ability to look after its own people, and its fear of being shamed by failure to do so.

CONCLUSION

The Hazara personal ideal is that of the "good" man, that is, the man who is honest, just, industrious, self-respecting, and considerate of the rights of his fellows. This concept of the good man appears to underlie both the formal and unformalized aspects of social control which we have discussed. The headman and the malik are selected by the people because they are good men and promptly lose their influence if they indicate a lack of the proper qualities. The influence of the mullah and the seyeds in upholding the standards of "goodness" in the group cannot be overemphasized. The relations of one individual to another, to his family and to the group, are based ultimately on the feeling for the appropriate behavior of the "good" man in any particular circumstance.

The ideal of the good man is maintained by two principal incentives to conformity, both instilled in childhood. The first is pride, evidenced in the honor of the family and in the self-respect of the individual; the second is fear, the fear of being publicly shamed in the eyes of the community by conduct unworthy of the good man. An additional incentive is the "fear of God," which is constantly emphasized by the mullahs in reminding the people that they will be answerable for their deeds on the Day of Judgment, if not before.

We hesitate to attempt an explanation, which would necessarily appear facile and superficial, of the cultural origins and history of this ideal which the Hazaras seem so successfully to maintain. The Hazaras are among the heirs of two proud and austere cultures, the Mongol and the Arab, to which one may look for at least a partial explanation of their social philosophy. The Quran time and again[26] impresses upon the believer the necessity of truth, charity, and love of kindred, and the Hazaras take its exhortations literally. Those who read are few, but oral tradition is strong. In the winter especially, when it is impossible to work outdoors and deep snow isolates the villages, the people gather together to talk. Among the Jaguri the family circle assembles in the home, where they sing and tell stories, or, if anyone among the group is literate, he reads passages from the Quran. Among the Timuri it is customary for all the men to gather in the local mosque, as in a clubhouse, for warmth or companionship. In whichever setting, home or mosque, there is a strong moral tone to the conversation. The Jaguri songs and stories tell of past heroes, the "good" men of the tribe, or gossip of the unfortunate people who deviated too greatly from the ideal. The Timuri mullah has ample opportunity to advise the men on details of their conduct and to guide them in the paths of what we can best describe as a kindly puritanism, ascetic but not fanatical.

Without wishing to push too far the argument for geographical determinism, one might suggest that the isolated mountain environment, even perhaps the invigorating climate of

---

[26] For example, "Righteousness is not that ye turn your faces towards the east or the west, but righteousness is, one who believes in God, . . . and gives wealth for His love to kindred, and orphans, and the poor, and the son of the road, and beggars, and those in captivity; and who is steadfast in prayer, and gives alms . . . " (Palmer, *The Koran (Qur'an)*, II 172, p. 22).

the Hazarajat,[27] may have been conducive to a selecting out and stressing of certain basic tenets of Islam which in the cultural centers of the Moslem world have become obscured by theological controversy and non-Islamic custom.

The general stress on group responsibility and mutual cooperation among the Hazaras may perhaps be derived ultimately from their Mongol cultural heritage. Any attempt to trace such a derivation must however be made with extreme caution. In a previous paper[28] it has been indicated that by the time of Chingis Khan there had developed among the Central Asian nomads "a type of patriarchal feudalism in which the relationship of master and man tended to absorb the relationship based on common membership in a blood group" and in which "the solidarity of the blood group was expressed not as a generalized responsibility of all its members for one another but rather as a personal dependence of the weak upon the strong."

It has been shown above that the original Hazaras entered Afghanistan with the army of Chingis Khan. Presumably therefore they were exposed to the general tendency toward feudalization. How then are we to account for their present condition in which the most typical groups show the least evidence of a feudal social structure?

It appears significant that among the Urazgani, who by other Hazaras are considered the most backward and old fashioned, feudal institutions prevailed to the present time. This suggests that the forms of group responsibility among the Jaguri, Besud, and Timuri are, to a great extent, not "survivals" of a pre-feudal era but rather a fresh development to meet new conditions following their settlement in Afghanistan.

The most forcible of new conditions would have been those of physical environment. Instead of living on the open steppe, the Hazaras found themselves hemmed into narrow steep valleys which isolated not only one group from another but the Hazaras as a whole from all other Turkic and Mongol tribes. Mongol feudalism, which was based not upon land but upon mobile men and herds may well have broken down under such restrictive conditions and given way to small self-contained democratic agricultural communities with a social life based on cooperation.

We do not, of course, suggest that such a renaissance of group responsibility was entirely, or perhaps even largely, *sui generis*. Despite the development of feudalism among the Mongol tribes, the tradition, and probably in many instances the actuality, of the cooperative social structure remained in force. Of equally great importance may be the similar traditions and actualities of Arabian culture which reached the Hazaras through the medium of Islam.

Much remains to be done before the points which we have touched upon can be fully

[27] In this connection it may be of interest to note in passing that some of our informants appear to be convinced environmentalists. Our principal Jaguri informant said that when he is at home in the Hazarajat he feels ten times stronger than when he is in Meshed. This he attributed to the water, the air, and the soil, and told a story of a chief who, when traveling abroad took with him a bag of earth from Afghanistan so that when things were going badly he might stand on it and regain strength.

[28] Hudson, *Kazak Social Structure*, pp. 104–05.

clarified. It is hoped that in future field work it will be possible to enlarge upon the implicit aspects of individual relationships in which Dr Sapir showed so great an interest and so penetrating an insight.

BIBLIOGRAPHY

BEVERIDGE, ANNETTE S. *The Babur-nama in English (Memoirs of Babur) by Zahiru'd-din Muhammad Babur Padshah Ghazi* (2 vols., London, 1921).

BROWNE, EDWARD G. *A History of Persian Literature under Tartar Dominion (A. D. 1265-1502)* (Cambridge, 1920).

ELIAS, N. (ed.), and E. DENISON ROSS (tr.) *A History of the Moghuls of Central Asia; being the Tarikh-i-Rashidi of Mirza Muhammad Haidar, Dughlát* (London, 1898).

VON DER GABELENTZ, H. C. *Ueber die Sprache der Hazaras und Aimaks* (Zeitschrift der deutschen morgenländischen Gesellschaft, Vol. 20, pp. 326-35, Leipzig, 1866).

HOWORTH, HENRY H. *History of the Mongols from the 9th to the 19th Century* (5 vols., London, 1876-1927).

HUDSON, A. E. *Kazak Social Structure* (Yale University Publications in Anthropology, No. 20, 1937).

KHANIKOFF, NICOLAS DE *Mémoire sur le partie méridionale de l'Asie Centrale* (In *Recueil de Voyages et de Mémoires publiés par la Société de Géographie*, Vol. 7, Part 2, pp. 239-451. Paris, 1844).

LEECH, R. *A Vocabulary of the Language of the Moghal Aimaks* (Journal, Asiatic Society of Bengal, Vol. 7, pp. 785-87, Calcutta, 1838).

LONGWORTH DAMES, M. *Hazara* (In *Encyclopaedia of Islam*, Vol. 2, p. 297, Leyden and London, 1913-34).

D'OHSSON, C. *Histoire des Mongols, depuis Tchinguiz-Khan jusqu'à Timour Bey ou Tamerlan* (4 vols., Le Haye and Amsterdam, 1834-35).

OUSELEY, WILLIAM (tr.) *The Oriental Geography of Ebn Haukal, an Arabian Traveller of the Tenth Century* (London, 1800).

PALMER, E. H. (tr.) *The Koran (Qur'an)* (London, 1938).

PETIS DE LA CROIX *The History of Timur-Bec* (2 vols., London, 1723).

RAMSTEDT, G. J. *Mogholica: Beiträge zur Kenntnis der Moghol-sprache in Afghanistan* (Journal, Société Finno-ougrienne, Vol. 23, Part 4, Helsingfors, 1906).

UNIVERSITY OF WASHINGTON
SEATTLE, WASHINGTON

THE SOCIALIZATION OF THE HOPI CHILD

By WAYNE DENNIS

INTRODUCTION

IT IS A TRUISM that the individual at birth has no behavioral characteristics which mark him as the member of any social group, and that a few years of residence in one society serve to cause him to resemble other members of his social world. But the processes by which the developing individual is caused to conform, to some extent, to the customs of his fellows are far from being thoroughly understood. Notwithstanding the fact that the recognition of the existence of a process called socialization is old, the social sciences in the past have often ignored it, or given it scanty attention. Anthropology and sociology have been concerned with the description of societies. They have seldom directed their attention to the socialization of the individual. Psychology, which might have been expected to investigate the process, was driven into a social blindness by the glare of the laboratory. If today these sciences are directing their attention to a greater degree than has been the case in the past to the individual within society and to the psychological aspects of social life, we must name as one of the instigators of this movement Sapir, who saw the inevitable woodenness of findings derived from disciplines which treated man as if he were a marionette and who urged that social sciences not ignore the emotional and intellectual life of the individual.

In those instances in which the socialization of the child has been dealt with, authors not infrequently have written as if there were no real psychological processes to be observed. Human nature has sometimes been characterized as plastic to such a degree as to possess no other attributes. The fitting of man to a social pattern has been likened to the pouring of wax into a mold, as if human material were not at all refractory. The simile infers that the metaphorical wax, neurological, glandular, and otherwise, which comprises the human individual has no tendencies toward shapes of its own. At times a pseudo-psychological impulse to imitate or to conform has been hypothesized. This advances the wax-mold analogy one step farther in the direction of absurdity, for when an impulse is added to the wax, the wax does not have to be poured into the mold—it jumps in of its own propulsion. Sapir criticized theories which hold that the plasticity of human nature is unlimited. His interest in psychoanalysis, we believe, grew partly from his recognition of the need of a psychology which gave cognizance to human tendencies and desires. Through the influence of such ideas there is emerging a social psychology which will do better justice both to cultural patterns and to individual tendencies than have the discussions of the past.

The aim of the present paper is to contribute in a small way toward the development of such a social psychology by suggesting how the child becomes adjusted in one small

society—a Hopi village in northern Arizona.[1] While our information is specifically concerned with Hotavila,[2] the account is descriptive of nearly all of the Hopi villages, and a
great deal of it may also be characteristic not only of the Hopi but of the majority of the
Southwestern Pueblos. Just how widely distributed are the practises to be described we
do not know because the details of child rearing and of child development have received
but little attention in anthropology. Within the limits of this chapter we must avoid a
comparative or an historical interest and deal solely with Hopi child-rearing without
discussion of its relationship to the practises of other groups. It is to be understood that we
specifically disclaim any notion that the Hopi originated the child-rearing customs which
they observe.

NECESSITY FOR SOCIALIZATION

If it were doubted that the Hopi child requires an active socialization, observation shows
that such doubts are in error. Hopi parents are very lenient and Hopi customs impose
almost a minimum of frustration and repression upon the child, yet the child may fail in
many respects to meet Hopi standards. Only after a series of social influences are brought to
bear upon him does he gradually approach the Hopi norms. A comparison of Hopi child
behavior with the behavior of children of other groups would show that conformity to
Hopi standards is not spontaneous and universal.

Foremost among the expectations of the Hopi parent is the requirement that the child
shall work. The industry of the Pueblo peoples is well known, and is a precondition of
existence in the arid region in which they live. The child is expected to join in the work
of the household, although his contribution is proportionate to his size. Despite the model
of his parents, the child does not do his tasks with the same willingness with which he
plays; work, in the beginning, has no "functional autonomy" and we shall need to examine
the means whereby the child is caused to perform his assignments.

Next to work in importance is the ceremonial life, which in native ideology is allied
with work, for without proper attention to the ceremonies, industry would not be productive. The child's place in ceremonial life is small; nevertheless, it is necessary that he
acquire some knowledge of ceremony and of the supernaturals who are associated with it,
and that he have the proper attitude and demeanor in regard to the performances which
take place in the plaza and in the kiva. Few difficulties seem to be encountered in the

---

[1] The material of this study was derived from informants and from direct observation in the course of two
summers' residence among the Hopi. In the present connection our findings have been much abbreviated and our
presentation has been limited to those topics which bear upon the question of socialization. A full account of
the child-rearing practises of Hotavila and of New Oraibi, together with observations on Hopi child behavior,
will be found in a book by the author, entitled *The Hopi Child* (New York, 1940). We are indebted to the Social
Science Research Council and to the Institute for Research in the Social Sciences at the University of Virginia
for financial assistance in the field study from which the following account is derived.

[2] Many data similar to those presented here, but for the village of Mishongnovi, are contained in the
monograph by Ernest and Pearl Beaglehole, *Hopi of the Second Mesa* (Memoirs, American Anthropological
Association, No. 44, 1935), p. 65.

child's adjustment to the religious observances, but socialization is no less important when it operates smoothly than it is when it proceeds with difficulty. The religious training of the Hopi child is interesting not only in itself, but also because the impersonators of the supernaturals are employed to encourage industry and good conduct as well as to inculcate respect for the gods.

A further general field in which the Hopi child requires socialization is the avoidance of open conflicts and the respect for the rights and the property of others. Hopi men seldom display strong emotion and almost never fight or quarrel, but the Hopi child has temper tantrums in which he screams and kicks and throws himself on the ground as no adult Hopi ever does. The child comes into conflict with other children over property, and these conflicts lead to hitting with the hands and with sticks, to pushing and shoving, and to the throwing of dirt and of stones. The pugnacity and aggressiveness of the child must be overcome so that in adulthood the behavior of the Hopi will approximate the Hopi ideal of a person who causes no trouble.

This list of the ways in which the Hopi find it necessary to modify child behavior is of course fragmentary. In addition to the socialization mentioned above, weaning must be accomplished, toilet habits must be established, taboos against indecent exposure must be inculcated, and many other standards of conduct must be interiorized. In discussing Hopi socialization within a limited space, we must of necessity restrict our treatment to those items which seem to us to be of greatest importance. A discussion of other topics is to be found in another publication by the author.[3] The present discussion will be limited to the topics named above: work, ceremonial life, and avoidance of conflict.

HOPI MEANS OF SOCIALIZATION

Parental Approval and Disapproval. Until he or she marries and establishes a separate home, the Hopi is a dependent member of his parents' household. The house belongs to his mother. The mother also possesses and dispenses the stored food supply of the entire family, while the father brings this supply into the possession of the mother and is directly responsible for clothing the family. Formerly the clothing was provided by his own work with skins and with textiles, but at the present time part of the clothing is obtained by purchase. The housing, feeding, and clothing of the child by the parents, and other less tangible services of the parents to the child, create bonds of love and of gratitude and of dependence which are used to influence the child toward observance of the parents' wishes. In some cases the desire to please the parents which grows out of the parent-child relationship may be almost sufficient in itself to cause the child to do what the parents wish in regard to helping with the work of the family and in conforming to the family pattern of religion and of deportment. If this is not sufficient, the parents have means of reward and punishment which can be brought into play. The child may be praised for his actions, although praise does not seem to be utilized to a great degree. One sees no indication of ex-

---

[3] *The Hopi Child.* Appropriate references to the literature on the Hopi are also cited in this work.

cessive pride on the part of parents or of much emphasis upon the superior qualities of one's own offspring; such feelings are restrained, and praise, too, is restrained in its forms.

Gifts are sometimes given to reward a task well done or to encourage an interest in work. The boy may be given a ewe, whose offspring will be his if the sheep receives proper care. The girl may have a small vessel for water-carrying which is all her own. Other rewards are received from the hands of the impersonators of supernaturals, the kachinas, as we shall see later.

On the negative side, scolding and nagging must be set down as of common occurrence. The child is quickly told when he displeases, although his parents are moderate in their expression, not raising their voices greatly in pitch or loudness and not losing their tempers easily. But scolding is very persistent; the child who has committed a misdeed is reminded of it at appropriate times for years afterward. The following illustrative incident occurred at Zuñi, but we feel that it expresses the spirit of Hopi discipline as well. Two boys who were playing with matches accidentally set fire to a barn and a team of horses was killed by the flames. We asked our informant in what way the boys would suffer for their offense. She said that for years they would be reminded of the great loss which they had caused the family, and that this would be brought to mind particularly when the boys needed new shoes or new shirts, or when they wished anything which must be purchased, for the horses could have been sold for money.

The Hopi are not averse to corporal punishment, although corporal punishments are not cruel or excessive. They are administered to young children, never to boys and girls of twelve or more years of age. The most usual form of corporal punishment is whipping the legs with a withe or a strap. The chastisement ordinarily is administered by that parent who has been disobeyed or offended, but, since the small children remain in the village and do not go to the fields, this is usually the mother. The mother would not be able to get the father to punish for her. She can, however, ask one of her brothers to punish the children, as we shall see later. No one except the parents and the maternal uncles has the right to punish the child, although anyone in the village may inform these persons of the child's misbehavior. The parents are financially responsible for any damage which is done by the child, and they, not the person whose property has been damaged, would discipline the child in such a case.

The most frequent cause of punishment, however, is not damage to property but failure to do the tasks which it is the child's duty to perform. The boy may be whipped for neglecting to keep the prairie dogs from the cornfield, or the girl for failing to come home to take care of the baby. Talking back to the parent or speaking impolitely to a parent are other causes of punishment, as are stealing and lying.

The parents may punish the child by withholding, or by threatening to withhold, some favor. Food, however, would never be denied in any case. To withhold food which is already in the house is never done, although the parent might refuse to buy candy or some other delicacy from the trading post. The most usual threat of deprivation is to threaten to leave the child behind when the family goes to a dance in a kiva. Occasionally this threat is carried out. To execute it is considered very severe, for all children want to go, and practically everybody in the village is in attendance. If the dance is one which is held out of doors in the child's own village such a threat is not made, for children are never kept at home under these circumstances.

The Role of the Maternal Uncle. As in many other societies, descent is matrilineal. Since the child belongs to the mother's clan, he shares the traditions and the history of that clan. Although the child is related to his father's people also, he is distinctly a member of his mother's household. While the child's parents jointly occupy the home, the home belongs to the mother. In case of separation, the father departs and takes up residence with his mother or with one of his sisters. Because the child belongs to a lineage which is not that of his father, it is felt that some male member of the child's lineage should be responsible for his conduct. The men who are most closely related to the child are the brothers of the child's mother, and they are responsible in a measure for the child's behavior. Any maternal uncle has the right to correct or to punish a child, but this duty is likely to be assumed by the oldest uncle, or by a particular uncle who is willing to accept the responsibility. The uncle, who is married into another family, comes to the homes of his sisters on winter evenings to lecture the children on their duties. He also punishes them if they fail in their duties, coming either at the mother's call or on his own initiative.

He does not correct minor and occasional offenses, but only misdemeanors which are serious or persistent. He may take disciplinary action if a boy injures other children, or if a son will not do as his mother tells him, or if the boy steals. If he thinks the offense requires it, he may whip the child severely, or he may punish the child by holding him in a smudge. The latter is considered the most severe form of Hopi child punishment. The uncle builds a small fire of green juniper twigs and holds the child, face downward, in the stifling fumes. This punishment is seldom used, perhaps only once in two or three years in an entire village, and it is never employed by a parent, but only by a maternal uncle. It is used for both boys and girls.

The uncle often punishes an entire group of brothers, though he may know that only one boy was guilty of the offense and may even be able to identify the culprit. Whether he similarly punishes a group of sisters we did not learn. When group punishment is used, it may take the form of whipping or of use of the cedar smudge. The boys are treated in proportion to their size, the young ones being punished only slightly.

Our informants gave no native rationalization of group punishment but we wish to suggest one way in which it fits into Hopi patterns of thought.[4] The Hopi often state that misbehavior, especially on the part of a participant in a ceremony, will cause the supernaturals to bring retribution not only upon the offender but upon the entire village. Group punishment for the offense of one boy would seem to be an effective way of illustrating the principle that the bad behavior of one person brings ill results to others. This sort of

[4] Group punishment is found elsewhere, and may, of course, be made to conform to quite different ideologies.

interpretation, on the part of the child, would be furthered by the fact that group punish-ment is not practised by his parents but by a representative of that large group of relatives, the clan.

Kachina Reward and Punishment. From the age of four months, when he is old enough to be taken out of doors, the Hopi child may witness the performances of the kachinas. These events take place in the months between February and July. The kachinas are men who impersonate the supernaturals, but the young child is told that they are the real gods. The kachinas have bodies like men, but their heads are different from those of men, being cylindrical, and having extraordinary eyes, ears, noses, and mouths. (These masks are care-fully and skilfully made.) There are many kinds of kachinas, each kind having a distinc-tive head and often other distinctive characteristics as well. The kachinas are richly dressed in embroidered kilts and foxskins, and they wear a great deal of turquoise and silver jewelry.

The child is told that the kachinas come in the clouds and also travel in the regions under the earth. They govern the rain and wind and snow; they control good and bad fortune generally. The Hopi must please them, for unless this is done, the rains will fail, the springs will disappear, and the Hopi will perish. To please the kachinas, one must lead a good life and faithfully perform the ceremonies.

The kachinas are described as living in the San Francisco Peaks, which, although many miles away, are visible from Hotavila. There the kachinas have villages and fields much like their Hopi counterparts, but the kachinas have the power to grow beans even in the wintertime and to produce corn and melons when the Hopi plants are still immature. Dur-ing the autumn and the winter, the kachinas remain in the mountains, impervious to cold. But in spring and summer they visit the Hopi from time to time, performing the dances in which the Hopi find so much pleasure.

The kachinas do not forget the children. When they first visit the Hopi each year in February, in the so-called Bean Dance, they bring the children bunches of fresh bean plants and also gifts of kachina dolls to the girls and of shinny sticks and tops to the boys.

Each child is given presents by one of the kachina impersonators, who may be the father or some other relative of the child but who the child thinks to be a supernatural. The child is told by his mother, or by others, that the present is brought because he has been a good child. The child looks forward expectantly to these occasions on which he receives fine gifts. He is warned by his parents that if he misbehaves the kachinas will bring him nothing. Such a threat is seldom executed, but a child who has been so warned may not receive his present until the kachinas make their last appearance of the day, which is near the hour of sunset. This entails an entire day of doubt and suspense, as the first public dance occurs shortly after sunrise. During this interval the child will have been reminded of his offenses by his parents, and he will have repented and promised to reform, whereupon the omniscient kachinas will take cognizance of his better heart and bring him a present. The possibility of not receiving gifts when all other children publicly receive them is said by informants to insure good behavior during a large part of the season of kachina dances. The kachinas bring presents to the children not only at the Bean Dance but at other dances as well.

At the public dances the kachinas are in the village in large numbers. At other times they appear singly and in small groups to perform other ceremonial functions. The child is thus frequently reminded of their presence in the vicinity, and he is impressed by the respect and the obedience which is given to them even by the adults. The child is thus surrounded by immediate supernaturals who take a direct interest in the affairs of the village and, he is told, in the child's personal behavior as well. The impressiveness to the child of these appearances of the gods in person can scarcely be overlooked.

To make this impression still more personal to the child, there occasionally appears a horrible female kachina, Soyoko, who with equally terrifying cohorts, goes about in the village demanding the children. At the first glimpse of these ogres parents and children alike wildly scramble inside and bolt the doors. But Soyoko and her companions, who are armed with saws and other vicious instruments, and who carry ropes and baskets with which to take away the children, come to each door, call the inhabitants by name, and loudly demand the sons and daughters. In order to render the parents willing to part with a child, the sins of the child are recited. "She does not grind enough meal." "He is lazy in the fields." "He is always fighting." The parents, who have informed Soyoko in advance in regard to what should be said about the child, hold the door against the invaders and defend their offspring and promise that he will do better in the future. After the passage of minutes which seem like hours to the child, the parents persuade the kachinas to leave by the device of giving them food, which lessens their appetite for children. The act is repeated at each door in the village.

The tradition of Soyoko is in every town and all children are afraid of Soyoko because they know that this personage does exist. In Hotavila Soyoko has not appeared for several years, but the mention of her name is still effective.

Initiation. When the child is between six and ten years of age he undergoes an impressive initiation which contains all of the elements of the elaborate Hopi ceremonialism. At the close of this he learns that while the real kachinas formerly came to visit the Hopi, they do not do so today. He learns that instead of the kachinas dancing for the pleasure of the Hopi, as he had thought, in reality the Hopi dress in the manner of the supernaturals and dance to please the gods. This secret must not be revealed to the uninitiated under pain of a very severe flogging by the kachinas. He learns that kachina presents have been the work of his own relatives, and that Soyoko, like all other kachinas, is impersonated. He is told that he himself may now please the gods by taking part in the masked dances, an art which he never before knew that a mere man could perform.

Our informants state that while knowledge of the nature of the masked dancers is often the cause of great disappointment to the child, it does not cause disillusionment or bitterness. The gods become not less real but more distant. The figures who dance in the village are mere men, not the powerful personages that the child once thought them to be, but the real gods are now free to become more powerful than the child could have conceived them as being in the form in which they danced in the plaza. It is more important to please the gods, now that the child is older, than it was when his powers of understanding and his possibilities of misbehavior were at the infantile level.

The impersonations, while they are recognized as such, still recall much of the emotional reaction which they did when they were thought to be real. A twenty-five year old informant from Mishongnovi, who had been terrified as a child when Soyoko on one occasion suddenly appeared near her without warning, confessed that she is still frightened when certain kinds of kachinas appear. The threat of calling Soyoko is effectively applied even to children who have been initiated.

Initiation is a milepost in the child's socialization. Not only does it mark a change in his conception of the gods, but it introduces a change also in his ideas concerning himself. Since early childhood he has heard of and dreaded the whipping with yucca blades which is a part of the children's initiation. He is now successfully past the ordeal. He possesses information which is not dreamed of by the uninitiated, and which he must keep from them. He may even dance in the kachina dances. He has risen one step toward adulthood; he is no longer a small child, and he should not act as one. This new feeling of maturity and of superiority encourages a control of tantrums, of shirking, and of dislike for hard tasks, because he is told that such things are characteristic of the uninitiated.

At a much later date, from sixteen to twenty years of age, the boy (but not the girl) undergoes a second initiation whose details are kept from the uninitiated (including anthropologists) with great secrecy, and which is said to be very much more important than is the first initiation. The second initiation marks the boy's entrance into manhood, and he is obligated, in order to be worthy of his new status, to put aside all childish things. He may no longer play with young boys, may not quarrel and fight as boys sometimes do; he should assume the character of a Hopi man. Refraining from quarreling and from malicious talking is not expected of the Hopi woman, because she does not undergo this second initiatory ceremony.

Other Children as Socializing Agents. The child's playmates and companions have little or no formal part in his socialization. Even his older sister who takes care of him when he is very young does not have the right to punish him, but is supposed to appeal to the parents to make him behave. Nevertheless, there is no doubt that in an informal manner the children exert an influence upon each other. We have seen young girls sufficiently exasperated to spank their younger siblings, regardless of their theoretical inability to do so. No doubt a child who does things which are displeasing to other children will have occasion to discover this fact. Hopi children ridicule each other, and they dislike very much to be ridiculed. However, not all of this ridicule works in the direction which the parents would wish. In New Oraibi recently one boy would not wear a clean shirt to school because the boys called him a woman when he did so. His father had to whip the boy in order to make him wear the laundered article of apparel.

Training in Games. Among the Hopi eternal vigilance is the price of security, a security which at its best is precarious. Corn may grow nearly to maturity to be washed away by a thundershower or to be stunted by a final failure of moisture. Crops are threatened at all times, not only by unfavorable weather but by worms and by prairie dogs, and by any burro or sheep or goat which escapes the watchfulness of its owner. Harvests are never safe until they are in the storage bin; not until then can the Hopi be certain of a season's yield.

One is tempted to draw a parallel between the training toward unceasing effort which characterizes adult life, and the rules of certain boy's games which may be said to embody a principle of difficult victory. These games exemplify the demand for continuous application and constant alertness which typify Hopi agriculture. In these games, success in the early phases is meaningless unless it is followed by success later in the game. Failure at any point causes the player to lose credit for his earlier successes.

This is illustrated in a stick-throwing game. The contestants are divided into two sides. The leader of one side throws the goal stick in a fashion such that it goes out of sight behind some obstacle. The other players must then throw without being able to see the goal. The team which owns the stick which falls nearest to the goal receives a score of one point. If a stick touches the goal two points are scored. When either side reaches a score of four, it is in a position to try for a victory. If in the course of the next trial the leading team wins the fifth point, it is declared winner. If, on the other hand, the team fails to earn the final point, both teams lose all of their points, and a new game must be started.

A similar principle is seen in an archery contest in which the participants direct their arrows at the rim of a small hoop of cornhusks. When one boy hits the target, the members of the opposite team must take the position of the successful archer and let go at the hoop from that position. The arrows which miss go to the boy who originally hit the target, but he retains them only if he can hit the target with the same arrows with which the opponent missed. At the close of the game he must shoot at a new target all of the arrows which he has temporarily won, and may keep only those that hit this second target. However, a great deal depends on the final shot, which is made with one of his own arrows. If the final arrow hits the target, he may keep not only those arrows which have hit this target but the ones which have missed it as well. A game of the same sort is played with darts. Among the girls there are no similar games.

Reciprocity. The Hopi child performs many services because he wishes to receive the services or gifts which will accrue to him in return, or because he feels obligated to recipro- cate for favors which have been done for him in the past. Hopi life is full of reciprocal obliga- tions; we can present here only some instances. The boy catches small game for the captive eagles because he will receive feathers in return when the eagles are killed. He helps his fa- ther's brothers, since when he marries he will wish them to make wedding garments for his bride. The girls make a special corn pudding when they are asked to accompany the boys on a rabbit hunt, for the game secured on such a hunt becomes the property of the girls. At a grinding party, the girl will grind meal for her godmother who saw her through the children's initiation and who inducted her into a woman's society. There are many such ex-changes of services in childhood as well as in later life, and these are important forces toward conformity.

SUCCESS AND FAILURE IN SOCIALIZATION

The success of socialization may be measured by determining the relative number of successes and failures. We obtained from our Hotavila informants and from informants at Mishongnovi and New Oraibi a complete census of children, listing them by households. We then had our informants go through this list in regard to several kinds of problem be-havior while we marked each individual who was said to possess each of the undesirable characteristics. The census includes all unmarried persons up to 22 years of age, a total of 525 cases, about equally divided as to sex. At the lower age levels there are approximately 30 children at each year; at the older levels, about 20 at each year.

Temper tantrums are found to be much more common among boys than among girls, as 21 boys and only 7 girls are said to have tantrums. The age range for tantrums is from two to twelve years of age, with the greatest incidence falling in the two to five year old level. It would appear, therefore, that Hopi methods succeed in getting rid of tantrums, and that they usually succeed at a fairly early period.

Fighting shows an even greater predominance of boys over girls than do tantrums, the numbers being respectively 22 and 5. The five girls who are reported as fighting are between four and nine years of age. The boys who fight are sometimes as old as sixteen, but none are older than that, a fact which tends to show that fighting ceases as the age of second initiation approaches. The greatest incidence of fighters is between eight and thirteen years of age (ages are inclusive). In this interval, approximately one-fifth of the boys are said to engage in fights.

In regard to stealing, the boys outnumber the girls 27 to 15. Beyond four years of age, when the taking of other people's property begins to be considered intentional stealing, there is no consistent trend with age, until the age of eighteen is reached, when the rate drops markedly. This again supports the view that the age of second initiation may be an impor-tant one. Girls do not have a second initiation, hence this cannot be evoked as an explanation of their conduct. However, the girls contribute only a minor part of the problem behavior. If fighting and stealing do become less common as adulthood is approached, it may well be that it is not due to the initiation itself but to a change in social position which begins to af-fect boys and girls alike. As the time for marriage approaches, both the boy and the girl may be anxious to gain the approval of persons beyond the circle of relatives. It should be pointed out, however, that at all ages the children who misbehave form only a small minor-ity, since only a small proportion of the 525 cases engage in each form of misconduct.

A few words may be said with regard to the fact that in the census of behavior problems the boys contribute more cases than do the girls. This situation is so much like the condition which prevails in our own very different and quite unrelated society that we are likely to see this similarity as the result of fundamental differences between the sexes. In regard to the behavior of Hopi girls, we must call attention to a few facts, some of which we have had no occasion to mention at an earlier point in this discussion. During the early years, girls have the responsibility of caring for younger siblings. This fact may affect the likelihood of a girl's fighting since her contacts are predominantly with a younger child. Her position as nurse-maid certainly affects her opportunities for stealing, since she has an almost constant com-panion who cannot be trusted to keep secrets and whose presence would make deception difficult. Beyond the approximate age of ten years, the Hopi girl is expected to remain at home almost continuously, and to go about only when accompanied by a woman. This per-sistent supervision of the girl has no counterpart in the boy, and renders an interpretation of sex differences in biological terms very dubious.

It is the native belief that family attitude and family discipline determine the behavior of the child. Examination of the means of social control which were described earlier will show that the parents and the maternal uncles provide practically all of the disciplinary in-fluences. The control by the kachinas is no exception, for while the young child does not identify the kachinas with his relatives, they are in effect the same persons. It is the parents who threaten that the kachinas will withhold gifts from a child who steals, just as it is the parents who provide the gifts and interpret them as a reward for good conduct. A dancer takes no responsibility for training or disciplining a child unless the child is his son, daughter, nephew, or niece, or unless the parents have given the dancer instructions. In effect, there-fore, all forms of child training, except those lessons which are administered by playmates, are received directly or indirectly from relatives. It is no one else's responsibility. There are no policemen, no truant officers, no youth organizations, no adult leaders of the young.

Examination of our census of behavior problems in Hotavila shows, in line with this analysis, that the instances of misconduct, especially of the more serious forms, occur chiefly in a few families. This is especially true of stealing.

The most outstanding example is a household all members of which are said to steal and lie. The parents are very poor. The husband is described as peculiar in behavior and his own wife says that he is a witch. There is a daughter of five years who has tantrums, and who steals and lies. She is the only five year old girl in our records who possesses all of these faults. Next in age are three boys, six, eight, and ten years old. They also lie and steal, and fight among themselves. Last winter they were rolled in the snow and whipped by their older sister. It is very unusual for an older sister to punish, and our informant did not know why she did so. It may have been because the parents had failed to do it themselves. The worst problem in the family is a boy of seventeen, who is possibly feeble-minded. He once robbed the trading-post: the chief and the members of the council did nothing about it, nor did anyone else. Last spring he and three other boys stole corn by boring a hole into a stor-age bin. When they tried this technique a second time, the owner of the bin caught them red-handed. The parents of the boys should have punished them, but they did not. It is even claimed that the parents of the boys encourage them to steal. The father of the seventeen year old boy whom we are discussing says his son is a witch. These recriminations show that there is little love or unity within the family. The boy is very slow in school and it is claimed that he is guilty of stealing a teacher's watch. We have no record of misbehavior on the part of the oldest child, a girl of eighteen. She is married and has a son eleven months of age, but she is still living in her mother's household.

There is a second family of which likewise it is claimed that parents and children alike engage in thievery. They go into neighbors' houses when no one is at home, a thing which no Hopi should do. They steal corn and sheepskins; the children steal toys as well. Even the two youngest boys, three and five years of age, steal; in addition they have tantrums. The youngest sucks his thumb. A boy of eight, who has the family weakness for other people's property, has the further fault of fighting and has ceased attending school. The next in the family, a boy of seventeen, steals, stutters, and is stupid in school. A girl of eighteen is sexually immoral. Again the oldest, a girl of nineteen, is the best in the family, nothing being recorded against her present behavior.

These cases constitute the two worst families of Hotavila and are very decided exceptions. That delinquent families make up but a small part of the population is shown by the fact that of the sixty-six Hotavila families which appear in the census of children, only twelve families have any children who are said to steal. There is only one other family, in addition to the two treated above, in which almost all members of the household steal.

These cases bring out clearly the fact that when the family of the child fails in his socialization, the Hopi community has no systematic means of attempting to do the work for itself. The majority of families, however, succeed fairly well in getting their children to conform to their ideals.

In discussing failures at socialization, we have said nothing at all about laziness. It is difficult to get any measure of parental success in inducing work habits. For one thing, failure in this direction affects only the parents, whereas since stealing and fighting involve other persons they are to a greater extent common knowledge. It is our impression that nearly every boy and every girl is induced to help to some extent with the work of the household, but we are unable to measure the degree of industriousness.

In the field of religion, there is little possibility of failure. In Hotavila, there are no conflicting doctrines, although missionaries have entered other villages. Furthermore, the child has practically no religious duties. The child does not doubt what he is told. His attitude toward the supernaturals is one of awe and respect. He may dance if he wishes but there is no feeling that he should do so. Childhood is the period in which the elementary religious ideas are implanted, but religious observances come later.

SUMMARY

The Hopi Indians expect the child to perform part of the work of the household, to avoid conflicts, and to respect property rights. Other demands upon the child, while real, are of less importance. That he will absorb the chief religious ideas of the Hopi is so certain that it is taken for granted and does not become a cause of parental anxiety.

To insure conformity to Hopi patterns, parents make use of approval and disapproval whose effectiveness is based upon the strong personal ties within the family. The father is no more potent a disciplinarian than is the mother. The duty of lecturing and chastising the child falls upon the maternal uncles of the child. In the matrilineal Hopi society, they are expected to correct the behavior of their sisters' children, who are of their lineage and clan. Some of the forms of corporal punishment which are at the disposal of the maternal uncles are relatively severe.

While the correction of the child is in reality the function of the parents and of the maternal uncles, the child is made to think that the supernaturals, whom he identifies with the kachinas or masked dancers, also take a direct interest in his conduct. The kachinas bring gifts as rewards for good behavior and threaten the child with abduction and cannibalism when he is bad.

The children's intiation gives the child a higher status in the community, disabuses him of his belief that the gods appear in person, and grants him the privilege of impersonating the supernaturals and of participating in the ceremonies. By drawing a line between the initiated and the uninitiated, it encourages the former to give up "childish" ways.

The performance of many of the duties of the Hopi child is encouraged by the strong custom of reciprocity; nearly every action brings a well-defined reward, or creates an obligation on the part of the recipient of the favor.

A census of cases of problem behavior shows that failure to conform occurs in a small number of instances. Since the responsibility for socialization is familial and is not a function of the community or of community agents, it is not surprising that the majority of problem cases come from families whose adult members themselves fail to conform to expectations of the village as a whole, and whose child training is defective. Some misbehavior, however, arises in "good families," presumably because among the Hopi, as elsewhere, not all individuals are equally susceptible to socialization.

University of Virginia
Charlottesville, Virginia

ATTITUDES TOWARD FOOD AND HUNGER IN ALOR

By CORA DU BOIS

DR SAPIR'S great respect for the subtlety and complexity of human beings acted as a sobering influence on the growing interest of anthropologists in psychology and upon the contributions they made to social psychology. As an anthropologist he minimized in no way the tremendous power of society in shaping people but he never permitted his interests as a social scientist to blind him to the infinite variety of individuals within a culture. He went even farther and in conversation, at least, would support the probability of innate personality types. This sound caution against the environmentalists' inclination to overvalue conditioning was a great advantage to his students. At the same time he laid full stress on studying the socialization of the child.

It seems possible to combine these two principles in a preliminary and tentative fashion by making certain assumptions, following certain methods of reasoning and thereby arriving at certain generalizations about people within a given cultural framework, without at any time denying that the processes and symbols are going to have tremendously different values in the total economy of the individuals involved. It is with this in mind that I should like to discuss attitudes developed toward food and hunger in a particular culture.

It can be reasonably assumed that all human beings have certain physiologically determined tensions. One of the most obvious of these is hunger. But nowhere do human beings discharge this or any other basic tension directly. All societies have devices whereby such tensions are delayed, redirected, and often elaborated. To acquire these devices children everywhere must be subject to disciplines. Such disciplines may be of various types and undoubtedly the question deserves close comparative study. For our purposes it will suffice to point out that they may be permissive, restrictive, or absorptive. By permissive disciplines are meant those by which children are encouraged to acquire certain behaviors through a variety of immediate or delayed rewards. By restrictive disciplines are meant those which definitely deny the child certain types of activity by punishments ranging from physical violence to withdrawal of approval. The absorptive disciplines are those not consciously imparted, as are the permissive and restrictive, but rather those behavior patterns so consistently observed in other members of the group that the child acquires them by a kind of psychic osmosis.

It is important to stress that a single discipline of childhood or a single traumatic experience is rarely sufficient in itself to set cultural personality types. Repeated experiences in different behavioral, value, and institutional contexts alone will create personality constellations of such force and consistency that they may become apparent to ethnologists who, with the best will in the world, can never have more than a superficial insight into peoples of an alien culture.[1]

Lastly, there is so far no very definite knowledge of what ego mechanisms will be employed by the individual in reacting to frustrations associated with different kinds of disciplines and discipliners. However, from the psychoanalysts and the psychiatrists there is a growing insight into personality processes like projection, introjection, sublimation, and so on. I assume these processes to be universal to mankind, although I should expect variations in weighting from culture to culture.[2]

The procedure, therefore, is to consider a basic physiological tension, see how it is acted upon by disciplines of childhood, what repetitions it finds in a variety of contexts and how it is crystallized by (or into) institutional behavior through those personality mechanisms I have assumed to be universal to mankind.

Hunger, as one of the basic and obvious tensions of human beings, everywhere subject to delayed, redirected, and elaborated gratifications, suggests itself as a point of departure for testing the procedure outlined above. The people used for this purpose are the Atimelangers, who belong to a cluster of five mountain villages on the island of Alor in the Netherlands East Indies.[3]

The experiences of the Atimelang child with hunger and food are to be considered first. Immediately after birth the mother takes the child in her arms and offers it the breast to suckle at will. From four to six days after birth the mother remains in the house with the infant rather constantly in her arms. When the umbilical cord has dried and dropped off, the mother and child leave the house for the first time and from then onward the child is offered in addition to its mother's milk many different kinds of premasticated foods and vegetable gruels. Any refusal of the child to nurse freely and frequently when opportunity offers during this first period of life is considered a serious symptom of ill health and gives rise to considerable concern in parents. After the first week the child is given adult diet as fast as it will take it, and a child of about eighteen months can often be seen at a feast alternately nursing and sucking a cube of boiled pork fat.

Since, however, women are primarily responsible for garden work and the subsistence economy of the Atimelangers, they return to regular field work often ten days to two weeks after the birth of a child. It is not customary for the mother to work with the child on her back or even near her, as it is in some societies, so the infant is left at home in the care of some kin, usually the father or older sibling. There is great variation in solicitude and effectiveness of feeding care received by infants from these substitute mothers. Also some wom-

---

[1] I am indebted to Dr A. Kardiner and some of his colleagues for their insistence on the need of repetition in many contexts to set certain personality trends.

[2] For a discussion of these mechanisms see Anna Freud, *The Ego and the Mechanisms of Defence* (London, 1937).

[3] The material used in this article was collected by the writer during eighteen months of residence on the island of Alor, extending from January 1938 through June 1939. Acknowledgments are gratefully made to the Social Science Research Council of Columbia University and to Dr A. Kardiner who made this work possible.

en have greater responsibilities than others in the number they must provide for and are therefore more pressed by field work. On the other hand some women may have given birth during the middle of the dry season when labor in the fields is slack. Still others may be lazy about gardening. As a result some infants receive more care and food during the first months of life. If an infant is left in the hands of a father or sibling, it is going to be fairly hungry part of that time. The person caring for the child may give it gruel or premasticated food more or less conscientiously, but to judge from the frequency with which infants spew out such nourishment, one may suggest that such feeding is not very effective or satisfactory. One repeatedly sees infants trying to nurse at the breast of a father or immature sibling only to be pushed away with an attitude of mild embarrassment.

Rilpada told an anecdote of his childhood which reveals both the frustration infants may suffer from this type of feeding as well as the older sibling's frequent resentment of the role of nurse maid.

Once mother and I were living in a field house near our gardens. She told me to carry Senmani [younger brother] while she worked. At noon he was hungry and wanted to nurse. I gave him food but he only vomited it. He cried and cried and wouldn't stop. I cried too. Finally I went and told mother to come and nurse him but she wouldn't. So I took Senmani, laid him down on a mat in the house and ran off to Folafeng. There from the ridge I shouted, "Mother, your child lies in the house. If you want to care for it, good. If you don't want to, that is also good. I am going to Atimelang to play."

The point to be made is that even during infancy, when children are quite generally de-lighted-in, and when they are rarely out of someone's arms, or at least someone's carrying shawl, gratification of hunger is frequently a disappointing experience. Feeding is irregular; intervals between nursing are so long that acute hunger may arise with either no means of gratifying it or gratification is offered in foods obviously less satisfactory than that which the mother offers. When the mother is home and not too busy, she will offer the child the breast whenever it is restless. However, I never heard any woman speak of the pleasure of nursing, which probably means no more than that the culture has not maximized this particular physical pleasure. Women, when asked, did generally say that they preferred child bearing to intercourse but almost invariably added, "Because children will give my funeral feasts." There were several women who said that they did not wish any more children because feeding them meant so much work. Economic organization, therefore, acts directly upon attitudes toward children and conditions the child's earliest experiences in respect to food in this society.

In Atimelang, therefore, the hunger tension of infants is not maximally met as in some societies where children are constantly in contact with their mothers and where the pattern of nursing is a consciously fostered gratification of both mother and child.

A still more serious feeding problem may arise when the child begins to walk, approximately between the thirteenth and eighteenth months. By the time it can manage to get about alone, it is left to play near the house or on the dance place in the center of the village.

An older sibling, real or classificatory, or an old woman may be near and will care for a whole group of children in a desultory fashion but no one is responsible for feeding the child and no one is greatly incommoded by his crying. When the mother goes off to work, the child is left from about eight in the morning until five in the afternoon without regular provision of food. This does not mean that he is left entirely without food, but that all he gets during that time may be odd bits an older child cedes more or less willingly and generously to him when he begs for it. Again, of course, there is marked variation in children's experiences during this period. They may have a solicitous older sister who can be spared from field work and who will provide relatively good care. There may be a grandmother who works less hard and frequently in the gardens. But, in any case, after the child learns to walk, his frustrations with respect to hunger are increased, and simultaneously he loses the constant handling and support he had during the first stage of life in the carrying shawl. That the acquisition of his first skill in the independent mastery of the outer world, i.e. walking, should be associated with two severe deprivations may well have larger personality repercussions in the realm of ego development than there is space to consider in this paper.

To add to the strain of this period and to reinforce it further, the weaning of the child may be hastened at this time because another sibling is expected. Rarely does one see a child of three or four still nursing. Although weaning is done simply by pushing the child away gently or placing the breast beyond its reach, there is no doubt that difficulties accumulate at this stage of development. Anal training, walking, and talking have not yet been deliberately instituted. They are allowed to take their own course. In other words, the child has acquired few skills during the first two or three years of life. Those which he has acquired have been by means of restrictive or absorptive disciplines. It is not surprising that this is the time par excellence of temper tantrums. These continue, as might be expected, with marked individual variation up to the ages of five to eight. Adult reactions to childrens' tantrums are characterized by great inconsistency. One day a mother will ignore the child; the next she may be irritated and strike it; on still another occasion she may deceive it into thinking she is not deserting it, only to slip away when the child has been diverted; or on still other occasions, especially at night, the child may be threatened with the local bogy-man who, incidentally, is not a very fearsome figure. In addition then to their inconsistency, all active disciplines are of the restrictive type. I have never seen a mother promise a child a reward for being good and then keep her promise.

A clear example of the needs of early childhood and the uncertainties of the persons on whom the child depends for its gratifications is found in a series of statements contained in Tilapada's autobiography. She tells of caring for a younger sister called Maliemai.

On the way [to the fields] Maliemai cried a lot, so I put her down and slapped her. Then I talked nicely to her and we went on when she was quiet. . . . When Maliemai was a little older, she would cry to go to the fields with me. If I were not angry with her, I would take her along with me to dig sweet potatoes. I would give her the big ones and keep the small ones. She was always crying. She cried to be fed; she cried to go places. I hit her on the head with my knuckles and then I would feed her. She cried because she was hungry.

The inconsistent and restrictive quality of discipline which pervades the child's life might well be expected to breed in it a sense of insecurity and suspicious distrust. It has at its disposal only one weapon with which to meet frustration and that is rage. The alternative idea of being good in order to gain one's ends is not presented to the child. But that rage is an ineffectual weapon is learned at very latest during the first decade of life.

While the child is discovering the futility of protest, he is also discovering his own resources. He may expect his mother to prepare a morning meal at about seven o'clock and another at about the same time in the evening. During the intervening twelve hours he learns to forage for himself. He learns this from five or six onward in the fluid play groups of free roving children. Remnants may be scraped from the cooking pot. A variety of insects usually spurned by adults can be found. In the fields near the village are mangoes, bananas, sweet potatoes, young corn, and squash. They can be eaten raw or easily cooked. As a rule adults do not object to the minor depredations of their own children or their playmates, but if the raiding is too constant or if the crop is scarce, children may be scolded for it. Such objections are most apt to be voiced when children are reaching the age at which their labor might be expected and is not forthcoming. There are several anecdotes of reproaches on this score, and in one instance a mother and half-grown son came to blows over the matter. But an additional factor in adult objections to children using garden crops too freely is that it may actually disrupt friendships between age-mates. Mangma, in his autobiography, gives several such anecdotes, one of which is quoted below.

Manimale said, "Let us go to the fields to dig sweet potatoes." My mother and father were away and I was hungry. For a month we played together going every day to dig sweet potatoes. But his mother was angry because we went to her garden to dig them. So after that first day we always went to my garden to dig them. Then my potatoes were finished. I was angry because we always went to my garden. I said to him, "You have lots of potatoes but we only went once to your garden and your mother was angry. Now you have many and you can't come to dig mine any more." I splashed water on him. Manimale said we would not play together any more.

Parental objections also pave the way for the thieving in which play groups of boys frequently indulge. The whole system of feeding reinforces one of the marked intracultural tensions centering on theft and fear of theft.

During this preadolescent play period boys may get occasional meals as guests. When an adult man visits a house in which a woman is at home, it is customary to set a calabash of food before him and any little boys who are about are invited to join him. Little boys very soon learn to attach themselves to any man who seems to be setting out on a "business" trip and in this way undoubtedly learn a great deal of the role expected of them as adults. Hunger is a motivation which leads to the acquisition of adult male skills. Little girls are not fed on these occasions, except rarely when they pick up a bit of food on the side while it is being prepared. There are still other sources of food available to small boys. During feasts those who help with the butchering are given the entrails or other less desirable bits of the pig to roast on the spot. Rat hunting, in which several boys assist a grown man or two, is another

BROILING ENTRAILS, A SMALL BOY'S REWARD FOR ASSISTANCE IN BUTCHERING.
THE MEAT FOR THE FEAST IS BEING BOILED IN THE POT

A LITTLE GIRL LEARNS HER ADULT TASK AS WATER CARRIER

[Facing page 276]

RICE CONES FURNISHED BY THE HOST IN A HOUSE BUILDING FEAST

CONTRIBUTIONS FROM THE WIFE'S FAMILY IN A DOWRY FEAST

[Facing page 277]

source of food. The rats are often roasted on the spot, and the children are given the bellies, entrails, and other less choice portions of the kill. In any event the day's food is as precariously and inconsistently procured as discipline is administered. Further, the food secured is the less choice kind which may, in conjunction with many other attitudes, help to produce in the child, the feeling of being undervalued.

As compared with this free play group period for boys, there is a slightly different adjustment for girls. Their play period is neither as long nor as free. They are more closely attached to their mothers, have more rigorous training in their adult role as providers for the family. They go out to work in the fields with their mothers and have therefor more regular access to food. I know of no cases in which little girls have been accused of pilfering from gardens, whereas such charges give rise to frequent if minor frictions with boys. On the other hand a girl does not have the guest privilege of the small boy. She gets no tidbits during butchering unless an unusually indulgent and thoughtful male kin happens to notice her on the edge of the group and gives her a bit of meat. Similarly, the meat at feasts is always distributed to the women but only in terms of the males in their household. That is, women get meat for their husbands and sons, but not for themselves or their daughters. Since food is taken home and eaten there, the women naturally get a share, but only as dependents of men. Also, since meat is eaten only in connection with a feast and is definitely a "treat," it becomes set in the children's minds as a symbol of masculine prestige. This coincides with theories of property which grant men the ownership of all flesh food as opposed to women who own the vegetable foods. The system of meat distribution at feasts helps to reinforce early in life and on a very basic level the role of masculine prestige in the culture. It is not that men are the providers; in fact they are quite the contrary. They are the ones provided for; yet they are the purveyors of a delicacy.

The girl, then is set during the preadolescent years in the essential and intimate relationship to the food cycle which she will follow all her life. Further, she has more systematic and deliberate training than boys in the role of adult existence. There is no sharp break in her life except the change of residence at marriage. It is significant that only after marriage is she allowed to make, independently of her mother, a food contribution to a feast. Public food contributions are the symbol of female adulthood.

Boys find themselves undervalued in comparison to men. Girls are valued in much the same terms as the adult women. Their role will always be somewhat underprivileged, but at least they do not experience the same marked discrepancy between childhood and the adult role expected of them as the boys do. The adolescent boy has a sudden adjustment to make and there are no crisis rites, no initiation ceremonies to help him. His change is not institutionalized or dramatized, and certainly he gets no direct education in it. At about fifteen he begins to ponder the purchase of a wife and that means entering upon the whole complex financial game which is the man's chief labor and honorific occupation. In the course of a few months he drifts away from the play groups, becomes a much more solitary figure, and interestingly enough often insists at this time on a midday meal, even if he must cook for himself.

Three meals a day is the symbol of adulthoood. It is significant that food as a status symbol should be used at the time that adult sex drives and financial responsibilities first become pressing.

This situation at the end of a long series of childhood experiences probably helps to set the wife as a mother figure. The wife, like the mother, is the responsible provider of food. A high degree of identification between the parent-child and husband-wife relation is actually conscious and valued in the culture. When older men lecture a young couple who have quarrelled, they invariably tell the young woman that she should be a mother to her husband and tell the young man that he should be a father to his wife. One of the strongest expressions of this sentiment was given by a young informant who may have made the identification a little more strongly than was customary.

Wives are like our mothers. When we were small our mothers fed us. When we are grown our wives cook for us. If there is something good, they keep it in the pot until we come home. When we were small we slept with our mothers; when we are grown we sleep with our wives. Sometimes when we are grown we wake in the night and call our wives "mother."

The mother is definitely the provider but, as we have seen, she is an uncertain one in many cases. It is not surprising therefore to find the relationship between spouses a precarious and mistrustful one. Even though the whole weight of the masculine financial system acts to stabilize marriages, Atimelangers average approximately 1.9 divorces apiece. This seems a high average when one considers the elaborate and cumbersome monetary negotiations involved in divorce.

So far I have been concerned with sketching briefly some of the hunger experience of childhood, the associated restrictive disciplines of adults, and the devices through which the culture somewhat negatively permits children to satisfy this basic need. There has been some indication how all of these affect human relationships. I should like to turn now to a series of institutionalized food attitudes and behavior.

The first and most striking is sacrifice, which is a matter of almost daily experience, representing practically all relationships to the supernatural. The word for sacrifice means literally "to feed," and every supernatural object is so placated. Individual and village tutelary spirits, the graves of the dead, the spirits of ancestors who have cultivated a field, wealth-bringing supernaturals, are all given their share of chicken blood, rice, and pig meat. Realistically enough, the offering is small and purely symbolic. The bulk of the sacrificial food is consumed by the people. In myths the sky heroes are always fed rice, millet, and eggs. Their revivification is achieved by pouring a pot of millet over their heads. The building of lineage houses must be accompanied by feasts at every stage of construction, and its importance is proportional to the number of pigs slaughtered in the course of building it. Newly purchased gongs or mokos[4] must be fed. It is, in fact, difficult to find any aspect of religious and social ceremonial which does not involve "feeding." In this connection it is not without signifi-

---

[4] Metal kettle drums used as currency.

cance that throughout Indonesia is the concept of man's creation from molded clay. In Atime-lang this widespread motif is altered so that man is created from molded rice and corn meal; that is, man is made from food.

Also food, rather than native currencies, is generally considered adequate pay for labor. The guest-workers who help cultivate a large rice field, who assist in erecting a lineage house who attend memorial funeral ceremonies, or who participate in similar ceremonial activities are all fed in return for their participation. When cooperative groups are formed for work in fields, the host of the day must furnish the midday meal.

There are other attitudes toward food which are perhaps less dramatic and institu-tionalized, but just as telling. If women are pounding rice or corn, any kernel which falls from the mortar is carefully picked up. Children of five or six have already absorbed this at-titude and are as meticulous as the adults of both sexes. A single bean left in a pod during shelling will be retrieved by children as well as adults. In clearing ground even isolated food plants will be carefully preserved. The meticulous fashion in which all food articles are saved and used does not coincide with any actual scarcity.

The natives also refer frequently to the annual "hungry period." This is the end of the dry season when there is no actual want but only less of the preferred foods. For a month or two natives depend more on cassava and sweet potatoes than on corn. Yet the culture phrases this as a period of food stress. In addition there were references to periods of famine as though they were an ever present threat. Careful inquiry revealed only two periods of shortage within the memories of people between forty and fifty. Both of these were due to factors which had disorganized the community so that for one season the fields had not been as extensively planted and as carefully weeded as is customary. There is no doubt that food, especially of the preferred sort, was scarce on these two occasions, but it was procurable by purchase in nearby communities and there is no evidence that anyone died of hunger. There is, in fact, no indication that hunger is ever necessary if a proper amount of foresight and in-dustry has been exercised. Perhaps one of the best indications that the concern over food scarcity is of psychological origin and not realistic is that there is no land hunger. No one ever expresses poverty or wealth in terms of land, although there is actually great variation between consumption units in the number and fertility of fields owned. This is so despite a strong preoccupation with wealth as status in the culture. Data on the yield of the fields in-dicate that crops are good and on the whole adequate not only to feed the consumption units but also to provide surpluses for contributions to feasts.

In addition there is a singular agricultural fiction in Alor. This concerns the so-called "good years" and "rat years" which come in alternate seasons. Theory has it that there is no use planting rice fields or any outlying plots during "rat years" because rodents will eat up the crop before it can be harvested. In the "good years" there are supposed to be fewer rats and there is a chance to lay in surpluses for large feasts. The theory of alternating years of rat plagues has no basis in reality. Essentially the idea is a fiction that every other year you are the helpless victim of depredations on your food supply. As one might expect, there are a few people who ignore the theory and plant extra corn fields or even occasional rice fields during "rat years." Yet the social fiction seems almost a rationalization of basic food attitudes in the individual. It appears to be almost an expression of infantile deprivation and help-lessness. However, it is only with the utmost caution that I would suggest in any particular case that individual psychology is the direct source of an institutionalized form.

Theft and fear of theft are ramified phenomena whose implications extend beyond their application to food, but the most common type of theft is from gardens. This may be ex-plained on two bases: one is the early theft habits of foraging play groups of boys; the other is that food is one of the few types of property which cannot be absolutely identified and which can be used without much fear of detection. For these reasons, perhaps, one sees the use of curses against theft erected most frequently in fields. These curses, made by spe-cialists, are bamboo poles into whose cleft top are inserted the necessary combinations of magical objects. They are erected in fields where theft has occurred or where the owner fears such an occurrence. Once there, they are supposed to work automatically. A thief would develop leprosy or some other fatal or debilitating illness, and even the owner should call the specialist to remove the curse before harvesting the field. Although these curses are widely used, they seem actually to engender very little fear among most people. Certainly they in no way effectively stop pilfering. Many people are more realistic in the face of depredations and keep armed guard on their fields. A thief caught in the act runs the risk not only of hav-ing to pay a fine but also of being shot.

Another important food attitude is shown by the limited range of generosity in dis-tributing it. An occasional guest is fed, but soon enough anyone who is obviously sponging is no longer asked to eat. In case a family runs short of corn or rice it has to buy or borrow from those who may have a surplus. But if food is borrowed, it is at rates of interest running as high as one hundred percent. This holds even between brothers. Thus Fanseni wanted a hundred-ear corn bundle. He got it from his brother but had to repay it at harvest time with two corn bundles of the same size. Even feasts, which at first blush appear to be generous food distributions, are far from lavish in actuality. Each female guest brings to the feast a contribution of food. Everything brought by guests is pooled with the hosts' contributions and then redistributed so that women may carry back home but little more than they brought in the first place. Of course they do receive meat in addition, but most often the meat consists of only three or four cubes of boiled pork about two inches square. However, the quantities displayed are considerable and the hosts derive satisfaction therefrom.

I have been concerned with describing a series of childhood experiences and a series of institutionalized adult food attitudes. The experiences of individual children with respect to hunger gratifications and disciplines vary greatly; it is to be expected, therefore, that in adults these cultural attitudes toward food will vary in "the depth or shallowness of meaning in the individual's total economy." Mangma began his autobiography with early memories of a period of hunger, whereas Tilapada, who was the same age and of the same village, began the story of her childhood with quarrels between herself and other children.

One man is conscientious and regular in making food sacrifices to his familiar spirits; another neglects them until illness indicates that he has angered his tutelaries. I have been concerned not with an attempt to uniformize personality among Atimelangers but with an attempt to show how individual childhood experiences with respect to hunger find constant outlets in institutionalized fields which reinforce early socialization and which persons may then invest with greater or lesser emotional energy.

Also, one must be careful not to use such nexi as exclusive causal sequences. I do not believe that the childhood food experiences of the Atimelangers have given rise to the system of sacrifice. They have merely reinforced and made significant to many individuals that widespread Indonesian custom. I would suggest, however, that it would be very difficult to eradicate sacrifice in Alor as long as its individual symbolic value can be so high. For example, a child who has learned that the gratification of hunger is a precarious and uncertain thing may well become an adult who shows obsessional attitudes toward the waste of food, especially if he sees adults who already reveal these attitudes. He has learned as a child that food is hard to get, that it can be stolen, and he has had no positive training in being generous with it. In fact, the whole pattern of discipline has been weighted on the restrictive rather than permissive side. All these individual experiences are reinforced by being reflected in adult behaviors (absorptive disciplines) and thereby become stable complexes that may have little relation to the reality of subsistence economy.

To avoid the possibility of simplistic interpretations, it must be stressed again that no single tension like hunger and the habits associated with its gratification will explain either the totality of the culture or the dominant and stressed personality traits of its bearers. It will be only by examining the whole variety of such individual life experiences and searching for the formalized and unformalized cultural correlates that any progress will be made, not only in defining more sharply the interaction of personality and culture, but also in elucidating the stability of attitudes and value systems. Institutions which may be invested with high emotional value because of patterns in child training are not the ones which can be lightly legislated out of existence. To eliminate such institutions without altering standardized methods of education, may well produce serious social and personal dislocations. The implications of these statements, if true, cannot be ignored by colonial administrators and legislators. It is possible that when we understand better our own culture we shall have learned that basic social changes of a non-disruptive nature must be anticipated in the early and intimate conditioning of children.

SARAH LAWRENCE COLLEGE
BRONXVILLE, NEW YORK

PERSONALITY DEVELOPMENT IN PUKAPUKAN CHILDREN

By ERNEST AND PEARL BEAGLEHOLE

I

ONE OF THE MOST memorable aspects of Edward Sapir's genius was his ability to think in terms of problems rather than within the academic limits of orthodoxly defined subjects. Ethnology, linguistics, and psychology thereby became cross-fertilized. Schools and methods became of secondary importance, or rather, were evaluated not in terms of narrow fields of investigation, but in the light of the help they promised for the solution of broadly conceived significant scientific problems. It was typical of Sapir, therefore, that he should have sensed in the problem of personality formation one of those major scientific orientations that direct the research and thinking of a generation or more of scientists. It was also typical of him that he should realize that no continuing research problem is worth the candle unless it breaks down into a 'series of hypotheses that stimulate and direct research not so much on several minor fronts but on one major front that draws to itself the support of sometimes independently conceived disciplines. The major problem for Sapir was the impact of cultures on personality. One of the linking hypotheses was his conception of culture, not as "something given but something gradually and gropingly discovered." The key to the way in which the individual personality discovers culture obviously lies in the field of child development. Lesser minds, having arrived at this point, might have washed hands and tossed the problem across to a field of study called "child psychology." Not so Sapir. He studied children himself (who of his students does not recall those memorable seminar discussions when the heart and mind of a child were examined with consummate skill). And as a second best, he suggested to some at least of his students that primitive children were quite as worthy of study as material culture or kinship systems. Again, however, the emphasis was always on problems rather than mere description of what children say or do or think.

It was directly under the stimulus, therefor, of Sapir's teaching that one of us undertook before a Polynesian field trip to draw up a series of notes and queries designed to serve as a guide to the study of the factors involved in the socialization of the primitive child.[1] By socialization was meant generally all those factors, influences, and processes, formalized or implicit, which the culture of the group acting through parents, elders, or other children brings to bear upon the neonata and continues through maturation to adolescence in order gradually to mould the raw stuff of human nature into conformity with group patterns of thought, feeling, and behavior. It was felt that material collected to answer such queries would throw some light on the influence of cultural factors in personality development and that further, viewing such material against the background of documented life histories, evidence might

---

[1] Pearl Beaglehole, *Some Notes and Queries for the Study of Personality Development in Primitive Societies* (Ms., 1934).

present itself regarding the factors bearing upon the development of personality differences.

The following material in no sense represents the fulfilment of a somewhat ambitious project. Owing to various exigencies of fieldwork[2] over which we had no control it was neither possible to study Pukapukan children with the detail they deserved, nor solve all the problems and hypotheses which we took with us into the field. Enough material was collected, however, to prove without doubt the fruitfulness of this aspect of Sapir's approach to the problems of personality. Some of this material is summarized here. If it raises more problems than it suggests answers to, this again is but tribute to Sapir's scientific acumen. After all, no new scientific approach is worth much unless it, at one and the same time, both suggests questions that should be asked and opens up wide fields of investigation. The sterile problem is the one that can most easily be answered.

II

The process of growing up in Pukapuka, as viewed from the vantage point of custom and institution, is for the average child an uneventful and straight-forward business. Children are eagerly desired by almost all parents. Male children are necessary to establish the continuity of descent and lineage. Both male and female children provide a form of old age insurance. Both, too, help to increase the flow of food into the family that results from regularly recurring village food divisions. Both sexes are also desired because the Pukapukan has real love and affection for children in themselves. The child of an unmarried mother is at no particular disadvantage. His maternal grandparents welcome the infant, giving him social status in the community. When his mother marries, as she surely will after thus establishing irrefutable proof of her child-bearing abilities, her child is almost always adopted by her husband and thus given paternal lineage status.

The new-born child is taken to the sea and washed, then oiled and wrapped in soft pandanus mats. For two or more days until the mother's milk comes the child is fed on coconut cream whenever it cries. For the first few days of life also the infant is cradled in the arms of female relations most of the day and night. It is given the breast whenever it cries. The mother sits while nursing, the child cuddled in her arms. Feeding is a leisurely procedure. The child is not hurried in any way but is allowed to satisfy itself fully and doze off to sleep still at the breast. When the infant is older it is held upright to nurse, its feet resting on the mother's lap. Older infants still adopt any attitude in feeding from the breast that suits them. Soft coconut flesh is introduced into the infant's diet at an early age, never however as a substitute for the leisurely and warm intimacy of breast feeding. The infant, though never left alone whether sleeping or awake, is rarely carried about. The mother remains inactive for some weeks after delivery. Thereafter when she participates more fully in gardening and domestic duties she leaves her child within the house in the care of an older child or female relative. The infant is carried about only when the guardian is a young girl who cannot resist

[2] Fieldwork was carried out on the Polynesian atoll of Pukapuka, one of the northern Cook group, for seven and a half months. The culture has been described in some detail in Ernest and Pearl Beaglehole, *Ethnology of Pukapuka* (Bulletin, Bernice P. Bishop Museum, No. 150, 1938).

the temptation of watching a group of her companions playing games on the beach. Then she carries the infant along with her, comforted gently in her arms.

As the infant grows older, it is gradually stripped of its baby coverings and lies naked on its mat. It then spends most of its time lying, sitting, and wriggling round beside the mother while she sits at her cooking or mat plaiting or else asleep within the cool house a few feet away. At this early age the child is good humoredly cleaned whenever it soils itself. Any older person in the household, male or female, who happens to be near the child at the time performs this task. Besides being fed whenever it shows signs of hunger, the child is always given the breast to comfort it and pacify it whenever it appears frightened or in pain. The child is comforted and petted in this way whenever it falls during the process of learning to walk.

The household into which the child is born consists on an average of between six and seven persons. The basis of this group generally consists of the biological family of mother, father, and one or more children. The most common additional member is generally an adult son's wife. Thereafter adopted children and relatives of almost every possible degree of relationship help to add to the group's number.

The composition of this household remains relatively stable throughout the child's life. Such breaks in the social fabric as death, marriage, divorce, birth, adoption, weaning cause a slight rearrangement of numbers, rarely of fundamental composition. Children practically never change their residence or feeding house among a larger kindred group according to personal whim. It may be noted from this that the Pukapukan child is brought up in a definite type of household group; its contacts while young within the household are rather narrowly defined in range. The child is mainly cared for by its mother. The father has no specific duties to perform. He is sympathetic and lavish in his affection for his child, caring for it, however, only when it is necessary or convenient. During much of its waking life the infant is fondled and carried by any male or female relatives or friends who happen to be visiting or working at the parents' house. Authority over the infant is largely focussed in the mother. Love, dependence, and affection on the other hand tend to diffuse themselves among many members of or visitors to the household. This fact and those patterns relating to infancy already given may well be emphasized because they do suggest that up to the time of weaning the infant is enabled to develop emotional attitudes that give the utmost possible psychological security. And this security stands the infant in good stead not only throughout the gradual process of building up its early habit patterns, but also at the time of weaning. Pukapukan infancy up to the time of weaning, that is, seems to be marked by a very minimum of frustration in regard to basic physiological and emotional needs.[3]

[3] In Pukapuka, we also strongly suspect, but cannot document, the fact that the lineage (here a paternal lineage) extends and deepens the sense of belongingness and safety secured first by the infant from a mother's cuddling. Besides its many sociological functions, therefore, the Pukapukan lineage tends to serve as a psychological device in this culture whereby a security and place of belonging are obtained by the child which transcends the immediate confines and experience of the family-household. Compare Beaglehole, *op. cit.*, pp. 229–33; James S. Plant, *Personality and the Culture Pattern* (New York, 1937), pp. 152–53.

The degree to which the process of weaning is traumatic depends somewhat on the type of weaning carried out. There are two methods of weaning in Pukapuka. The first is used if the mother becomes ill, or if the milk fails, or if she becomes pregnant again. In such case, the child is suddenly and immediately removed from its mother's presence and care and placed entirely in the care of a feeding parent, usually the father's sister or the mother's mother. The breaking off is complete and absolute. The feeding parent carries the child about day and night, trying to pacify it and feeding it coconut water, grated coconut, and grated taro. For some children this weaning may take a week to complete. For children more dependent upon their mothers, weaning may take two or more weeks. The second method of weaning is more gradual. The infant is taken to feeding parents in another village and left with them for a whole day at a time. The feeding parents fondle the child, feed it solid foods, and try to keep it happy and pacified. This occurs once or twice a week over a period of about two months, the mother meanwhile trying to accustom the child to solid foods, feeding him co-conut and taro before giving the breast. By the end of these months, the child is walking fairly well. He is encouraged to identify himself with the activities of his siblings, to play away from his mother as much as possible. More and more the mother refuses to give the breast at the child's demand. The weaning is thus accomplished by a series of gradual steps in which other interests and other foods assume an importance in the child's mind because both are associated with the status and prestige of a group of elder children with whom the child's lot is more involved. Any hesitations over taking the steps of the weaning process are overcome for the child by the well-directed and unmistakable ridicule of elders, both adult and children.

Again it may be noted that by the time the weaning stage is passed and the child is ready to join the children's play groups there has been little physical frustration and a lack of any discipline that could be called severe. The child has been a center of interest during infancy. Now it has been gently eased out of infancy and into the status of a relatively self-dependent childhood. Thumb sucking, incidentally, as distinguished from object sucking, is unknown among Pukapukan infants or children. This gradual process of growing up is continued dur-ing the early years of childhood (from the age, say, of two to seven or eight). Young children form mixed-sex gangs. They are relatively free from adult demands or adult interference of any sort. These gangs, consisting of perhaps six or more children drawn from neighboring households, roam about bush, reef, or beach by day or night. Their plays are either imitative games mimicking adult activities—fishing games, domestic games, "family games" (realistical-ly acting the roles of husband and wife)—or else the free-energy activities apparently char-acteristic of children everywhere—laughing, dancing, racing, singing, and swimming. Hungry, the children drift back to the village for food; tired, they throw themselves down in the house for a sleep of one hour or eight. The gangs have a relatively stable existence. They appear to be based mainly on age level. Children of the upper age gradually drift out to join groups of still older children. Their places are taken by the "weaners" who drift into the group from below. Adults are generally tolerant of these children's gangs. As long as they keep to themselves, amuse themselves with their own activities, and in general are rarely seen or heard, then the children have the utmost freedom to explore at leisure their brave new world of physical events and human relationships.

By the time the child has reached the age of about ten years the gangs have become single-sexed and the responsibilities and duties of fitting into an adult world begin to limit their earlier freedom. Boys and girls go around in their own gang groups whenever they have time or the opportunity. But now much of their activity is devoted to learning adult tasks through more constant association with adults. While the boy associates with his older male relatives and absorbs a knowledge of fish and fishing, of such male craft activities as the making of hooks, houses, canoes, nets, and fishlines, the girl stays closer at home with her adult female relatives and in turn learns the preparation of foods and the plaiting of baskets, food containers, mats, and clothing. Attitudes both central and incidental to the Pukapukan psychology of the sexes also tend to sink deeper and stabilize themselves at this period, both boy and girl learning, by largely unconscious repetition, the specific attitudes of their own sex and absorbing from example, talk, and gossip expectancy attitudes in regard to the behavior, feeling, and thinking of the opposite sex. These attitudes receive a fairly explicit exemplification in the old chants that both sexes learn by heart for recital at recurring festival occasions. After puberty the young take every opportunity (opportunities are generally many and easily come by) to school themselves in the sex patterns of their culture by processes of experiment that end with the more stable relationships of marriage.

It is in the pre-puberty period in particular, however, that there is a hardening of discipline and control which seems to come as a shock to many children. For children of this age, girls as well as boys, physical beatings are common. Children are whipped with apparent severity—though the onlooker must sometimes be deceived into assuming that loud shouting and wailing accurately indicate intense pain—for various types of activity which either parent or other relative of equivalent status in the household interprets generally as disobedience to commands or laziness or lack of expected skill. These beatings are given mostly by the older women of the household. Their long range effect and the discipline they subserve are probably of a dual nature. The control, that is, tends to jolt the child out of an earlier freedom attitude; it also hastens the fuller participation of the young person in adult economic activities, thus increasing the productive economy of both the household group and the close-knit village community. With the acquisition of adult status, marked formerly by observing simple group ceremonies and the formal donning of waist girdle or woman's kilt, the young person is considered a full-fledged adult member of the community: eligible to marry, to receive adult food shares in village food divisions, to perform all the economic duties associated with the age grading of young adults. The gradual process of learning the ins and outs of Pukapukan culture is now, in theory at least, well on to becoming a finished task.

III

So far the pattern, as it has been stated, has run itself along with an easy but, of course, deceptive simplicity. Mention of stresses and strains incidental to the process of becoming socialized have been confined to generalized statements about weaning and pre-puberty. These two periods are undoubtedly two formalized crisis periods in the life of the Pukapukan child. But there are others as well that are common but which probably have a differing impact, depending somewhat on obscure factors in the life of this particular Pukapukan child or that. Study of all the behavior records collected by direct observation of Pukapukan children in a wide variety of situations suggests that the most frequent of these stresses in the socialization process order themselves into the following rough and non-exhaustive classes: behavior difficulties over weaning; behavior stresses through discipline; behavior problems in adoption; fear situations of various kinds, such as fear of objects, fear of ridicule; aggressive behavior in the effort to control objects; aggressiveness towards siblings. It will be worth while to characterize these difficulties in some detail in order to illustrate both the situations that give rise to frustration and the behavior that is typical of the Pukapukan child in these circumstances.[4]

Two observations will serve as examples of weaning stresses. These and other observations throughout this section are given in the form of field note records.

Mata, a childless married woman is minding her sister's baby, William (0:8),[5] for the day while his mother works in the taro gardens. The child is soon to be weaned and has already started to eat taro and nuts: Mata's keeping the child for a whole day is part of the weaning process. The child gets restless and fretful, so Mata picks it up in her arms and rocks it violently, cuddling it fiercely, bumping it about and patting it with no gentle hand. To soothe the child further she gives it her dry breast to suck. The baby sucks hard and then when he can get no milk, he stands up, suddenly bites Mata's neck. Then he returns to her breast and ends by giving her nipple a severe nip with his teeth. Mata slaps the child on the head. The child cries hard, throws itself about in her lap. It is given some coconut flesh to eat but continues to whimper for some time thereafter.

Liaki (1:3) is the youngest of six children living with their unmarried mother. He walks but is not yet completely weaned. His mother is just recovering from a chill and fever. She tries not to let Liaki have the breast because she fears her fever may have made her milk bad for the child. She puts Liaki to sleep on the section of the sleeping platform occupied by his sisters. He repeatedly gets up in the night, however, crawls over to his mother, cries loudly and tries to get at her breast. He is crying this afternoon. His mother tells me she has again tried to put him to sleep without breast

---

[4] The material on children given here is summarized from specific observations made throughout our Pukapukan fieldwork on thirty-one children in Yato village, the village in which we lived. This is more than half the children in the village between the ages of six months and twelve years. The children studied grouped themselves in age grades as follows: under 1 year, 4; 1-2 years, 4; 2-3 years, 4; 3-4 years, 5; 4-5 years, 4; 5-6, 6-7, 7-8, 8-9, 10-12, 2 children each. Twenty-two of the children were male, nine were female. There is no reason to think that this group as a whole (and its age distribution) does not represent a fair sample of Pukapukan children—except for the fact that an ideal sample would demand approximately equal sex representation. Specific record taking of these thirty-one children was, of course, supplemented by more casual observation of many children in our own as well as in the two other villages on the atoll, together with long discussions with informants over childhood problems. One of us, it should also be noted, could use the Pukapukan dialect with sufficient confidence to make the native language the means of communication with both children and adults.

[5] Figures in parenthesis after names indicate the child's age. A figure before the colon indicates years; one following the colon, months.

feeding. Each time she puts him down, he sits up, cries and crawls onto her lap. Kneeling in her lap he tries to grasp her breast. She pushes his hand away. He rolls onto his belly on the ground, kicks his toes into the sand for a few minutes and then falls asleep. Whenever he is seen these days he is playing continually with his penis. Sometime later, when he wakes, his mother puts him outside the cookhouse. The railings of this are too high for him to climb over. He finally succeeds in entering the house by bending back the screen-mat tied to the railings, poking his head through a gap in the railing and tumbling into the house headfirst. His mother says he always enters the house in this way, "just like a baby getting born." She says weaning time is hard for the child. He cries all the time because he cannot get what he wants.

Discipline of children is secured in two ways: either by physical punishment or else by threats designed to arouse fear in the child. Discipline-frustrations are of the following order:

For bodily hygiene: as soon as a child is old enough to walk, an older person, either parent or sibling, leads it to a proper place outside the house. A child old enough to be about by itself is expected to leave the house to attend to its bodily needs. Should it fail to do this, parents scold, threaten to whip and often do whip the child across the buttocks.

Physical punishment: A mother sends her son (12:0) to feed the family pigs. The boy goes off in the right direction but stops to play a game of marbles. His mother keeps her eye on him, continually calling out to him to get along to the pigs. After about half an hour, with the boy still playing marbles, the mother asks a man going in that direction to bring the boy back to her. The man carries the boy back on his shoulders. The mother puts down the infant she is nursing and whips the boy severely with a coconut leaf switch. A group of her friends sit around unconcerned. The boy finally runs from her into the house where he picks up an empty coconut and hurls it at his mother. It goes wide. His mother pays no more attention to him. Crying, the boy rolls on the ground for a while, then goes off to feed the pigs.

Threats: Parents threaten toddlers by telling them that animals, e.g., pigs or ducks, will get them if they disobey commands, or else that ghosts will eat them. Ghost threats are common at nightfall. (Fear of supernaturals is very strongly grounded in Pukapukan psychology.) Spitting or pretense of spitting at misbehaving children is also a common method of discipline.

In connection with all types of discipline the eldest boy in the family has special privileges and powers over his younger siblings. He may whip his younger brothers or sisters if they disobey any of his commands.

Aggressive behavior towards younger or older siblings of the same or opposite sex appears to be common in Pukapuka. According to one excellent informant most children were unhappy if there were no younger brothers and sisters in the family. When her eldest son was about eight years old, he asked his mother to give birth to a sister for him. His mother said she would and when she later told the boy she was pregnant, he was very happy and assured her many times that she was going to bear a female child. According to his mother this boy never showed any jealousy towards his younger siblings while they were still infants but when they reached the age of two or more years and began to run about he would become angry with them and very aggressive in their presence. Two examples will again show the form in which this aggression expresses itself among children.

Pita (10:0) has a drinking nut which his two younger siblings, Talatini (8:0) and Langatila (3:6), wish to share with him. Langatila grizzles and cries at his brother while Talatini struggles with Pita to secure possession of the nut. Pita fights him off with one hand at the same time swallowing the coconut water as quickly as possible. Then when the nut is nearly empty he throws it on the ground and walks off. Talatini picks it up and goes to crack it open. Langatila cries harder than ever. Pita comes back, picks up a coconut switch and beats Langatila with it. Pita says he does this "without reason, just for fun." He goes inside the house and finds Langatila there. He whips him again, continuing the whipping as crying Langatila first climbs a house post unsuccessfully trying to escape the punishment, then slips down the post and falls on the ground. He finds a coconut spathe there and tries to hit Pita with it. While this is going on, the father of the two boys comes into the house. Langatila without a word to, or a glance in the direction of, his father slips out of the house and walks away to the beach, muffling his sobbing as he goes. The mother of the boys has been in the cookhouse next door throughout this scene, within easy hearing range, but she has not bothered to interfere with this aggressive behavior.

The second example shows this sibling aggression in another context. The children of Pulotu are sitting on the beach eating their food. Ngatokalua (5:0) is crying. His elder sister Nunui (12:0) volunteers that she has just whipped him. After a while Ngatokalua stops his weeping, turns to Nunui and calls such insults at her as "stinking vagina." Nunui slaps his face. He repeats the insult and this time Nunui hits him hard across the mouth with her hand. He begins to cry once more. Nunui meantime has been minding her still younger brother (1:3) who is fretful and troublesome. She makes a slip knot in a coconut leaflet, slips the noose over Liaki's penis and pulls the leaflet so hard that Liaki falls to the ground. Nunui then tries to rock Liaki to sleep by cradling him in her arms and manipulating his penis. When she thinks Liaki is asleep, she carries him towards the house but Liaki wakes and cries out. Nunui runs back to the beach carrying the crying Liaki suspended by an arm and leg. She runs down to the sea, playfully dips Liaki's head under the water, then sits down on the sand and begins her rocking of Liaki all over again. Tinomana (2:6), another brother, comes up. He sees his younger brother being rocked to sleep. He picks up a long coconut midrib from the beach and makes as if to hit Liaki with it. He ends by pounding the midrib against a log of drift wood, then holds it up in the air, shouting out that it is his spear.

Frustrations arising from a conflict of loyalties consequent upon adoption would seem to present major difficulties in the lives of many Pukapukan children. There are two types of adoption in the culture: complete adoption and partial or feeding adoption. Complete adoption involves change of residence and change of patrilineal descent. Feeding adoption usually involves change in residence but never change in descent line. To show the incidence of Pukapukan adoption it may be noted that of 348 persons included in a household census, 80 (22.9%) have at some time been completely adopted. Of 209 persons of a generation below that of mother and father in the households, 43 (20.5%) are completely adopted, 13 (6.22%) are partially adopted. Adoption of both types, therefore, has involved over 25% of the individuals in one generation-stratum. The motives for adoption are both personal and economic. The personal motive is the desire of a childless man to ensure the continuation of his patrilineal descent line; economic incentives include the desire of a childless couple for the food shares and property that an adopted child brings into the household, or for someone to care for them in their old age. The range of possible relationships between adopting parent and child is almost infinite. Study of census material, however, shows that adoptions by maternal and paternal relatives are almost equal; the father's sister, mother's brother, and mother's father are likely to adopt more frequently than any other relatives.

The process of complete adoption generally begins with the bespeaking of a child before its birth. The adopting couple feed the mother from the third month of pregnancy onwards. They present her family with special food gifts each time there is a food division. They name the child and provide the birth feast, taking formal possession of the child at weaning. This method of pre-natal adoption is looked upon as the best method of ensuring complete social and emotional control of the child. A divided loyalty in the child is looked upon as fatal to the complete success of the economic and psychological security desired by the parents. On the other hand it is recognized that adoption at a later age gives the parents a chance to evaluate the capabilities of the adopted child. Hence some parents favor a partial or feeding adoption at the beginning: the adopting parents take the child at weaning time into their household; if at a later date they wish completely to adopt the child, they do so by mutual arrangement with the blood parents, accompanied by a renaming of the child.

All our Pukapukan informants sensed the conflict situations involved in this extensive practise of adoption. The adopted child is considered to be the child of the adopting parents in everything except the accident of conception and gestation, though the fiction is that the adopting parents become sociological parents before birth through their pre-natal feeding of the mother. The adoption is held to break all kinship ties based on blood and new kinship obligations are established according to the relationships of the adopting parents. As the child grows up, however, he soon learns to know his blood parents. He may be permitted to visit them, to work with them, to care for them in sickness, but it is to his adopting parents that the child owes primary social and affectual obligations and on whom he is supposed to lavish all his interest and support. Because of the complete sociological break that adoption is supposed to occasion, the conflict situation which blood parents, either through motives of natural affection or economic advantage, may stimulate by encouraging their child to visit them, by petting him, lavishing affection over him, saving choice food for him, is regarded with dismay and hostility. Blood parents who in any way try to revive blood ties are regarded as black traitors. If a child shows more than a formal interest in his blood parents, the latter are expected to show in every possible way, even by resorting to violent whippings, that the child is unwanted. Similarly, adopting parents are justified in severely disciplining an adopted child who persists in sneaking off to a blood parent's household. The following examples will illustrate these points:

Lima (7:0), the adopted child of Mata and Leleau, comes back to Mata's house from working in the bush with Leleau, eats some food, throws off his lavalava and then starts to walk down the village path in the direction of the next village where his blood parents live. Mata screams after the boy to return immediately; then noticing he is not paying any attention to her, she runs after him. She comes back driving the crying boy in front of her with heavy blows from a thick stick. Lima runs into the house and Mata barricades him inside, telling him not to try to move from the house on pain of another beating. In explanation of this scene, Mata complains that Lima slips away from her house as much as possible, visiting his blood parents by preference. She is enraged with the boy and takes a long time to calm down again. Lima, incidentally, is forever pulling at his penis and masturbating. Mata is almost the only Pukapukan parent who is worried by this. She does not allow Lima to go naked as do the other boys of his age but keeps him dressed in the lavalava skirt. It is perhaps significant that Lima tossed aside his lavalava before trying to steal away from his adopted mother's house.

The second example of frustration is more indirect in that it refers to the reaction of a child to other children in the household who have been adopted, but it provides a case of play behavior that is clearly symbolic and probably only to be intrepreted in terms of a deep-seated conflict over being a member of a household in which the adopted children enjoy a favored position.

Ta (7:0) is the youngest of eight children. He lives with his now elderly parents who have adopted their two grandchildren (Ta's niece and nephew) into the same household. The parents give all their favors and affection to their adopted grandchildren. Ta is obviously unwanted in the household. He is an unsmiling, lonely child, hanging precariously onto the fringes of a gang that has no particular welcome for him. On this occasion he was seen playing marbles with two other boys and a girl, the oldest of whom was four and a half years.

Ta drops out of the game. He strolls off into the bush but is soon back again with a long narrow immature coconut. He cuts a nick out of the center bottom of this nut with his knife and says, "This is the penis of my child." Then he turns the nut over and makes another nick saying, "This is the hole of the anus for defecating." Now he scratches a few rough marks on the nut to represent eyes, nose, and mouth, and lays the nut down on the ground. He says his child has lived for one day only and is now dead. He says he is going to bury the child. (But for adoption, Ta's nephews, whom he now calls "brother" would be called "son" or "child" by him.) He begins to dig out a hole in the ground with a coconut shell. The other two boys now drop their marble game and join in the burial play. When he has finished digging, Ta goes off to find some "mats" for his corpse-child. He brings back some large dried leaves which he carefully wraps round the child. The three boys now place the corpse on strips of coconut leaf and lift it up to place in the grave. As they do so, they fumble. The corpse drops off the leaves onto the ground. Without comment, all three boys kick the corpse and hole to pieces, trampling on both with their feet.

While his two friends begin other games, Ta picks up a small piece of coconut wood and starts to cut out what he calls a coffin. He whittles away for almost an hour, carefully shaping the box and hollowing out the inside. From another portion of the same piece of wood Ta shapes what he says is his "child"—a longish piece of wood with a knob representing the head. He inserts the child in the coffin. Finally, he makes a lid and with it carefully covers over the child inside the coffin. When he has finished he stares at his work for a while. Then he removes the child and proceeds to cut coffin and lid into small sections. These sections he throws away into the bush. Now he cuts up his child-corpse, handing round pieces to several boys who have come up to play saying, "Eat my child here!" His own share of the child's body he places in his mouth and chews vigorously. He spits out the macerated wood, stamps on it, and goes away.

Burying games played by children are not uncommon. They generally follow immediately upon a death in the community when the children's interest is turned to corpses by fringe-participation in the funeral wake and burial. Ta's play, however, bore no relation to any actual death. It appears to have been quite spontaneous, unmotivated by immediate imitation. It is nonetheless significant, however, for the insight it gives into the adoption-frustration situation in Pukapukan society; specially significant if Freud's conceptualizations be used for approximate explanation.

IV

Enough has perhaps been said to suggest some of the overt conflict situations that the Pukapukan child has to surmount in the slow process of socialization. It may be of interest now to discuss briefly the attitudes of children to the facts of sex and also the attitudes of parents and elders in regard to the sex knowledge and sex plays of children. The dissussion will show clearly that conflicts over sex are certainly not conflicts that in any way appear to ruffle the surface of Pukapukan child development. The metaphor may well be emphasized in so far as it still leaves as an open question the nature and extent of unconscious conflict and repression.

Two points may well be kept in mind in considering the sexual attitudes of Pukapukan children. First, the general attitude of the culture towards sexual activities is that these are pleasurable play activities. The attitude is realistic, sensuous but not sensual. For the Pukapukan all activities lead naturally to some form or other of sex expression. Secondly, all members of the household sleep in the same sleeping house. Where there is only one mosquito net in the house, parents and children all sleep under it. In a few houses in which a rough partition separates two rooms, parents and small children sleep in one room, older children in the other. A group of older women informants said that some parents make an effort not to let their children witness them in coitus but other parents make no effort to conceal their actions. Particular parents wait until they assume their children are asleep or else go to the bush to have intercourse. These precautions, however, prevent little. It is certain that children witness the sex act at one time or another, usually at a very early age, and are fully conversant with all that relates to sex and childbirth.

Many conversations with children between the ages of three and six years record detailed but volunteered accounts of childbirth. The children assume that childbirth is as neutral a topic of discussion as any other; just as their parents have no objection to their being present at childbirth—no objection that is, so long as they do not insist on pursuing a kitten between the legs of a parturient woman or hindering the midwife by tangling her up with a pig that is being chased. Similarly in regard to the sex act: the familiarity of children with this phase of behavior as recorded in their conversations or activities is striking in its completeness. Words referring to the sex act are continually on their tongues either by way of comment, gossip, or insult, just as they are continually on the tongues of adults, whether children are present or not. Typical field records are the following:

As a gang of children (ages 3 to 8) are sitting on the beach towards evening watching the fishing canoes come back from their day outside the reef, a single-seater canoe goes past. When asked who is in the canoe the children reply, "It is Elia." Lima (5:0) goes on to add: "It is Elia who copulated with Tala." He then improvises a song to the words, "It is Elia who copulated with Tala. They walked. They copulated. They played about." As Lima sings his song, the other children join in. All are sitting on the ground and as they sing, they accompany the rhythm of the song with movements of their bodies.

Olani (3:6), a girl, is sitting on the railing of the cookhouse. Her mother is inside the cookhouse nursing a baby and nearby is an older brother. Olani sings a song which all seem to enjoy. She has taken the tune from one of the hymns she hears in church and has adapted it to the following words: "They went through the bush. I guess they copulated!" This song she repeats over and over again. Her mother explains that the children playing in the bush often see couples going to, or coming back from, the back beach of the island (favourite place of assignation in Pukapuka). The children note the names of the couples and come back to the village singing improvised songs about the incident. Olani's song was looked upon by the mother as a very ordinary type of expression for her daughter.

Masturbation is extremely common among children of both sexes to the age of about 12 years. Equally common is manipulation of the sex organs, either in situations which seem to cause shyness in a child or else as a game among children. There is probably no particular point in documenting such behavior in detail. Field records include for example the following situations: three boys, the youngest 3 years, the others 6 and 7 years respectively, manipulating each other's penises when they are supposed to be observing Sabbath rest; a group of six boys between the ages of four and six years manipulating their penises and then trying to demonstrate to each other whether they can micturate with erect penises; a girl aged 12 years minding her brother (1:3) and amusing herself by making a slip knot in a coconut leaflet, slipping the noose over the boy's penis and then dragging on it hard enough to pull the boy to the ground; family plays in which a child pairs off with another of the opposite sex, the two playing at being husband and wife by manipulating each other's sex organs and imitating the sex act.

The general attitude of adults to masturbation in children and sex organ manipulation is one of good-humored toleration; that is, it is considered amusing if called to their attention. But for the most part adults never feel called upon to notice. Two exceptions only were noted to this generalization: one has been already mentioned for the boy Lima; the other exception occurred when a mother drew attention to her masturbating son in order to amuse an audience (not, however, to shame the boy). All adults know that masturbation goes on among children. It is regarded as their game, natural to children of certain ages, and that is all there is to it. There is only one reference in the folk tales to adult masturbation. This concerns the fate of certain Pukapukan husbands whose wives all left them, attracted by a gang of exceedingly handsome young men. The tale relates in great detail the practises of the deserted husbands before they summoned up enough courage to attack and kill the young men. No Pukapukan can tell this tale without commiserating with those husbands of long ago.

The material just summarized suggests clearly the Pukapukan practises of, and attitudes to, sex among children. They may be summarized for boys as a good deal of play with the sexual organs, including masturbation and manipulation of the sex organs of other children, usually but not exclusively of the same sex. For the girls much the same holds. These generalizations hold for children up to the age of eleven or twelve. Towards the end of this age period boys and girls are both caught up into an increasing participation in adult activities: fishing, coconut collecting, food preparation, and mat making. The character of plays, at this age, does not differ from the typical wrestling plays, organized games, and imitative plays of children of younger age levels. It has seemed impossible to characterize on the basis of field records any flight to reality or any repression of parentally directed hostility theoretically expectable from the concept of the latency period. There are likewise no records to be added concerning Pukapukan adolescence. Casual observation suggests no adolescent conflicts, no cultural storm and stress period. Nor does knowledge of the culture suggest any psychological reason or basis for possible adolescent conflicts. There is a total absence of motifs, incidents, or allusions to adolescence in the chants and folktales. The only coming of age with which the Pukapukan seems to be familiar is the assumption of sociological adulthood when the old judge the young to be ready to take on the economic and social responsibilities of adult life.[6]

V

Enough field data have been given, we hope, to outline the main patterns of childhood socialization in Pukapuka and some of the stresses incidental to this process of growing up. Certain theoretical points emerge from this material. They relate on the one hand to field methods and on the other hand to interpretations of the field data.

On the completion of our field work we summarized for Sapir our experience and conclusions in regard to field methods.[7] There is no need to retraverse these in detail. They related principally to an analysis of the kind of culture in which we thought children could be

[6] There are naturally occasional deviants who do not fit easily into this pattern. In *Brief Pukapukan Case History* (Journal, Polynesian Society, Vol. 48, pp. 135–43, 1939) we have outlined one adolescent's growing up that illustrates interesting variations on the pattern as here stated. It should also be noted that in Pukapukan culture, before conversion to Christianity broke down some of the old personal tapus, one situation alone was likely to have caused personal stress at this period. This was the strict tapu that formerly held between a man and his cousins-in-avoidance (females only). The tapu was not observed in childhood. Its incidence was first felt during adolescence. The functioning of this tapu and the stresses it brought about have been noted in the *Ethnology of Pukapuka* (pp. 259–63). This tapu is preserved today among old people. The young bother about it little. Among the younger generations several marriages have even occurred among kin who were formerly rigidly tapu to each other—an utterly inconceivable situation according to old-time patterns, and one today that causes great disapproval among the old.

[7] Ernest and Pearl Beaglehole, *Some Methodological Implications in the Study of Primitive Children* (Ms., 1935).

most fruitfully studied, the kinds of situations, observations of which would lead to the most valuable data, the type of training most desirable for those studying primitive children, an evaluation of case-study possibilities in primitive cultures, and a final emphasis on the importance of long-continued study of selected children over a period of years.[8] This last conclusion we take to be fundamental. One assumption of our *Notes and Queries* was that by studying children of different age levels problems incidental to a time series might at least be overcome. But the time series itself appears to be of spectacular importance if we wish thoroughly to understand personality development and socialization processes. By observation of children for a few weeks at a time, even by repeating such observation periods at regular or irregular intervals, it is possible to compile a formidable set of data relative to sex life, play, relations to other children and adults, and so on. But the question of interpretation still remains. How are these data to be interpreted as bearing upon the production of certain personality types or upon the theory and practise of child development? Only, we assume, by studying selected children over measurable time periods. In terms of theory, analytic or otherwise, it may be possible to infer that certain strains, inhibitions, repressions should result from the conditioning processes that a culture approves. The next step in method must always be to see if such strains and blockages do occur. And unless the same individual is studied over a long period of time, how can one be sure what happens and what the processes at work really consist in? We believe "retroactive" case histories that work backwards from the present are of great value. But of greater value still would be forward-working case histories that took the infant from birth, several particular infants in fact, and studied them with a day to day care, as they interacted with their personal and cultural environment. This would be a difficult task even for the most heroically conscientious and psychologically sophisticated anthropologist. But until it is done we will always be guessing at the key which solves the problem—guessing with some probability doubtless but never being sure the key has been found. The first five years of life are generally considered of importance in our own society for establishing the main personality reactive patterns in the child. A five year case history of a primitive child, starting from the first hour of life or before, would give the key that would open many of the doors that at present lock away the inner processes of personality socialization.

Turning now more specifically to the interpertation of field data, one point among many may be emphasized. A survey of recent psychoanalytic and anthropological literature suggests some conflict of opinion over the relative importance of cultural factors in stabilizing personality patterns. Admittedly everything turns upon the question of what is psychologically given. If the hypothetical raw stuff of human nature is essentially plastic, easily to be molded this way or that, then culturalization must play an overwhelming part in personality development. Even should the individual be born with a basic personality type,

[8] See Ernest Beaglehole, *Polynesian Anthropology Today* (American Anthropologist, Vol. 39, pp. 213-21, 1937), p. 220. Kluckhohn has also commented on this point among others in his paper: *Theoretical Basis for an Empirical Method of Studying the Acquisition of Culture by Individuals* (Man, Vol. 39, No. 89, July 1939).

nevertheless as long as this type is not polar, much importance must be attached to cultural factors in defining the success with which the basic psychological personality adjusts itself to the status personality.[9] If on the other hand, as psychoanalytic theory appears to hold, the psychological nature of man is everywhere the same—that is if the infant in Siberia or in Africa or Polynesia is heir to emotional and sexual drives (libido) that must find outlet on object or self according to predetermined developmental stages—then it would seem that cultural factors can do little but accentuate here or play down there. The psychoanalytic contention that the nuclear complex is of universal occurrence is perhaps a case in point.[10] Psychoanalytic theory in this matter is still in a formative stage and doubtless it may be possible to adduce evidence in conflict with the preceding statement. Roheim, for instance, in his analysis of Australian materials, concludes that the Australian aborigine is predominantly of the oral character type,[11] a personality development that can be due to conditioning and to this only.

On the other hand Dr Susan Isaacs[12] inclines rather strongly to the opinion that cultural factors are of slighter importance than libidinal drives. She would expect to find in Pukapuka, personality types similar to those found in our own society. It would seem in support of this view, as careful study of all our records indicate, that Pukapukan children engage in behavior activities in frames of reference that are analogous to, or even identical with common behavior activities of American children. There are alternations of love and hate, object sucking, nipple biting, plays with sand and water, "cosy places" plays, genital manipulation, "family plays"—to name but a few. In this sense, and generalizing broadly, the major difference in the socialization process between Pukapukan and American children lies in the

[9] See for instance Ralph Linton, The Study of Man (New York, 1936), specially Chapters 8 and 26, and Plant, op. cit., pp. 109-20.

[10] Compare Ernest Jones, Mother Right and the Sexual Ignorance of Savages (International Journal of Psychoanalysis, Vol. 6, pp. 109-30, 1925) with Malinowski's analysis in Sex and Repression in Savage Society (London and New York, 1927), sp. pp. 135 ff. Benedict, also, believes that an Œdipus complex is quite impossible among the Zuñi. See her Patterns of Culture (New York, 1934), p. 101.

It may be noted that since our article was completed (November, 1939) M. F. Ashley Montagu has summarized the relevant cultural material bearing on the Œdipus complex in his paper Nescience, Science and Psycho-Analysis (Psychiatry, Vol. 4, pp. 45-60, 1941, see pp. 48-49). Reference may also be made to Margaret Mead's recent survey of comparative work on character structure: Cultural Change and Social Surrogates (Journal of Educational Sociology, Vol. 14, pp. 92-109, 1940). The relative importance of biological drives as compared with cultural factors in determining character structure and personality development has also become a matter of active recent discussion. See in this connection Harry Stack Sullivan, Conceptions of Modern Psychiatry (Psychiatry, Vol. 3, pp. 1-117, 1940), Ernest Beaglehole, Interpersonal Theory and Social Psychology (Psychiatry, Vol. 4, pp. 61-77, 1941), A. Kardiner, The Individual and His Society (New York, 1939), and finally, the more orthodox point of view and the references given in Ernest Lewy's article, The Return of the Repression (Bulletin, Menninger Clinic, Vol. 5, pp. 47-55, 1941).

[11] G. Roheim, The Study of Character Development and the Ontogenetic Theory of Culture (in Essays Presented to G. C. Seligman, London, 1934, pp. 281-92). Horney gives a good summary of the present position in her Neurotic Personality of our Time (New York, 1937), pp. 16-20.   [12] From personal communication.

fact that the Pukapukan attitude to overt sex expression among children is the very reverse of our own. This means that Pukapukan children say and do things that American children only phantasy about. The fundamental libidinal drives are the same. The difference is that what the children of one culture do, the children of the other culture dream. Our own feeling is that the implications of this difference for the culturalization-personality process are still unclear.

A similar suspension of judgment would also seem to be in order over the psychology of the so-called latency period. In our own society psychoanalysts conclude that repressive cultural attitudes towards sexual expression have the effect of so controlling libidinal development that the years of middle childhood, say from seven to twelve, are characterized by an absence of overt sexual behavior. Freud himself apparently inclined to the view that whether or not a latency period is found in a particular culture depends upon attitudes in that society to sexual expression or repression.[13] The data summarized here on Pukapukan children would appear to support this view. Again however Dr Isaacs, on the basis of her very extensive work with children, conceptualizes the latency period in somewhat different terms. According to her,[14] it is best understood as referring to the child's repression of its central unconscious conflicts with regard to his parents, the consequent lessening of emotional tension and stabilization of attitudes towards adults and other children. In terms of this definition it is plain, as Dr Isaacs herself suggests, that the latency period is just as characteristic of Pukapukan children as of those of American culture.

One further note may perhaps be added in regard to interpretations. The adult Pukapukan character, as judged by cultural ideals, seems to be one marked by much aggressiveness. Evidence for this is found in intense village rivalries over sport (but not in economic matters), in innumerable personal chants that glorify individual prowess in love and other pursuits, in an at times turbulent island history marked by bloodshed and violence.[15] This aggressiveness might be directly due, on a theoretical analysis, either to specific patterns of childhood conditioning or else it might conceivably represent an over-compensation for fundamental insecurities and inadequacies brought about by the conditioning of other patterns. One's inability decisively to infer the types of adult character formation likely to result from childhood patterns even in our own society is presumably due to the fact that we are working with a social psychology that is as yet not as powerful as it may sometime become. One's difficulty is increased immeasureably when any sort of definitive analysis is attempted for a primitive society.[16] We confess a present inability to show the linkages within

[13] See for example Sigmund Freud, *An Autobiographical Study* (London, 1935), p. 66 fn.

[14] Susan S. Isaacs, *Social Development in Young Children* (London, 1933), pp. 259, 397-99, appendix 2, pp. 458-61.

[15] The role of this aggressiveness in Pukapukan culture and the mechanisms whereby it receives institutionalized outlet have been briefly characterised: Ernest Beaglehole, *Emotional Release in a Polynesian Community* (Journal of Abnormal and Social Psychology, Vol. 32, pp. 319-28, 1937).

[16] G. Gorer has recently attempted this type of analysis in his *Himalayan Village* (London, 1938). Cf. Margaret Mead's review-article on this book in Oceania, Vol. 9, pp. 344-53, 1939.

Pukapukan culture that join childhood patterns to the patterns of behavior that set the norm for adult activities. In very general terms one can annotate four stages of Pukapukan child development: an infancy marked by maternal solicitude and consequent security; a weaning that sends the child a-packing in the company of his fellows; years of childhood that mean a large measure of independence and freedom from parental or adult control; a pre-adolescence that sees a reassertion of adult control and a tendency to force the child along the path to adult status. These seem to be the main stages in the process of growing up. Should they tend to produce an aggressive adult character? The answer to this question might well lie in a deeper analysis of the pre-adolescent period, where one senses the Pukapukan urge to push the child willy-nilly into adulthood. But perhaps the question is not one rightly asked. If it is, it surely brings us back once more to the necessity of forward-looking life histories. Only through these can we see the pattern actually at work molding the life of the individual. Only in terms of data so gained could one surely present the inner story of how the socialization process actually works. Only in this way could one tell the story of how the individual measures himself up to the ideal standards of a culture and works out his personality pattern in terms of his felt achievement.

Again therefore one returns to the question, what is the psychologically given and what the nature and importance of cultural conditioning? It is tribute to Sapir's insight into the ways of culture and of man to note the way in which he sensed that the study of primitive children would ultimately provide clear solutions to many difficult problems. The answers are not yet at hand. The problems are only beginning sufficiently to clarify themselves in such a way as to present workable hypotheses as leads for investigation. Sapir's theory of culture led him inexorably to certain inferences regarding the processes of culture acquisition. It is now the privilege of the psychologist-anthropologist by using this lead to enrich his own field work and thus his understanding of what culture means to man.

VICTORIA COLLEGE
WELLINGTON, NEW ZEALAND